CINEMATIC FICTIONS

Cinematic Fictions

David Seed

LIVERPOOL UNIVERSITY PRESS

First published 2009 by
Liverpool University Press
4 Cambridge Street
Liverpool
L69 7ZU

British Library Cataloguing-in-Publication data
A British Library CIP record is available

ISBN 978-1-84631-212-0

Typeset by XL Publishing Services, Tiverton
Printed in Great Britain by the MPG Books Group, Bodmin and King's Lynn

For Joanna

Contents

Introduction

This book asks a simple question: given their fascination with the new medium of film, did American novelists attempt to apply cinematic methods in their own writings? There have been a number of studies of individual writers' close involvement with the cinema and with movie production, and I draw on these, in several cases adding to this historical documentation. But these details offer a necessary preamble to my main subject of methodological influence and congruence. Notwithstanding the invaluable studies by Garrett Stewart and David Trotter, I argue throughout for an interchange between the media, recognizing of course that any such interchange can only be approximate, as were the aesthetic analogies between fiction and painting in the latter half of the nineteenth century. The time frame of this study extends from the turn of the nineteenth century up to the Second World War.

From its very beginnings the cinema has played a special role in defining American culture. Indeed Amy Kaplan has tied the new medium to the emergence of the USA as an imperial power: 'A majority of these films showed Americans in motion: marching, riding, sailing, embarking on ships, and returning home'.[1] The presentation of mobility thus had a political point to make in suggesting the dynamism of the nation itself. By the 1910s, Norman K. Denzin has argued, 'American society became a cinematic culture, a culture which came to know itself [...] through the images and stories that Hollywood produced'.[2] Novels played their part in this transformation. Indeed it has a historical symbolism that in the 1890s Thomas Edison considered collaborating with the writer George Parsons Lathrop on a science fiction novel dealing with space travel, to be called *Progress*.[3]

The emergence of film occasioned a heated debate throughout the 1910s over high art as against the 'democratic art' of the cinema, a debate which to a greater or lesser extent influenced the novelists who were drawn to film.[4] The attraction was there despite the suspicion that literature risked being superseded by the new medium. In 1925 the poet Vachel Lindsay, who was also one of the first US commentators on film, declared: 'we are sweeping into new times, in which the eye is invading the province of the ear, and in which pictures are crowding literature to the wall'.[5] The extent of this anxiety varied from author to author; it was a real concern for F. Scott Fitzgerald, for instance. More generally, Lindsay's McLuhanesque diagnosis of what was happening in the media helps to explain the self-evident emphasis on the visual which will be traced throughout this study.

Of the relation between narration in fiction and in film Seymour Chatman and Robert Scholes have theorized resemblances and differences, though Scholes has argued that the reader's goal of visualization is a point of convergence.[6] Similarly Kamilla Elliott has not only argued for an interdependence between 'figure' and 'image' whereby verbalizing and visualizing prove to have a far closer relation than was thought, but also proposes a 'parallel and overlapping dynamic' between the two modes so that we can speak of a 'novelistic cinema' as well as of the cinematic novel.[7]

The earliest monograph to apply cinematic approaches to American fiction was Claude-Edmonde Magny's *The Age of the American Novel* (1948: English translation 1972), which was written against the background of the growing popularity of American fiction in post-war France. Concentrating primarily on Dos Passos, Hemingway, Steinbeck and Faulkner, Magny identifies a parallel evolution, a congruence between common aims. Thus, the novel's 'aim is to *show* rather than to *say*, and it is therefore related to the cinema even when it is not in the least influenced by it.'[8] Magny argues that the cinematic dimension to US novels emerges in the influence of behaviourism on their methods: thus, 'they give us not their characters' feelings or thoughts but an objective description of their acts, a court record of their speeches, the minutes of their "conduct" in a given situation'.[9]

Magny identifies two further characteristics which link US fiction to the cinema: ellipsis and impersonality. The first involves a disciplined selectivity of information, the second reflects a broad shift from the individual to collectivities. Predictably, this position leads Magny to invest two novels with special importance: Dos Passos' *U.S.A.* and Steinbeck's *The Grapes of Wrath*. When she discusses Dos Passos Magny avoids one of the besetting weaknesses of her study, namely its lack of detailed discussion. For her *U.S.A.* is the supreme example of the 'impersonal novel' because it attempts to portray a whole epoch, and she gives an invaluable account of how the characters are constantly being swallowed up by their surroundings. Much the same argument is mounted for *The Grapes of Wrath* though with a looser focus on film.[10]

In his 1987 survey article on the cinematic novel, Steven G. Kellman declares that 'it is pre-eminently as an emblem of modernity that authors first hailed the cinema'.[11] Most studies of the relation between these two media have tended to concentrate on modernism. Alan Spiegel's *Fiction and the Camera Eye* (1976) focuses his discussion on 'concretized form' in modernist fiction and dates this back to Flaubert, who for him was a formative figure in foregrounding the visual. Spiegel goes on to examine the visual dimension to the narratives of Hemingway, Faulkner ('perhaps the most elaborate and prodigious exponent of the cinematized narrative'), Nabokov and Dos Passos.[12] Spiegel shows how they break down the visual field into components for analysis. They are all thus 'anatomists' as he puts it, in their different ways dismembering appearances.

Spiegel's approach resembles that of Keith Cohen's *Film and Fiction* (1979), which gives an invaluable and more documented account of the convergence between cinematic and literary methods growing out of impressionism. For him, in impressionism 'all is reduced to one and the same level of phenomena, as background fades into foreground, the near into the distant, the exalted into the mundane'.[13] Cohen's study focuses specifically on literary modernism and he discusses four cinematic aspects of fiction: the 'vitalization' of objects, temporal distortion, point of view and discontinuity. His emphasis falls mainly on writers such as Joyce, Woolf and Proust, the only American writer to receive any detailed consideration being Gertrude Stein. Here he addresses her use of repetition as a means of dismantling traditional description and achieving a flow of aspects within an extended present.

Cohen's discussion of modernism has inspired two subsequent studies of its relation to film. P. Adams Sitney's *Modernist Montage* (1990) applies that cinematic method to literature in order to explore the following paradox: modernists 'stress vision as a privileged mode of perception, even of revelation, while at the same time cultivating opacity and questioning the primacy of the visible world'.[14] Taking examples from cinema and literature alike, Sitney demonstrates the recurrence of special moments of vision where exactly what is seen remains either obscure or absent. His study gives an exceptionally clear account of disjunctive and conjunctive montage, and throughout he demonstrates how problematic the notion of visuality was for the modernists. Once again Gertrude Stein is the main exemplar from American prose fiction and Sitney shows how she at once showed the 'most impressive resistance to visual representation in modernist literature', but also created a kind of 'imaginary cinema' to express the 'temporal duration of an entity'.[15]

The second work to have taken its lead from Cohen is Susan McCabe's *Cinematic Modernism* (2005). Like Laurence Goldstein's *The American Poet at the Movies* (1994), *Cinematic Modernism* does not limit itself to poetry.[16] To avoid any crude suggestion of linear influence, McCabe uses a triple analogy in her study, that between experimental cinema, hysteria (for her, the 'disease exemplary of modernity') and modernist discontinuity. What vision was for Sitney, the body is for McCabe. Once again we have paradox: the modernists show a 'desire to include bodily experience and sensation along with an overpowering sense of the unavailability of such experience except as mediated through mechanical reproduction'.[17] McCabe offers a suggestive and skilful exercise in comparison. One of the main values of her monograph lies in its capacity to map out connections between diverse cultural phenomena. Once again the method is juxtaposition, used to draw out the evident similarities of cinematic and literary practice through tropes of embodiment. Her central subjects are Gertrude Stein, William Carlos Williams, H.D. and Marianne Moore. In all these cases except the last experiments in poetry overlap into or have clear implications for these writers' prose fiction.

The genre 'cinematic fiction' has been defined rather restrictively by Gavriel Moses, whose 1995 study *The Nickel Was for the Movies* hypothesizes a different category, that of the 'film novel', which he defines as showing a 'firm notion about the art of cinematography as a whole, intermittent and sometimes extensive attempts at the creation of film-mimetic literary passages, and an exploration through narrative means of the place this medium has in human experience'.[18] Moses' main American examples are Fitzgerald, West (briefly), Walker Percy and – depending on where we locate him – Nabokov. A film novel emerges as one which incorporates such a sophisticated awareness of cinematic techniques that its meta-subject is representation itself. Every novelist chosen by Moses is in effect a film theorist.

One of the problems in examining cinematic fiction lies in the retrospective application of this approach to fiction which predates the cinema. Reviewing early critical works in this area, Caroline Geduld has complained: 'what kind of descriptive writing would *not* be comparable to film technique? Where does the cinematic imagination begin?'[19] Geduld's question was triggered by the famous case of Eisenstein's use of Dickens and Zola to construct an archaeology of the cinema.[20] Eisenstein also demonstrates an approximate congruence between some techniques of nineteenth-century fiction and what were to become central methods in film. Jean Normand has used the cinematic analogy to good effect in examining the lighting, perspectives, and mirror-screens in Hawthorne's fiction.[21] The issue of visualization has its own history, as John Conron has shown in his classic study *American Picturesque* (2000). What is striking in relation to the present volume is Conron's retrospective use of cinematic terminology to describe the nineteenth-century vista ('a means of plotting the gaze kinematically'), montage in Thoreau's *Walden*, and the speed of impressionist sketches by Stephen Crane and others.[22] We shall see in the next chapter how Crane is a transitional case in rendering visual dynamics with reference to contemporary visual technology. Where Conron charts the development of American representations in the visual arts, William Meyer identifies a similar national tradition of the 'hypervisual' in American literature emerging from a Protestant notion of vision and being extended by the cinematic impulse towards ever more detailed or extensive visualization.[23] In the views of Conron and Meyer the cinema essentially accelerates a process already active in American art and literature. In a similar spirit, Paula Marantz Cohen has argued that early film realized the American myth, articulated by figures such as Emerson and Whitman, of that nation having a 'privileged relation to reality'. The new medium fulfilled calls from earlier writers to circumvent language and enact direct vision, thereby giving a new status to the observer.[24]

This study is not an exercise in transposing the critical discourse of film onto literary material. The processes described are more complex and selective than that model would suggest. The cinema was not a single or stable entity. Some novelists drew on silent film; others looked to the Russian theorists for inspiration; and yet others turned to continental film-makers rather than to Hollywood. Film itself was constantly evolving during the first decades of the twentieth century and the writers discussed here engaged in a kind of dialogue with the new medium, selectively pursuing strategies of montage, limited point of view and scenic composition towards their different ends. Chapter 1 addresses early treatments of films in the writings of Edith Wharton, Thomas Dixon and their contemporaries, considering how the cinema gradually assumed its central cultural status. Chapter 2 turns on the modernist experimentation of Gertrude Stein, e. e. cummings and William Carlos Williams. Chapter 3 extends this discussion to H.D. (Hilda Doolittle), who was actively involved in continental art cinema and who applied the notion of memory film in her fiction. Chapters 4–6 consider the works of Hemingway, Fitzgerald and Faulkner, examining how these writers draw on film to shape their representational techniques and, in Fitzgerald's case, the nature of spectacle. Chapter 7 turns to montage in Dos Passos, a method he found reinforced by the Soviet film-maker Sergei Eisenstein. I then address in Chapter 8 the involvement with movie-making and the movie business generally of Theodore Dreiser and Upton Sinclair, next moving on to the incorporation of documentary techniques in writing of the thirties. This forms a context for John Steinbeck, the focal figure of Chapter 10, in which his relation to the film-maker Pare Lorentz will be examined as well as his own film-making. Chapter 11 turns to the particular problems encountered by African American writers such as Henri Micheaux, Zora Hurston and Richard Wright in cultural representation. Chapter 12 extends the earlier discussion of modernism to consider the use by Henry Miller and Anaïs Nin of continental Surrealist cinema to compose dream narratives. Finally in Chapter 13 I turn to the emergence of the Hollywood novel, which ironically redeploys the methods of film to depict the life of the movie capital.

NB. Short titles are given in the notes. Full publication details can be found in the bibliography.

Notes

1   Amy Kaplan, *The Anarchy of Empire*, pp. 149–50.
2   Norman K. Denzin, *The Cinematic Society*, p. 24.
3   Robert Sklar, *Movie-Made America*, p. 11; Marcus, *The Tenth Muse*, p. 44.
4   For commentary on this debate, see Raymond J. Haberski, *It's Only a Movie!*, pp. 15–32.
5   Vachel Lindsay, *The Progress and Poetry of the Movies*, p. 181. This work was not published until 1995. For a full discussion of Lindsay's writing on the cinema, see Marcus, *The Tenth Muse*, pp. 188–201.
6   Robert Scholes, 'Narration and Narrativity in Film' in Mast and Cohen, *Film Theory and Criticism: Introductory Readings*, 3rd edn, p. 399.
7   Kamilla Elliott, *Rethinking the Novel/Film Debate*, pp. 222, 125, 113–14.
8   Claude-Edmonde Magny, *The Age of the American Novel*, p. 48. The other novelists discussed in this study are Dashiell Hammett, Elmer Rice, James M. Cain, John O'Hara and F. Scott Fitzgerald – all briefly.
9   Magny, *The Age of the American Novel*, p. 40.
10 Magny sees in Steinbeck and others a sign of American writers' tendency to turn from fiction to reportage (*The Age of the American Novel*, p. 170), but this is simply erroneous since from the late nineteenth century onwards (in cases like that of Stephen Crane) it has been common for American writers to have parallel careers as novelists and journalists.
11 Steven G. Kellman, 'The Cinematic Novel: Tracking a Concept', p. 472.
12 Alan Spiegel, *Fiction and the Camera Eye*, p. 117.
13 Keith Cohen, *Film and Fiction*, p. 22.
14 P. Adams Sitney, *Modernist Montage*, p. 2.
15 Sitney, *Modernist Montage*, pp. 146, 163.
16 Laurence Goldstein's *The American Poet at the Movies* (1994) includes Nathanael West and Delmore Schwartz among other writers of prose fiction in its discussion.
17 Susan McCabe, *Cinematic Modernism*, p. 3.
18 Gavriel Moses, *The Nickel Was for the Movies*, p. xvii.
19 Caroline Geduld, 'Film and Literature', p. 126.
20 Sergei Eisenstein, *Film Form: Essays in Film Theory, and The Film Sense* [paginated separately], *Film Form*, p. 208. Eisenstein's lead has been productively followed by Grahame Smith in his *Dickens and the Dream of Cinema* (2003). For Eisenstein's comments on Zola, see *Film Essays*, p. 80.
21 Jean Normand, *Nathaniel Hawthorne*, pp. 308–33.
22 John Conron, *American Picturesque*, pp. 199, 299, 314.
23 William E. H. Meyer, Jr, 'From *The Sun Also Rises* to *High Noon*', pp. 25–37.
24 Paula Marantz Cohen, *Silent Film and the Triumph of the American Myth*, pp. 6–8. Cohen substantiates her argument by addressing the aestheticizing of the body, the dramatic representation of landscape, the 'narrative of the face' and the emergence of the star system.

1

Beginnings

Literary Impressionism: Stephen Crane and Others

As early as 1891 Thomas Edison began experiments with a 'kintoscope' (later called 'kinetoscope'), which would become the first movie camera. Only three years later this device featured as a 'visual telegraph' in John Jacob Astor's novel *A Journey in Other Worlds*, where it has become elaborated into a means of transmitting live video sequences. The instance is symptomatic of the 1890s, when references to visual technology began to be evident in American fiction. The period from the mid-1890s to 1920 marks a transition between such early references to a situation in which film has become fully recognized as a cultural medium. This chapter addresses features of this transition.

Stephen Crane's 1895 classic *The Red Badge of Courage* is frequently taken to be one of the most important examples of literary impressionism, in which the narrative information is limited to the sensory horizon of its protagonist Henry Fleming. His point of view is rendered in terms similar to that of a mobile camera. The composition of scenes shows a proto–cinematic aware-ness of movement. Take for example the opening of chapter 11. First Crane gives us an atmospheric establishing shot in which first clouds – traditionally a sign of foreboding – and then men are described: 'Great brown clouds had floated to the still heights of air before him [...] The woods filtered men and the fields became dotted'. Then Fleming discovers the action near him: 'As he rounded a hillock, he perceived that the roadway was now a crying mass of wagons, teams, and men.' Suddenly everything seems to be happening near him and what is his reaction? To run with the men in flight? No. Instead we are told: 'he seated himself and watched the terror-stricken wagons'.[1] Fleming processes the scene as a spectacle detached from himself. Although we are told that he feels relief at not being the only one to retreat, his relish of the sight before him is of a visual spectacle whose interest increases once a band of cavalry appears moving up the road in the opposite direction. Commenting on such effects in Crane and the impressionists, Keith Cohen argues that 'the fidelity to surface, shape, and aura is less a means of giving an impression of reality than a means of revealing some deeper, hidden essence: in brief, the mechanism of the symbol'.[2] What this account fails to explain in Crane is how this process of revelation is dramatized by positioning the reader as observer close to Henry Fleming, who is himself an observer. Again and again, Fleming acts like a spectator to his own experience and part of learning to see involves him in trying to decide how relevant scenes are to himself.

Of course Crane died in 1900 before the cinema was properly established but there are signs in his writings of a recognition of visual technology. In his story 'The Blue Hotel' an Easterner witnesses a fight but his mind can only register 'like a film […] lasting impressions' of the men, which in cinematic terms resembles a 'freeze' whereby the narrative is temporarily suspended while the men's features can be observed.[3] Another example is even more modernistic and anticipates Dos Passos' use of montage news-effects. The sketch 'Heard on the Street Election Night' is sometimes subtitled 'Passing Remarks Gathered in Front of "The Press" Stereoptikon'. Although this device was designed to give an early form of dissolve from one scene to another, Crane's method of representation is one of fragmentation. His sketch consists of sequence of snatches of speech within which a 'magic lantern man' is attacked for trying to con the audience with his advertisements.[4]

'The Blue Hotel' would tend to confirm Jonathan Crary's assertion that the early technology of the cinema (and of photography) was seen as an 'extension of existing forms of verisimilitude'.[5] Indeed, James Nagel cites a 1934 study which describes impressionism as 'sensory kodaking, a confused mosaic of details, a rivulet of hyphenated photographs'.[6] The only confusing thing here is the bewildering medley of metaphors, and in fact the main analogy between mental impression and Kodak snapshot had been used at least as early as 1905. In that year the novelist W. D. Howells opened his collection of travel sketches London Films with the following statement: 'whoever carries a mental kodak with him (as I suspect I was in the habit of doing long before I knew it) must be aware of the uncertain value of the different exposures'. Then follows an elaborate comparison between the development of a film and the maturing of personal impressions. Howells worries that he might have confined himself to the 'surfaces of things' – a recurrent anxiety in early literary commentary on film and photography – and also reveals that he thinks of his films serially, as in the case of the 'succession of meteorological changes quite past computation' in an English spring.[7]

In London Films Howells figures himself as a sensitized surface registering the sights of London. More importantly, he records the *moving* spectacles of the city, such as the ladies taking walks in Hyde Park or the view from Greenwich across the Thames towards the Isle of Dogs.[8] Howells' main analogy is with the camera, but the visual dynamics of his scenes makes it no surprise that he should describe a weekend excursion as filmic. There he explains that 'villagers in their church-going best [...] our lightning progress suffered us to behold in a sort of cinematographic shimmer'.[9] When commenting on the cinema in 1912 for one of his *Harper's Magazine* editorials, Howells had no doubts about the fact that film was here to stay, rather regretted its apparent descent from pantomime ('it is a convention of the moving picture that life is mostly full of farce'), but then gave his article a Wellsian twist by reflecting how useful the cinema could be for American schools.[10]

Howells, like his friend Henry James, belonged to a pre-cinematic generation, but, just as Howells easily assimilated the camera and film, so Alan Nadel has argued that the famous account of the 'house of fiction' in Henry James's 1908 preface to *The Portrait of a Lady* (with its discourse of apertures, angles and optical instruments) anticipates the cinema in projecting a narrative assembled out of partial visual views. 'James's fiction and mainstream narrative film,' he declares, 'both exploit an imaginary "elsewhere", never fully revealed and rendered with implicitly infinite complexity'.[11] The year after the preface James published the 1909 story 'Crapy Cornelia', where the protagonist's anxiety about proposing marriage is articulated as a blockage of his visual field (his 'view') through a process of close-up: 'the incongruous object was a woman's head, crowned with a little sparsely feathered black hat [...] that grew and grew, that came nearer and nearer, while it met his eyes, after the manner of the images in the cinematograph'.[12] David Trotter has related this scene to James's visit to see 'biograph' war-pictures in 1900 as showing a displacement of the protagonist from the scene of a marriage proposal through the quoted close-up.[13]

Point of View and Spectatorship: Frank Norris and Edith Wharton

References to film technology in turn–of–the–century novels alert the reader to important visual themes in those narratives. One of the first descriptions in American fiction of an early film show occurs in Frank Norris's *McTeague* (1899), where a San Francisco family go to a show whose climax is the kinetoscope. Amid the general hubbub we only get glimpses of the film:

> The kinetoscope fairly took their breaths away.
> 'What will they do next?' observed Trina in amazement. 'Ain't that wonderful, Mac?'
> McTeague was awe-struck.
> 'Look at that horse move its head,' he cried excitedly, quite carried away.

'Look at that cable-car coming – and the man going across the street. See, here comes a truck. Well, I never in all my life!'[14]

Alfred Litton has pointed out that Norris misnamed this show since the kinetoscope was a peepshow; McTeague's family would actually have seen a vitagraph display.[15] The novelty of the show for McTeague lies in the film's conversion of fragments of everyday life into spectacle and in that respect it reinforces Norris's depiction of the sights of the city, although, as David Trotter points out, he is unsure what to do with this unsettling combination of sensory immediacy and technological depiction.[16] One of McTeague's favourite occupations is to watch the street from his first-floor dentist's surgery. He comes to associate each phase of street life with a particular time of day and Norris describes the scene as a spectacle presented for the dentist's benefit: 'day after day, McTeague saw the same panorama unroll itself'.[17] On the one hand the sights catch the observer's attention for a time; on the other, the analogy suggests repetition of the same. The street thus simultaneously attracts and confines. It is only when McTeague finds himself in the open space of the city shoreline that he can begin constructing fantasy images of his own future prosperity, specifically the acquisition and display of a huge gold tooth outside his surgery.[18]

Although McTeague is not the narrator, his perspective dominates the novel. Thus, early perspective shots articulate his growing desire for material success. By the same token, after he begins his flight from the law for murder the composition of his visual field reflects McTeague's increasing isolation and gradual slide into mania. His journey into Death Valley suggests an abandonment of life itself. McTeague becomes dwarfed by the sheer expanse of space: 'miles upon miles to the east and southeast the desert unrolled itself, white, naked, inhospitable, palpitating and shimmering under the sun, unbroken by so much as rock or cactus stump'.[19] It is as if McTeague is a tiny being on a huge organism with a mysterious life of its own. As the heat increases visual clarity collapses into mirage and the fugitive is thrown into prominence as the only figure moving across this huge landscape scanned by the eye of the sun. McTeague's consciousness of his surroundings becomes hallucinatory and intermittent, so that when he has his final fight with the deputy pursuing him, his sense of sight seems to have become temporarily suspended, only returning when he realizes ironically that he is now handcuffed to a corpse. Thus, although McTeague supplies a tight focalization of the novel's scenes, from the 'kinetograph' show onwards he is 'incapable of deciphering the significance of events in his life'.[20] As Mary Lawlor has shown, Eric von Stroheim's film adaptation lost this claustrophobic narrowness of perspective by broadening the point of view away from McTeague himself.[21]

Where Norris uses visual techniques to articulate McTeague's sexual and monetary appetite, Edith Wharton incorporates one of the earliest references to film in *The House of Mirth* (1905) in order to highlight the collective social gaze in her novel. The key episode is a fashionable wedding organized by one of the richest families of New York. Guests are ferried in by special trains; casual onlookers kept at a distance by the police. The description is focalized through the eyes of Lily Barth the protagonist: 'in a church packed with fashion and festooned with orchids, the representatives of the press were threading their way, note-book in hand, through the labyrinth of wedding presents, and the agent of a cinematograph syndicate was setting up his apparatus at the church door. It was the kind of scene in which Lily had often pictured herself as taking the principal part [instead of being] merely a casual spectator, instead of the mystically veiled figure occupying the centre of attention'.[22]

The fact that the event is going to be filmed is of course one of the many displays of wealth here; but more importantly, it is one of the key mechanisms for transforming the scene into a spectacle which can be seen by others. The same is true in verbal terms of the press-man, who will be filling the society columns of his paper. Throughout Wharton's novel there is a constant oscillation between performance and spectatorship. Indeed, the two things merge together in Lily's imagination since she has mentally rehearsed – specifically 'pictured' – such a scene in which she is both leading performer and observer of herself. Film here joins two other analogies – the theatre and art-objects – in articulating this double consciousness on Lily's part of seeing and of being seen.[23] Like the expensive flower she is named after, Lily is a figure constantly on display before judgemental female eyes and a collective male gaze which can shift rapidly from aesthetic appreciation to sexual desire.

It proves to be impossible to separate the sensuous from the aesthetic even when Lily goes to see the wedding presents. In moving close-up Lily's fascinated gaze ranges across the jewels laid out on display: 'Lily's heart gave an envious throb as she caught the refraction of light from their surfaces – the milky gleam of perfectly matched pearls, the flash of rubies relieved against contrasting velvet, the intense blue rays of sapphires kindled into light by surrounding diamonds'.[24] The images are double. They show stones harmonized with their settings. In that sense they show the taste of an invisible 'composer' and at the same time they tantalize Lily by suggesting an ideal state for herself, which she will never achieve. If she were the performer here she would wear the jewels on her body; and if she were wealthy enough to possess the jewels she would have achieved one of her main desires. For Lily dreams of the perfect setting for herself, constantly composing situational images for herself that are denied by crude reality. The present marriage scene collides with Lily's ambition for social stardom. Locked into the position of spectator, she blanks out the couple at the centre of the event, tacitly attempting through this suppression to see the marriage as a fantasy setting for herself. The inclusion of a cine-camera within the marriage scene thus draws the reader's attention to how extensively the novel's action is revealed through a sequence of scenes which are constructed and scrutinized by the novel's characters.

Although Edith Wharton's fiction was adapted for the cinema quite early in her career, references to film are comparatively scarce in her work.[25] In 1914 she went to the cinema in Bilbao with Walter Berry and evidently enjoyed the experience.[26] Three years later Wharton wrote this experience into *Summer*, which describes the bemused experience of a New England librarian being taken into a 'glittering palace' and being subjected to 'blinding alternations of light and darkness'. The sheer variety and pace of scenes prevents her from merging into the audience: 'All the world has to show seemed to pass before her in a chaos of palms and minarets, charging cavalry regiments, roaring lions, comic policemen and scowling murderers; and the crowd around her [...] all kindled with the same contagious excitement, became part of the spectacle, and danced on the screen with the rest'.[27] The young woman's incomprehension alienates her from a situation in which film and spectators merge and 'dance' before her eyes.

1922 and 1923 were years when Wharton sold movie rights to a number of her novels – *The Glimpses of the Moon* (for which Scott Fitzgerald wrote a script) and *The Age of Innocence*, among others.[28] Later in the same decade Wharton expressed her admiration for Anita Loos's *Gentlemen Prefer Blondes* and for Charles Merz's 1928 collection of satirical sketches *The Great American Band-Wagon*.[29] The latter included a section on 'The Silver Screen' which ironically pointed out how marginalized the novelist had become within the Hollywood system and also how the American cinema was making an 'attempt to state life as simply as possible'. Merz continues: 'all primary things are reduced to manageable units in the movies. Human nature itself has been subdivided, catalogued, and card-indexed'.[30] Given her preference for fiction which depends on nuances of character, Wharton would have endorsed Merz's parodic version of Hollywood.

Despite this, we can observe a gradual increase in Wharton's allusions to film during the 1930s. In that decade she formed a friendship with the American novelist Louis Bromfield, a resident in France since 1925 and also a screenwriter for MGM. Wharton complimented Bromfield on his movie projects, wryly contrasting his success with her own situation: 'I have had several cinema proposals,' she admitted, 'but they seem to fade away after a time, and so far no cash has resulted'.[31] Wharton herself was keen for *Ethan Frome* (1911) to be adapted, perhaps because it had so many cinematic quali-ties.[32] In an essay of 1929 on 'Visibility in Fiction' Wharton unconsciously shared Sergei Eisenstein's view of Dickens as a proto-cinematic writer, commenting that 'the startling visibility of Dickens's characters is indisputable; they are "close-ups" before the cinema'.[33] Wharton even uses the same analogy in her 1934 autobiography to express the relation of a finished work to its writer: 'the result of his toil too often presses on his tired eyes with the nightmare weight of a cinema "close-up"'.[34] As Parley Ann Boswell has shown, film offered Wharton a means of exploring her relation to popular culture. In *The Children* (1928) the focalizer Martin Boyne resembles a movie-goer observing the spectacle of modern types. Of one such figure we are told: 'Life's a perpetual film to those people. You can't get up out of your seat in the audience and change the current of a film.'[35] Here film suggests a tempo and a serial sequence of vivid scenes in the life of 'those people'. By the time of her late stories Wharton included the cinema in the signs of modernity which her characters struggled to digest: 'sky-scrapers, advertisements, telephone, wireless, aeroplanes, movies, motors, and all the rest of the twentieth century', reflects the protagonist of 'Pomegranate Seed' (1931).[36] And in 'Charm Incorporated' (1934), the brother-in-law of the American protagonist, having failed in his attempts to become a film star, decides to marry Halma Hoboe ('the greatest of them all').[37] Seen from a distance, the protagonist imagines his relative entering a world of glamour and fabulous wealth but the reality is that his simply becomes the latest in a series of short-lived marriages. 'Charm Incorporated' reflects Wharton's arm's-length engagement with the subject of Hollywood.

Southern Spectacle in Thomas Dixon and *Gone with the Wind*

We have tended to think of Thomas Dixon's relation to the cinema in very simple terms as the man who supplied the narrative for D. W. Griffith's *The Birth of a Nation* but since the publication of Anthony Slide's biography of Dixon, *American Racist*, in 2004 it has become possible for us to see the true complexity of that relation. Dixon began his literary career writing plays, then turned to novels, and finally to film-making; but it was the latter to which he gave priority. The coming of the cinema, he declared in 1923, marked a 'revolution in the development of humanity'.[38] And accordingly the film writer or director should take himself more seriously as leading that revolution. From around 1910 onwards Dixon became ever more enthusiastic about having his writing adapted for the cinema, then began that adaptation himself, and ultimately set himself up in the business of film production, being especially prolific in the 1920s.[39]

In a talk given just before *The Birth of a Nation* (whose title was suggested by Dixon) Griffith outlined one of his main principles of cinematic construction. 'No one questions for a moment the superiority of the cinema for the presentation of spectacles', he declared, but these had to be balanced against the 'smaller things, the scenes in which a smile and a tear are combined'.[40] This alternation between small and large scenes can already be seen in the novel on which *The Birth of a Nation* was based, *The Clansman* of 1905. Setting his novel at the end of the Civil War, Dixon contrasts the national spectacle of the Capitol lit from top to bottom with the smaller personal dramas of those seeking news of war casualties. The climactic scene of Lincoln's assassination shows Dixon's capacity to pace an event through a rapid sequence of 'shots'. Before anyone understands what has happened there is a sequence of events: the crack of the pistol, the first sight of the assassin, and finally a scream from a spectator. Appearance and gesture define the latter's role as the indicator, to point out the assassin: 'Leaning far out of the box, from ashen cheeks and lips leaped the piteous cry of appeal, her hand pointing to the retreating figure'.[41] This would be the point where a title card would convey her words, which in turn trigger a scene of chaos in the theatre. Dixon makes no bones about the visual symbolism here because the collapse of order in the theatre prefigures a larger national collapse. But first Lincoln must die and here Dixon uses a close-up to maximize the pathos of the event: 'Within the box, the great head lay in the surgeon's arms, the blood slowly dripping down, and the tiny death bubbles forming on the kindly lips'.[42]

   Even before he became properly involved in the cinema, scenes like this show that Dixon was already demonstrating a sense of pace and of how to control the scene before the reader. His sequel to *The Clansman*, *The Fall of a Nation* (1916), brings the two media together more closely. The novel was written simultaneously with the screenplay and was published to coincide with the first screening of the film. The prologue assembles a sequence of historical scenes in line with Dixon's conviction that 'the motion picture is the finest vehicle of historical exposition ever devised'.[43] The point which Dixon is eager to establish early in the novel is that the fall of the USA is a disaster waiting to happen. Although a professed republic, the nation's real power lies in the hands of the banker Waldron and this must be shown visually. First through the mise-en-scène we see the luxury of his mansion: 'the crown-embossed electric lantern above the massive table in the centre of the room flooded the gold and scarlet cloth with light'.[44] Again and again Dixon achieves his effects with a broad brush as if the reader were viewing a visual spectacle. Here the image suggests an incongruous monarchism, wealth, and – through the very size of the table – power. Waldron and his fellow conspirators draw together within the circle of light, which in turn makes a scenic comment on the surrounding darkness. The conspiracy to hand over America to an imperial power happens 'off-camera'. The tangible signs of this conspiracy coming to a head are sudden visual disruptions to normal life: the bombing of a cab, the appearance of a 'company of soldiers in dull brown uniforms' and so on. Then come the battles. These are Dixon's set scenes and he takes care to locate his point of view at a high vantage point – in a balloon, for instance. Dixon uses counterpoint in *The Fall of a Nation* to maintain narrative impetus and pace. The political schemings of Waldron alternate with his attempts to persuade a young woman into marriage and once war breaks out sequences of military action alternate with more domestic scenes. The effect is similar to the parallel montage for which Griffith became known.

Dixon's repeated theme of the fall of the nation stands at the centre of his last novel *The Flaming Sword* (1939), which also tried to demonstrate through narrative the power of film. Once again the USA hovers at the brink of collapse. Images of disorder demonstrate the ruin of the South; unemployment rises dangerously, as do the machinations of the Communists. And then there enters the narrative a 'great motion picture' which is brought over from California and shown first to the President, then to the Chief Justice. The proponent of the film explains: 'in scenes of vivid life we have told for the first time the Southern white man's story of the crucifixion of the defeated South by the politicians of 1867'.[45] Both President and judge are astonished by the film, which is of course none other than *The Birth of a Nation*, and Dixon's novel could thus be read as a fantasy of the impact he hoped his films and Griffith's would have on the nation. Furthermore, he planned the novel to be 'bigger and more sensational' than his earlier works, hence the proliferation of violent scenes of civil strife: shootings in Houston, a battle between blacks and whites in Tulsa, and an uprising to produce the 'Soviet Republic of the United States'.

Dixon played his part in shaping the imagination of Margaret Mitchell, who in her youth produced a dramatization of Thomas Dixon's *The Traitor*, before going on to become in the 1920s film critic for the *Atlanta Journal*.[46] The evocation of spectacle in the famous set pieces of *Gone with the Wind* (1936) and the novel's alternation between military and domestic action draw on Dixon's novels and probably his films too.[47] The retreat to Atlanta, for instance, when an 'army of refugees' precedes the Confederate troops, is narrated through panning shots without any frame to evoke the sheer scale of the event: 'Planters and Crackers, rich and poor, black and white, women and children, the old, the dying, the crippled, the wounded, the women far gone in pregnancy, crowded the road to Atlanta, on trains, afoot, on horseback, in carriages and wagons pile high with trunks and household goods'.[48] The trailing sentence captures through its cumulative syntax the length of the human procession, whose movement is measured against the few remaining women standing by the road to help.

With the burning of Atlanta, Mitchell follows a different strategy of gradual approach to the viewpoint of Scarlett O'Hara. In the episode discussed above the point of view is that of an imagined witness to historical events. Now the perspective is narrowed down to that of Scarlett. At first the fire is perceived as a distant transformation of the night sky from black to red. As the fire approaches Scarlett, the noise (screams, explosions) increases until her climactic flight with Rhett Butler is reached. Unlike the earlier retreat or the hospital scenes, the viewpoint now narrows down to a single perspective shot at street level followed by a temporary chaos of light, sound and motion: 'Ahead of them was a tunnel of fire where buildings were blazing on either side of the short, narrow street that led down to the railroad tracks. They plunged into it. A glare brighter than a dozen suns dazzled their eyes, scorching heat seared their skins and the roaring, crackling and crashing beat upon their ears in painful waves. For an eternity, it seemed, they were in the midst of flaming torment and then abruptly they were in semidarkness again'.[49] Mitchell skilfully captures the temporary confusion and drawn-out duration of this flight, which has the symbolism of a rite of passage. All the earlier scenes of landed domesticity are wiped out in scenes like this which evoke destruction and loss.

Action and the Film Business

Starting from his first encounter in 1908 with a French camera crew on Guadalcanal, in other words during the very period when the cinema was first developing into a mass entertainment industry, Jack London became convinced that films were going to supersede the novel. In an interview of 1914 he stated: 'in the portrayal of action, which often is [a] fight, the motion picture is supreme as a medium of expression and it carries the underlying motive, perhaps, better than the alphabet could'.[50] Supreme or not, London had already started incorporating cinematic allusions into his fiction by 1914. In *Martin Eden* (1909), the development of the protagonist's imagination is expressed as an expansion of his visionary sense projected in a visual realization: 'on the screen of his imagination he saw he saw himself and this sweet and beautiful girl [his lover Ruth], facing each other and conversing in good English [...] while ranged about and fading away to the remote edges of the screen were antithetical scenes, each scene a picture, and he the onlooker, free to look at will upon what he wished'.[51] 'Picture' here is misleading because what Eden sees are scenes in violent motion where he drinks with cowboys or witnesses an attempted mutiny. Later, when Eden himself engages in a fight, his heightened visual consciousness results in a double self-consciousness: 'it was to him, with his splendid power of vision, like gazing into a kinetoscope.

He was both onlooker and participant'.[52] London here gives early expression to a double consciousness we will encounter throughout this study: a consciousness of the self as agent and as spectator. Even at moments of intense physical activity, Eden converts himself into spectacle, already imagining how he will appear to a hypothetical future reader/viewer.

In 1916 London developed his interest in film even further, composing the novel *Hearts of Three* in collaboration with the screenwriter Charles Goddard, who would supply London with completed episodes for him to work into novel form. The result was applied cinema: 'the formal structure of the novel adopts the conventions of the movie serials, which kept audiences hanging on the proverbial edges of their seats in anticipation of the next episode'.[53] In his foreword to *Hearts of Three* London records how his novel marked a new departure for him, in line with the 'rise of moving pictures into the overwhelmingly most popular form of amusement in the entire world'. The plan was that he and Goddard would compose episodes independently, then revise them jointly. In the event, Goddard – 'the master of action and lord of speed', as London calls him – worked much faster than London, who acknowledged this in describing the book as a 'novelization of Mr. Goddard's scenario'.[54] This must be one of the earliest instances of the term subsequently used to describe a novel which is an adaptation of a screenplay. *Hearts of Three* is indeed an action narrative. Set in Central America, it combines the lost world theme, updated piracy (one character is a descendant of Henry Morgan), commercial enterprise, and love interest. Apart from his use of sudden reversals, cliff-hanging chapter endings and similar devices, London describes his narrative as a sequence of 'episodes', each containing about ninety 'scenes', which suggests that he conceived it in terms of cinematic scenes containing distinct shots.

London seems to have developed such a strong conviction that film narratives – i.e., in his terms, film *action* narratives – were the way the culture was moving that he not only assimilated cinematic techniques into his fiction, but also tried to arrange to have a film released to synchronize with the appearance of his last novel *The Little Lady of the Big House* (1916).[55] A number of factors converged here. Not only was London fascinated by the medium; he also patently enjoyed his status as literary 'star', and even saw a political dimension to a medium breaking down artistic exclusivity. In *Paramount Magazine* for 1915 he declared 'the motion picture spreads it [the artistic message] on the screen where all can read and understand – and enjoy. No more are the pleasures of the theatre for the rich alone'.[56]

London was one of the first novelists to realize the commercial potential of the cinema, not only in the sale of film rights but in a close involvement with the business of movie-making. As early as 1913 he signed a contract for adaptations of his works.[57] The novelist Rex Beach, who served as president of the Authors' League from 1911 to 1918, similarly urged novelists to put a film clause in their publishing contracts.

Like Jack London, Edgar Rice Burroughs was initially attracted to the cinema by the enormous sums he could make in selling the film rights to his stories.[58] However, Burroughs' interest by no means stopped there. He immediately tried his hand at writing for the screen, of which more in a moment. Like L. Frank Baum of Oz fame, he formed his own company, in his case to make Tarzan films, even buying up land to construct movie sets; he wrote his own Hollywood novel (*The Girl from Hollywood* of 1923 warned about the drug problem); contributed articles to film journals such as *Hollywood Screenland* and *Screen Play*; in 1925 he considered starting a gossip column about the movie capital. In short, Burroughs was fascinated by every aspect of film production.[59] It was his attempts to write scenarios ('synopses' as he called them) in 1915 which were most relevant to his fiction. As he struggled with this unfamiliar genre Burroughs expressed uncertainty whether he should supply a skeletal outline or narrative summary and he made a point of adding love interest to some of his scenarios in order to bring them into line with the conventions of the Western. Early in these attempts Burroughs received the following advice from an official at the Selig Polyscope Company: 'The chief purpose in writing a scenario is to get as much action in each reel as possible and each reel is to contain a strong punch, all leading up to a final climax.' His correspondent continued on the paramount need for the visual to take priority: 'anything that can not be photographed should not be written'.[60]

The prioritization of action was entirely congenial to the journalist and novelist Richard Harding Davis, who reported on the Spanish–American War and then in 1913–14 returned to the same places in Cuba to help Augustus Thomas with a film adaptation of *Soldiers of Fortune* (1897).[61] This was one of the earliest examples of filming on location and was only one of several adaptations of Davis's works. In 1915, one year before his death, Davis was filmed by a Vitagraph crew for the film (now lost) of an invasion of the USA, *The Battle Cry of Peace*. Davis's fascination with the cinema emerges clearly in a 1915 story, 'Billy and the Big Stick'. While in Haiti, the narrator meets the 'King of the Movies', a star on site to help with a US government film called *The Man Behind the Gun*. Davis at once demonstrates a shrewd awareness of the potential in film for national propaganda and the emerging stereotypes which will support that purpose. The film in question is nothing less than a promotional project for the US navy at a moment when the USA was acquiring Caribbean possessions, and is described as follows: 'in moving pictures, in the form of a story, with love interest, villain, comic relief and thrills, it would show the life of American bluejackets afloat and ashore, at home and abroad'.[62] Unfortunately, death cut short Davis's interest in the new medium.

The activities of London, Burroughs and their contemporaries reflect the emerging attractions of California as a focus of the movie industry. Among many others, it attracted Julian Hawthorne, the son of the novelist Nathaniel, who moved to the Hollywood area in 1915 and who spent the rest of the decade writing screenplays (unsuccessfully) for his own earlier stories.[63] It was during the 1910s that the impact of the cinema began to be widely registered. This impact was made the subject of Carolyn Wells' 1919 novel *Patty and Azalea*, which schematically contrasts two courses of life for young women. Patty is a newly married housewife puzzled by the mysterious behaviour of her relative Azalia, who comes from the West to visit. Her secret ambition to become a 'moving-picture actress' is demonstrated when she is recognized in a local film show riding ponies bareback and rescuing a baby from a fire. The contrast with Patty's sedentary domestic life could not be starker, but it is a sign of the times that even she is persuaded to pose in studies by a director. Here the motive is not money so much as the excitement of the medium itself, which is shown to challenge routine stereotypes of female lifestyles.

The Professionals and the Commentators

The lure of the cinema, which initially in the USA meant the lure of Hollywood, was an amalgam of glamour, success, and of course money. Some novelists tried to realize this dream, as we shall see in succeeding chapters; a small number became established professional writers, figures such as Anita Loos, Ben Hecht, and Fannie Hurst. In addition to short fiction, Loos started writing for films as early as 1912 and speedily developed a talent for writing sketches to suit stereotyped subjects such as 'the highbrow' or 'comedy drama'. More importantly, in 1920 she published, with her husband John Emerson, a practical manual entitled *How to Write Photoplays*. Throughout this guide, she stresses the need for clarity and simplicity of action, expressive scenes ('introduce as many tableaus as possible into your story'), a revelatory climax ('make your denouement sudden'), and a final fade-out ('the most artistic close').[64] This manual is in effect a compendium of the early operative conventions in silent film of the period and gives a warning which many novelists found difficult to digest: the primacy of action and story. 'Don't squander time on literary style', she declared.[65]

Ben Hecht, who became the highest paid screenwriter in Hollywood, had a different career. Before he went to Hollywood in 1925, Hecht established himself as a journalist and avant-garde novelist in Chicago. While there, he was invited by Theodore Dreiser to collaborate in a film-writing project which never materialized. He almost certainly encountered the works of poet Carl Sandburg, who was a regular movie reviewer in the 1920s. Hecht's screenplay for Sternberg's *Underworld* (1927) is thought to have been influenced by Sandburg. Following the popularity of gangster films which this helped create, Hecht also wrote the script for *Scarface* (1930), directed by Howard Hawks.[66] Hecht himself (disingenuously) summed up screenwriting in 1929 as an entirely mercenary activity whereby the movie moguls hoax themselves. Of the movies, he wrote: 'I am chiefly interested in how much money I can wangle out of them'.[67] Despite this pose of cynicism, Hecht worked in the movies right up to his death in 1964, collaborating on the script for *Gone with the Wind* (1939) and adapting Steinbeck's treatment for Hitchcock's *Lifeboat* (1944). In 1932 Hecht wrote an adaptation of *Back Street* by Fannie Hurst, who by then was well established in her own right as a screenwriter. Hurst came to Hollywood in 1925 after winning a screenplay competition and for the next ten years became a leading figure in screen- and story-writing for the movies. She sat on the committee to preview the film of Dreiser's *An American Tragedy* and became a close friend of Zora Neale Hurston, championing the cause of African Americans in her novel *Imitation of Life*.[68]

The sustained period of work by Loos and Hecht especially was uncharacteristic of novelists' experience of Hollywood, which was typically sporadic, unpredictable and in some cases fleeting. James T. Farrell, for instance, was a relative late-comer, being invited in 1941 by Twentieth Century-Fox to work on a new script for *Common Clay*. When his script was rejected, Farrell told a friend: 'I am frankly proud to announce that I am a failure in Hollywood'.[69] This sounds as if Farrell's contact with film was very brief, but in fact he devoted substantial space in his 1945 essay collection *The League of Frightened Philistines* to film. In considering the influence of Hollywood on the novel he cites Louis Bromfield as a hack author writing for the cinema and also notes the 'stimulation it has given to a kind of hard-boiled realism', a mode we will encounter later in relation to William Faulkner.[70] In the present study we will encounter a considerable range of opinion about the cinema and Hollywood practice, by no means all negative. The novelist Daniel Fuchs, for instance, came to Hollywood in 1937 and one of his first assignments from Warner Brothers was to work with Faulkner on an adaptation of Eric Ambler's *Background to Danger*. In 1938 he published a fictional sketch called 'Hollywood Diary', in which a young aspiring screenwriter repeatedly registers a dreamlike quality to his experience because he knows so little about what is really going on. This is more of a reflection on the writer's inexperience than on the system. Indeed, looking back on his Hollywood years, Fuchs recalled: 'I found the life in the studios most agreeable'.[71]

He found no intrinsic opposition between novel and film; on the contrary, Fuchs found the collective work of the studios a welcome relief from the solitude of novel-writing.

Lastly, there were those purists who viewed Hollywood as synonymous with cultural corruption. This was the line taken in Edmund Wilson's 1941 booklet *The Boys in the Back Room*, in which he attacked those writers such as John O'Hara who had been touched by 'Hollywood lightheadedness'. He complained particularly of encountering the 'wooden old conventions of Hollywood' in James M. Cain, such as the use of gags and reversals of fortune.[72] The author of a 1937 article 'Writer in Hollywood' warned: 'After two years or even less of dissolves, cuts, fades, irises, montage, tempo, pace, rhythm, zooms, sterilized dialogue and situations, wipes, trucks, sound, scenery, and all the rest, a novelist's style and approaches are almost certain to be impaired and probably ruined. Few, if any, respectable novels have ever come out of Hollywood or from people who have spent much time there.'[73] We hear these sentiments surprisingly rarely – they were shared up to a point by H. L. Mencken, for instance – but it will be the burden of this whole volume to demonstrate that, far from impairing their work, cinematic techniques were eagerly adopted by American novelists as helping them towards new possibilities of representation.

Notes

1 Stephen Crane, *The Red Badge of Courage*, p. 54.
2 Cohen, *Film and Fiction*, p. 37.
3 Crane, *Tales of Adventure*, p. 159.
4 Crane, *Tales, Sketches, and Reports*, pp. 333–37.
5 Jonathan Crary, *Suspensions of Perception*, p. 344.
6 James Nagel, *Stephen Crane and Literary Impressionism*, p. 7. The work quoted is Harry Hartwick's *The Foreground of American Fiction* (1934).
7 W. D. Howells, *London Films*, pp. 1–2.
8 The photographs illustrating *London Films*, courtesy of the London Stereoscopic and Photograph Company, show the city when the horse was the only means of road transport. Cecelia Tichi (*Shifting Gears*, p. 233) cites an Eastman Kodak promotional brochure from about 1914 called *Motoring with a Kodak* in which the new attraction of speed is stressed.
9 Howells, *London Films*, p. 153. Howells began introducing film allusions in his writings from 1913 onwards. According to Edward Wagenknecht, Howells praised the novels of Kathleen Norris as 'a moving-picture show', but Wagenknecht does not cite his source (*William Dean Howells*, p. 147).
10 W. D. Howells, 'Editor's Easy Chair' in Harry M. Geduld, ed., *Authors on Film*, pp. 77–85.
11 Alan Nadel, 'Ambassadors from an Imaginary Elsewhere', pp. 194–95. James similarly stresses presentation from the outside, the importance of point of view, and insists: 'the essence of any representational work is of course to bristle with immediate images' (*The

Art of the Novel, pp. 60, 300, 331).

12 Henry James, *The Complete Tales: Volume 12*, p. 343. Cf. Adeline R. Tintner's 'Henry James at the Movies' for commentary on his story 'Crapy Cornelia'.

13 David Trotter, *Cinema and Modernism*, pp. 21, 115–16.

14 Frank Norris, *McTeague*, p. 62. In *The Octopus* (1901) Norris also uses the kinetoscope analogy to describe the sequence of a day's remembered events passing before the protagonist's 'imagination like the roll of a kinetoscope' (*The Octopus*, p. 209).

15 Alfred G. Litton, 'The Kinetoscope in *McTeague*', pp. 107–12. The advertisement in the theatre for the kinetoscope quotes from W. K. L. Dickson's 1895 *History of the Kinetograph* without revealing that the latter machine had become obsolete, for Litton one of the novel's ironies at the audience's expense.

16 Trotter, *Cinema and Modernism*, pp. 17–18.

17 Norris, *McTeague*, p. 9.

18 George Wead comments on Norris's cinematic use of the 'small, telling detail' in 'Frank Norris: His Share of *Greed*', in Peary and Shatzkin, eds., *The Classic American Novel and the Movies*, p. 149.

19 Norris, *McTeague*, p. 230.

20 Litton, 'The Kinetoscope in *McTeague*', p. 111.

21 Mary Lawlor, 'Naturalism in the Cinema: Eric von Stroheim's reading of *McTeague*', in Norris, *McTeague*, pp. 393–94.

22 Edith Wharton, *The House of Mirth*, p. 69.

23 Gary Totten describes this double consciousness as a reciprocal gaze which is demonstrated in the episode in which Lily acts out a tableau vivant ('The Art and Architecture of the Self', pp. 71–88).

24 Wharton, *The House of Mirth*, p. 71.

25 For full details on movie adaptations of Wharton's fiction, see Scott Marshall, 'Edith Wharton on Film and Television'. See also Kathleen Fitzpatrick, 'From *The Children* to *The Marriage Playground* and Back Again'. John Jobst notes allusions to the cinema in Wharton's *The Marne* (1918), which suggest a false glamorization of war (*Cinematic Technique in the World War I American Novel*, pp. 22–23).

26 R. W. B. Lewis and Nancy Lewis, eds., *The Letters of Edith Wharton*, p. 325.

27 Wharton, *Ethan Frome and Summer*, p. 193.

28 Shari Benstock, *No Gifts from Chance*, pp. 371–72.

29 Lewis and Lewis, eds., *The Letters of Edith Wharton*, pp. 491, 517. Of Merz's book, Wharton wrote: 'it's the best thing of the kind I've seen yet'.

30 Charles Merz, *The Great American Band-Wagon*, pp. 175, 176. Merz presents the American cinema firstly as very big business but his main argument focuses on the secure predictability of films: 'what the movies have done has been to create character-types as easily recognized and as dependable as Harlequin and his merry friends in the old commedia dell'arte. As a nation, that is the way we like our character; a man is one thing or another, and never something in between' (pp. 179–80).

31 Daniel Bratton, ed., *The Correspondence of Edith Wharton and Louis Bromfield*, p. 31. In contrast, Bromfield received story credits for *The Rains Came* (1939) and *Brigham Young* (1940). Details of the movie adaptations of his works are given in David D. Anderson, *Louis Bromfield* (1964).

32 Benstock, *No Gifts from Chance*, p. 438. *Ethan Frome* starts, like *The House of Mirth*, with an establishing shot of the protagonist, who has his history inscribed on his features. We witness Frome, as an outsider, gazing in through the window of the village hall at the dancing. His growing intimacy with Mattie is expressed through an exchange of looks and

their sledge journey builds up to a climactic crash followed by a dissolve. Every phase of the action is expressed scenically through variations on the novella's winter landscape.

33 Edith Wharton, *The Uncollected Critical Writings*, p. 165.

34 Edith Wharton, *A Backward Glance*, p. 197.

35 Parley Ann Boswell, *Edith Wharton on Film*, pp. 63–64; Edith Wharton, *The Children*, p. 101.

36 Edith Wharton, *Collected Stories, 1911–1937*, p. 683.

37 Wharton, *Collected Stories, 1911–1937*, p. 653. The story was originally called 'Kouradjine Limited', then re-titled 'Bread Upon the Waters' for the American serialization, finally being changed yet again to 'Charm Incorporated' in the 1936 collection *The World Over*. Universal produced *Strange Wives* (1935) based on this story, but the film is lost.

38 Anthony Slide, *American Racist*, p. 6.

39 Dixon's library included a copy of John Emerson and Anita Loos's *How to Write Screenplays* (1920).

40 Slide, *American Racist*, p. 100.

41 Thomas Dixon, *The Clansman*, p. 76. Dixon's attention to expressive gesture almost overwhelms his dialogue, as in the climactic scene in *The Sins of the Father* (1912) in which a girl is told that she has a black mother. As the first signs of this 'horror' emerge 'the girl lifted her hand as if to ward a blow'; the carefully paced revelation next triggers a gesture of supplication: 'the girl clenched her hands and sprang in front of him'; finally as her father reveals all and leaves, she 'clung desperately to his arm' (Dixon, *The Sins of the Father*, p. 216).

42 Dixon, *The Clansman*, p. 77.

43 Slide, *American Racist*, p. 95.

44 Thomas Dixon, *The Fall of a Nation*, p. 14.

45 Thomas Dixon, *The Flaming Sword*, p. 209. The episode with the President is probably an allusion to the White House viewing of *The Birth of a Nation* organized for Woodrow Wilson.

46 Anne Edwards, *The Road to Tara*, pp. 31–32, 96, 110–11.

47 When her novel was published, Mitchell received a very complimentary letter from Dixon and a correspondence started between them in which she admitted that she was 'practically raised' on Dixon's novels: Gerald Wood, 'From *The Clansman* and *Birth of a Nation* to *Gone with the Wind*', p. 123. Wood's essay addresses the permutations of the myth of the old South in Dixon, Griffith and *Gone with the Wind* (novel and film).

48 Margaret Mitchell, *Gone with the Wind*, p. 299.

49 Mitchell, *Gone with the Wind*, p. 386.

50 Tony Williams, *Jack London, The Movies*, p. 2. Interview quoted in Marsha Orgeron, 'Rethinking Authorship', p. 93. Williams (chaps. 1–3) gives a detailed account of the early adaptations of London's works, including those in which he himself made brief appearances. The period 1909–1912 was marked by the popularity of action films, taken from narratives like London's.

51 Jack London, *Novels and Social Writings*, pp. 630–31.

52 London, *Novels and Social Writings*, p. 678.

53 Orgeron, 'Rethinking Authorship', p. 104.

54 'Foreword', *Hearts of Three*, pp. vii, ix.

55 *Hearts of Three* makes use of flashback, parallel editing and even dissolves like the following transition: 'it seemed to him that the picture of his forebear faded into another picture' (Orgeron, 'Rethinking Authorship', pp. 107–108).

56 Jack London, 'The Message of the Motion Pictures', in Geduld, ed., *Authors on Film*, pp.

106–107.

57 R. Barton Palmer, ed., *Nineteenth-Century American Fiction on Screen*, p. 210.

58 London became involved in a protracted lawsuit to protect his rights in the 1910s. For full details see Robert S. Birchard, 'Jack London and the Movies'. London was impressed by the educational potential of the new medium, writing in 1915: 'Again the cycle of evolution comes with pantomime and pictures – motion pictures. It batters down the barriers of poverty and environment that obstructed the roads to education, and distributes knowledge in a language that all may understand' ('The Message of Motion Pictures', in Geduld, ed., *Authors on Film*, p. 106).

59 In order to promote his books, in 1908 L. Frank Baum formed a travelling show called 'Fairylogue and Radio Plays', which included short films, lantern slides and stage performances. In 1910, through the Selig Polyscope Company, Baum released four one-reelers, three based on the Oz stories and all scripted by Baum himself. That same year he moved to Hollywood and in 1914 founded the Oz Film Manufacturing Company, which released longer Oz films, again scripted by Baum. When the venture failed Baum sold his company to Universal. For information on Baum's film activities, see Linda McGovern, 'The Man Behind the Curtain'. For commentary on Burroughs' formation of a Tarzan company, Hollywood novel, film articles and proposal to write a Hollywood gossip column, see Irwin Porges, *Edgar Rice Burroughs*, pp. 486, 544–45, 565–66 and 684, 577 respectively.

60 Porges, *Edgar Rice Burroughs*, pp. 365–66.

61 Described in Davis's 'Breaking into the Movies'.

62 Richard Harding Davis, 'Billy and the Big Stick'.

63 Maurice Bassan, *Hawthorne's Son*, pp. 221–22.

64 John Emerson and Anita Loos, *How to Write Photoplays*, pp. 87, 91, 106. Loos worked closely with D. W. Griffith for years and knew many of the novelist-screenwriters in Hollywood, including Scott Fitzgerald. Her short fiction and film treatments are collected in *Anita Loos Rediscovered* (2003). Loos was an important social figure in Hollywood, numbering the expatriate Aldous Huxley among her friends. Her best-selling novel *Gentlemen Prefer Blondes* (1926) spoofs the emerging culture of style and image through the eyes of a would-be film actress. Loos's memoirs include *A Girl Like I* (1966), *Kiss Hollywood Goodbye* (1974), and *Cast of Thousands* (1977).

65 Emerson and Loos, *How to Write Photoplays*, p. 33.

66 William MacAdams, *Ben Hecht*, pp. 5, 101–102, 124–25. This biography includes a full filmography and bibliography. Hecht's screenwriting, including his collaborations with Howard Hawks, is discussed in Richard Corliss, *Talking Pictures*, pp. 2–24. Sandburg's film reviews are collected in *'The Movies Are'* (2000). In 1943 Sandburg signed a contract with MGM to write a novel and help produce a feature film about the USA to be called *American Cavalcade*. The project instead developed into Sandburg's only novel, *Remembrance Rock* (1948).

67 MacAdams, *Ben Hecht*, p. 115.

68 Brooke Kroeger, *Fannie*, pp. 174, 189–90, 206–207. Hurst was involved in Dreiser's plagiarism suit over *Back Street*. The controversy over the 1934 film *Imitation of Life* is discussed in Anna Everett, *Returning the Gaze*, pp. 218–32.

69 Robert J. Landers, *An Honest Writer*, p. 257.

70 James T. Farrell, 'The Language of Hollywood', in *The League of Frightened Philistines*, p. 147. The example he cites of the hard-boiled mode is *The Postman Always Rings Twice*. In this essay and its companion, 'More on Hollywood', Farrell attacks the overwhelming commercialism of Hollywood.

71 Daniel Fuchs, 'Strictly Movie: A Letter from Hollywood, 1989', in *The Golden West*, p. 238. 'A Hollywood Diary' is collected in the same volume (pp. 29–38). On Fuchs' work for the studios, see Gabriel Miller, 'Daniel Fuchs', in Robert E. Morsberger et al., eds., *American Screenwriters*, pp. 109–14. Fuchs' own contribution to Hollywood fiction was a short novel about a film actress undergoing a crisis, *West of the Rockies* (1971).

72 Edmund Wilson, *Classics and Commercials*, pp. 26, 21. Cain started working as a screen-writer for Paramount in 1931, but was never very successful although he enjoyed the Hollywood ambience. Cain's novels will be discussed in Chapter 5. O'Hara began movie reviewing in 1931 and in 1934 moved to Hollywood, working initially for Paramount. He does not seem to have developed much interest in the film medium, being saddled with what he called 'polish jobs' (Frank MacShane, *The Life of John O'Hara*, pp. 101–102).

73 Phil Stong, 'Writer in Hollywood', *Saturday Review of Literature* (10 April 1937), p. 14; quoted in David King Dunaway, *Huxley in Hollywood*, p. 67.

2
Modernist Experiments:
Gertrude Stein and Others

Gertrude Stein's Serial Descriptions

The simultaneous emergence of modernism and the cinema helps to explain why writers found in the new medium possibilities of representing and recording experience.[1] In her survey of the impact of the cinema on modernist practice, Laura Marcus has stated that 'new ways of seeing and animating the object world entered into and shaped literature in the early decades of the [twentieth] century'.[2] Recent studies of modernism have all linked literary experimentation with the new technology of visual representation and David Trotter has argued that the new media promised direct representation of experience while at the same time putting the nature of that existence in doubt.[3] Virtually every writer discussed in this volume was influenced by modernism but the three American writers who will be considered in this chapter – Gertrude Stein, e. e. cummings and William Carlos Williams – all responded directly to the cinema as part of their broader experiments across visual and verbal media. Gertrude Stein's writings can thus be approached as an assault on habits of seeing. In *The Geographical History of America* (1936) she writes: 'They used to think that the world was there as we see it but this is not so the world is there as it is human nature is there as it is and the human mind.'[4] The question of how we see and, even more importantly, how to represent becomes the subject of Stein's experimental prose from an early point in her career.

In 1934, riding high on the popularity of *The Autobiography of Alice B. Toklas* the year before, Gertrude Stein toured the USA delivering lectures. Recording her first impressions of the USA after a long absence, the first event she described was cinematic: 'the first thing that happened was what they called a newsreel' and she continued: 'I just never had seen a talking cinema, and when they said to me will you make one, it was just to me like nothing at all.' Although the making of the newsreel had little impact on her, seeing herself on the screen was another matter, especially in contrast with the earlier experience of seeing her name in print: 'imagine what is that compared to never having heard anybody's voice speaking while a picture is doing something, and that voice and that person is yourself'.[5] This disturbing experience ('it upset me very much', she recalled) has a symbolic importance here because, as we shall see, her visit to the United States impressed Stein with the importance of the cinema and as a result led her to revise her view of her own earlier writings.

Her *Lectures in America* (1935) shed new light on her writings up to that point in their stress on motion: 'the American thing is the vitality of movement', she declares.[6] Not just movement, however. Again and again in this series Stein mediates motion through images of technology: the motor car, aeroplane, and cinema. Looking back on the composition of her plays Stein may well have had her newsreel experience in mind when she considers the complex relation between sight and sound: 'I suppose one might have gotten to know a good deal about these things from the cinema and how it changed from sight to sound, and much before there was real sound how much of the sight was sound or how much it was not. In other words the cinema undoubtedly had a new way of understanding sight and sound in relation to emotion and time.'[7] Unlike her research mentor at Harvard, Hugo Munsterberg (who viewed sound on film with suspicion), Stein characteristically turns her mind to the perceptual implications of sound, speculating whether it can replace visual representation or vice versa; and, more importantly, she speculates about the relation between representation and technology, how seeing can be represented rather than *who* is seeing.[8] The lecture 'Portraits and Repetition' is the central text in Stein's works for establishing an analogy between her methods of writing and film. The latter offered her a new way of articulating her belief in a continuous compositional present: 'Funnily enough the cinema has offered a solution of this thing. By a continuously moving picture of any one there is no memory of any other thing and there is that thing existing, it is in a way if you like one portrait of anything not a number of them.'[9]

Before addressing the importance of this statement, we need to remember the argument Stein had earlier mounted in her famous 1926 lecture 'Composition as Explanation'. Here she retrospectively gives an Emersonian account of how she constructed her early portraits: 'in the meantime to naturally begin I commenced making portraits of anybody and anything. In making these portraits I naturally made a continuous present an including everything and a beginning again and again with a very small thing. That started me into composing anything into one thing.'[10] 'Begin' is the key term here and is crucial for conveying Stein's notion of making her portraits new. It is as if each statement within her descriptions captures a fresh aspect, as if she is observing her subject each time from a fresh angle. On the one hand this ties

Stein's descriptions to the process of seeing; on the other it further implies the fugitive nature of her subjects, especially the human subject.[11]

In *Lectures in America* Stein shifts her concern from beginnings to motion. Process is still in the foreground of her discussion but now she pays more attention to the position of the observer. She begins to ask questions about portraits: does a picture move or the viewer? Does a painting live outside its frame? Her concern with motion and with the relation of figure to ground resembles at times the discussion of the photoplay by Hugo Munsterberg. Stein had participated in psychological experiments at Harvard under Munsterberg's direction in the late 1890s and these experiments undoubtedly left their mark on her early attempts to incorporate characterological measurement in her descriptions. In his *The Photoplay: A Psychological Study* (1916), Munsterberg's general emphasis on the processes of perception would have been congenial to Stein, especially in the 1930s. Munsterberg's considerations of the perception of depth, movement, and the relation of foreground to background, and his assertion that 'the photoplay obeys the laws of the mind rather than those of the outer world', all resemble Stein's explanation of the processes of observation in *Lectures in America* and indeed would shed further light on her adoption of the cinematic analogy.[12] Failing any concrete evidence that she had read *The Photoplay*, however, this connection must remain conjectural.

Casting round in 'Portraits and Repetition' for a way of expressing the relativity of motion, Stein draws an analogy between portraiture and a moving train.[13] Stein's moving pictures are made possible by modern technology, that of the car, the train, and above all the aeroplane. Where the first two offer speed, the last offers a qualitatively different experience which Stein describes in her first portrait of Picasso: 'One must not forget that the earth seen from the airplane is more splendid than the earth seen from an automobile', she declares.[14] For her this kind of view is the very embodiment of modernity. A journey by motor car simply accelerates the experience of travelling by wagon whereas aerial views became a visual symbol of the twentieth century.[15] Stein ran technology and art together in this perception. Looking back on her American journeys in *Everybody's Autobiography* (1938), she drew an analogy between the wandering lines of post-Cubist painting and the shapes of the American landscape seen from the air.[16]

Of course Stein does not suggest that Picasso, Matisse and others went up in planes and then recorded their impressions. Similarly, she does not argue that she was consciously applying cinematic methods in the early 1900s. Stein herself has recorded that she was taking her lead from painters such as Cézanne and subsequent Stein scholars such as Jayne L. Walker have established conclusively that the dominant influence on Stein at the time of composing her early works was the experimentation of Picasso and his contemporaries. What happened in 1934 was that Stein realized an analogy with her practice of repetition – which, she never tired of insisting, was not simple repetition but always the addition of some new element. The transitions of film of necessity compelled the reader to concentrate on the moment of observation. In 'Portraits and Repetition' she writes: 'In a cinema picture no two pictures are exactly alike each one is just that much different from the one before, and so in those early portraits there was as I am sure you will realize as I read them to you also as there was in The Making of Americans no repetition.'[17] The reader will make up his or her own mind about whether or not there is repetition in *The Making of Americans*, but it appears in this description that Stein wanted to insist on the dynamics of portraiture by seeing a diachronic analogy between the movement of prose and film sequence.

In her 1935 essay 'How Writing Is Written' Stein repeats essentially the same argument about repetition in prose being cinematic. Considering how the situation of narrating varies from occasion to occasion, she realized that this was 'the same as the idea of the cinema' and continued: 'the cinema goes on the same principle: each picture is just infinitesimally different from the one before'.[18] 'Picture' is ambiguous here: does Stein mean frame or shot or scene? Later in the same essay, Stein appears to be using the term 'cinema' in a different sense again. Looking back on how she struggled to condense her word-portraits, she recalled: 'I used three or four words instead of making a cinema of it'. With some justification Laurence Goldstein has commented: 'here "cinema" is a term for continuity, for verisimilitude in the representation of reality'.[19] In fact, it is used locally to contrast with Stein's sense of an economy of expression, whereas in the earlier more important passage her analogy is with serial expression. As Wendy Steiner notes, film helped Stein articulate her sense of process: 'the movie metaphor [...] implies that the subject is whole not because one perceives *him* as a whole, but primarily because one *perceives* in a uniform mode'.[20] In fact, as we shall see, by placing her emphasis on representation (and therefore, for the reader, perception) as process, Stein risks showing the elusiveness of her subjects.

Thus in Stein we have the case of a writer recognizing the importance of the cinematic analogy in retrospect, and in what follows I shall be following the lead of Stein herself in considering a cinematic dimension to her early writings. Cinema for her was one aspect of a more general innovation which she summarizes as follows: 'The characteristic thing of the twentieth century was the idea of production in a series, that one thing should be like every other thing, and that it should all be made alike and quantities of them.'[21] In 'Portraits and Repetition' Stein insists that 'any one is of one's period' and that 'this our period was undoubtedly the period of the cinema and series production'.[22] Serial descriptions characterize her first substantial narratives.

Three Lives (completed in 1906 and published in 1909) is a transitional work incorporating two quite different methods of description. The first and third narratives freeze their subjects in non-narrative moments while their portraits are constructed and the subsequent narratives simply confirm the precision of the portraiture. The epithets Stein attaches to her characters fix them as type-figures whose characteristics are confirmed by events. As Keith Cohen has noted, 'the repeated narrative elements function literally to *frame* the intervening diegetic development. The precise repetition engenders in the reader the paradoxical feeling of having witnessed a certain series of events and yet now of being thrust back to the borderlines of the fictional world, right back where he started from'.[23]

This not the case with the central, and by common consent most engaging, narrative of *Three Lives*, the tale of the young African American Melanchtha. Here Stein begins to make use of a descriptive method through serial and apparently repetitive statements about her character. Thus we are told: 'Melanchtha Herbert was always losing what she had in wanting all the things she saw. Melanchtha was always being left when she was not leaving others. Melanchtha Herbert always loved too hard and much too often.'[24] Whereas the 'Good Anna' and the 'Gentle Lena' are framed or contained by their epithets, Melanchtha as a character constantly escapes definition and as a result engages our attention more effectively. The repetition of 'always' in the quoted passage does not carry a force of defining finality. Instead, each statement adds to the reader's sense of aspects of Melanctha which never ultimately add up to a total view of her. Instead of being seen (like Anna and Lena), now she herself sees, and Stein identifies looking with desire, with 'wandering' in every sense: 'Melanchtha liked to wander, and to stand by the railroad yard, and watch the men and the engines and the switches and every-thing that was busy there, working'.[25] Melanchtha is not defined by any single situation and it becomes symbolic that she is drawn to places of transit: the railroad yards and later the dockyards. Stein repeatedly uses the railway and roads as images of transition and this bears directly on Melanchtha's mobility of character.[26] By this point she has appropriated the narrator's own descriptive idiom and appeals to a sub-verbal dimension to behaviour not susceptible to representation. Stein's transition away from the more conventional realism of the frame tales in *Three Lives* can thus be seen as a move away from the straightforwardly visual towards a serial descriptive method whereby each statement about her central character positions the reader slightly differently in relation to her subject.

The Making of Americans (written 1906–11 but not published until 1925) is Stein's massive contribution to the American family novel. Despite its extreme length, Stein's novel ironically demonstrates the difficulty of knowing ('perhaps no one will ever know the complete history of every one') as reflected in the difficulty of composition. At one point the narrator reflects: 'Every one to me just now is in pieces to me'.[27] But there is another, even more striking aspect of this novel which suggests a paradox in Stein. When we consider the visual dimension to prose we expect details of appearance, colour, setting and so on; but it is exactly these circumstantial details which Stein's method excludes. Because she pays so much attention to characters' subjective life and because she is constantly categorizing characters, she leaves no space for the data that would enable us to visualize them. In trying to cope with the fact that Stein's cinematic method actually led her away from visual detail some critics have even proposed an analogy between single descriptive statements and strips of film.[28] In *The Making of Americans* the narrative abstracts characters as type-figures whose relations are examined in the course of the novel. The result is not just abstract, but also clinical. Julian Murphet has argued persuasively that the very title of *The Making of Americans* suggests a process of assembly like that on a factory production line and sees the novel as demonstrating a 'series production' of humanity.[29] He relates the sequences of resemblance which Stein traces out to the mass production methods which F. W. Taylor was introducing in the period. The 'making' in the title therefore suggests the 'lab-work of the narrator herself who constructs Americans from models down to interchangeable "pieces", pieces which are objectively calculable and invariant: snapshots, gestures, habits, "bottom natures"'.[30]

This account of composition by interchangeable parts fits the metafictional statements Stein makes on seeing in *The Making of Americans*. Firstly she explains how we perceive an individual through resemblances: 'Everybody is a real one to me, everybody is like some one else too to me. Almost every one in looking at any one mostly feels that that one they are then seeing, is like some one else they have known in their living'; then she admits the unavoidable subjectivity in vision: 'Every one has their own way of seeing every one, every one has some that are more complicated to them than other ones'.[31] Stein's austerely objective language in the novel could be read as an attempt to exclude this subjectivity. Janet Hobhouse comments that '*The Making of Americans* was in Gertrude's mind to some extent a scientific work. It was to set forth a theory of behaviour.'[32] The novel's scientific dimension emerges through its prose, which at no point assimilates the point of view or idiom of the characters. All the novel's data is scrutinized from a distance, as if by a scientific observer. P. Adams Sitney, whose *Modernist Montage* (1990) was the first study to pursue the cinematic analogy in Stein, warns the reader what not to expect in her work, declaring that 'Stein's imaginary cinema is not essentially a mode of visual representation but a rhythm capable of articulating the temporal duration of an entity'.[33]

Sitney's view of the complexity within Stein's filmic comparisons was picked up and developed significantly by Susan McCabe, whose *Cinematic Modernism* (2005) constructs a three-way analogy between modernist poetic practice, experimental film, and hysteria. Of her case studies, that of Stein works well (the others are H.D., William Carlos Williams, and Marianne Moore) because she demonstrates a continuity of interest in motor automatism (the subject of her psychological experiments at Harvard under Hugo Munsterberg in the 1890s), stylistic repetition, and the comically mechanistic movements of Charlie Chaplin. The latter she sees as showing an 'intricate cooperation between automatism and will'; and she compares Henri Bergson's notion of comic stiffness with Chaplin's performances, which render 'life as a repeating mechanism'.[34] The comparison with Chaplin is not at all fanciful since he was admired by a number of the modernists (Hart Crane, Delmore Schwartz and others). Indeed Laurence Goldstein argues that Chaplin became an international sign of modernism and presented an 'ingratiating symbol of American mass culture'.[35] Stein and Chaplin met in Hollywood during the former's 1934 tour.[36] In his autobiography Chaplin himself parodied Stein as an elephantine *grande dame* being fêted by the company. Her reported comments on film are relevant here: 'She theorized about cinema plots: "They are too hackneyed, complicated and contrived." She would like to see me in a movie just walking up the street and turning a corner, then another corner, and another.'[37] Naturally enough, this suggestion reminded Chaplin of Stein's repetitive prose style. For her part, Stein explained her desire to write a drama in which nothing happened and it seems as if they agreed to differ: 'he wanted the sentiment of movement invented by himself and I wanted the sentiment of doing nothing invented by myself, anyway we both liked talking but each one had to stop to be polite and let the other one say something'.[38]

So far I have been suggesting that Stein 'discovered' the cinema in the 1930s, but one of her least-discussed works would question that argument. In *The Autobiography of Alice B. Toklas* we are told that William Cook, an American painter who was forced by poverty to become a taxi-driver, 'inspired the only movie Gertrude Stein ever wrote in english [sic]'.[39] The result was a brief scenario, laconically entitled 'A Movie', which Stein wrote in 1920. The text is introduced by a modernist gloss on language with lines such as 'Eyes are a surprise' and 'Printsess a dream' which, Beth Hutchison argues, indicate a paradox in that Stein is writing 'words which would become invisible (neither seen nor heard) were the scenario to be filmed'.[40] In fact this paradox is more apparent than actual because – in these pre-talkies years – Stein is sketching out a sequence which would incorporate title cards. She expresses through reported speech those actions which could be performed through gesture and through direct speech (not, however, separated typographically from the rest of the text) those expressions which would probably need titles. As Sarah Bay-Cheng argues, 'the script is composed of a series of visual moments or exchanges'.[41]

It is striking throughout how Stein understands the needs of the medium. She introduces sequences with establishing shots and action cues. The story is simple. Since his wallet is empty, our hero decides to become a taxi-driver in 'gay Paree' and, once America enters the war, is drafted into the Secret Service. Up to this point we have had a preamble. Then the action proper begins: 'Back tomorrow. Called up by chief of secret service. Goes to see him. Money has been disappearing out of quartermaster's department in chunks. You've got a free hand. Find out something.'[42] Each of the first three sentences would correspond with a shot and the very tempo of Stein's prose is unusually brisk. The short sentences and paragraphs set a pace, which corresponds with the action, an action depending on the speed of the taxi. Setting off on his mission, the protagonist collides with two men on motor-cycles near Avignon and is taken to the nearby hospital. On his (surprisingly rapid) recovery, he learns that the two officers have set off for Pont du Gard and sets off in pursuit. The chase, a standard feature of silent action movies, reaches its climax with the capture of the two men, at which point Stein reveals the fact that they were the thieves. Her management of pace shows a shrewd awareness of action and also of when to disclose information to the reader/viewer. The scenario concludes with a finely patriotic tableau with the protagonist in his taxi bringing up the rear of a victory parade while American and French flags flutter in the breeze. The rapid tempo of the action suggests a debt to slapstick comedy and overall Sarah Bay-Cheng sees the script as a 'jokeless, humourless gag film'.[43]

Stein's second excursion into film-writing was a brief scenario called 'Film: Deux soeurs qui ne sont pas soeurs', which appeared in the *Revue Européenne* in summer of 1930. Prior to that, in 1927 she had contributed two essays – 'Mrs Emerson' and 'Three Sitting Here' – to the film journal *Close Up*, but there is little critical agreement about their cinematic dimension.[44] There is no dialogue in 'Film', which is partly an exercise in specifying appearance and movement without any explanatory contextualizing. In a Paris street a laundress is gazing at a photograph of two poodles, whereupon two women get out of a car and demand to see the photograph. A further elegant young woman enters the car but is ejected by the first women, who leave. At this point the laundress discovers that she no longer has the photograph and begins to tell her story to a young man. End of first scene. The action now shifts to a second Paris street, where a second laundress is accosted by the original two women who thrust upon her the photograph of the dogs. The two women then leave and the second scene concludes. In the third and final scene, two days later in the original street, the first laundress once again meets the elegant young woman and the young man; the two women in the car pass holding in their arms a poodle and an unidentified packet. Although words pass between some characters, the sketch resembles a scenario for a silent film, where all is movement and where emotion is revealed through expression. No character is named and the sequence takes on a surreal dimension from the apparently chance encounters in the French metropolis. Duplication teases the reader with a significance which remains out of reach. In short, we are in the position of the three on the pavement: 'les trois sur le trottoir le [the car] regardent passer et n'y comprennent rien'.[45] Ironically, the sequence of action is in itself quite clear and easy to visualize. Unlike Stein's earlier screenplay which cues in comic recognitions, *Film* for Beth Hutchison 'exemplifies a more hermetic style [...] privileging the creators of the film over its spectators'.[46]

The Surreal Caricatures of e. e. cummings

Despite e. e. cummings' lifelong interest in the cinema, this has been largely neglected by his critics. Two of his closest friends from Harvard no doubt strengthened this interest: John Dos Passos (discussed in Chapter 6) and James Sibley Watson, who took over *The Dial* in 1919, transforming it into a major literary journal.[47] Gertrude Stein, however, exerted a formative influence. In 'The New Art' (1915), an essay published while he was still at Harvard, cummings praised what he saw as the triumph of line over realism in Cubist and Post-Impressionist art, and took Stein's *Tender Buttons* as a work symptomatic of the direction prose might take following the lead of Cézanne or Matisse. cummings also praised Amy Lowell's writing as a 'clear illustration of development from the ordinary to the abnormal'.[48]

cummings was determined to move away from realist representation and he drew on visual technology to help rationalize that move. 'The artist who represents is bad,' he asserted in 1920, 'because he represents something which a camera can represent better.'[49] Accordingly, his view of the cinema was ambivalent. In 1924 he briefly held a post at the Famous Players-Lasky Corporation studios in Astoria near New York but wrote his mother that he had been 'very busy doing absolutely nothing'.[50] When he visited Hollywood in 1935 he took an intense dislike to the people in the business, though claimed to have tried to sell a scenario to MGM.[51] During the 1920s the editor of *Vanity Fair* encouraged cummings to contribute a series of comic sketches or 'turns', among which two commented on the cinema. In 'A Modern Gulliver Explores the Movies' cummings adopts the mask of an intrepid 'English explorer' who penetrates the wilds of the Astoria studios where the local customs are described as if belonging to an alien barbaric culture.

The most important of these sketches, however, is 'Vanity Fair's Prize

Movie Scenario', which burlesques the kind of writing competitions promoted by magazines such as *Photoplay*. Here cummings presents 'A Pair of Jacks' as the 'most perfect example of the "popular" type of movie'.[52] Indulging his love of the grotesque, he plays throughout on incongruities: a Chinese setting with Mexican names, a mayor who is a young woman with a red beard, a 'hero' arriving at the gates of Heaven wearing a nightie and smoking a pipe. Similarly cummings juxtaposes slapstick, melodrama, and domestic scenes without making any attempt to link them. Barbara Seidman comments: 'By blending these stories in such irrational ways, cummings strikes at the heart of straightforward causal narrative structure. He deliberately thwarts the formulaic simplicities which are the cornerstone to melodramatic narrative at the same time that he uses their surface characteristics.' But does cummings simply ridicule film here? Not so, according to Seidman, because, as he parodies film practice, cummings 'permits his readers to glimpse the abstract potential of the medium once it has been freed from the obligation to tell a story'.[53] This is exactly the self-liberating move cummings made when he was preparing to write his novel *The Enormous Room*, but there is another characteristic of the comic scenario, which can be shown from the following excerpt:

> SCENE 10. Exterior Town. Tampalinas Guerrero, nursing his snake bite, puts down the telephone to die.
> TITLE: *And the sun's last rays reflected the passing of a good Indian.*
> SCENE 11. Exterior Deck. Shot of Jack Clinto with Elizabeth Bilge in his arms lowering himself from the rail to the open sea [...]
> SCENE 12. Exterior Home. MEDIUM SHOT of Grandma standing gracefully on a piano stool [...]
> SPOKEN TITLE: *'Don't worry, birdie, Granny won't hurt your babies!*[54]

cummings' parody is based on an expert knowledge of filming. He shows an awareness of when to introduce titles, the length of shots, close-ups, the function of irises and fades; in short, he demonstrates a knowledge of how a film sequence could be constructed and – through ridicule – a familiarity with scenic composition which is reflected in his own novel.

Up to this point it might sound as if cummings' attitude to film was mainly negative, but to balance this account we need to consider his 1930 essay 'Miracles and Dreams' which makes his major statement on the cinema. Here cummings praises *Battleship Potemkin* and Chaplin as giving relief from the 'habitual idiocy' of modern films and finds the following saving grace: 'it is thanks to the progenitors of the animated cartoon that the miraculous eyes occasionally wink and monotonous mobility forgets itself in fabulous clowning'.[55] For cummings animated cartoons are a medium of miracle in which reality can be suspended or transformed. Here he offers yet more examples of his preference for the absurd, for games which destabilize reality. In his 1950s' lectures he states of himself: 'like a burlesque comedian, I am abnormally fond of the precision which creates movement'.[56] This relish for comic mobility helps to explain his special feeling for Chaplin (one of his art collections included a sketch of that actor) and helps further to explain the method cummings used to depict his temporary imprisonment by the French authorities during the First World War, which was described by one reviewer as being 'jerky, rather like a Chaplin movie'.[57]

When *The Enormous Room* was published in 1922 cummings claimed that 'the appeal of the book is largely documentary', but nothing could be farther from the novel's method than documentary.[58] The most predictable narrative model for expressing his experiences would have been a prison diary but this is rejected as being false to a prisoner's sense of time. For reasons quite different from Gertrude Stein's, the narrator situates the reader within a continuous present in which there is no necessity for sequence: 'I shall [...] lift from their grey box at random certain (to me) more or less astonishing toys'.[59] cummings casts himself as a producer, introducing particular effects for the reader's entertainment. Thus, at one point he explains: 'And now, just to restore the reader's faith in human nature, let me mention an entertaining incident'.[60] The reason for cummings' strategy must have been compensatory. During his imprisonment cummings would have been passively subject to the whims of the French authorities. In his novel, however, cummings retrospectively takes control of his experiences, orchestrating them according to his sense of the absurd.

If this is so, cummings must cast himself as an observer within his narrative, like a camera in the sense that he is within the situation but somehow not of it. He has no past before the narrative, nor any future afterwards. He simply functions as a narrative means in shaping descriptions. As we shall see, his skill at painting comes out repeatedly in the portraits he presents, but cummings feeds a cinematic consciousness into his narrative at every point through his evocation of the mobility of observation. A character with particular interest or energy he terms a 'kinesis'; he intermittently uses the present tense to convey immediacy; and at an early point divides the description into 'shots' designated 'glance one' and 'glance two'. The most explicit allusion to the cinema occurs when the narrator finds himself the possessor of money – a very rare case since all possessions have been impounded. Instantly a crowd gathers round him. Cautiously he pockets his banknote. 'Then I gazed quietly around with a William S. Hart expression calculated to allay undue excitement. One by one the curious and enthusiastic faded from me.'[61] Hart was the first film star to establish the Western genre, projecting himself as one not to be meddled with.[62] Of course, the narrator's self-comparison is tongue-in-cheek because by no stretch of the imagination is he a tough guy. The effect is as if a director has given himself a brief cameo role within his own movie, again a brief fantasy of power, which can only be comic within the general situation of imprisonment.

cummings' exploitation of space underpins his scenic sense. Although he alludes to *The Pilgrim's Progress* in the novel, the analogy is awkward since Bunyan's is a linear, end-directed narrative. In practice, cummings defines his action spatially. The prison as a whole, with its yard, passages and rooms, functions like a set within which characters appear and disappear abruptly. The most startling instance of this is the director who habitually bursts out of his office:

> And BANG! would a door fly open, and ROAR! a well-dressed animal about five feet six inches in height, with prominent cuffs and a sportive tie, the altogether decently and neatly clothed thick-built figure squirming from top to toe with anger, the large head trembling and white-faced beneath a flourishing mane of coarse blackish bristly perhaps hair, the arm crooked at the elbow and shaking a huge fist of pinkish, well-manicured flesh, the distinct, cruel, brightish eyes sprouting from their sockets under bushily enormous black eyebrows, the big, weak, coarse mouth extended almost from ear to ear and spouting invective, the soggy, brutal lips clinched upward and backward showing the huge horse-like teeth to the froth-shot gums.[63]

Although this figure is shouting, the scene is so overwhelmingly visual that it resembles the sudden entrance of a caricature villain in a silent film. cummings carefully guides the reader from an overall initial impression of size through individual features from fist to eyes and mouth.

The suddenness of this entrance is typical of events in *The Enormous Room*. cummings implies that nothing has a meaningful connection with anything else and this perception authorizes him to present every scene as a bizarre and bewildering spectacle. Estrangement effects are constant, like his arrival at a station by night on the way to the prison: 'The yellow flares of lamps, huge and formless in the night mist, some figures moving to and fro on a little platform, a rustle of conversation: everything seemed ridiculously suppressed, beautifully abnormal, deliciously insane'.[64] The syntax mimics the disconnection between the narrator's visual data, which he relishes as absurd. Because he supplies the lens for the reader, the narrator determines dimension. Thus, his first perception of the communal room shared by the prisoners expands until it has become enormous. Similarly the characters he sees mutate bewilderingly. They might segment into different coloured aspects, transform into animals, or their features might seem to disintegrate.

The composition of scenes helps this effect. At one point the narrator sees guards carrying 'two girls, who looked perfectly dead' out of the women's cells which are on fire. Then out of the smoke emerges a prostitute who here embodies vitality itself: 'shouting fiercely through the darkness – stood, triumphantly and colossally young, Celina'.[65] The delay of her name until the very end of the sentence and the brief pause after that ending give an effect like a freeze where the central figure stands out in defiance against a background of smoke and darkness. Here and elsewhere, cummings strikingly contrasts figure with ground. The privileging of characters' appearances, however grotesque, over the physical detail of their surroundings softens the impact of the latter and correspondingly reduces the effect of claustrophobia we might expect from a prison setting.

cummings' 1933 record of his trip to Russia also includes an intermittent cinematic element, which this time actually pulls against his main technique in *Eimi*. Shortly after his arrival in Russia cummings records the following detail: 'a kindly little man reassures with slowed-up-movie wavings'.[66] This is one of the earliest in a series of film allusions, which cummings uses to convey his sense of image and movement, an effect increased by the use of the present tense throughout. At one point he is describing the approach of a tram, literally using a kind of mobile Cubism: 'imagine a cube , black and with silver edges ; if you can visualize the gradual prodigious tumescence of this cube, whose substance meanwhile turns through greedy red toward fatal green while its six facets curl with some huge inner strain [...]'.[67] cummings exactly captures the growth in the size of the image which is the visual sign of its movement within the observer's visual field, and also the permutations of colour through which the tram passes as it draws near. The effect is at once dynamic and abstract, but the abstraction of the image does not in any way compromise the reader's comprehension; instead, its abstraction is part of its visual immediacy.

This is an example of a moving object. Compare it with an image of caricatures, which harks back to *The Enormous Room* and where the film comparison is explicitly incorporated into the description: 'in stagger 2 extraordinary caricatures (1 grim little ratfaced chap swamped beneath somebody's much too big overcoat , somebody else's differently much too big shirt, Charlot's pants, and a hatlessly dripping hat remarkably similar to some recently tossed custard pieless pie: 1 big , ungainly, gruesome, horribly everywhere who from a far too tight boy-scout uniform protrudes – and more especially aloft, via lumps of totally hairless skull)' [sic].[68] With his usual sharp eye for appearance, cummings plays on incongruity here, on the mismatch between the body size of these two figures and their outlandish dress. The first is physically small but swamped in huge (presumably cast-off) clothes, whereas the second seems to be squeezed out of his bizarre scout's uniform. We should remember the context here in the Revolutionary

Literature Bureau and then we can recognize a satirical effect behind cummings' obvious relish of these two figures. Throughout *Eimi* he is dismayed by the visible poverty of Russia and also by the Soviets' unrelieved solemnity, especially towards culture. This solemnity characterizes the manner of the two men which is grotesquely at odds with their appearance. The passing comparison with Chaplin not only helps the reader to visualize the smaller man but also draws an ironic analogy with an actor who repeatedly ridicules authority figures in his films. Such passages are relatively rare in *Eimi* because cummings constantly indulges in verbal and typographical pyrotechnics to give visual dimension to the text itself rather than to the figures within it.

William Carlos Williams' Segmented Sequences

Again and again in this study we see how writers' reactions to the cinema are inseparable from their scrutiny of visual representation. The cinema might suggest a way forward; it might offer a useful analogy; or it might present a negative phenomenon which in itself can help a writer take a new direction. cummings is clearly drawn to slapstick for its potential to ridicule officialdom visually. Like cummings, William Carlos Williams expressed suspicion of the cinema for a number of reasons. In surveying early twentieth-century culture for his unfinished study *The Embodiment of Knowledge* he saw the cinema as symptomatic of the replacement of scientific enquiry with services: 'at such a time multiplication of services takes the place of serious effort, and the type of genius represented by Thomas Edison is predominant, the theories of "service" (not the fact), the pragmatism, and philosophical (cinematizations) (slow motion) amateurs were turned up'.[69] Then there was the problem of film's superficial popular appeal, which Williams saw as encouraging a vagueness of perception or a factitious glamour. In *The Great American Novel* (1923) he cites Vachel Lindsay as arguing that 'America needs the flamboyant to save her soul' and notes the general craving for excitement in the vogue for jazz and the flapper, continuing: 'even the movies, devoid as they are of colour in the physical sense, are gaudy in the imaginations of the people who watch them; gaudy with exaggerated romance, exaggerated comedy, exaggerated splendour of grotesqueness or passion'.[70] In the novel a girl embodies this need by dreaming of a 'saviour of the movies' to lift her out of her humdrum existence while travelling on the subway. Throughout his career Williams remained hostile to popular film. In 1960 a series of photographs for Whitman's *Leaves of Grass* only confirmed his attitude. 'As photograph after photograph was uncovered for me to spend my eyes upon,' he wrote, 'I realized for the first time how much we are losing in the movies. I have long realized its triviality compared with for instance a painting – but also a still.'[71] Despite Williams' hostility to popular film, he was unwavering in his admiration for the writings of James Joyce, who arguably had already incorporated a cinematic dimension within his fiction, and Williams was particularly impressed by the techniques of fragmentation used by the Surrealists.[72]

In his prose improvisations of 1920, *Kora in Hell*, Williams incorporated the cinema in his meditations on visual perception. Waking one morning, he tries to record the first sights of the day but 'a vague cinema lifting its black moon blot all out'. Briefly the morning sun is smothered by the 'head's dark'. The rich light of the external scene is displaced by internal images and this leads Williams on to the following meditation: '*In the mind there is a continual play of obscure images which coming between the eyes and their prey seem pictures on the screen at the movies. Somewhere there appears to be a mal-adjustment. The wish would be to see not floating visions of unknown purport but the imaginative qualities of the actual things being perceived accompany their gross vision in a slow dance, interpreting as they go*' (italics in original).[73] This passage shows none of the social anxieties expressed in the earlier quotation, but rather forms part of what Susan McCabe argues is a cinematic technique which Williams uses throughout *Kora in Hell* to estrange the reader's perception of the body: 'his mythic transit [into a symbolic underworld] points towards cinema's capacity to make the body "continually other" [...] and to intensify sensation in the spectator'.[74]

Kora in Hell presents a montage of images, miniature narratives and brief meditations all linked by a guiding narrative voice which is constantly urging on the reader with expressions such as 'stand aside' or 'pass it over' which give a situational immediacy to each segment. And even within each segment Williams frequently uses 'cuts' to prevent a factitious continuity from emerging. Before his comment on cinematic mental images quoted above, for example, he describes a scene of childbirth in such a way that each sentence repositions the reader in relation to the local subject. Thus, the narrator enters the building and registers the striking difference of temperatures between rooms: 'one room stove-hot, the next the dead cold of a butcher's ice box. The man leaned and cut the baby from its stem. Slop in disinfectant, roar with derision at the insipid blood stench: hallucination comes to the rescue on the brink of seriousness: the gas-stove flame is starblue, violets back of L'Horloge at Lancy. The smile of a spring morning trickles into the back of his head and blinds the eyes to the irritation of the poppy red flux. A cracked window blind lets in Venus. Stars.'[75] In the second sentence Williams includes himself within the scene as if watching his own actions. The woman giving birth is depersonalized into a physical organism producing child and blood, implicitly less important than the imagistic memory links which further detach the narrator from the immediate situation. A flower from the past temporarily 'blinds' him to the 'flower' of the present in the poppy-red blood. But Williams never allows the actuality of the situation to lapse and so a blind actually lets in a glimpse of stars. He plays on a complex sense of the visual whereby each sentence moves forward with fresh segments of sense-data which remind the reader of the narrator's selective perceptions.

For Susan McCabe 'the descent and regeneration Williams imagines operates through cinematic metaphors'.[76] And she draws suggestive comparisons between Williams' method and that of Surrealist cinema, a method of progression through isolated sections. Williams was preoccupied with giving shape and meaning to what he called the 'inevitable flux of the seeing eye' and he attempted to realize this aim by cutting into sequences.[77] The result is that, as in Gertrude Stein, the reader is constantly made aware of the compositional process. In *Kora in Hell* at one point Williams offers a 'portrait of a disreputable farm hand made out of the stuff of his environment', constructed out of glimpses of domestic activity.[78] The description then cuts into an account of domestic cleanliness in a brief, quasi-documentary sequence. Here again the reader never loses the sense of being positioned as an observer and, as we shall see later, the question of the reporter intruding on the privacy of the observed was to become a major issue in 1930s' documentary.

The speed of visual impressions is crucial to Williams' method and Cecelia Tichi has situated his writings within a machine aesthetic which was emerging in the USA between 1910 and 1930. Specifically she argues that *A Novelette* (written in the early 1920s, published 1932) demonstrates 'cultural conditions of speed and acceleration', and she cites the following city scene as being 'explicitly photographic': 'As the gates closed and the bridge slowly swung open wasting his time enforcing a stand-still, he thought again of "Juan Gris," making a path through the ice. That was the name of the approaching tug boat seen through the branches of a bare beech tree. It had a white cabin and a black stack with a broad yellow band around it.'[79] While Tichi is surely right to see a connection between this image and Stieglitz, whom Williams greatly admired, her general assertion that Williams was practising a 'kinetic' method implies that he is concerned to express movement, as he does here through the closing bridge and approaching tug. The more relevant comparison then would not be with a photographic still but with a brief cinematic sequence. It is the movements of the bridge which catch Williams' imagination.

When Williams started his novel trilogy in the 1930s he reduced the cuts in his narrative and by avoiding the use of speech marks ran together description, summarized thought, and speech into a single continuum of data. *White Mule* (1937) moves away from the machine aesthetics of Williams' earlier work, instead thematizing the machine in gigantic printing presses and juxtaposing them with organic processes like the birth which opens the narrative. There is a new quality of vision in this novel which could partly be explained as a medical perspective, though that sounds inappropriately clinical. What Susan McCabe saw as a voyeuristic quality in his poetry now features as a sustained attention to all the physical processes of childbirth, its aftermath, and the first years in a child's life. Consider how *White Mule* opens: 'She entered, as Venus from the sea, dripping. The air enclosed her, she felt it all over her, touching, waking her'. The child's birth is not presented as an exit from the mother's body, rather an entry into the scene and therefore into life itself. Then the child is given an elementary sentience which further privileges her centrality in the situation and which resists her designation by adults as an 'it'. The first person to speak is the midwife, the second the mother, and the third the father, 'at the door'.

The positioning of the only male present at a distance from the bed is important because Williams is giving us visual data unavailable to any male character. Thus, the midwife cuts the umbilical cord: 'in prehistoric ooze it lay while Mrs D wound the white twine about its pale blue stem with kindly clumsy knuckles and blunt fingers with black nails and with the wiped-off scissors from the cord at her waist, cut it – while it was twisting and flinging up its toes and fingers into the way – free'.[80] The close-up is near to Mrs D's point of view but the attention spreads away from the baby to include the signs of her lack of hygiene and, by inference, her poverty. Williams never allows the visual detail to dehumanize the baby nor does he attempt a photographic accuracy. Indeed in 1938 he expressed his misgivings, in relation to the painter and photographer Charles Sheeler, about the 'too facile copying by the camera'.[81] Williams avoids this in the scene we were just considering by shifting the visual angle, drawing back from the bed to render dialogue near the door, and by drawing out the act of cutting. He implicitly refuses here the social convention of making childbirth an exclusively female scene and by so doing foregrounds the physicality of the baby herself. This sets going a major motif and a descriptive method, which returns constantly to the vulnerability of Williams' characters to poverty, hunger and illness.

Williams, Surrealism and the Revolution of the Word

Like Stein and cummings, Williams conceived his work in visual terms. In 1927 he noted 'I will make a big, serious portrait of my time'; and four years later he added that experimental writers were seeking a language that would 'embody all the advantageous jumps, swiftnesses, colours, movements of the day'.[82] The qualities Williams added in 1931 focus on speed and rapid transitions, in other words on cinematic qualities. In his survey of the impact of

American film on the French avant-garde Richard Abel stresses exactly these characteristics. It was, he argues, the films of Chaplin, William S. Hart and others which suggested possibilities of rapid scene change and then fragmentation to writers such as Blaise Cendrars, who was to be an important influence on Dos Passos and whom Williams met and knew.[83] Williams' writing appeared in literary journals such as *Transition* and *Pagany* which regularly carried articles on the cinema and experimental pieces which attempted to convert film methods into prose. One of the most extreme examples of this sort of experimentation was Rob Brown's 'Readies'. These were to be works printed on a reading film with a minimum of punctuation to disrupt the flow of words. Brown's idea was an unusually literal application of a machine aesthetic which took its lead from the cinema. In 1930 he declared: 'with written matter moving before the eyes new forms of expression will develop naturally'. He was explicit about his analogy: 'the Readies are no more unusual than the Talkies, and not a scratch on television'.[84] Bizarre as the idea sounded, it was a logical offshoot of a growing concern with speed in experimental literature. Brown was influenced by Stein in devising his Readies and he numbered among his contributors Williams, Stein and James T. Farrell.[85] His idea of a rapid reading machine is an extreme sign of his interest in the process of textual production and consumption which concerned Stein, cummings and Williams alike.

It was Surrealism which particularly engaged Williams' imagination. 'Surrealism does not lie. It is the single truth', he declared in 1929 and among other films he saw Léger's *Ballet Mécanique* in 1926.[86] However, the most direct confirmation of Williams' interest in the Surrealists lies in the fact that in 1929 he translated a novel by Philippe Soupault – *Last Nights of Paris*. Soupault was a leading commentator on the cinema, wrote prose scenarios himself, and in 1923 contributed an article to the journal *Broom* on American film, in which he wrote that 'the "U.S.A." cinema has thrown light on all the beauty of our time, all the mystery of modern mechanics'.[87] This essay was later expanded into a pamphlet called *The American Influence in France* (1930). Here he repeated his belief that American film had 'brought to light all the beauty of our epoch', and in poems such as 'Cinema-Palace' he attempted to employ what David E. Shi has described as the 'cinematic technique in which seemingly unrelated shots are projected on the screen in rapid succession'.[88] In that respect Soupault was typical of French experimental writers: 'in their search for new forms and techniques relevant to the Machine Age, the Cubist painters and poets found American film techniques such as cross-cuttings, fade-outs, and close-ups thoroughly "modern"'.[89]

Soupault's *Last Nights of Paris* is the narrative of a *flâneur* trying to understand Paris from its transients, prostitutes, and even dogs. It is a very visual narrative using close-ups, panoramas and rapid scene shifts. At one point the narrator toys with the appearance of the Eiffel Tower: 'I amused myself, with memory as an aid, by indefinitely varying her silhouette as if I were examining her through a kaleidoscope'.[90] Just for a moment Soupault creates a Cubist visual effect, as if the tower is seen through a series of stills, each from a different angle. This is only one instance of a general concern throughout the novel with rendering visual dynamics and the priority given to the visual could not have been lost on Williams. He had already taken a lead from collage in incorporating advertisements in *The Great American Novel*; Surrealism had suggested the potential in a method of fragmentation; and Soupault must have helped to show how narrative could be given a cinematic dimension. We will see similar influences at work in the writings of Williams' contemporary John Dos Passos.

Notes

1   On the relation between modernism and film, see Sitney, *Modernist Montage*; McCabe, *Cinematic Modernism*; and David Seed, 'British Modernists Encounter the Cinema', in Seed, ed., *Literature and the Visual Media*, pp. 48–73.

2   Laura Marcus, 'Literature and Cinema', p. 337. On the relation between modernism and film, see Sitney, *Modernist Montage*; McCabe, *Cinematic Modernism*; and David Seed, 'British Modernists Encounter the Cinema', in Seed, ed., *Literature and the Visual Media*, pp. 48–73. Laura Marcus's *The Tenth Muse* remains a model of intellectual breadth in relating modernism to the new medium, although she does not discuss many American authors.

3   See studies by Maggie Humm, Susan McCabe, and Michael North. David Trotter 's basic hypothesis throughout his *Cinema and Modernism* (2007) is that there was a shared conviction that new media made it possible to record existence but that the 'superabundant generative power' of the media put that existence in doubt (p. 181).

4   Gertrude Stein, *The Geographical History of America*, p. 82.

5   Gertrude Stein, 'I Came and Here I Am', in *How Writing Is Written*, ed. Robert Bartlett Haas, p. 68. Another first for Stein on this visit was that she made a radio broadcast.

6   Gertrude Stein, *Lectures in America*, p. 173. This sentiment is echoed in 'How Writing Is Written' (1935), in which Stein declares: 'in the Twentieth Century you feel like movement': *How Writing Is Written*, p. 153. The writer Stein felt had invented this kind of modern motion was Walt Whitman.

7   Stein, *Lectures in America*, pp. 103–104.

8   Munsterberg published a pioneering study, *The Photoplay: A Psychological Study* (now usually called *The Film: A Psychological Study*) in 1916, in which he analysed the ways in which film appealed to different psychological faculties such as attention and recall. There is no evidence that Stein ever read his study but it is a strong possibility, and both Julian Murphet and Tim Armstrong discuss the link between the two writers. Murphet argues that Munsterberg's writings on mechanism have a suggestive importance: 'Gertrude Stein's Machinery of Perception', in Julian Murphet and Lydia Rainford, eds., *Literature and Visual Technologies*, p. 73. Armstrong places a similar emphasis on the mechanism of production: *Modernism, Technology and the Body*, p. 199.

9   Stein, *Lectures in America*, p. 176.

10 Gertrude Stein, *Writings and Lectures 1911–1945*, p. 26.

11 In *The Autobiography of Alice B. Toklas* Stein recorded how she was 'tormented by the problem of the external and the internal' and reflected that 'after all the human being is essentially not paintable' (p. 127).

12 Munsterberg, *The Film: A Psychological Study*, p. 41.

13 Here and in *Paris France* (1940) Stein records how one of the first pictures she remembered was a huge circular panorama in San Francisco of the Battle of Waterloo, one in which the scene would come alive as the viewer turned.

14 Gertrude Stein, *Picasso: The Complete Writings*, p. 88.

15 John L. Fell has shown that aerial views were fashionable in writings by H. G. Wells and others at the beginning of the century: *Film and the Narrative Tradition*, pp. 66–67.

16 Gertrued Stein, *Everybody's Autobiography*, p. 164.

17 Stein, *Lectures in America*, p.177. In the mid-1930s Stein was drawing on the cinema for a number of aspects of literature including its emotional impact. In *The Geographical History of America* she asserts 'and now there are no tears in reading', giving as her evidence the following anecdote: 'A movie star said, no matter how much or how many cry on the screen the audience remains dry eyed. Has that something to do with the fact that now there is no connection no relation between reading and the human mind' [*sic*] (p. 89).

18 Stein, *How Writing Is Written*, p. 158.

19 Stein, *How Writing Is Written*, p. 159; Goldstein, *The American Poet at the Movies*, p. 70.

20 Wendy Steiner, *Exact Resemblance to Exact Resemblance*, p. 52, italics in original.

21 Stein, *Paris France*, p. 61. It is characteristic of her identification with modern technology that one of Stein's earliest memories in this volume was of being photographed.

22 Stein, *Lectures in America*, p. 177.

23 Cohen, *Film and Fiction*, p. 121.

24 Gertrude Stein, *Three Lives and Q.E.D.*, p. 56.

25 Stein, *Three Lives and Q.E.D.*, p. 61.

26 In 'Ida' (1940), for instance, Stein explicitly uses a road as an emblem of present transition within a larger serial sequence in which 'there was never any beginning or end': *Writings and Lectures 1911–1945*, pp. 361, 382.

27 Gertrude Stein, *The Making of Americans*, pp. 454, 520.

28 The analogy with the film strip is drawn in Marianne DeKoven, '"Why James Joyce Was Accepted and I Was Not"'.

29 Murphet, 'Gertrude Stein's Machinery of Perception', in Murphet and Rainford, eds., *Literature and Visual Technologies*, pp. 75, 72.

30 Murphet, 'Gertrude Stein's Machinery of Perception', in Murphet and Rainford, eds., *Literature and Visual Technologies*, p. 75.

31 Stein, *The Making of Americans*, pp. 334, 380.

32 Janet Hobhouse, *Everybody Who Was Anybody*, pp. 38–39.

33 Sitney, *Modernist Montage*, p. 163. Sitney's general argument is that the modernists constantly 'stress vision as a privileged mode of perception, even of revelation, while at the same time cultivating opacity and questioning the primacy of the visible world' (p. 2).

34 McCabe, *Cinematic Modernism*, pp. 78, 81. McCabe's account remains one of the most thoughtful considerations of the cinematic analogy in Stein's different portraits.

35 Goldstein, *The American Poet at the Movies*, p. 48. For commentary on Chaplin's popularity among writers, see Gorham Munson, *The Awakening Twenties*, pp. 232–39; and also Charles J. Maland, *Chaplin and American Culture*, pp. 84–93. Chaplin was a close friend of Upton Sinclair and Waldo Frank, among other novelists; the latter included a

portrait of the actor in his 1937 collection *In the American Jungle (1925–1936)* (1937), pp. 61–73. Sherwood Anderson wrote Chaplin into his essay-narrative *Perhaps Women* (1931). Composing it as a protest against the encroachment of the factory production line, Anderson describes visiting a factory where he adopts the persona of Chaplin to retain his humanity: 'I became a Charlie Chaplin that night by the mill gate. I was, to myself at least and for the time there in the half darkness, just the grotesque little figure Chaplin brings upon our screen [...] the little figure with the cane [...] standing blinking thus before a world he does not comprehend, can not comprehend' (*Perhaps Women*, pp. 95–96). John Emerson, the husband of Anita Loos, was an old friend and in 1918 gave Anderson a token job at the studio of John Emerson-Anita Loos Productions in Fort Lee, New Jersey (Kim Townsend, *Sherwood Anderson*, pp. 149–50).

36 Among the other figures Stein met were Dashiell Hammett, with whom she discussed compensatory glamour in the male protagonists of novels, and Harry Leon Wilson, the author of the Hollywood novel *Merton of the Movies* which Stein greatly admired (see *Everybody's Autobiography*, pp. xxiii, 250). Stein was an avid reader of detective stories, especially those by Edgar Wallace: see 'Why I Like Detective Stories' (1937) in *How Writing Is Written*, pp. 146–50. For a discussion of Hart Crane's fascination with Chaplin, see Goldstein, *The American Poet at the Movies*, pp. 39–55. According to Alice B. Toklas (*What is Remembered*, p. 152), a number of film directors gathered round Stein, curious about her popularity, but were put off by her sarcasm.

37 Charles Chaplin, *My Autobiography*, p. 330. Stein may have had in mind G. W. Pabst's 1925 film *The Joyless Street* which was reviewed in *Close Up* by H.D. P. Adams Sitney sees an allusion to Fernand Léger's *Le Ballet mécanique* (1924) in Chaplin's account (*Modernist Montage*, p. 161).

38 Stein, *Everybody's Autobiography*, p. 246.

39 Stein, *The Autobiography of Alice B. Toklas*, p. 176.

40 Beth Hutchison, 'Gertrude Stein's Film Scenarios', pp. 36–37.

41 Sarah Bay-Cheng, *Mama Dada*, p. 38.

42 Gertrude Stein, 'A Movie', in Robert Bartlett Haas, ed., *A Primer for the Gradual Understanding of Gertrude Stein*, p. 70. Stein's choice of a taxi-driver for her subject is probably an allusion to the use of six hundred Paris cabs in 1914 to transport troops to the front for the Battle of the Marne.

43 Bay-Cheng, *Mama Dada*, p. 38.

44 Maggie Humm, for example, finds a filmic element in the essays' serial presentation of aspects, writing of 'Three Sitting There': 'the sketch is written in a continuous but fragmentary form like a series of close-up stills or film shots' (*Modernist Women and Visual Cultures*, p. 183).

45 Gertrude Stein, 'Film: Deux soeurs qui ne sont pas soeurs', p. 601. A copy of this work can be found in the Gertrude Stein papers, the Beinecke Library, Yale University. Sarah Bay-Cheng comments: 'what characters see in *Film* often surprises them and is often incomprehensible both to the characters and to the audience' (*Mama Dada*, p. 44).

46 Hutchison, 'Gertrude Stein's Film Scenarios', p. 38.

47 Watson also made two experimental films: a short version of *The Fall of the House of Usher* in 1929 and *Lot in Sodom* in 1933. In cummings' public lectures of the 1950s he singled out Watson for particular praise.

48 e. e. cummings, *A Miscellany Revised*, p. 8. Amy Lowell's 'Towns in Colour' sequence in *Men Women and Ghosts* (1916) assembles a series of visual sketches to narrate the typical experiences of a day in the city. Breaking up her sentences into units of visual perception, Lowell gives a dynamic, cinematic rendering of the city in which focus, point of view, and

MODERNIST EXPERIMENTS: GERTRUDE STEIN AND OTHERS   47

accordingly colour are constantly shifting.

49   cummings, *A Miscellany Revised*, p. 19.

50   F. W. Dupee and George Stade, eds., *Selected Letters of E. E. Cummings*, p. 107.

51   Richard S. Kennedy, *Dreams in the Mirror*, p. 366.

52   cummings, *A Miscellany Revised*, p. 40.

53   Barbara Seidman, '"Patronize Your Neighborhood Wake-Up-And-Dreamery"', p. 12.
Seidman's discussion of this comic scenario and its context is particularly valuable.

54   cummings, *A Miscellany Revised*, p. 43.

55   cummings, *A Miscellany Revised*, p. 211.

56   e. e. cummings, *i: six nonlectures*, p. 64.

57   Kennedy, *Dreams in the Mirror*, p. 242. The reception of cummings' novel is discussed in
Paul Hendrick's '"Brilliant Obscurity": The Reception of *The Enormous Room*'.

58   Dupee and Stade, eds., *Selected Letters*, p. 88.

59   cummings, *The Enormous Room*, p. 103.

60   *The Enormous Room*, p. 176.

61   *The Enormous Room*, p. 99.

62   William S. Hart (1864–1946) acted in over 70 films and also directed, produced, and
scripted a large number, especially in the late 1910s. His is probably the role which Merton
Gill is trying to adopt in Harry Leon Wilson's *Merton of the Movies* (1919).

63   *The Enormous Room*, p. 137.

64   *The Enormous Room*, p. 45.

65   *The Enormous Room*, pp. 145–46.

66   e. e. cummings, *Eimi*, p. 8.

67   *Eimi*, p. 80.

68   *Eimi*, p. 105.

69   William Carlos Williams, *The Embodiment of Knowledge*, p. 113.

70   William Carlos Williams, *Imaginations*, p. 200. Williams made his complaints about the
US public's vague responses to art in the second issue of *Contact* magazine, January 1921.

71   William Carlos Williams, *A Recognizable Image*, p. 231.

72   For relevant commentary on Joyce, see Thomas L. Burkdall, *Joycean Frames*.

73   Williams, *Imaginations*, pp. 66, 67, italics in original.

74   McCabe, *Cinematic Modernism*, p. 99. McCabe then proceeds to give a cinematic reading
of the opening poem in *Spring and All* and argues further that Williams repeatedly
constructs a male observer (sometimes a 'voyeur physician') in his writings.

75   Williams, *Imaginations*, p. 66.

76   McCabe, *Cinematic Modernism*, p. 99.

77   The relevant passage in *Spring and All* states that the 'inevitable flux of the seeing eye
toward measuring itself by the world it inhabits' will tend towards humiliation unless the
individual rises to a 'co-extension with the universe' (*Imaginations*, p. 105), a statement
which identifies the problem more clearly than its solution.

78   Williams, *Imaginations*, pp. 70–71.

79   Tichi, *Shifting Gears*, pp. 242–43, 246; Williams, *Imaginations*, p. 284. Williams discusses
Stieglitz in his 1934 essay 'America and Alfred Stieglitz'.

80   Williams, *White Mule*, p. 9.

81   Mike Weaver, *William Carlos Williams*, p. 63.

82   William Carlos Williams, *Selected Essays*, pp. 62, 109.

83   Richard Abel, 'American Film and the French Literary Avant-Garde (1914–1924)'. Abel
credits Cendrars with publishing the first screenplay and he is also considered to be the
originator of the ciné-novel (see Eric Robertson, 'Writing the Alphabet of Cinema: Blaise

Cendrars', in Murphet and Rainford, eds., *Literature and Visual Technologies*, pp. 148–51). A further contemporary example of the *ciné-roman* can be found in Luigi Pirandello's *Shoot!* (1926), a narrative in the form of notebook excerpts from a cinema operative. Gubbio the narrator takes a Futurist glee in the consolidation of a frenetic tempo to action by the cinema apparatus, a tempo which finds its ultimate form in the USA: 'Long live the Machine that mechanises life!' (*Shoot!*, p. 9).

84 Rob Brown, 'The Readies'. Also in 1930 the novelist Meyer Levin unsuccessfully attempted to make a film with marionettes after studying with Fernand Léger in Paris (Alistair Cooke, ed., *Garbo and the Night Watchmen*, p. 89).

85 Brown's 'Readies' are discussed in Michael North's *Camera Works*, pp. 74–82. North proposes Brown's *What Happened to Mary* (1913) as the first example of a novelization from a film.

86 Williams, *Selected Essays*, p. 96; Weaver, *William Carlos Williams*, p. 69.

87 Philippe Soupault, 'The "U.S.A." Cinema', *Broom* 5/2 (September 1923), quoted in Abel, 'American Film and the French Literary Avant-Garde (1914–1924)', p. 85. Soupault's essays on the cinema are discussed in Marcus, *The Tenth Muse*, pp. 227–28.

88 David E. Shi, 'Transatlantic Visions', pp. 589–90. Shi demonstrates how French writers started appropriating the techniques of the American cinema even before the beginning of the First World War and wove these methods into their writings, where they were subsequently discovered by American modernists such as Stein and Dos Passos. Thus American writers came to appreciate their own cinema through the intermediary activities of the French Cubists and Surrealists. Soupault shared an enthusiasm for Chaplin with his compatriots.

89 Shi, *Transatlantic Visions*, p. 585.

90 Philippe Soupault, *Last Nights of Paris*, p. 53. Soupault records in his 1924 essay 'Cinema USA' how he would search the city streets for inspiration until American movies liberated him from an expectation of naturalism (Hammond, *The Shadow and Its Shadow*, pp. 55–56).

3

H.D. and the Limits of Vision

Unlike the writers considered in the previous chapter, the poet and novelist H.D. (Hilda Doolittle) was actively involved in film-making for a time. Throughout her career she remained obsessively preoccupied with the visual but constantly pushed against the limits of visibility. 'Vision' was a term which oscillated in her works between the physical and the transcendental, and for her film was a crucial medium for exploring this border area. Although she witnessed the shooting of scenes for a Mary Pickford film in Carmel in 1920, her closest involvement in the cinema took place between 1927 and 1933, and in the midst of her enthusiasm she declared: 'the world of the film to-day [...] is no longer the world of the film, it is *the* world'.[1] For H.D., as for Henri Bergson and Hugo Munsterberg, film offered a new means of articulating the dynamics of the mind.[2] In H.D.'s writings from the late 1920s onwards, perception is repeatedly referred to as a quasi-cinematic process. For example, in the short sketch 'Mira-Mare' (written in 1930), while a female character is watching a man on a beach, we are told: 'her narrowed squint widened like a camera shutter'.[3] Sometimes H.D. sets up an opposition between mechanical and organic perception; often she refers to the eyes as if they were unusual lenses registering different dimensions of reality.

Throughout her career H.D. was engaged with the symbolic nature of the image and, although she never completely identified the two, of hieroglyphics. For her, a hieroglyphic was always visual and always in need of decoding. She noted how the heroine in Lev Kuleshov's 1926 film *Expiation* had a 'way of standing against a sky line that makes a hieroglyph, that spells almost vividly some message of cryptic symbolism'.[4] Michael North has shown that during the nineteenth century photography and early film were imagined as a new alphabet 'between letters and pictures' which was routinely compared to hieroglyphics.[5] This analogy formed the subject of a whole chapter in the poet Vachel Lindsay's study *The Art of the Moving Picture* (1915, revised 1922), which anticipates Marshall McLuhan in seeing film as a challenge to logocentrism. The invention of the photoplay for him

thus represented a return to ancient pictorial script independent of alphabets
and therefore, in theory, accessible to any viewer. For Lindsay the rise of film
represented the realization of a democratic idea attempted by Whitman,
namely 'the possibility of showing the entire American population its own
face in the Mirror Screen'.[6] He found the nearest literary analogy to what he
witnessed on the screen in the practice of the Imagists, reflecting that every
photoplay has an Imagist element. Indeed, he further speculated that
Imagism might bring a necessary economy to film-making: 'the Imagist
photoplay will put discipline into the inner ranks of the enlightened and
remind the sculptors, painters, and architects of the movies that there is a
continence even beyond sculpture'.[7] Lindsay speculates further about the
desirable brevity of an Imagist film and its potential for original scenic
composition. Not only economy, but religion too can be invigorated by the
new medium, which could recapture a double sense of 'vision' under pressure
from modern materialism: 'we have maintained that the kinetoscope in the
hands of artists is a higher form of picture writing. In the hands of prophet-
wizards it will be a higher form of vision-seeing'.[8]

     To achieve this higher form of vision was one of H.D.'s aims throughout
her career. In her 1919 *Notes on Thought and Vision* she discusses two ways of
seeing: from the womb and from the brain. The higher consciousness she
designates the 'over-mind' and explains it through optical imagery: 'the over-
mind is like a lens of an opera-glass [...] the love-mind and the over-mind are
two lenses. When these are properly adjusted, focused, they bring the world
of vision into consciousness. The two work separately, perceive separately,
yet make one picture'.[9] Although H.D. is addressing a duality here, Adelaide
Morris argues that the lens introduces a third ocular dimension, and
Charlotte Mandel has gone further in reading the lens as a symbolic demonstration of H.D.'s conversion of an instrument of scientific investigation into
a means of spiritual enquiry.[10] A lens offers access to perceptions otherwise
inaccessible. In that sense it functions here as a liminal symbol, a threshold
similar to great works of art such as Da Vinci's *Madonna of the Rocks*, which
is a 'window into the world of pure over-mind'.[11] In *Notes* H.D. is essentially
sketching out a model of perception, which draws on optical instrumentation
but which must wait for her novels for its cinematographic embodiment.
Similarly, in her early novel *Asphodel* (written 1921–22) H.D. uses the model
of a stream-of-consciousness monologue. There are moments of visualization, as when the protagonist Hermione imagines a projection of names:
'names came and went like lights flashing on a white screen [...] Names and
fantastic backgrounds. America, the wilderness, the rockies'.[12] Because the
narrative works on a vocal rather than a visual basis, the implications of this
image are left undeveloped.

     In contrast, H.D.'s 1926 triptych novel *Palimpsest* transforms the concept of textual superimposition into a series of speculations about vision. The middle section, set in London in 1916–26, repeatedly evokes light behind light, 'shrines beyond shrines', 'faces overlaid now one another [sic] like old photographic negatives'.[13] The palpable impact of the past on the present is introduced through the opening section of the novel, set in 75 BC, and then is extended into a kind of double vision in the modern age. The character Raymonde struggles to see with mental acts analogous to the use of microscope or telescope (analogies we shall encounter later in *The Gift*, written 1941–44), but her experience is constantly compromised by her sense of flux, of no image being hard-edged or autonomous. It seems to her that every image carries the trace of another, but they pass so quickly that she can scarcely register them. This is where the film analogy enters *Palimpsest*. Reflecting on the fleeting impact of meeting others, she notes: 'even that wavering outline was blurred by other equally important, equally transient impressions and the whole went on and on like some swift cinematograph'. Sometimes the past is conceived through outlines behind actual images; at other points it is represented as momentary imagistic glimpses of another world, 'flashes of pure fire-blue, temple column and gold rimmed portico behind this eternally erratic cinematograph present'.[14] Nothing could be further from the static, hard-edged precision of H.D.'s Imagist poems than these evocations of a kind of impressionistic cinema of perception. Process is represented filmically as a loss of image clarity or as the sudden eruption of incongruous – what in the 1950s would be described as subliminal – images into the present.

In *Palimpsest* the present is constructed as the site of attempting access to the past and it is therefore absolutely consistent with H.D.'s theme that the concluding section should be set in the archaeological excavations of Egypt. The local dateline is 1925, when Carter's opening of the royal tombs was continuing and when the Great Sphinx of Giza was totally uncovered. Now the difference between past and present is no longer figured as confusion, but rather as a mental layering for the protagonist: 'she wanted to dive deep, deep, courageously down into some unexploited region of the consciousness'.[15] H.D. draws a distinction between the everyday recording of sights through newsreel and photography on the one hand, and an internalized 'filming' on the other. The novel's location here is a key tourist site and also a place which offers tangible access to a lost spiritual world. The protagonist experiences both modes of perception. Although she dislikes the business of tourism, she cannot help participating in its responses: 'her common or everyday eyes were recording the scene before her. The blacks and yellows, the inked-in shadows, the out of the way sifting of sun on sand'.[16] At moments like this her eyes become a camera recording sights on the same level of banality as the photographs taken by Captain Rafton, a British member of the group, who boasts: 'this one is particularly good. I got it standing just above the cinema crowd, luckily as the chariot wheel was brought out'.[17]

In contrast with this crude visual recording, the protagonist attempts a more spiritual response as she descends into the burial chamber of one of the kings. This descent seems to be taking her into the world of the dead; and then she sees the form of the dead king.[18] Intense contemplation transforms the king: 'the body, sublimated, had become some exquisite gem, black opal, a toy in the larger sense'.[19] What happens here is a process of exclusion whereby other circumstantial details and the presence of other visitors are blanked out. Her field of vision here is necessarily limited whereas two vista shots clearly indicate the modern perspective on the ancient; as instances of looking-towards they imply a desire to move beyond the prosaic actuality of tourism. In the first she looks towards the Nile from the garden door of her hotel: 'the door was exact frame for the patch of road across which passed casual donkey-boys in fez and blue [...] And behind the stone strip of the separating wall, the river. Yellow, with one umber square-set sail'.[20] Thresholds are privileged sites in H.D.'s fiction because they offer the promise of access to other worlds. Here the explicit framing of perspective suggests a plenitude of local life richer than that which can be crudely fixed in photographs. When she visits the avenue of the sphinxes by night the perspective works in reverse, backwards from the stone shapes to the approach road, the carriage horses and driver, culminating with her own registering consciousness. Unlike the previous perspective shot, this experience becomes uncanny from its lack of visual clarity. The road disappears, the walls the group climbs seem to be part of the desert, and she feels displaced from this location to similar Greek antiquities. Seen in the daylight, the sphinxes seem much more familiar, 'as a scene, stage-set properly and subtly lighted, looks commonplace'.[21] The scenic alternation is characteristic of the visual oscillation, in the last part of *Palimpsest*, between precise 'realist' viewing and a more mythic form of vision.

Visions of Liberation in *Her* and *Bid Me to Live*

Two novels written in 1927 when H.D. was beginning her professional involvement in film already make use of filmic methods to support their accounts of their protagonists' process of self-liberation. In *Her* (US title *HERmione*) Hermione Gart attempts to find an identity through her visual perceptions. By shortening her forename ('I am Her') she in effect divides herself into subject and object. As Rachel Blau DuPlessis argues, she is 'both "cinematographer" and main subject, behind the camera and in front of it, actor and *auteur*.[22] In the early chapters of the novels objects are described as 'gelatinous' as if they have no clear form and one of Hermione's drives throughout the narrative is to give shape to things, to shape images. We are told: 'precinematic conscience didn't help her. Later conscience would have. She would have seen form superimposed on thought and thought making its spirals in a manner not wholly related to matter but pertaining to it'.[23] *Her* contains numerous allusions to psychoanalysis as a practice post-dating the narrative and by the same token this allusion to film gives the reader a signal that cinematic techniques will be woven into the novel without damaging its pre-cinematic realism.

Her describes how Hermione seeks to escape the claustrophobia of her American family life first through a relationship which might lead to marriage with the eccentric poet George Lowndes (modelled on Ezra Pound) and later through a different erotic bonding she forms with a young woman called Fayne Rabb. Before the entry of these catalysts into the narrative the novel takes scrupulous care to trace out the shifts in Hermione's visual perceptions. The point of view resembles a camera lens which is constantly shifting focus and angle; at one point, when she goes into a dark hallway out of bright sunlight her vision blurs into patches of colour. At another moment taking tea is reflected through a 'convex Victorian mirror' which transforms the characters into an 'exaggerated puffed out little Dutch group of them and cloth and careful lines of the oblong pattern where the folded cloth had been carefully unfolded, making two careful lines, bisecting teacups clustered and teacups scattered'.[24] The distorting mirror has the parodic effect of making the group resemble earlier formal artefacts, an effect which is strengthened by the abstract lines of the tablecloth folds, which become a further imagistic confirmation of formality. The constant visual shifts in this novel make it even more unstable, for Susan Friedman, than a stream-consciousness method. In the latter the reader's sense of an individuating source gives an implicit fixed point to the narrative, whereas now Hermione constructs and deconstructs her experiences through shifting imagistic sequences.[25]

With the arrival of George Lowndes the visual perspective shifts to that of a supine Hermione looking up at the poet's head, i.e. in a posture of submission. The distorting mirror figures again, symbolically, in relation to his implicitly threatening overtures to Hermione. Indeed, Lowndes' impact is to trigger a greater self-consciousness in Hermione. She visualizes herself sitting up in bed like a marble form during a storm. We are told 'she saw things' with a suggestion of new-found clarity, as when she freezes her father in an image like a daguerrotype as he enters the house; Lowndes' mother is caricatured as a waxwork; and a figurine on a piano increases and decreases in size as if the vantage-point were oscillating. Hermione visualizes herself through partial images, synecdoches of her body such as a 'phosphorescent

and white' arm emerging from her dress.[26] This partial self-figuration paves
the way for the appearance of Fayne Rabb.

With Fayne's arrival, the cinematic dimension to Hermione's perceptions
becomes more strongly pronounced. The image of the street, like a 'stage
street going on, not there, getting nowhere', gives a perspective shot of the
newly acquired pace to Hermione's account.[27] However, the most dramatic
moment in the novel is the following account of Fayne:

> Her bent forward, face toward Her. A face bends towards me and a curtain opens.
> There is swish and swirl of parting curtains. Almost along the floor with its strip
> of carpet, almost across me I feel the fringe of some fantastic wine-coloured
> parting curtains. Curtains part as I look into the eyes of Fayne Rabb [...] Curtains
> fell, curtains parted, curtains filled the air with heavy swooping purple. Lips long
> since half kissed away.[28]

Not surprisingly, this scene has attracted more critical comment than any
other moment in the novel. Jean Gallagher has described it as a 'screen close-
up' and Rachel Connor has explained how the curtains 'allude to the *framing*
that is central to visual representations of the female body in the cinema', here
specifically evoking the opening of a film.[29]

Feminist critical accounts of such passages in H.D. tend to take bearings
from Laura Mulvey's famous essay 'Visual Pleasure and Narrative Cinema',
in which she argues that 'the presence of woman is an indispensable element
of spectacle in normal narrative film, yet her visual presence tends to work
against the development of a story-line, to freeze the flow of action in
moments of erotic contemplation'.[30] One feature of H.D.'s modernism was
her studied avoidance of linear narrative and therefore erotic moments like
that quoted cannot be read as disrupting a flow. Furthermore, as is often the
case in H.D., the nature of the scene's actuality is problematic. The site of the
visual encounter is only metaphorically rendered through curtains parting –
not that this reduces the erotic impact of the image – and the distance
between the subject and object of the gaze closes up, not just as the faces
approach each other, but through a more radical appropriation of Fayne by
Hermione. Prior to this passage she describes how she takes possession of
Fayne's eyes, adjusting them like an opera glass to her own needs. If Laura
Mulvey's argument depends on the preservation of a spectatorial distance
between the male gaze and its female object, then clearly H.D.'s account
presents a radically different kind of visual encounter. The symmetry in the
first sentence of the quoted passage suggests a mirroring process: Hermione
bends towards the other, the other bends towards Hermione. The difference
from earlier episodes is that now the mirroring effect is not distorting or
parodic, but rather suggestive of an equilibrium between the two female

characters. This encounter exemplifies what Jean Gallagher has described as the 'literally entrancing effects of lesbian desire' in H.D.'s work.[31]

At no point in *Her* is Fayne compared to a film star. Film analogies are implicit here whereas the earliest account of movie-going in H.D.'s fiction occurs in *Bid Me to Live*, written the same year that she became involved in plans to contribute to the journal *Close Up*. In June 1927 she wrote to her friend Viola Jordan: 'I feel it is the living art, the thing that WILL count but that is in danger now from commercial and popular sources'.[32] This enthusiasm feeds straight into the novel, where movie-going is a major liberating experience for the protagonist Julia Ashton. Set in London towards the end of the First World War, the novel depicts Julia's life in that city as drab and restrictive, until that is Julia's lover-to-be takes her to the 'pictures'. Their box seats give an awkward view of the screen but this has the result of including the audience within the spectacle: 'below her, below them, were the thousands; it seemed that all the soldiers in the world, symbolically were packed into the theatre'.[33] Though separated spatially from the figures below her, Julia's readjustment of vision to see the film better results in an identification with the rest of the audience. The scene before them shows a car racing along a road in the Italian mountains and every viewer gets caught up in the physical immediacy of that race: the car 'swerved, it bent, they swerved, they bent with it. The multitude, herself, Vanio [her companion Vane], all of them swerved and turned. She was part of this.'[34] Where the earlier chapters of the novel are mostly set within domestic interiors, this scene takes Julia out of herself and enables her to participate in a larger action. Loss of self-consciousness does not initially mean that Julia loses her sense of context. In place of a soundtrack (this is of course a silent film), an organ plays 'It's a Long Way to Tipperary' and thereby offers a counter-narrative to the story unfolding on the screen. The soldiers join in singing the song of departure, just as they will be shortly leaving England, perhaps going to their deaths; whereas the film story is read by Julia as a return home, for reasons still to be revealed.

H.D.'s description of the cinema in *Bid Me to Live* is extremely selective in its circumstantial details and this must be strategic. In her contribution to the first issue of the film journal *Close Up* (July 1927, again the same year as the novel), she refers scathingly to the crowds, 'suffocation, pink lemonade, sawdust even' associated with movie-going.[35] All these aspects are blanked out in the novel and the most striking visible sign of the audience – the smoke – becomes transformed into the incense being offered to Beauty by the devotees in the stalls. A gradual concentration of attention takes place in the novel as the focus progresses from car to driver and destination. By the time the female star is introduced, the spectators' presence has been elided in the act of rapt contemplation. The novel's text briefly transforms itself into a shot-by-shot summary of the action. The actress herself emerges as a person-ification of Beauty going through a series of postures which evoke different mythic guises: Persephone as the woman with the flowers, a hooded Demeter once she wraps her scarf around her head, and so on.

The narrative tense shifts into the present to convey this perceived immediacy and thereby briefly resembles a screenplay:

> She climbs marble stairs out of a fairy-tale [...] she staggers toward her mirror. Pushing back the wet stuff of the palpably mermaid garment she regards her face, the same face from a mirror [...] she pushes back the dark hair from the white forehead, and as the screen veers to show her reflected image at still closer range, one sees the flower-scattered rain-drops on her face. The camera swerves, the flower-tears have vanished and she lifts, as if in replica, to replace them, a diadem of brilliants.[36]

Throughout this description H.D. gives us a serial sequence of shots, which capture the actress's self-consciousness. The subject of the audience's gaze, she transforms herself into an image for her own contemplation. At the moment of this contemplation the camera has closed up on her face and sets up a brief imagistic sequence from raindrops to tears to jewels which culmi-nates in what resembles an act of self-coronation. Here the identification between the female spectator (Julia) and the actress seems complete. Strik-ingly, the carefully paced sequence of movements is relatively detached from any clear film narrative and this is an effect further increased by the mythic parallels woven into the account.

There is a hidden polemic in this description. In her 1927 *Close Up* essay H.D. waxed indignant over the American censors' attempts to stereotype the female: 'a beauty, it is evident, from the Totem's stand-point, must be a vamp, an evil woman'. By the Totem she means a fixed perception which has become set in stone and observed unthinkingly. Where this rule resembles a primitive object, in her counter-assertion H.D. presents beauty as a living principle passed on from age to age: 'Beauty was made to endure, in men, in flowers, in hearts, in spirits, in minds'.[37] We are now in a position to under-stand why, in *Bid Me to Live*, H.D. through her protagonist describes the beauty of the film actress without reference to any historical specifics such as hairstyle or dress. By so doing and by deploying mythic analogies, she performs an act which, in the *Close Up* essay, she can only identify in the abstract, namely rescuing the actress (and therefore the medium) from the restricting stereotype of beauty. Julia's experience of the cinema has the effect of liberating her sense of vision. After she goes to Cornwall with Vane she becomes a 'see-er' finely attuned to the hieroglyphs inscribed in that ancient landscape.

H.D., Film Critic

In 1927 H.D. was involved in the setting up of POOL Productions, a small Swiss-based film company founded by herself, Kenneth Macpherson and Bryher, the heiress of the shipping magnate Sir John Ellerman. The group made a number of films, the most important of which was *Borderline*, starring Paul Robeson in the story of an interracial love triangle set in a small village. As well as acting in *Borderline* and other films, H.D. took an active part in the filming and cutting of *Borderline*.[38] From 1927 to 1933 the POOL group also published a journal of film criticism, *Close Up*, in which H.D. produced a number of essays and which numbered among its contributors Eisenstein, Gertrude Stein, and the English novelist Dorothy Richardson.[39] Looking back on these years, Bryher recorded how film appealed because of its independence of the nineteenth century and because it seemed to offer a visual vocabulary independent of particular languages and cultures: 'the film was new, it had no earlier associations and it offered occasionally, in an episode or single shot, some framework for our dreams. We felt we could state our convictions honourably in this twentieth-century form of art and it appealed to the popular internationalism of those so few years because "the silents" offered a single language across Europe'.[40]

H.D.'s essays in *Close Up* provide valuable documentation of how she was working out her notions of film and also how she speculated on the relation between that medium and prose fiction. In a series of three pieces entitled 'The Cinema and the Classics' she asserts the need for what she calls 'restraint', ie economy, in the composition of scenes. Thus, in conveying a laurel tree it would be sufficient to present 'one branch, placed against a soft back drop, or against a wall of any empty room, with suitable cross-effect of shadow'. The play of light against dark would be one way of engaging with the element which defines film: 'light speaks, is pliant, is malleable. Light is our friend and our god. Let us be worthy of it'.[41] Here film is reinforcing the lessons H.D. learnt from Ezra Pound during her Imagist period of precision and economy; her speculations on scenic composition were to bear fruit in later novels such as *Nights*. Her reverential celebration of light explains why she believed the cinema had a social role to play: 'the cinema has become to us what the church was to our ancestors'.[42] Unlike Dorothy Richardson in her 'Continuous Performance' articles, H.D. had relatively little to say about the social function of film.[43] The assertion just quoted is by no means made to lament the secular spirit of the modern age but rather to insist on the spiritual dimension to film, a concept which H.D. develops in a number of different areas.

H.D. had no doubt about the importance of film for suggesting new kinds of modernist structure. She was impressed by *The Passion and Death of a*

Saint (1928) by the Danish film-maker Carl Dreyer, which she describes as 'one of the most exquisite and consistent works of screen art and perfected craft'.[44] But – and there is a large but with this film – H.D. expresses real restiveness over Dreyer's detailed documentation of Joan of Arc's suffering, which she begins to see as tantamount to sadism. For Susan Friedman, the issue was one of gender, although H.D. never quite spells it out: 'her review demonstrates her ambivalence as a woman to the visual forms of male modernity in which the director invites the viewer to join in his gaze at female victimization'.[45] Hence H.D.'s resistance to the film, which for her precluded the possibility of any kind of impartial viewing.

H.D.'s work with the POOL group revealed to her the complex artistry of film construction. In her *Borderline* pamphlet she pointed up the lesson: 'the professional writer, seldom if ever stops to puzzle out the difficult reasons for time-limits, effect of light and shadow that may or may not mean to him what it must inevitably man to the director or the man behind the camera'. She idealized Kenneth Macpherson as multi-skilled craftsman who could combine writing with film-making and who, among others, managed to compose his film using a 'meticulous jig-saw puzzle technique'. At present she finds movie-going and interest in film to be too passive, reflecting: 'when we get past this sedative period, we will perhaps begin, "write" our novels and plays in "pictures". That is the aim psychologically to be striven towards'.[46] This is one of H.D.'s most explicit statements of her desire for picture-writing, for a kind of imagistic script which exploits film's raw material – light.

Her work for *Borderline* and other films gave H.D. necessary training with the film apparatus. In the final issue of *The Little Review* for May 1929 the editor Margaret Anderson published the results of a questionnaire she had sent to contributors. In her response H.D. declared her enthusiasm for the *Borderline* project and for film in general:

> Just at the moment I am involved with pictures. We have almost finished a slight lyrical four reel little drama, done in and about the villages here some of the village people and English friends. The work has been enchanting, never anything such fun and I myself have learned to use the small projector and spend literally hours alone here in my apartment, making the mountains and village streets and my own acquaintances reel past me in light and light and light. At the moment I want to go on in this medium working with and around pure types, pure artists, pure people, experimenting with faces and shadows and corners. [She then speculates on solitary travel with a camera where she would] wander in and about the Italian and Swiss hills making light do what I want.[47]

It is striking that H.D. articulates this dream, apparently never fulfilled, as an individual activity analogous to fictional composition. However enthusiastic she became about the small POOL group, the collective aspect of film-making was the first to go in her application of its methods for her own purposes. Furthermore, for Anne Friedberg the passage just quoted does not so much show H.D.'s interest in film-making as in a 'privatised form of reception, of viewing'.[48]

Many commentators on H.D. have extrapolated the concepts of border-lines and projection from her POOL activities to argue for their centrality in her oeuvre. Adelaide Morris, for instance, has traced out the different senses of 'projection', from film showing to an opening up of the 'boundaries of the self'. She finds a calculated pun in terms such as 'medium', which links film to psychic processes through an interaction between the physical and the spiritual.[49] For Susan McCabe, the act of crossing borders, with its multiple connotations of sexuality, transcendentalism, and so on, is central to H.D.'s negotiation of difference. Thus, for H.D. film functioned as a 'threshold space' and the relation between viewer and viewed collapses into a 'projection of bisexual space'.[50] One of the meanings to projection here would be the psychoanalytical one of externalizing psychic impulses and H.D. made no bones about insisting that 'the film is the art of dream portrayal'.[51] She read *Borderline* as having a dream logic, for instance in showing a café scene full of hostile observers as a nightmare for the African American protagonist, played by Paul Robeson. Similarly she praised Conrad Veidt's *The Student of Prague* (1926) for its depiction of doubling and its use of the mirror.

Lastly, we should note that, in keeping with many American writers, H.D. rejected the style and ethos of Hollywood, devoting her attention in *Close Up* to continental cinema. She reserved her special praise for G.W. Pabst's *The Joyless Street* (1925), which showed Greta Garbo in her second acting role, as the 'most astonishingly consistently lovely film I have ever seen'.[52] In particular, she admired the way in which Garbo's presence shone through despite the commercial influences that might banalize her. In a striking act of identification, H.D. read Garbo as a symbolic goddess reflecting back her beauty on the spectator.[53] It was the actress's stare which caught H.D.'s imagination because it suggested clairvoyance, whereas in her 1930s' sketch 'Mira-Mare' H.D. ridicules a character for wearing the trappings of a star: 'shoulders naked as a screen beauty, rose from new Derry & Toms saxe-blue'.[54] Similarly she praised Brigitte Helm's performance in Pabst's *The Loves of Jeanne Ney* (1927) because 'her eyes [...] are the wide staring eyes of the blind, but in her blindness she is alive, aware, acute, clair-voyantly attuned to every sound, every movement, every shade of light and every shift of sun and shadow'.[55] We shall shortly see the importance of the gaze in H.D.'s fiction, but the last description goes further than mere appre-ciation. H.D. is drawn to the paradoxical skill of Helm in playing a blind role in which she seems so sensitive to her surroundings that her perceptions verge on the preternatural. Like many of H.D.'s own characters, she seems to be a seer.

Film Mystery: *Nights*

H.D.'s *Nights* (1935) draws on her film-making experiences and the Swiss location of Kenwin (Bryher and Macpherson's house-cum-studio where the novel was written) for its setting. The novel presents a series of episodes in which a woman named Natalia, now deceased, attempts to regain control of her marriage after she has discovered her husband's infidelity. She does this by taking as lover a young Englishman named David. The sequence heads towards a conclusion without ever reaching one and is edited through a prologue by 'John Helforth', who writes scientific texts. This prologue presents Natalia's death as inexplicable, but strictly speaking Natalia herself is the central mystery of *Nights*, together with her own text.

The male narrator (the novel was originally published under the 'author-ship' of John Helforth) initiates the cinematic references in this work by describing the moment when he first heard Natalia's story as follows: 'the scene was as livid and unreal as any jerry-built film set'.[56] This analogy highlights the drama of the moment and at the same time implies scepticism towards the story he is being offered, and throughout the prologue filmic comparisons suggest false representation. The business of the prologue is partly to engage in a speculative reconstruction of Natalia's last moments – it is assumed she drowned in the local lake. Thus the narrator imagines her putting on her ice skates and then 'she swung out like a Nordic skating champion on a news-reel'. No sooner has this image been created than it is questioned: 'I do not visualize her skirt swirling and whirling like that ice-Pavlova – we all know her from our news-reel'.[57] Since no-one saw Natalia skating, the first comparison is contradictory in offering a fictional image compared with non-fictional film. This is then negated in the second comparison and the image is yet further complicated by the narrator's mention of a photograph of Natalia skating, again as if from a newsreel, but with the wrong caption. The film comparisons thus do not help to stabilize a subject, but rather do the opposite by problematizing the real. As Rachel Connor points out in relation to the ice-skating image, 'while Helforth indicates that the sight of Nat skiing is *unlike* the image of Anna Pavlova on the newsreel, the process through which her identity is constructed in Helforth's imagination, is similar to that of the film star on the silver screen'.[58] Helforth exploits his editorial function to engage in a quasi-cinematic 'production' of Natalia.

Natalia's narrative, according to H.D.'s daughter, consists of a 'restless dizzying montage', which deploys many cinematic devices to grapple with its subject.[59] Natalia herself shares the first narrator's cinematographic self-consciousness, as when she declares to the young woman Una: 'I know the sort of scenario you want, I know just the sort of screen thing'.[60] Una is defined by her wide staring eyes, a feature that could connote gullibility or the desire for a quasi-cinematic spectatorship. Similarly Natalia later reflects that Renne, a repressed and conventionally minded character, is composing a 'scenario' for Una. These instances demonstrate Natalia's caution about not allowing her own narrative to slide into conventional grooves. The main site for the novel's action is predictably her bedroom and she takes great care to prevent David's arrivals and departures resembling a social/sexual drama.

Instead, Natalia's scenes enact rapid sequences in which the reader moves to and fro between thought sequences and passages of description, between dream and waking life. Just as the narrative shifts between first and third person, so Natalia represents herself as the subject and object of her experience, characteristically using external images as springboards for flights of her imagination. Take the following sequence of sense-impressions which gradually lead us to one of her cherished symbolic objects: 'the shawl has tassels over her silk sleeping-coat. The coat is soft against her shoulder, her sleeves and the silk fringe of the shawl are dull rose. The shell in her hand is pearl. Out of the hollow of the shell, (held, reflecting the blurred edge of the upper inset line of concealed wall-lights) her world begins'.[61] The prose paces a gradual shift of images (shawl – coat – sleeves – hand – shell) culminating in that of a matrix. The shell is one containing space, as is her room, but it is described as a generative source, hence the care over light effects. The shell is a translucent object with lights behind it, one of many such privileged objects in H.D.'s prose.

The shell functions as a liminal object offering a portal to Natalia's impressions of the day and that progression is repeated throughout *Nights*. For instance, at one point Natalia and David are seated on either side of a table and David asks her if she loves women. This question is enacted imagistically through a gradual close-up on David's eyes as they approach Natalia. The pressure of the question becomes so severe that she hallucinates being trapped by eyes, a perception so acute that she can only continue the conversation by blindfolding David. At another point, Natalia registers estrangement from David in a desire to lie in her room alone: 'she must get away, must lie alone, must let lines and patterns of the two interlocked triangles of light and shadow [...] draw her out. She wanted to watch triangles of light and shadow, on her ceiling'.[62] The symbolism of the images is left implicit. They could be part of the dualities of the work; Natalia's husband is figured as darkness at the beginning of her narrative. At any rate, Natalia registers a desire to use her ceiling as a mindscreen for her contemplation in a situation of solitude in which David plays no part. *Nights* presents a kind of mental cinema characterized by rapid cuts from image to image, dissolves (she imagines her head 'melting' into a disembodied vision), near and long shots, and constant shifts in focus. Unlike the film analogies considered in the prologue, these techniques are functions of Natalia's self-directed thought.

The Working of the Memory Film: *The Gift*

The Gift, written in the early 1940s against the background of the London Blitz, represents an effort by H.D. to investigate her own spiritual origins and twins family history with that of the Moravian religion. *The Gift* also identifies a visionary inheritance culminating in H.D.'s appropriation of film. Her grandfather's use of the microscope ('he was the naked eye') passes on to the father's telescope and reaches the present in H.D.'s attempts at recall.[63] Thus both her progenitors are actively involved in technologically aided visual scrutiny, with the paradox that to the young H.D. what they were scrutinizing remained largely invisible to her. The opening section of her memoir is entitled 'Dark Room', a clear allusion to the London blackout but at the same time suggestive of the darkness of a movie house. In her 1941 story 'Escape' H.D. explores the strange interaction between a romantic film and the newsreels which follow it. The latter become 'fictitious' and the scene ambiguously poised between the real and the imaginary: 'I walk into a film-set [...] this unreal scene has its very real sound going on'.[64]

The 'dark room' of *The Gift* also suggests the site of photographic development and functions as a mental matrix out of which H.D.'s images will emerge. She repeatedly draws on the cinematic analogy to articulate the problem of dynamic continuity in her memoir. Thus her first memory images are isolated instances: 'in these flashes of flash-backs, we have the ingredients of the Gift'.[65] The title term is revealed to be a process of spiritual transmission rather than an object. Indeed, the reification of images in her grandfather's slides, reminiscent of those in a magic lantern, suggests an old-fashioned visual technology which has become superseded by mind cinema. Ultimately the gift comes to resemble the movement H.D. is aiming to capture in her memoir, virtually a principle of narrative composition: 'the trouble is, the process of this letting loose or letting flow, continuous images like a moving-picture, is a secret one can not, with the best will in the world, impart'.[66] Throughout *The Gift* H.D. draws on the film analogy to articulate her varying degrees of success at recall. Images and scenes may stand in isolation or may gel into local sequences. When she fits together a scenic narrative of her mother visiting a fortune-teller, H.D. notes with satisfaction: 'the film unrolls in my head'.[67] At another point, when she and others move from one lamp-post to another on a winter night, she projects the knowledge of film technique she acquired in the 1920s into the memory-scene: 'it goes on in what we later call slow-motion, at the moving-picture shows'.[68]

The evocation of memory flow is contrasted repeatedly with the effects of pre-cinematic devices such as a gyroscope, whereby images become 'almost continuous'. H.D. both constructs and questions her account. At a later point her brother turns the pages of a book of paintings so quickly that they seem to flow but actually 'did not fit together'. Resembling a kaleidoscope or an 'old round box' – presumably a kind of zoetrope – the effect is disconcertingly confusing for H.D. and is written into *The Gift* as a rapid sequence of paratactic images which resemble discontinuous film shots:

> Aunt Jennie gives me a Chinese-lily that you plant in a bowl with pebbles.
> The bowl Aunt Jennie gave me was blue and shiny [...]
> Eric puts his ash in the saucer, he throws the end of the cigarette down and it smokes beside the match-stick.
> The ash curls up and I go on looking at the smoke of the cigarette.
> Eric shuts the book.
> Gilbert is standing by the piano, looking at Papa's wallet.
> The table is round like a big wheel.[69]

Thematically the sequence opens with a gift which is contained within one circular form (the bowl) juxtaposed with others – the saucer and table – but the significance of particular images is left implicit. H.D. emerges here as a medium rather than a narrator.

Throughout *The Gift* H.D.'s spiritual search is informed by a conviction that she is the transmitter, not the originator, of her imagery. In her notes she recorded: 'I let the story tell itself or the child tell it for me'.[70] She demonstrates an explicit awareness that she might slide into the clichés of the film medium and carefully resists scenes that might be 'built up from a screenstory, or a hut constructed by that facile scene-designer, the unconscious mind'.[71] With memories of her recent period of therapy with Freud fresh in her memory, H.D. constructs a site of narration which repeats Freud's room in Vienna and when looking back on these experiences (in *Tribute to Freud*, 1944) she deploys pre-cinematic imagery, reflecting: 'these pictures are so clear. They are like the transparencies set before candles in a dark room'.[72] Despite H.D.'s interest in Freud's theories, she stolidly refused to reduce her mental imagery to symptom and instead read these images as emerging from a cultural pool: 'the picture-writing, the hieroglyph of dream, was the common property of the whole race'.[73] In *The Gift* this same conviction is reflected in the narrator's receptivity to her mother's stories, in the blurring between her adult friend Bryher and her mother, and in her deliberately relaxed posture to help the working of her memory: 'this, I could remember, through steadily and stealthily letting pictures flow fast and through me'.[74] Film ultimately comes to signify for H.D. the unrolling elsewhere of a destiny, which the individual can only glimpse intermittently.

Notes

1   Barbara Guest, *Herself Defined*, p. 135; H.D., 'Russian Films' (1929), in James Donald, Anne Friedberg and Laura Marcus, eds., *Close Up*, p. 135.
2   Henri Bergson describes the working of a mental cinematograph in *Creative Evolution* (1911). Hugo Munsterberg was one of the formative scholars of psychology at Harvard and was for a time Gertrude Stein's postgraduate tutor. In his 1916 study *The Photoplay: A Psychological Study* (now usually entitled *The Film: A Psychological Study*), he discusses depth and movement, the relation of the close-up to attention, the 'cut-back' to memory, and related issues of perception.
3   H.D., *Kora and Ka*, p. 66.
4   'Expiation', in Donald, Friedberg and Marcus, eds., *Close Up*, p. 126.
5   North, *Camera Works*, pp. 4–5. The analogy persisted throughout the silent film era, being used by the French film-maker Abel Gance in 1927 to designate a cinematic 'pictorial language' which the viewer need to learn (quoted in Walter Benjamin, *Illuminations*, p. 228). Laura Marcus has argued that the hieroglyphic analogy supported a view of silent cinema as 'thinking in pictures rather than in words' and continues: 'the dream of recapturing a prelapsarian, universal, pictographic language fed directly into early film aesthetics', citing Vachel Lindsay as one of the first to pursue the analogy: 'How Newness Enters the World: The Birth of Cinema and the Origins of Man', in Murphet and Rainford, eds., *Literature and Visual Technologies*, pp. 33, 42. For further discussion of the hieroglyphics analogy, see Armstrong, *Modernism, Technology and the Body*, pp. 227–28.
6   *The Prose of Vachel Lindsay*, Vol. I, p. 241. Lindsay was concerned to defend the film medium against attacks like the novelist Floyd Dell's criticism of the adaptation of *Ghosts*. H.D. certainly knew Lindsay's poems through the Imagist circle and may well have read *The Art of the Moving Picture*.
7   *The Prose of Vachel Lindsay*, Vol. I, p. 317. Lindsay's extrapolation of Imagism, though far less developed, resembles Sergei Eisenstein's discussion of the cinematic potential in the Japanese ideogram in *Film Form* (1949).
8   *The Prose of Vachel Lindsay*, Vol. I, p. 329.
9   H.D., *Notes on Thought and Vision*, p. 23. For a discussion of the relation between the overmind and H.D.'s 'jelly-fish' experience on the Scilly Isles, see Susan Stanford Friedman, *Penelope's Web*, p. 10.
10 Adelaide Morris, *How To Live*, p. 101; Charlotte Mandel, 'Magical Lenses: Poet's Vision Beyond the Naked Eye', in Michael King, ed., *H.D. Woman and Poet*, pp. 301–17.
11 *Notes on Thought and Vision*, p. 18.
12 H.D., *Asphodel*, p. 105. Though written earlier, *Asphodel* is a chronological sequel to *Her*, taking the characters to Europe during the First World War.
13 H.D., *Palimpsest*, p. 157.
14 *Palimpsest*, pp. 163, 164.
15 *Palimpsest*, p. 179.
16 *Palimpsest*, pp. 179–80.

17 *Palimpsest*, p. 191.
18 The tomb of Amenophis (Amenhotep) II which is visited is one of the deepest in the Valley of Kings and has an entire book inscribed around the walls.
19 *Palimpsest*, p. 183.
20 *Palimpsest*, p. 186.
21 *Palimpsest*, p. 228.
22 Rachel Blau DuPlessis, *H.D.*, p. 59. She comments further on the novel's filmic dimension: 'there are freeze frames, strange camera angles, intense close-ups of objects, fades, interesting montages or superimpositions of eyes, of pools, of concentric circles' (pp. 66–67).
23 H.D., *Her*, p. 60. The only challenge to the period realism of the novel comes when Hermione claims to have 'seen' someone on the telephone through a 'sort of mirror television' (p. 76).
24 *Her*, p. 51. Rachel Connor suggests (*H.D. and the Image*, p. 25) that the distorting mirror is drawn from Germaine Dulac's 1923 film *La Souriante Madame Beurdet*.
25 Friedman, *Penelope's Web*, p. 107.
26 *Her*, pp. 91, 117.
27 *Her*, p. 150.
28 *Her*, p. 163.
29 Jean Gallagher, 'H.D.'s Distractions', p. 419; Connor, *H.D. and the Image*, pp. 56, 59.
30 Laura Mulvey, *Visual and Other Pleasures*, p. 19.
31 Gallagher, 'H.D.'s Distractions', p. 412. Gallagher seeks to relate the female stare to an aesthetic of stasis in H.D. whereby the female protagonist seeks the reciprocal gaze of the second female, and in which the field of vision is emptied of any distraction from the moment of erotic encounter.
32 Letter of 6 June 1927 quoted in 'Louis Silverstein's H.D. Chronology, Part Three (April 1919–1928)', at http://www.imagists.org/hd/hdchron3.html. Barbara Guest's *Herself Defined* (1984) remains the standard H.D. biography but the Silverstein Chronology gives a wealth of supplementary information and quotes extensively from unpublished letters.
33 H.D., *Bid Me to Live*, pp. 122–23.
34 *Bid Me to Live*, p. 123.
35 H.D., 'The Cinema and the Classics I: Beauty', in Donald, Friedberg and Marcus, eds., *Close Up*, p. 105.
36 *Bid Me to Live*, p. 125.
37 'The Cinema and the Classics I: Beauty', in Donald, Friedberg and Marcus, eds., *Close Up*, p. 107.
38 Connor, *H.D. and the Image*, p. 24. For critical commentary on the film *Borderline*, see Anne Friedberg, 'Approaching *Borderline*', in King, ed., *H.D. Woman and Poet*, pp. 369–90. Thomas Cripps explains the symbolism of the film as follows: 'in the end it is the white world turned upside down, the Negro made whole, the European idiom reordered with black the symbol of virtue and white the incarnation of evil' (*Slow Fade to Black*, p. 210).
39 Other contributors included Arnold Bennett, Marianne Moore and Upton Sinclair. In 1927 a contribution by William Carlos Williams was turned down. The essays by H.D. and Dorothy Richardson among others have been republished in Donald, Friedberg and Marcus, eds., *Close Up*. For valuable commentary on the context of *Close Up* and on H.D.'s film essays, see Humm, *Modernist Women and Visual Cultures*, pp. 130–56, 164–73.
40 Bryher, *The Heart to Artemis*, pp. 247–48. In addition to writing novels, Bryher also published *Film Problems of Soviet Russia* in 1929. H.D. shared her internationalism, asserting in 1929: 'we are no longer nations. We are or should be *a* nation' ('Russian

Films', in Donald, Friedberg and Marcus, eds., *Close Up*, p. 136).

41 H.D., 'The Cinema and the Classics II: Restraint', in Donald, Friedberg and Marcus, eds., *Close Up*, pp. 111, 112.

42 H.D., 'The Cinema and the Classics III: The Mask and the Movietone', in Donald, Friedberg and Marcus, eds., *Close Up*, p. 116. H.D.'s 'Projector' poems give one expression of this perception.

43 Katherine Hopewell argues that H.D. in her writing on film tends to adopt the position of a 'mandarin aesthete' ('"The Leaven, Regarding the Lump"'). For a detailed account of Dorothy Richardson's film writing, see Susan Gevirtz, *Narrative's Journey*, pp. 38–97.

44 H.D., 'Joan of Arc', in Donald, Friedberg and Marcus, eds., *Close Up*, p. 131.

45 Friedman, *Penelope's Web*, p. 14.

46 H.D., '*Borderline*: A POOL Film with Paul Robeson', in Donald, Friedberg and Marcus, eds., *Close Up*, pp. 229–31. Susan Friedman reads H.D.'s pamphlet as presenting the 'racial experience of marginality' as a paradigm for post-war cultural dispersal (*Penelope's Web*, p. 16). Susan McCabe reads the film as a reversal of 'Griffith's myth of American identity as the protection of white womanhood from "primitive" black sexuality' (*Cinematic Modernism*, p. 170).

47 H.D., 'Confessions and Letters: H.D.', pp. 38–39.

48 Anne Friedberg, 'On H.D.', p. 29.

49 Morris, *How To Live*, pp. 103–10.

50 McCabe, *Cinematic Modernism*, pp. 139, 48.

51 '*Borderline*', in Donald, Friedberg and Marcus, eds., *Close Up*, p. 232.

52 'The Cinema and the Classics I: Beauty', in Donald, Friedberg and Marcus, eds., *Close Up*, p. 107. Bryher described the film as the one which 'expressed our generation' (*The Heart to Artemis*, pp. 251–52).

53 See Charlotte Mandel, 'Garbo/Helen'. Mandel also surveys H.D.'s interest in film in her article 'The Redirected Image', which focuses particularly on cinematic techniques in her long poem *Helen in Egypt*.

54 *Kora and Ka*, p. 68.

55 'An Appreciation', in Donald, Friedberg and Marcus, eds., *Close Up*, p. 145.

56 H.D., *Nights*, p. 8.

57 *Nights*, pp. 13, 14.

58 Connor, *H.D. and the Image*, p. 56.

59 *Nights*, p. xii. Kenneth Macpherson told H.D. that the novel was 'Garbo in writing' (Guest, *Herself Defined*, p. 204).

60 *Nights*, p. 76.

61 *Nights*, p. 54.

62 *Nights*, p. 89.

63 H.D., *The Gift*, p. 41.

64 H.D., 'Escape (January 1941)', p. 9. I am grateful to Rachel Connor for drawing this story to my attention.

65 *The Gift*, p. 42.

66 *The Gift*, p. 50.

67 *The Gift*, p. 53.

68 *The Gift*, p. 117.

69 *The Gift*, pp. 204–205.

70 *The Gift*, p. 257.

71 *The Gift*, p. 111.

72 H.D., *Tribute to Freud*, p. 29.

73 *Tribute to Freud*, p. 71. Susan Edmunds notes that the Freudian reordering of stories closely resembles cinematic montage and connects the two in her study of H.D.'s long poems (*Out of Line*, pp. 128–29). H.D. drew on Freud for an explanation of a visionary experience she had in 1920, where she saw images on the wall of her hotel room. In *Tribute to Freud* these are read like hieroglyphics, as yet more instances of 'picture-writing' (pp. 44–56). For Adelaide Morris, the 1920 experience positioned H.D. 'as a hybrid human machine projector and viewer' (*How To Live*, p. 94).

74 *The Gift*, p. 212.

4

Ernest Hemingway:
The Observer's Visual Field

Although he does not extend his works in a transcendental direction, the writings of Ernest Hemingway, like those of H.D., emerge from a matrix of modernist experimentation in which the nature of visual perception is explored. Hemingway, however, presents the unusual case of a writer who rarely commented on film and who made a positive point of avoiding Hollywood, only becoming interested in film-making in the 1930s; yet whose work has long attracted commentary on his cinematic method. Probably the earliest instance is that of a French reviewer who declared, on the evidence of *A Farewell To Arms* (1929), that Hemingway was a 'man who is at once a camera and a phonograph'.[1] In 1934 Wyndham Lewis, by no means an admirer of Hemingway, quoted a passage from this same novel and reflected: 'I read this page as I came to it, just as I would watch scenes unfolding on the screen in the cinema'. Bemused by the unusual power of this method, Lewis described Hemingway's writing as a *'cinema in words'*.[2]

Since these early views it has become routine for critics to praise Hemingway's visual immediacy.[3] Here is Harry Levin in 1951 glossing a passage from *For Whom the Bell Tolls*: 'each clipped sentence, each preposi-tional phrase, is like a new frame in a strip of film: indeed the whole passage, like so many others, might have been filmed by the camera and projected on the screen'.[4] In repeating the analogy drawn by Gertrude Stein in the 1930s Levin is compounding the confusion over units within that comparison. What is being compared to what? The frame of a film is an entity which disappears with the film's motion, but a sentence does not become 'invisible' in the same way as we perceive its place within a larger sequence.

Although Edward Murray has dated Hemingway's cinematic fiction from the 1930s, his earliest prose was exploring modes of visual representation. A series of sketches called 'Paris 1922' represent his first attempt at blending journalistic reportage with the imagistic precision he had been learning from Gertrude Stein. The majority of the six sketches open with the phrase 'I have seen', which situates Hemingway as an observing presence, a kind of human camera recording brief events such as a collision at a race-course (later developed in the story 'My Old Man') or a police charge into a crowd. Hemingway in this respect seems to realize what Stanley Cavell has called the magic of the cinema 'not by literally presenting us with the world, but by permitting us to view it unseen'.[5] With the elision of the observer, we are given glimpses of larger actions and the sequence resembles a montage of shots of Paris life. Each mini-sequence contains two figures or images so that the reader is invited to speculate on their juxtaposition. For example, the fourth sketch reads as follows: 'I have stood on the crowded back platform of a seven oclock [sic] Batignolles bus as it lurched along the wet lamp lit street while men who were going home to supper never looked up from their newspapers as we passed Notre Dame grey and dripping in the rain'.[6] Eugene Kanjo rightly argues that these sketches work like cinematic shots and reads the quoted passage as a tracking shot of the cathedral.[7] Certainly Hemingway's vantage point here occupies the space of a moving camera, but the shot is actually of the street; the cathedral is only brought in at the end to supply a fixed point, against which movement is registered. The men buried in their newspapers are there to contrast with the observer's visual attentiveness: they are looking down while the observer's gaze implicitly rises towards Notre Dame. True to modernist practice, Hemingway avoids punctuation in order to maximize the flow of impressions – a strategy used by Dos Passos among others – and by introducing the pieces with 'I have stood' or 'I have seen', Hemingway suggests that that these are only a few of the examples the observer could produce.

In Our Time

In Our Time (1924) remains Hemingway's most innovative work in its alternation between stories and brief vignettes. Hemingway explained the latter's function in a letter to Edmund Wilson, namely 'to give the picture of the whole between examining it in detail. Like looking with your eyes at something, say a passing coast line, and then looking at it with 15X binoculars'.[8] It is important that Hemingway couches his explanation in terms of visual technology because seeing is an imperative throughout *In Our Time*, carrying with it connotations of confronting unattractive aspects of the modern world. In 'Indian Camp' the young Nick Adams (the intermittent protagonist of the stories) witnesses his father performing a Caesarean operation and its aftermath. This operation is a crucial event in the narrative but is a lacuna in the text because Nick turns his head away. The only moment of shockingly vivid description comes when Nick sees what has happened to the husband: 'The Indian lay with his face toward the wall. His throat had been cut from ear to ear. The blood had flowed down into a pool where his body sagged the bunk'.[9] Thus Nick's sight of the Indian is positioned early in a learning sequence. More importantly, we can already see how Hemingway is writing the observer into his narrative and ordering the visual data in a sequence determined by the movement of that observer's gaze. The brief pauses after each sentence mimic the series of shocks experienced by Nick in his first sight of death.

For all their differences of subject, each section of *In Our Time* repositions the reader/viewer in relation to the descriptive detail. Hemingway's second vignette, an example of reportage, draws on two dispatches he sent to the *Toronto Daily Star* in 1922 dealing with the civilian evacuation of Thrace. The first was a cable which compresses political and ethnic information into a limited length. In the vignette all this has disappeared, the sole remaining allusion being to the Greek cavalry. Similarly, in his first report Hemingway comments: 'It is a silent procession', while the version in *In Our Time* leaves this implicit.[10] Hemingway's longer dispatch situates the reporter within the scene: 'I walked five miles with the refugee procession along the road'.[11] The vignette clearly draws on some aspects of the dispatch form: it is brief, specific and visualized. But it also blanks out most of the contextual information and elides the observer/reporter to an implicit function, a presence assimilated into the visual ordering of the sketch. As Eugene Kanjo has rightly pointed out, the opening gives a marker of visual depth by using vertical objects to establish a long shot: 'minarets stuck up in the rain out of Adrianople across the mud flats. The carts were jammed for thirty miles along the Karagatch road'.[12] The progression in the sketch resembles a slow close-up from categories (people, animals) to differentiated groups (camels, women and children), to the specific instance of a woman in childbirth being helped by a girl 'scared sick looking at it'. Hemingway carefully mimics the gradual emergence of clarity as the focus approaches the vantage point.

In the sketch just described, the authenticity we expect from an eye-witness is dispersed into the scrupulous sequencing and growing specificity of the detail, but sometimes Hemingway positions us within scenes where no external observer is possible, as at the hanging of a criminal (Chapter XV) or the execution of ministers in Chapter V. In the latter case, the reader is implicated in an act carried out presumably in secrecy by an unnamed group of soldiers ('they'). Once again the progression is from the group to the individual, here to a minister so disabled by typhoid that he is sitting down when he is shot. The next vignette echoes this posture, to different effect. It opens as follows:

> Nick sat against the wall of the church where they had dragged him to be clear of machine-gun fire in the street. Both legs stuck out awkwardly. He had been hit

in the spine. His face was sweaty and dirty. The sun shone on his face. The day was very hot. Rinaldi, big backed, his equipment sprawling, lay face downward against the wall. Nick looked straight ahead brilliantly. The pink wall of the house opposite had fallen out from the roof, and an iron bedstead hung twisted toward the street.[13]

From Gertrude Stein Hemingway had received a lesson in economy and direct representation which has borne fruit in this sequence. There is a minimum of movement in this sketch. What we have instead is a sequence of images which, as in Cubism, slightly alter the perspective as we progress from one to the other. Nick's posture is given, then a close-up on his face. The shift to Rinaldi is effected through a general comment on heat, a descriptive equivalent to a brief dissolve as the focus moves. Rinaldi himself is lying face down, so cannot offer a point of view; hence the switch back to Nick. The final sentence in the passage has taken over his point of view to give us a symbolic image of war damaging private life: a private interior has become transformed into a grotesque external image of debris.

Without inflating Nick's importance as observer, Hemingway has used him to exemplify the sights and experiences of war. He is both seen and seeing; object and subject, as happens in other pieces. In 'The Battler' Nick (whose recurrence demonstrates the 'leakage' between vignettes and stories) offers us our initial perspective on the face of the punch-drunk ex-boxer of the title. Then the gaze is reversed as the other glares in his face before attacking him. 'Soldier's Home' gives us a different variation on point of view by opening with two photographs of the protagonist, one in his college fraternity, the other in uniform in Germany. These resemble the publicity photos of a film star, but Krebs is just too late to act out the role of the local hero returning from the war. As Eugene Kanjo points out, the descriptions of these photos 'stand to the short story as establishing shots stand to a film story', except that these images have an ironic relation to the narrative.[14] The photographs freeze Krebs in local moments of success which his homecoming undermines. Far from easing back into small-town life, Krebs finds himself estranged by the changes in fashion during his absence. The photos should be images of his typicality, but they only highlight his difference from the other townsfolk, even the other members of his family.

It would be ridiculous to describe Krebs as a returning hero or Nick in the earlier sketch as a glamorous war casualty, and yet Hemingway's understated detail plays his descriptions off against such stereotypes. Of his vignettes, Alan Spiegel comments: 'he makes you see everything – the peripheral and the central, the adventitious and the necessary – with an equal proportion of emphasis and therefore on the same plane of value'.[15] 'Everything' is sweeping and vague, and totally misses Hemingway's use of perspective like a camera to direct the reader's visual attention. In the vignette of Nick, the latter's immobilization by a wound forces him to be a spectator of war, but only within the limited range of his visual field.

Hemingway excels at evoking the physical immediacy of sequences of action. His fascination with sports skills, which was to develop into a fetish in his later works, reflects his desire to be as specific as possible about the actions of skiing, fishing, horse-riding, and of course bull-fighting. The last of these is given priority in a sequence of vignettes starting with long shots and then giving a close-up in Chapter XII: 'It all happened right down close in front of you, you could see Villalta snarl at the bull and curse him, and when the bull charged he swung back firmly like an oak when the wind hits it, his legs together, the muleta trailing and the sword following the curve behind'.[16] The formulation of witness through the second person could be taken as a colloquial variation on the first person or a hint at the typicality of the scene, as if the reader could repeat the experience. Although Villalta snarls, his is a *visual* action like all the details in this balletic sequence. Hemingway captures the theatrical elegance of the man's movements, which are a performance to the crowd. So, when the kill finally occurs, Villalta is frozen in a posture raising his hand to his roaring audience.

In this instance the bull dies, but one of the most important vignettes describes a toreador's death through an explicit cinematic analogy. Chapter XIV shows a bullfighter named Maera who has been gored. Immobilized by his wound, everything happens around him until his wound becomes fatal: 'Maera felt everything getting larger and larger and then smaller and smaller. Then it got larger and larger and then smaller and smaller. Then everything commenced to run faster and faster as when they speed up a cinematograph film. Then he was dead'.[17] Hemingway expresses the ultimate experience of death through modulations of perceived images. The magnification and contraction of Maera's visual field externalizes his physical situation and enables Hemingway to avoid the cul-de-sac of this perspective. The comparison positions the reader as 'viewer' of Maera's sensations, which become a narrative spectacle ended by his death.

The examples considered above demonstrate the local vividness of *In Our Time* rather than its progression. Robert M. Slabey has located a central 'metaphysical quest, finding a way to exist', while Richard Hasbany has subjected the volume to an imagistic reading, in which the parts gradually evoke a composite impression of the period.[18] While Hasbany is certainly right to stress the importance of Imagism for the visual specificity of Hemingway's method, his analysis keeps freezing his diachronic account into an 'image' or 'impression'. Understanding *In Our Time* involves us in reading *across* sections, following a montage-like sequence in which each scene is modified by its successor. Thus, the dead babies in the opening sketch 'On the Quai at Smyrna' (added to the 1930 edition) anticipate the childbirths of 'Indian Camp' and the evacuation vignette. 'My Old Man' builds up to a climax in which the father of the narrator dies in a riding accident. This is immediately followed by the vignette of Maera's death. Then the penulti-mate vignette, the description of a hanging, is situated within the gap between the parts of 'Big Two-Hearted River' as if it were a nightmare of the narrator. The recurrence of images and scenes from section to section blurs any sharp distinction between public and private, American and European. No experience, it seems, is unique; but neither is any overall 'image' gener-ated. We have instead a series of fragments from larger sequences in which causality is reduced to chance reversals.

In Our Time follows modernist practice in its use of montage, of decentred perspective (Nick Adams only recurs intermittently), and in its startling shifts of tone and subject. Its refusal of any grand narrative and its presenta-tion of partial glimpses anticipates William March's 1933 war novel *Company K*, which disperses narration among the members of the eponymous military company. March opens his novel with a private thinking back to his experi-ence of the Western Front and speculating how he could give sequence to all the different stories:

'I wish there were some way to take these stories and pin them to a huge wheel, each story hung on a different peg until the circle was completed. Then I would like to spin the wheel, faster and faster, until the things of which I have written took life and were recreated, and became part of the whole, flowing toward each other, and into each other; blurring, and then blending together into a composite whole, an unending circle of pain... That would be the picture of war.'[19]

The sheer difficulty of achieving a 'composite whole' informs *In Our Time* as well as *Company K*. Both titles point to shared predicaments, but March's irony is even greater than Hemingway's in showing how separate the members of the company are from each other. Their divided opinions over shooting German prisoners are symptomatic of a broader separation mimed in the spatial gaps between each section of the novel. In the passage quoted the wheel of fate is a traditional figure of shared suffering. It also resembles a pre-cinematic machine like the phenakistoscope, which simulated movement through an observer spinning a disk with mounted illustrations.[20] March's novel not only shows care over its long shots, close-ups, etc. but breaks the soldiers' experiences down into small units resembling a film shot, implying an analogy between fictional narration and a cinematic machine to give an effect (or illusion) of motion and continuity.[21]

Visual Horizons: *The Sun Also Rises* and *A Farewell to Arms*

Despite the assertions of Frank Laurence and Edward Murray to the contrary, we have already seen a cinematic dimension emerging in Hemingway's early prose. Although he ridiculed popular film's tendency to glamorize, like many of the other writers discussed in this volume, he attached his main priority to visual representation. Like Conrad, Hemingway defined clarity in visual terms. His 1935 'Monologue to the Maestro' stressed the need to see his experience and to 'write it down making it clear so the reader will see it too'; and he later insisted that the novelist 'writes to be read by the eye'.[22] We can see this priority feeding into some sections of *The Sun Also Rises* (1927). Here the narrator Jake Barnes ironically dismisses travel by declaring that 'all countries look just like the moving pictures', but deploys cinematic methods to give special value to topographical descriptions in which he is a *flâneur* of the Paris streets or a tourist in northern Spain.[23] During the coach journey to the Pamplona fiesta, the landscape gradually becomes more detailed, building up to the visual climax of arrival.[24] In this and similar sequences narrative commentary is obviated by the dynamic of the narrator's gaze directing the reader/viewer's attention to key visual features.

Despite the much-quoted passage in which a character accuses Barnes of having lost touch with the soil, the most animated descriptive sections of the novel are premised on the latter maintaining a distance from his cherished sights. The fact that he is a news-reporter only confirms Barnes's perception of Paris street life and the Spanish fiesta as spectacles to be relished visually. In 1926 Hemingway told his editor Maxwell Perkins that he had shot a film sequence of the Pamplona fiesta: 'we made a movie from inside the ring one year with a German portable camera [...] and had the rush of people coming into the ring, coming faster and faster and then finally falling all over themselves and piling up and the bulls jamming over them and right into the camera'.[25] The same attention to visual pace is registered in the novel when the bulls approach the narrator's vantage point and we are given a brief close-up of a man being gored. For a moment the tracking shot of the rush is suspended: 'both the man's arms were by his sides, his head went back as the horn went in, and the bull lifted him and then dropped him'.[26] And then we return to the general flow towards the bull-ring. Barnes watches the bull-fights through binoculars, in other words through a mechanical device for magnification analogous to the change in a camera's focal length. Obviously one purpose here is to give us another close-up like the vignette in *In Our Time* discussed earlier.

Our consciousness of the crowd lapses as the reader/viewer is directed to observe the drama between bull and bullfighter. Note the exchange of gazes in the following lines: 'the bull was watching. Seemingly he watched the white horse, but really he watched the triangular steel point of the pic. Romero, watching, saw the bull start to turn his head. He did not want to charge. Romero flicked his cape so the colour caught the bull's eye. The bull charged with the reflex'.[27] This sequence follows the logic of a shot/reverse-shot. The switch backwards and forwards between the bull and Romero creates, as in film, a shared visual field within which, once the bull charges, the two figures merge momentarily into a single image. Single, that is, but for the difference between the bull's sudden movements and the leisurely sweeps of Romero's cape. It was exactly this effect which Hemingway expressed in cinematic terms in his book on bull-fighting. In *Death in the Afternoon* (1932) he described how one bull-fighter 'can perform the usual movements of bull fighting so slowly that they become, to old-time bullfighting, as the slow motion picture is to the ordinary motion picture'.[28]

A Farewell to Arms (1929) is a self-edited narrative in which Frederic Henry isolates the story of his love for Catherine Barclay by detaching it from any personal context. Instead of placing it within his own life-story, the opening gives us a slow 'panning shot', which moves our gaze gradually away from the house to the far distance of the mountains.[29] In spatial metaphors, intimacy is rendered through proximity and detachment through distance. The opening thus uses visual movement to block off any close identification with the narrator. Like the descriptive sections of *The Sun Also Rises* and like *The Red Badge of Courage*, the visual limit throughout this novel is the narrator's perceptual horizon. Throughout the novel, action is expressed primarily through gesture, scene and image. Initially the narrator comes across as a pair of eyes giving a view of troop movements framed through a house window, i.e. of a distanced spectacle .

Of course this is our superficial first impression and, once the relationship with Catherine begins to form, time takes on more value, hence the extension of scenes, the lingering over small actions such as eating together, and the ominous allusions to the seasons. The latter punctuate every section of *A Farewell to Arms* and give scenic expression to the inevitability of the love subject's transience.

In controlling the visual syntax of his narrative Henry often appears to function like a one-man film production team. W. M. Frohock quotes a passage describing the ambulances in the mountains and comments: 'This is straight movie, complete with everything but the shooting directions, the lens being permitted to pick up more or less, and to hold it longer or shorter times, according to the mood of Frederic Henry'.[30] In the following passage from Chapter 16 the management of light and perspective is crucial for evoking the lovers' sense of comfort:

> That night a bat flew into the room through the open door that led to the balcony
> and through which we watched the night over the roofs of the town. It was dark
> in our room except for the small light of the night over the town and the bat was
> not frightened, but hunted in the room as though he had been outside. We lay and
> watched him and I do not think he saw us, because we lay so still. After he went
> out we saw a searchlight come and watched the beam move across the sky and
> then go off and it was dark again.[31]

The power of this passage comes from its lighting effects – what John Jobst
has called 'camera placement'.[32] Although set in semi-darkness, there is no
loss of visual clarity. The motion of the bat into the room cues in a reverse
shot of how the lovers watch the town. The image of the balcony repeats the
open window of the opening chapters, with the difference that now watching
is shared. There is also a desire for concealment, to see without being seen,
which gives suspense to the bat's entry (a small violation of their interior),
and which explains the final shot of the searchlight. The latter is literally an
image of searching, specifically for signs of the enemy but, because the war
cannot be separated from the love action, also an image of the surveillance
they try to avoid.

   A Farewell to Arms assembles a complex sequence of scenic and imagistic
recurrences, which constantly invite us to revise our view of the action as it
moves forward. The lovers' change of dress suggests changes in their role and
identity. Henry's personal retreat to Milan at the opening of Chapter 33
recapitulates his earlier entry into that city as a war casualty. Instead of being
transported by others and with other casualties, Henry moves under his own
volition. He enters a wine shop: 'The proprietor was behind the bar. Two
soldiers sat at a table. I stood at the bar and drank a glass of coffee and ate a
piece of bread. The coffee was grey with milk, and I skimmed the milk scum
off the top with a piece of bread. The proprietor looked at me'.[33] This
sequence contrasts strikingly with longer sentences suggesting a flow of
visual data. Now the sentences – each one a 'shot' – give a staccato montage
tracing the movement of Henry's gaze round the bar. Essentially he is placing
himself at a distance from the soldiers, a gesture of his withdrawal from the
army, and as his eyes sink in a close-up on his drink we become conscious of
the barman's gaze on him. Will he be exposed as a fugitive? These details
precede any dialogue and further demonstrate how far the novel depends on
scenic construction in representing its action.

   Hemingway's prose objectivism resembles the method of Thomas Boyd
in his own novel of the First World War, *Through the Wheat* (1923), which
was admired by Hemingway and actively promoted by Scott Fitzgerald. Here
the action on the Western Front is refracted through the soldier William
Hicks, who functions as protagonist but whose point of view is constantly

being swallowed up in the collective perspective of his platoon. Boyd writes a visual self-consciousness into his novel through two early comparisons. At one point we are told of a corpse: 'death, camera-like, had caught and held him fast'; and at another an officer's facial expression seems modelled on film: 'his eyes were narrowed as if he were registering "extreme wariness", for the motion-pictures'.[34]

These analogies indicate Hicks' function in the novel, which is to give a camera-like record of battle scenes, in particular to counteract popular images of military bravery with the unglamorous actuality. Bodies are repeatedly shown as fragmented, objects among other debris, or grotesque figures across which the observer's gaze ranges: 'some wore expressions of peace as if they were about to enjoy a long and much-needed rest; others sprawled with sagging chins, from which a stream of saliva had flown; one face grinned like an idiot's'.[35] Scott Fitzgerald, who helped to get this novel published, commented that Boyd 'must write about the external world' and the sign of this is the novel's scrupulous care over visual distance, close-ups, and lighting effects.[36]

In Boyd's novel, as in March's *Company K* and *A Farewell to Arms*, the impossibility of seeing a whole war front leads these writers to break down their descriptions to small scenic units authenticated but inevitably limited by their reliance on individual perspectives, units whose potential subjectivity is offset by objectivist representational techniques whereby the observer often attenuates into a disembodied point of view – in short a human camera. As a result, the scenes tend to become instances of modern warfare rather than signs of clear military progress or defeat in the field. It was partly Willa Cather's pursuit of clarity as well as her continuing commitment to military heroism that led Hemingway to complain to Ezra Pound that Cather's 1922 novel *One of Ours* showed a battle scene deriving from Griffith's *Birth of a Nation*. 'I identified episode after episode, Catherized', Hemingway declared.[37]

Multiple Perspectives in *To Have and Have Not*

During the 1930s Hemingway's interest in the cinema grew. Edward Murray rightly draws our particular attention to two stories from that decade: in 'The Capital of the World' (1936), he argues, 'the narrative mobility of the third-person point of view permits Hemingway to employ filmic crosscutting technique'.[38] This is achieved through a spatial separation between different levels of the Madrid pension (the 'set') in which the action takes place.[39] At one point a matador upstairs tries unsuccessfully to seduce a girl; downstairs the waiters ridicule the customers. Hemingway keeps the contrasts between scenes going through the spatial markers 'upstairs' and 'down'. There is an element of cinematic self-reference in this story since the 1930 film *Anna Christie* is being shown, in which Garbo plays a prostitute, exactly the role attributed to the girl by the matador. Just as the film-goers are frustrated by Garbo's failure to match up to a glamorous image, so the matadors (the 'stars' of Madrid society) and bullfighting in general are presented ironically as falling short of expectations. In 'The Capital' different actions are presented as if happening simultaneously, whereas in 'The Snows of Kilimanjaro' (also 1936) cross-cutting takes the form of italicized flashbacks occurring within the consciousness of the injured male protagonist; the editing is thus chrono-logical rather than spatial. Immobilized and fatigued in an African setting, his thoughts drift back into a montage of past scenes featuring snow: 'now in his mind he saw a railway station at Karagatch and he was standing with his pack and that was the headlight of the Simplon-Orient cutting the dark now and he was leaving Thrace then after the retreat [...] in the morning at breakfast, looking out the window and seeing snow on the mountains in Bulgaria'.[40] Recall is expressed as viewing a memory screen on which cherished scenes from the past are projected.

The 1930s not only saw Hemingway experimenting with cinematic techniques in his fiction; he also began to take an interest in film-making. In 1933 he discussed with Lewis Milestone the possibility of collaborating over a documentary on Spain which would not use professional actors. 'All must be shot in Spain,' he declared, 'No Hollywood. No studio'.[41] Nothing came of this project, but Hemingway's expression of interest helps explain his subsequent involvement in *The Spanish Earth* project, completed in 1937. This film will be discussed in Chapter 8.

Hemingway's willingness to experiment with perspective can be seen in his 1937 novel *To Have and Have Not*, which was completed and published against the background of the Spanish Civil War. Harry Morgan is liquor-runner between Cuba and the USA, approached as the novel opens about the possibility of smuggling human cargo. Unlike *The Sun Also Rises* and *A Farewell to Arms*, *To Have and Have Not* contains no preamble. The reader is plunged straight into an already existing situation between Morgan and the smugglers, the former refusing their business. The men leave the café, then: 'As they turned out of the door to the right, I saw a closed car come across the square toward them. The first thing a plane of glass went and a bullet smashed into the row of bottles on the show-case wall to the right. I heard the gun going and bop, bop, bop, there were bottles smashing all along the wall'.[42] Hemingway evokes what was to become a cliché-image in gangster movies by gearing his description closely to the pace of Morgan's perceptions. The window shatters before he can process the event, whereas once the focus shifts outwards to the square the shootings take on a slow-motion quality as one of the smugglers falls wounded: 'He flopped there, putting his hands over his head, and the chauffeur shot at him with the shotgun while the nigger put in a fresh pan [to the machine gun]'.[43]

So far it might sound as if Hemingway were merely following the practice of his earlier narratives in privileging the protagonist's perspective by making it our sole access to visual data. However, as the novel progresses the focalization shifts in Part Two to an anonymous third person and in Part Three to a friend of Morgan's named Albert. The latter section, the longest in the novel, is not even tied to that single point of view, but instead shifts constantly. The first effect of these shifts is to complicate the position of the protagonist. The sudden shooting we were just considering is only the first in a series which, we learn in Part Two, includes Morgan himself. In that brief section we see the aftermath of an unsuccessful attempt at liquor smuggling, which has left him wounded in his arm and his companion fatally shot. Hemingway here begins the process of objectification which will lead ultimately to Morgan's own death.

In Part Three of the novel the action is often broken up into brief cinematic shots. For instance, Chapter III focalizes its first scene through Albert; then it cuts to follow Morgan and the lawyer Bee-lips into a back room where no one else is present; finally the two men emerge and rejoin the others, and Albert's point of view is restored. The range of cinematic devices grows as Hemingway shifts perspective. He uses cross-editing as the narrative cuts between the writer Richard Gordon and Morgan's narrative, flashback to the Gordons interrupted during sex, scenic reprise between Morgan's boat and as coda a long shot across the sea showing a tanker in the distance. The only character to be linked with the cinema is Dorothy, the daughter of a Hollywood producer, who ignores her lover in favour of her own mirror-image ('she was extraordinarily pretty, with a small, very fine figure').[44] One of the most powerful images in the novel is the external view of Morgan's boat adrift after the Cubans have been shot. The perspective resembles that of the coastguards who find her, giving sharp visual detail without identifying the bullet-holes: 'there were a number of fresh, wood-splintered holes in the newly painted planking of her hull'. The verbal 'camera' then pans along the boat's sides: 'there was no sign of life on her although the body of a man showed, rather inflated looking, above the gunwale [...] and, from the long seat alongside the starboard gunwale, a man seemed to be leaning over to dip his hand into the sea'.[45] The whole sequence is brilliantly objectified as if through the eyes of an observer ignorant of Morgan's narrative. Indeed it seems as if Morgan himself is already dead and his narrative ended.

In 1939 Howard Hawks tried to get Hemingway interested in screenwriting for the cinema, in collaborating on a script for *To Have and Have Not* or on an adaptation of 'The Short Happy Life of Francis Macomber' to be shot in Africa.[46] During the Hawks adaptation of the novel William Faulkner was brought in to revise the subject into a conflict between Vichy and the Free French. Although the first section of the film stuck closely to Hemingway's text a number of major changes were made to his narrative, most notably in filling out the character of Marie to an independent presence capable of challenging Morgan at many points.[47] In the novel women are limited to minor stereotypical roles such as the acquiescent wife or the embodiment of glamour. Most obviously, they are excluded from Morgan's sea journeys and therefore from the most dramatic action sequences.

This exclusion changes in Hemingway's novel of the Spanish Civil War, *For Whom the Bell Tolls* (1941), in which the protagonist Robert Jordan has a brief passionate affair with a young woman named Maria. When first seen (through Jordan's eyes), she is caught in a series of still images which link her visually to the Spanish landscape. In one of the scenes in which the two make love we look down at Maria pressed into a bed of heather roots. Contrast this image with her own account of being cropped by fascist soldiers in a barber's shop. Here Maria is forced to watch her hair braids being cut off in the mirror, a displaced analogue for her rape, whereas Jordan's eyes provide her with a less threatening mirror. Jordan's perspective on her is benignly phallic, unlike the anonymous violence of the fascists. Indeed the difference between the two sexual acts suggests that Hemingway is setting up a metaphor of the rape of Spain by the fascist forces. If this is so, it inevitably situates Maria as a passive, reactive presence in the novel, unlike the older woman Pilar, who receives compliments from Jordan for her visual evocation of an earlier battle ('Pilar made him see the fascists die').[48]

There is further dimension to Maria which confirms Hemingway's consciousness of film in this novel. Jordan links her in his thoughts with Hollywood stars. Gazing at her as she walks before him, he begins to wonder whether she is real: 'maybe it is like the dreams you have when someone you have seen in the cinema comes to your bed at night and is so kind and lovely. He'd slept with them all that way when he was asleep in bed. He could remember Garbo still, and Harlow. Yes, Harlow many times. Maybe it was like those dreams'. As his reverie continues, Jordan recalls one particular dream in which Garbo comes to him 'like the old days with Jack Gilbert'.[49] It seems here as if Jordan is doubting his growing love for Maria, but the cinema dream suggests a half-formed fantasy of him starring in a leading role in the war; his romantic attachment helps to produce the pathos of the lovers' eventual separation and Jordan's own impending death.

The Hollywood allusions just considered confirm the cinematic organization of *For Whom the Bell Tolls*. Hemingway repeatedly demonstrates an awareness of point of view, which serves to produce suspense right from the opening scene. The 'camera' first locates the focalizer, then merges with his vantage point: 'he lay flat on the brown, pine-needle floor of the forest, his chin on his folded arms [...] The mountainside sloped gently where he lay; but below it was steep and he could see the dark of the oiled road winding through the pass'.[50] The observer need not be named yet because our attention is concentrated totally on his function. Unlike *To Have and Have Not*, this narrative is end-directed in that we wonder whether Robert Jordan, the observer here, will blow up the bridge he keeps under surveillance throughout this novel. Sometimes he watches with the naked eye, sometimes with binoculars. At other points physiology and technology merge in a metaphor which identifies purpose with visual clarity. A scene with Maria dissolves into an image of the bridge: 'he was walking beside her but his mind was thinking of the problem of the bridge now and it was all clear and hard and sharp as when a camera lens is brought into focus'.[51] What Jordan actually 'sees' in his mind's eye is a composite image of the bridge formed from many actual viewings, within which he sees himself place the dynamite charges.

Hemingway's use of the third person helps the shifts in visualization, which sometimes, as Laurence has pointed out, occur within a single sentence.[52] Furthermore, again, following Laurence, Hemingway's descriptions frequently demonstrate a 'sense of [...] camera placement, field of view, and range as when a weapon, or a camera, is aimed'. Laurence then demonstrates how a description could be broken down, as if for a film script, into shots of different length, thereby showing Hemingway's skill at conveying movement and posture. However, Laurence adds the following proviso: 'Jordan's way of seeing is not exactly like a camera's. His mind sees very particular details – the ammunition clip, the insigne – in a way that a camera at this distance could not select'.[53] The problem in this account is that the camera does not see, nor does it select. Those functions are performed by its user and Hemingway foregrounds the human agent in passages such as the one quoted in the previous paragraph in which attention is expressed as a shift in lens. The characteristic move is thus from lack of specificity – a general or 'soft-focus' effect – to sharp detail, as in a close-up. And because Jordan is a trained military observer, the details objected to by Laurence would be exactly the ones he would focus on particularly. We can see this working negatively in the last close-up on the bridge guard. Here the details become positively unwelcome. Jordan recognizes the guard from earlier observations: 'he was wearing the same knitted stocking-cap. And he had not shaved. His cheeks were sunken and his cheekbones prominent'.[54] Jordan lingers so much over the details of the guard's features that he feels his professional perspective is becoming compromised and has to put the glasses down.

In addition to representing surveillance, Hemingway deploys a range of cinematic devices to serve other devices. The dialogue passages with only minimal identificatory tags accustom the reader to a collective style of utterance characteristic of Spanish. The alternations in point of view give other characters' assessments of Jordan. Flashbacks contextualize the action, biographically when Jordan recalls leaving home.[55] Cross-cutting between proximate scenes within the same location starts from an early point and Hemingway broadens out the action by juxtaposing Jordan's group with a same-time montage of Republican headquarters in Madrid. As the time for the assault on the bridge approaches – and here we should remember Hemingway's stated admiration for *The Birth of a Nation* – tempo is built up by cross-cutting between two main narrative sequences: the preparations of Jordan's group and the efforts by Andres to deliver Jordan's dispatch to a Republican general. The latter set up tracking shots of Republican forces massed along a mountain road, but these images are offset by the contents of the dispatch, which warn that the enemy already knows of a planned Republican assault. In short the final drama of the novel is expressed through rapid perspective shifts (along the mountain road, downwards through the girders of the bridge, up into the sky for fascist planes) and through changes in location. The novel ends at a point of imminence at which the reader cuts between the perspective of the wounded Jordan and that of an approaching cavalry officer: 'Lieutenant Berrendo, watching the trail, came riding up, his thin face serious and grave. His sub-machine gun lay across his saddle in the crook of his left arm. Robert Jordan lay behind the tree, holding on to himself very carefully and delicately to keep his hands steady'.[56] This quiet note of suspense is not Hollywood and the 1943 adaptation adds the following: 'The film cuts to a close shot of Jordan aiming directly into the camera. Suddenly the weapon is firing violently. As the smoke obscures the screen, there is a shot of a tolling bell'.[57] This sort of violent climax is out of key with the novel and also confusing since Jordan's point of view is privileged throughout. The tolling bell clearly suggests death, but whose? Jordan's seems inevitable but that makes the last shot unnecessary, except as an obvious image of the title.

The ambiguity of the final imminent encounter between representatives of the opposing forces in Spain is consistent with Hemingway's use of montage, especially in the last sections of the novel. The shifts in location cut across the narrative line focusing on Jordan and offset his single-minded purpose with suggestions that the Republicans are divided or incompetent. These scenic juxtapositions complicate the reader's view of the Spanish conflict, complications which the emphasis in the Paramount adaptation on the love subject and its new ending were clearly aimed at simplifying. The simplifying effect of Hollywood adaptation seems to justify Hemingway's suspicion of the American film industry. However, these reservations were far more muted in his friend and contemporary F. Scott Fitzgerald.

Notes

1   Meyers, *Hemingway: The Critical Heritage*, p. 149.
2   Wyndham Lewis, *Men Without Art*, p. 33, italics in original. This was the famous account of Hemingway which branded him a 'dumb ox'.
3   An unusual exception is Michael North's argument against seeing emingway's journalism as formative for his fictional style. Within the context of a discussion of photography and film, this argument makes minimal reference to the visual (*Camera Works*, pp. 186–207.
4   Harry Levin, 'Observations on Hemingway', in *Contexts of Criticism*, p. 159.
5   Stanley Cavell, *The World Viewed*, p. 40.
6   Ernest Hemingway, *Complete Poems*, p. xxiii. The sequence here is entitled 'Paris 1922, Auteiul Auteiul'; 'Auteiul' is a misprint for Auteuil, the Paris race course which Hemingway visited.
7   Eugene Kanjo, 'Hemingway's Cinematic Style', in Charles M. Oliver, ed., *A Moving Picture Feast*, pp. 4–5.
8   Ernest Hemingway, *Selected Letters*, p. 128.
9   Ernest Hemingway, *Complete Short Stories*, p. 69.
10 Ernest Hemingway, *Dateline: Toronto*, p. 232.
11 Hemingway, *Dateline: Toronto*, p. 251.
12 Hemingway, *Complete Short Stories*, p. 71; Kanjo, 'Hemingway's Cinematic Style', in Oliver, ed., *A Moving Picture Feast*, p. 7. In Thrace Hemingway travelled for a time with two cameramen who were filming the evacuation. One of these, Shorty Wornall, gave Hemingway his story about the Greek king (whom he had filmed), which subsequently became the coda to *In Our Time* (Carlos Baker, *Ernest Hemingway*, p. 149). While they were travelling across Thrace, Wornall told Hemingway: 'Got some swell shots of a burning village today [...] Shoot it from two or three directions and it looks like a regular town on fire' (*Dateline: Toronto*, pp. 249–50). Also in 1923 Hemingway reported on the French propaganda films about their occupation of the Ruhr (*Dateline: Toronto*, p. 294). Hemingway's vignettes were published in 1924 with the lower-case title *in our time*; the following year appeared the volume which alternates stories with vignettes.
13 *Complete Short Stories*, p. 105.
14 Kanjo, 'Hemingway's Cinematic Style', in Oliver, ed., *A Moving Picture Feast*, p. 8.
15 Spiegel, *Fiction and the Camera Eye*, p. 100.
16 *Complete Short Stories*, p. 141.
17 *Complete Short Stories*, p. 161. In her 1913 story 'Forsythe & Forsythe', Charlotte Perkins Gilman uses the same analogy to articulate a character's sense of time passing in his life: 'That was eight years ago, eight years that were now scurrying through his mind like a quickened cinematograph' (Carol Farley Kessler, *Charlotte Perkins Gilman*, p. 196).
18 Robert M. Slabey, 'The Structure of *In Our Time*', in Linda W. Wagner, ed., *Ernest Hemingway: Six Decades of Criticism*, pp. 65–76; Richard Hasbany, 'The Shock of Vision: An Imagist Reading of *In Our Time*', in Linda W. Wagner, ed., *Ernest Hemingway: Five Decades of Criticism*, pp. 224–40.
19 William March, *Company K*, p. 2.
20 The phenakistoscope dates from the 1830s, as does the cylindrical zoetrope, which was redesigned in the 1860s. Both were superseded by flexible film in 1889 and of course by the first movie film in 1895.
21 March uses cinematic imagery to show the secularized world of his characters. One soldier sees a Catholic print of the Bleeding Heart, then hallucinates a Christ figure emerging across the trenches. The following section repeats the same need for prayer, but this time

directed towards a cinematic icon of Lillian Gish torn out of a movie magazine (*Company K*, pp. 27–30).

22 Ernest Hemingway, *By-Line*, p. 212; Matthew J. Bruccoli, ed., *Conversations with Ernest Hemingway*, p. 120.

23 Ernest Hemingway, *The Essential Hemingway*, p. 13.

24 Cf. W. M. Frohock, *The Novel of Violence in America*, p. 169: 'the procession and pace here are essentially emotional'. Jeffrey Meyers finds an analogy with Conrad in this sequence, noting how each instance 'resembles a cinematic tracking-shot' ('Conrad's Influence on Modern Writers', p. 189).

25 In Matthew J. Bruccoli, ed., *The Only Thing That Counts*, p. 52.

26 *The Essential Hemingway*, p. 148.

27 *The Essential Hemingway*, p. 163.

28 Ernest Hemingway, *Death in the Afternoon*, p. 21.

29 Cf. Jobst, *Cinematic Technique in the World War I American Novel*, pp. 140–41.

30 Frohock, *The Novel of Violence in America*, p. 177.

31 Ernest Hemingway, *A Farewell to Arms*, p. 92.

32 See Jobst, *Cinematic Technique in the World War I American Novel*, pp. 32–33 and *passim*.

33 *A Farewell to Arms*, p. 211. Unlike Nick Adams in 'The Killers' (1927), Henry is here both witness and protagonist; Adams functions mainly to supply the visual perspective on two gunmen seeking a Swede in a restaurant. As Frank M. Laurence points out, 'almost everything in the text that is not dialogue is simple and direct observation, what a witness to the drama of the story would see' (*Hemingway and the Movies*, p. 202). For valuable commentary on how film adaptations filled or expanded on perceived absences in this story, see Oliver Harris, 'Killing "The Killers": Hemingway, Hollywood and Death', in Seed, ed., *Literature and the Visual Media*, pp. 74–95.

34 Thomas Boyd, *Through the Wheat*, pp. 67, 69.

35 Boyd, *Through the Wheat*, p. 147.

36 Andrew Turnbull, ed., *The Letters of F. Scott Fitzgerald*, p. 218. In 1926 Hemingway told Maxwell Perkins that Boyd's novel was an 'awfully good book' (*Selected Letters*, p. 202).

37 Hemingway, *Selected Letters*, p. 105.

38 Edward Murray, *The Cinematic Imagination*, p. 220. Frank M. Laurence counters Murray's selection of stories by noting that cross-cutting occurs in the early story 'Up in Michigan' (*Hemingway and the Movies*, p. 217).

39 Bernard Olsey argues that this spatial division of the action was suggested by Garbo's 1932 film *Grand Hotel*, in which the destinies of apparently unrelated guests intersect, and that Hemingway draws on this film to set up his theme of breaking illusions ('*El Pueblo Espanol*: "The Capital of the World"', in Jackson J. Benson, ed., *New Critical Approaches*, pp. 238–44).

40 Hemingway, *Complete Short Stories*, p. 42.

41 Hemingway, *Selected Letters*, p. 385.

42 Ernest Hemingway, *To Have and Have Not*, p. 11.

43 *To Have and Have Not*, p. 12.

44 *To Have and Have Not*, p. 177.

45 *To Have and Have Not*, p. 132. The grim spectacle of this boat of corpses is pushed towards black farce when it is towed ashore and Albert's screaming widow adds an appropriate 'sound effect' for the gaping crowd.

46 Bruce F. Kawin, ed., *To Have and Have Not* [screenplay], pp. 15–16; Hemingway, *Selected Letters*, p. 485.

47 For detailed commentary on the changes in adaptation, see Kawin's introduction to the

screenplay of the Howard Hawks adaptation; William Rothman, 'To Have and Have Not Adapted a Novel', in Gerald Peary and Roger Shatzkin, eds., *The Modern American Novel and the Movies*, pp. 70–79; Thomas Hemmeter and Kevin W. Sweeney, 'Marriage as Moral Community: Cinematic Critiques of Hemingway's *To Have and Have Not*', in Oliver, ed., *A Moving Picture Feast*, pp. 64–75. For further commentary on film adaptations of Hemingway's fiction see Gene D. Phillips, *Hemingway and Film*, and Laurence, *Hemingway and the Movies*. A. E. Hotchner has published his screenplay *Ernest Hemingway's 'After the Storm'*.

48 Ernest Hemingway, *For Whom the Bell Tolls*, p. 131.
49 *For Whom the Bell Tolls*, pp. 133, 134. Jean Harlow established herself as the original 'blonde bombshell', playing romantic leads until her death in 1937. Garbo and Gilbert played together in *Flesh and the Devil* (1927) and subsequent films. Garbo wore a woollen sweater, like that referred to in Jordan's dream, in *Susan Lenox: Her Fall and Rise* (1931), in which she co-starred with Clark Gable.
50 *For Whom the Bell Tolls*, p. 5.
51 *For Whom the Bell Tolls*, p. 157.
52 Laurence, *Hemingway and the Movies*, p. 220.
53 Laurence, *Hemingway and the Movies*, pp. 219–20.
54 *For Whom the Bell Tolls*, p. 407.
55 Expressed through a receding perspective shot of his home station as Jordan watches from the rear platform of his train.
56 *For Whom the Bell Tolls*, p. 444.
57 Frank M. Laurence, 'Death in the Matinee: The Film Endings of Hemingway's Fiction', in Oliver, ed., *A Moving Picture Feast*, p. 28.

5

Success and Stardom
in F. Scott Fitzgerald

A Rival Career

F. Scott Fitzgerald was the supreme novelist of style. Throughout his writings he paid particular attention to how his characters constructed their social personae and what self-image they strove to project. Unlike Hemingway, he was drawn to all aspects of the movie business and one of his keenest disappointments came from his failure to achieve success in Hollywood. In 1936 Fitzgerald expressed his perception that the craft of the novel was 'becoming subordinated to a mechanical and communal art [...] in which words were subordinate to images, where personality was worn down to the inevitable low gear of collaboration. As long past as 1930', he continued, 'I had a hunch that the talkies would make even the best selling novelist as archaic as silent pictures'.[1] Like many of his fellow writers Fitzgerald feared a loss of autonomy in Hollywood and could never come to terms with the collaborative screenwriting system. Despite those anxieties, he never wavered in his conviction that 'the movies are a tremendously important question', as he declared in a 1923 interview.[2]

Fitzgerald became a keen movie-goer in 1906 but it was around 1919 that his professional involvement in the cinema began with writing film scripts.[3] The next year he sold the film rights to his story 'Head and Shoulders' to Metro and, by his own account, approached D. W. Griffith with a proposal for a film about film-making, Griffith's reaction being 'immediately contemptuous'.[4] The following year, in an interview with *Shadowland* magazine, Fitzgerald was already inventing a would-be career for himself when he declared: 'I used to try scenarios in the old days [...] Invariably they came back'.[5] Fitzgerald's comments on the cinema tend to have an implied self-reference. For instance, he was surely opening up an opportunity for himself when he complained in 1923 of the poor calibre of screenwriters then being used. Although he admitted that 'the movies have accomplished two wonderful things' – comedy and action films – he insisted that the studios should take on 'younger good writers' to improve the quality of their films.[6] The following year, Fitzgerald wrote a critical article on Hollywood directors called 'The Most Pampered Men in the World', in which he dismissed most directors, with the honourable exception of figures suh as Chaplin and Griffith, as an 'utterly incompetent crew'.[7]

Allusions to the cinema appear in Fitzgerald's writings from the very beginning. *This Side of Paradise* (1920) at one point presents the drunken memories of Amory Blaine in filmic terms as a sequence of images between dissolves: 'His head was whirring and picture after picture was forming and blurring and melting before his eyes'. A fresh drink makes the images more coherent and the analogy becomes explicit: 'as the new alcohol tumbled into his stomach and warmed him, the isolated pictures began slowly to form a cinema reel of the day before'.[8] The strategy of expressing coherence of recall through the film analogy was one which Fitzgerald later used in looking back on New York in the 1920s. 'My Lost City' (1932) assembles a montage of newsreel-like images of returning troops and parties, then cuts to gloomier private scenes of Fitzgerald alone, all forming part of what he described as 'my own movie of New York'.[9]

The Beautiful and Damned (1922) is the first of Fitzgerald's novels to apply cinematic techniques and to investigate the phenomenon of stardom. Book One carries sub-headings similar to the titles for a silent film; indeed, at this time Fitzgerald was working on the titles for the film adaptation of Edith Wharton's novel *The Glimpses of the Moon*.[10] Also in the opening section is placed 'A Flashback to Paradise', an inset quasi-mythical dialogue sequence with the personification of Beauty who was going to appear in a 'new country' in the guise of an 'actress in the motion-pictures', but who is now going to appear as a society girl. It was this flashback which Fitzgerald's friend John Peale Bishop suggested resembled 'elevated moments of D. W. Griffith'.[11] Whatever the specific influence, Fitzgerald has explicitly transposed a cinematic technique for representing the past into his narrative to introduce his female 'siren' (his term) – Gloria Gilbert.

The daughter of a manager in a mid-western film production company, Gloria pursues a career initially as a socialite, later as a would-be film actress. Like her namesake Gloria Swanson, she tries to act out the lifestyle of stardom before she even takes a screen test.[12] The analogy between social and cinematic performance is made explicit again and again. One of Gloria's friends is compared to the 'vamp' Theda Bara; a film director discovers Gloria just before her marriage; and the marriage itself is presented through the medium of a dialogue-only 'script'. Come the day of her screen test, Gloria cannot objectify herself and instead becomes caught in a self-conscious sense of being graceless: 'with a definite effort she forced herself to act – and she had never felt that the gestures of her body were so banal, so awkward, so bereft of grace or distinction'.[13] Already living out her life as a social spectacle, with her husband as her most appreciative audience, Gloria fails to capitalize on this performative skill. When the expected letter of rejection comes, she tries to locate the reason in her features. She gazes anxiously into the mirror:

> She strained to see until she could feel the flesh on her temples pull forward. Yes – the cheeks were ever so faintly thin, the corners of her eyes were lined with tiny wrinkles. The eyes were different. Why, they were different! ... And then suddenly she knew how tired her eyes were.
> 'Oh, my pretty face', she whispered, passionately grieving. 'Oh, my pretty face! Oh, I don't want to live without my pretty face! Oh, what's *happened*?'
> Then she slid toward the mirror and, as in the test, sprawled face downward upon the floor – and lay there sobbing.[14]

Self-scrutiny has become a reprise of the screen test. Ironically the reader, positioned here as an invisible observer, recognizes the authenticity of her melodramatic gesture of self-estrangement from her own ageing mirror image. The expected continuity from socialite to actress fails to materialize. For a fuller investigation of the relation between the two roles the reader has to wait until *Tender is the Night*. For Edwin T. Arnold, examples like the above demonstrate Fitzgerald's evocation of a 'world in which the real and the unreal, the illusion and the mechanics of the illusion not only existed side by side, but actually intertwined in their own complex way'.[15]

Fitzgerald was aware from the beginning of his career of the financial value of film rights to his short stories and novels; indeed Alan Margolies has argued that up to 1925 he wrote his stories with one eye on the Hollywood market, making sure to include appropriate visual effects.[16] Fitzgerald visited Hollywood three times: briefly in 1927 and 1931, and finally for a longer period from 1939. The various projects in which he was involved during these visits have been well documented and four of his screenplays have been published.[17] The vast majority of his assignments were either minor (contributing to the script of *Gone with the Wind*) or failures; the only writing credit Fitzgerald received was for Joseph L. Manckiewicz's *Three Comrades* (1937). *Lipstick: A College Comedy* (1927) was designed for Constance Talmadge and the surviving version is neither a synopsis nor a screenplay, but rather resembles a short story narrated mostly in the present tense. Aaron Latham describes the result as a 'convincing slapstick of manners' but notes that it probably had far too much dialogue for a silent movie.[18] We can, however, see Fitzgerald making a visible effort to articulate action primarily through visible movement. Specifically, Fitzgerald makes elaborate play on the eponymous lipstick, which functions as an erotic trigger for the beautiful

protagonist Dolly, leading her into a series of relationships. It is typical of
Fitzgerald's treatment of glamorous romance that he never loses sight of the
role played by this commodity object; in fact the lipstick itself becomes a
secondary protagonist as the reader/viewer watches its movements from
character to character.

In Fitzgerald's early stories the many references to the cinema serve to
highlight themes. For example, the wealth and style of the mansion in 'The
Diamond as Big as the Ritz' is shown in the fact that it offers guests a private
'moving-picture machine' (an early home video) and that the rooms were
designed by a 'moving picture fella'.[19] Later stories incorporate cinematic
effects, for example 'Magnetism' (1928), which is set in Hollywood and
which narrates events through the perspective of a Hollywood actor. George
Hannaford mentally composes scenes as if they were part of an ongoing
movie. His feared separation from his wife is imagined as a melodramatic
scene in which Kay declares: '"promise me you'll remember," Her tears were
falling. "I'll be different, but somewhere lost inside me there'll always be the
person I am tonight"'. George, however, can't hold this last scene from a
romantic melodrama: 'the scene dissolved slowly'.[20] Each scene between the
couple has a histrionic self-consciousness, which his wife recognizes,
declaring: 'Oh, we're such actors, George – you and I', a line which will recur
in *Tender is the Night* within a similarly theatrical context.[21] In 'Crazy
Sunday' (1932), also set in Hollywood, the focal character is a film continuity
writer who extends the visual to a paranoid degree where everyone is
watching everyone else to assess their 'performance'. Even the natural
environment is drawn into this sense of all-encompassing performance: in
one scene 'the full moon over the boulevard was only a prop'.[22] No area is
exempt from the artifice of cinematic representation, it seems.

In the lecture on Hollywood he wrote for Sheilah Graham in 1939
Fitzgerald stressed the role of the director as a negotiation from one medium
to another: 'A writer's instinct is to think in words. The director has got to
work with the writer and turn the writer's words into visual images for the
camera. We can do without speeches, but we've got to see, for on the screen,
seeing is believing, no matter what the characters say'.[23] In effect Fitzgerald
personifies the two roles he attempted to juggle in his writing for the cinema,
and the tortuous history of Fitzgerald's screenwriting could be seen as a
prolonged struggle with dialogue and scene. In virtually every case, he was
adapting the work of others for the screen, but in 1940 he was given the rare
opportunity to adapt one of his own narratives.[24]

That year Fitzgerald was approached over the possibility of producing a
film based on his 1931 short story 'Babylon Revisited'. He threw himself into
the task with enthusiasm because for once he seemed to have complete
control over the script. The story describes the efforts of a young man to

regain lost connections with Paris and his daughter, who is living there with relatives. The rupture with the past has been brought about by the Wall Street crash and the simultaneous collapse of the protagonist's marriage. The protagonist Charlie negotiates with his sister for his daughter's guardianship. Just when he seems about to succeed, a couple reappear from his past and the project collapses. Even when Charlie dreams of his dead wife approving his plan, this is expressed cinematically through image: 'She said a lot of other things – very friendly things – but she was in a swing in a white dress, and swinging faster and faster all the time, so that at the end he could not hear clearly all that she said'.[25] As if the soundtrack has been lowered, our attention falls squarely on the image of the wife as child (does he want his daughter back as a substitute?) which accelerates towards nightmare.

For his screenplay Fitzgerald retained few of the original scenes and changed the action, as he explained in an author's note, in an 'attempt to tell a story from a child's point of view *without* sentimentality'.[26] Now Charlie's daughter determines the point of view, even the camera angle, as she looks up at adult figures. As Aaron Latham points out, Fitzgerald experimented with separating soundtrack from image within scenes. We *see* with the child's point of view but *hear* adult conversations so that 'the child's vision has become a kind of test of the adult vision'.[27] Fitzgerald demonstrates his skill with cinematic techniques in his use of flashback, montage to show the acceleration of time, and of close-up. One of the problems with the script, however, lies in its melodramatically explicit showing of the mother's suicide and the father's collapse.

Image Management in *The Great Gatsby*

In 1919 Fitzgerald began a serious study of Joseph Conrad's fiction and subsequently cited the latter's preface to *The Nigger of the 'Narcissus'* as summing up his artistic credo that 'the purpose of a work of fiction is to appeal to the lingering after-effects in the reader's mind', as he put it in a 1934 letter to Hemingway.[28] In this preface Conrad insists that the novelist should 'arrest' or detach a sequence from the flux of experience so that the reader can respond to its 'surrounding vision of form and colour'; more importantly in the present context, he also asserts the priority of the visual: 'my task which I am trying to achieve is, by the power of the written word to make you hear, to make you feel – it is, before all, to make you *see*'.[29] In 1923 Conrad gave a talk in New York called 'Author and Cinematograph'. Fitzgerald knew of the visit but did not attend the talk, contenting himself with dancing on the lawn of Conrad's American publisher, where he was staying.[30]

Conrad simultaneously asserted the primacy of vision and at the same time showed its elusive nature. Vision for his narrators remains an ultimate goal despite the visual specificity of Conrad's narratives. Similarly, in *The Great Gatsby* (1926) Fitzgerald constructed an account which he himself subsequently criticized for lacking visual clarity. In answer to a detailed letter on the novel from John Peale Bishop, who criticized its lack of a 'quality of clear visualization', Fitzgerald admitted that Gatsby remained 'blurred and patchy', adding: 'I never at any one time saw him clearly myself'.[31] Seeing in fact becomes a major part of the novel's subject, even of its location. The action is set in West Egg, Long Island, a renamed version of Great Neck where the Fitzgeralds were living at the time of the novel's composition. The famous lists of Gatsby's party-goers suppress the presence of what Edmund Wilson called the 'movie crowd'. Visitors to Fitzgerald's weekend parties included Gloria Swanson and the film-writer and playwright Sidney Howard.[32] In 1923 Fitzgerald sold the movie rights to his story 'Grit' which was released the following year.[33] When Nick Carraway rides into New York in Gatsby's car, we are told: 'with fenders spread like wings we scattered light through half Astoria', not mentioning that in 1922 (the year of the novel's action) the Astoria Studios of Paramount had been producing films for the last two years.[34]

Despite the suppression of Astoria's significance, the movies feature in the novel as offering glamour (the stars' apartments near Central Park), relief from heatwaves, and, for Myrtle Wilson, dreams to compensate for her humdrum life. They thus figure as part of the visual environment of the novel, along with photography and advertisements demonstrating the cultural priority of the image. The movies thus induce a modern, technologically aided way of seeing described by Michael North as 'spectroscopic'.[35] It very quickly becomes apparent that Nick Carraway is an expert on visual representation: he introduces the setting cinematically 'with the sunshine and great bursts of leaves growing on the trees – just as things grow in fast movies'.[36] In his valuable discussion of photography in *The Great Gatsby*, Lawrence Jay Dessner points out that the reference here is to time-lapse photography, an important detail because it reflects Nick's awareness of duration.[37] It also introduces a major theme running throughout the novel, whereby characters are compared with representations, a point to which I shall return in a moment. Suffice it to note here that in the first two chapters Nick demonstrates his familiarity with perspective ('life is much more successfully looked at from a single window'), pace (Daisy and Jordan Baker approach their dinner table in studied slow motion), and delivery (in seeing through Daisy's pose of cynicism).[38] As he gets used to the New York crowd he comes to enjoy the spectacle as the passers-by 'flicker' before his gaze.[39]

In his summary of cinematic elements in this novel, Wheeler Dixon states: 'the visual sensibility apparent in *Gatsby* is, from a filmic standpoint, that of the spectator'.[40] Essentially Dixon is restating Nick's role in the narrative, which is that of the informed outsider, but in so doing he oversimplifies the visual effects Fitzgerald is setting up. These effects are repeatedly ambiguous and contradictory. Take the single most vivid icon in the novel, the massive hoarding showing the eyes of Doctor T. J. Eckleburg. This is an image of a gaze, of eyes writ large; it is also an advertisement, offering as a commodity an aid to vision. Wilson the garage-owner comments towards the end of the novel 'God sees everything', whereas his assistant reassures him: 'that's an advertisement'.[41] The two meanings refer to the opposing ends of a visual perspective: the vantage point from which things can be seen and the eyes as an object to be looked at. Nick sometimes seems to approach events as a film viewer, exploiting his familiarity with technique to elaborate romantic fictions for himself (with Jordan Baker) or for Gatsby.[42] He is neither insider nor outsider, but a shifting combination of the two, as in the first New York scene. Looking out of an apartment window, he imagines a second observer returning his gaze: 'high over the city our line of yellow windows must have contributed their share of human secrecy to the casual watcher in the darkening streets, and I was him too, looking up and wondering. I was within and without'.[43] In film terms a shot/reverse-shot is used to unify the visual field between two characters; here, however, Nick fractures his perspective so that he simultaneously becomes observer and observed. This image sums up an uncertainty he shows in how to situate himself within the scenes he presents. Like Conrad's Marlow, Nick is a contradictory narrator, sometimes claiming great insight, at other points admitting his ignorance.

Seeing for Nick, of course, involves cultural scrutiny since the characters have all constructed their own appearances and therefore identities.[44] Gatsby's fluidity is simply the most versatile instance of a general conception of identity which Nick sums up performatively as an 'unbroken series of successful gestures'.[45] But gesture might be caught by the camera and photographs are unusually important in the novel, so much so that Fitzgerald includes a would-be photographer (McKee) in the first New York scene. Lawrence Dessner reads him as an example of failure and therefore an anti-Gatsby; more generally, he sees photography as tied in with the question of time: 'ageless, forever new, the photographic image incessantly implies that the life it captures is itself subject only to the desires and manipulations of the photographer'.[46] The photograph could thus represent an attempt by the subject to freeze time at a point of glamour, and certainly characters' obsession with their youthfulness is a recurrent subject in Fitzgerald's writings. We should, however, remember how photographs are caught up in the commercial imagery of the novel. Richard Godden has shrewdly asserted that 'to see in 1925 was to see through the stencil of commodity'.[47] This insight bears directly on photography. McKee prides himself as the technician of appearance; when it is suggested that he take a portrait of Myrtle Wilson, he declares: 'I should change the light [...] I'd like to bring out the modelling of the features'.[48] For him the body is the raw material that can be shaped to present desired features. In this respect he resembles Nick who is also trying to construct images with features, in other words with meaning.

McKee performs an important function in drawing the reader's attention to the ways in which a photograph can reify appearance. 'Doing something' with his subjects, as he puts it, suggests commodifying them to their best advantage. Daisy and Jordan, for instance, offer two interchangeable images: 'the only completely stationary object in the room was an enormous couch on which two young women were buoyed up as though upon an anchored balloon. They were both in white, and their dresses were rippling and fluttering'.[49] White here suggests a blank on to which Nick can inscribe meaning; it also suggests coolness as a metaphor for sophistication. Once the two young women start talking to Nick, he notices that their words have no real meaning; they merely support their pose as glamorous, languid beauties.

Nick recognizes Jordan Baker from her publicity pictures and his final comment on her returns to this connection: 'she was dressed to play golf and I remember thinking she looked like a good illustration'.[50] Dress is costume throughout, changed from scene to scene, sometimes even within a scene; and characters are repeatedly perceived as imitations of representations, images of images frozen in postures emblematic of style but quite distinct from function. It just isn't relevant whether Jordan is going to play golf or not. Photographs and illustrations thus draw our attention to the visual self-consciousness of the main characters who, like actors in a film, are determined to play leading parts. Gatsby could thus be viewed as the star performer in Nick's projected (pun intended) fiction. He has appropriated his own setting – a huge house built to mimic a French town hall – and the novel makes much of the initial irony that Gatsby remains unknown to the vast majority of his guests. Unlike Dick Diver in *Tender is the Night*, he is not evident as a social organizer but is rather a producer behind the scenes, visible through the consumables for his parties. For this reason Joss Lutz Marsh argues: 'Gatsby imagines himself, in film terms, the director of the action. First he has constructed Jay Gatsby. More, the marvellous set scenes of the novel are precisely that – set'.[51] Nick sees Gatsby as a star; Gatsby takes upon himself the initiatives of a director. A visitor to Gatsby's house makes the theatre/film analogy explicit by exclaiming over the 'realism' of using actual books in his library; and when Daisy is given a tour of the house as a prelude to restarting her romance with Gatsby, she bursts into tears over his beautiful shirts. The displacement of feeling from person to possessions is ironic but actually confirms our suspicion of a larger displacement. Gatsby's house (bought, not created by him) reminds Nick of a public building elsewhere;

Gatsby's well-thumbed photo of his house seems more real than the house itself, which 'seems more visual than concrete'.[52] Nick is inconsistent in his scepticism. He alternates between seeing through Gatsby and applauding (as if he were in the latter's audience) the sheer scale of his fictions.

As he gets to know Gatsby, Nick figures him more and more in cinematic terms. His party is represented through a montage of disconnected episodes. Then Gatsby emerges from his own created scene through a speech mannerism ('old sport'), an isolated feature (his smile is lingered over) and then an abrupt cut to the apparition of an 'elegant young rough-neck'.[53] Initially Nick tries to compose Gatsby as a figure against a ground but the information he receives from and about Gatsby is too diverse to gel. Nick then turns to gesture and movement. When Gatsby meets Daisy in Nick's house he leans against the latter's clock:

> 'We've met before,' muttered Gatsby. His eyes glanced momentarily at me and his lips parted with an abortive attempt at a laugh. Luckily the clock took this moment to tilt dangerously at the pressure of his head, whereupon he turned and caught it with trembling hands and set it back in its place.[54]

The business with the clock enacts Gatsby's attempts to revive the past. Literally and metaphorically he puts the clock back, with one eye on Nick as if sizing up audience reaction.

The cinematic equivalent of putting the clock back would of course be a flashback and in two cases Fitzgerald uses a filmic method. In her history of the flashback, Maureen Turim notes that one function is to show the 'haunting of the past – representing a certain character's obsession with the past'.[55] The first time this happens is in Chapter 4 where the narrative suddenly cuts to Jordan Baker's 'voice-over' describing events from 1917. The transition is abrupt, but explained, whereas the shift into the past at the end of Chapter 6 is more ambiguous. Gatsby is reminiscing to Nick and expresses his desire to return to a point in the past. Through the device of ellipses the text creates a 'dissolve' whereby the reader is displaced back to a moonlit autumnal evening when Gatsby and Daisy kiss under the stars. Despite Nick's gestures towards Gatsby's 'appalling sentimentality', the stagy nature of the scene is not offset by any references to Gatsby's narrative style. Its provenance remains suspect. Did Nick compose it to embody his perception of Gatsby's romantic dream? The scene passes before we can even register its ambiguity.

With the denouement of the novel, Gatsby rapidly recedes into memory images. Even Nick's eye-witness account of finding his corpse in the swimming pool is striking because of Gatsby's absence. Just at the point at which the reader is expecting an account of the body Nick studiously keeps our eyes diverted onto the movement of the water: 'A small gust of wind that scarcely corrugated the surface was enough to disturb its accidental course with its accidental burden. The touch of a cluster of leaves revolved it slowly, tracing, like the leg of a compass, a thin red circle in the water'.[56] The pacing of the passage is extraordinarily careful in keeping Gatsby's corpse off camera. Instead we get an image of flux and transience. It is as if Gatsby is already fading from the narrative. The final scene of the narrative is an even more radical dissolve, as if the tangible signs of the modern age 'melt away' to an unspoilt pre-industrial green land. But this is Nick's dissolve, of course, not Gatsby's.

Directing the Life Script: *Tender is the Night*

From the beginning Fitzgerald's plans for *Tender is the Night* included a film dimension. In the first version of 1925–26 he designed as protagonist one Francis Melarky, a former Hollywood technician travelling in Europe with his mother. Then in 1929 Fitzgerald hit on the 'new angle' of having instead a 'brilliant young motion-picture director taking time out from his success with his wife in Europe'.[57] Despite the final changes Fitzgerald made to the protagonist, the presence of film in *Tender is the Night* is felt at every level of theme and treatment. Film companies in France and Italy are participating in the American cultural invasion of Europe and even the opening of the novel on the Riviera has its appropriate symbolism. In Fitzgerald's 1932 story 'Crazy Sunday' the coast near Hollywood is called the 'American Riviera' and the novel's first setting is described in cinematic terms in order to establish the main theme of Book I, namely façades and frontages. From a general panorama of the coast, the focus falls on Gausse's Hotel, then on its beach, which will figure as the site of the first action in the novel.

Into this prepared scene steps Rosemary, the young film star and initial female protagonist of the novel. She embodies the 1920s' ideal of the child-woman summarized by Alexander Walker as 'small, very feminine, skilful or child-like, yet vigorous, energetic, resilient and, above all, young'.[58] Fitzgerald pauses briefly on her mother (who plays the role of manager, as happened with stars such as Mary Pickford), but then writes the reader into the text as an appreciative (and implicitly masculine) observer: 'one's eyes moved on quickly to her daughter, who had magic in her pink palms and her cheeks lit to a lovely flame [...] Her fine forehead sloped gently up to where her hair, bordering it like an armorial shield, burst into lovelocks and waves and curlicues of ashe blonde and gold. Her eyes were bright, big, clear, wet and shining, the colour of her cheeks was real'.[59] This description encapsulates Rosemary as image, exemplifying Walter Benjamin's assertion in 1936 that 'the cult of the movie star' preserves 'the phony spell of a commodity'.[60] At the beginning of the novel the phoniness of Rosemary's image has yet to emerge.

As an accomplished film actress, Rosemary professionally assesses appearances for the reader, at the same time incorporating her self-consciousness at being under observation. Just as we have scrutinized her, so she sizes up Nicole Warren, first as an icon (a 'Viking madonna') and then as a romantic rival for Dick. Rosemary's point of view then involves a self-consciousness about the gaze which spreads among the characters on the beach – hence their question whether Rosemary is 'in the plot'. Like Nick Carraway, she assesses behaviour as performance.

A visit to the Gaumont studios near Monte Carlo offers an interpretive perspective. At one point Rosemary and the others suddenly witness a scene in action: 'they came across the white crackling glow of a stage, where a French actor – his shirt front, collar, and cuffs tinted a brilliant pink – and an American actress stood motionless face to face. They stared at each other with dogged eyes, as though they had been in the same position for hours'.[61] Pink is an over-determined colour term in this novel, connoting youth, the frontage of Gausse's hotel and the colour used for black and white photography in film.[62] The scene actually resembles a still or freeze-frame, in posture raising the question of whether Dick and Rosemary will ever get together. While at the studio, Rosemary is met by an American director who sizes her up sexually and professionally. His gaze alerts us to the commodification of Rosemary which has already taken place by her participation in film and more generally suggests that looking, in this novel even more than in *The Great Gatsby*, involves possession and ownership. Rosemary is only too willing to be exploited by her director, but Dick baulks when she arranges a screen test for him, because this seems to be removing his own prerogative. The episode which follows this visit to the film studios draws implicit analogies between film practice and the domestic life of the Divers. We see Nicole, for instance, walking slowly and silently round her cherished setting – her garden – and then being called by Dick, who uses a megaphone, part of a director's standard equipment in the silent era. Indeed he orchestrates his parties like a directed performance, one of which is compared in its tempo with a 'slapstick comedy'.

Within such contexts Rosemary sizes up Dick sexually and professionally (the two areas overlap repeatedly) as a kind of social director, and accordingly begins to make overtures to him by feeding him cue lines which he initially ignores. Ruth Prigozy argues that 'Rosemary's vision is the key to the book'. She embodies the contradictions of American culture – its hard-headed commercialism and its façade of innocence. She is both product and agent. Prigozy continues: she is 'present and future in one: she is the Frankenstein created by American industry. Her mask of innocence conceals the last act in American history'.[63] Rosemary is a type figure and that typicality reflects her cinematic role. In an interview for *Motion Picture Magazine* in 1927 Fitzgerald surveyed film actresses of the period and declared that 'just as the screen exaggerates action, so it exaggerates type': the naïve girl becomes the 'dumb-dora', 'the exotic girl becomes bizarre', and so on.[64]

Rosemary combines the Griffith girl-woman, the self-interest she has learnt from her mother, and an element of the 'vamp' as played by figures such as Pola Negri.[65] It is irrelevant to accuse Rosemary of naivety when she leans towards Dick and breathes 'take me' because she is well aware of its theatricality; and by the same token Dick turns to implicitly cinematic analogues when he says of her declaration 'let's drop it out of the picture'.[66] Just for a moment he is attempting to regain control of their romantic script. But there is no doubt who is in control. Commenting on the scene at the Paris hotel between the two, Richard Godden states that Rosemary's love is 'gestural and involves careful self-direction, a dance of camera angles culminating in the ultimate movie-still'.[67] The two ascend a staircase slowly, Rosemary in the rear, come to a clinch and then separate equally theatrically with a close-up of hands sliding apart on the banisters. Fitzgerald made a wise choice in allowing Rosemary and sometimes Dick to supply the point of view, but without taking over the narrating. This enables him to stress even further the self-conscious staginess of Dick and Rosemary's brief affair. Even at a moment of intimacy Dick's connoisseurial perspective on his own experience is evident, as in the following close-up. Briefly the point of view shifts to Dick: 'Presently she kissed him several times in the mouth, her face getting big as it came up to him; he had never seen anything so dazzling as the quality of her skin'.[68] Instead of yielding to sensation, this image demonstrates the dominance of sight in this section of the novel.

Rosemary's role is to embody power through her control of Dick's perspective. She thus establishes a gender theme which Fitzgerald had identified in 1928 (three years after starting work on *Tender is the Night*): 'American life today easily lends itself to satire: women absolutely dominate. They are organized against the men, whose intelligence, it seems to me, moreover, is becoming feminine'.[69] The 'romantic' interplay between Dick and Rosemary then can be seen as a quasi-cinematic struggle for control of their script (graphically symbolized in Nicole's attempt to wrench control of the family car from Dick), a struggle which Dick loses (when he hears of Rosemary's sexual activities on a train, his evasive reaction resembles an attempt to conceal a screen: 'do you mind if I pull down the curtain?').[70]

The focus of action in Book I on Rosemary and the cinema alerts the reader to less prominent visual details in the subsequent sections of the novel. We note that Dick wears a variety of outfits ranging from a military uniform to Swiss lederhosen and ski suit. Each costume signifies a role, or at least a *would-be* role; and in this way his fragmentation before the final slow fade at the end of the novel is signalled in visual terms. Similarly, Dick's consummation of his affair with Rosemary takes place within the context of her filming in Rome, specifically against the background of a 'huge set of the Forum, larger than the Forum itself'.[71] This imagistic triumph of simulation over actuality drains the intensity from Dick's affair, which has already receded into the past.

Despairing of getting *Tender is the Night* made into a film, in 1934 Fitzgerald wrote his own 'Summary Movie Treatment' with Charles Warren.[72] This treatment greatly simplified chronology and action by having a single linear sequence in which Dick is immediately set up as a competitor for Nicole's favours against an émigré Russian aristocrat. As Aaron Latham points out, the treatment is crudely melodramatic, starting with a funicular accident to occasion the first meeting between Dick and Nicole.[73] Fitzgerald had planned to use music in constructing his drama, but otherwise the outline loses most of the novel's psychological intricacy. Fitzgerald's new ending makes a stark contrast with the low-key conclusion to the novel. Having helped arrange the release of the aristocrat who, instead of Dick, gets involved in a brawl with the police, Nicole is taken to hospital with a mysterious illness. Dick (in the treatment a surgeon) diagnoses a disease of the brain and operates:

> In the quiet, mechanical smoothness of the operating room, in the midst of his delicate work – with the newness and mystery of this particular operation – and the burning sensation that he is trying to save Nicole for another man, Dick's nerve fails.
>
> But Nicole, deep in the oblivion of the anesthetic murmurs once 'Dick' and his hand does not falter after that.[74]

The aristocrat is palmed off with Baby Warren, Dick and Nicole face a 'brighter' future together, and Fitzgerald's 'Hollywoodization' of his novel is complete with a tableau ending.

Working the Hollywood System: Fitzgerald and Budd Schulberg

Fitzgerald's last and unfinished novel not only engages with Hollywood as subject but also applies cinematic methods in its organization. Thanks to Matthew J. Bruccoli's newly established text of 1993, we are able for the first time to trace Fitzgerald's plans for the novel's composition. Bruccoli substituted a new title, *The Love of the Last Tycoon: A Western* (which for convenience here will be shortened to the familiar *The Last Tycoon*), as suggested by Fitzgerald's lover Sheilah Graham for the following reason: Fitzgerald 'wanted it to sound like a movie title and completely disguise the tragic-heroic content of the book'.[75] By the time that Fitzgerald started writing this novel in 1939 he had gained considerable experience in screen-writing and so it is scarcely surprising that the latter inflected his method. Bruccoli specifies a number of key signs of this influence: 'the technique of the screenplay is scenic and episodic. The screenwriter is writing for the camera, with the knowledge that the structure and pacing of the movie will be achieved through editing the film. Moreover, many screenwriting assign-ments are piece-work, requiring the writer to work on individual scenes [...] After Chapter 1 Fitzgerald was not writing chapters, but episodes for the novel.'[76] For this reason, the sections of the reconstituted *Last Tycoon* are numbered as episodes following the practice of screenplays. Another sign of this influence is Fitzgerald's economy of expression and his relative avoid-ance of discursive description. Among his working notes is a warning to himself not to let an episode degenerate into a 'piece of character analysis'.[77] The resulting text is neither a script, nor a conventional novel, but something closer to a *ciné-roman*, a novel which imitates the formal discipline of a screenplay.

The eponymous last tycoon is a producer named Monroe Stahr, loosely modelled on Irving Thalberg in the early 1930s, who is at the peak of his success, i.e. a star of the film business.[78] Stahr is the focus of interest throughout, in his control of all aspects of movie production and in his brief love affair with a young woman who reminds him of his dead wife. To ensure a tight narrative focus Fitzgerald presents events through the daughter of another movie tycoon. He explained his plan in the prospectus for the novel: 'by making Cecelia at the moment of her telling the story, an intelligent and observant woman, I shall grant myself the privilege, as Conrad did, of letting her imagine the actions of the characters'.[79]. He uses her as delegated author as well as to establish a mode of engaged visual scrutiny. As Wheeler Dixon puts it, she becomes a 'narrative recorder with the capacity for both point-of-view shots and the ability to assume the standpoint of the ideal spectator'.[80]

The opening scene of the novel establishes Cecelia's credentials as narrator and establishes the heightened significance of visual detail. Distracted by the screenplay analogy, Wheeler Dixon has insisted that Fitzgerald gives us visual 'notes', which require 'filmic translation and mediation', but this is not the case.[81] *The Last Tycoon* opens in a plane where a certain Mr Smith is sleeping alone in the 'bridal suite', a special cabin for VIPs. After the plane has been temporarily grounded, Mr Smith gives Cecelia a gold ring which he has noticed her staring at. Mr Smith turns out to be none other than Monroe Stahr, but Fitzgerald through Cecelia has

already roused our interest in him through the carefully paced release of
descriptive details, which suggest his status and power. Unlike those of Pat
Hobby, who will be considered in a moment, Stahr's eyes are among his most
expressive features. Cecelia yields to his gaze: 'his dark eyes took me in'; then
he hands her his ring (a 'gold nugget with the letter S in bold relief') and
explicitly takes possession of her: 'Stahr folded my hand over the ring'.[82]
Fitzgerald's imagery does not come across as annotations so much as
economic details which cue in Cecelia's construction of a romance in which
she plays alongside Stahr.[83]

Stahr is not only the protagonist of the novel. Fitzgerald even writes in a
scene exploring the relation of film to the novel, in which Stahr meets a
disgruntled novelist who has had enough of movie melodrama. Stahr's
response is to convert the writer's office into narrative: he asks him to imagine
a typist coming into light his stove. Unconsciously fascinated by the description, the novelist asks 'What happens?' Stahr's reply: 'I don't know [...] I was
just making pictures'.[84] Stahr's improvisation suggests that he, as well as
Cecelia, is the co-creator of Fitzgerald's story. Situations and images are
evoked as local fields for narrative extrapolation. They are the bases of
possible narratives rather than the narrative itself. Thus there is an important
self-reflexive dimension to *The Last Tycoon* which comes out, for instance,
when Stahr is watching the rushes (the unedited film sequences) of a particular day. As each shot or sequence ends, actors step out of their roles while
the camera is running. The construction of films here becomes an analogue
for the composition of Fitzgerald's own narrative.[85] Cecelia 'freezes' the
actual Stahr into a framed glamour photo ('he was my picture') and Stahr
judges another character 'as he would a shot in a picture'.[86]

The Last Tycoon presents a personification of movie success, whereas the
short stories which Fitzgerald published in 1940–41 to raise money while
working on his novel all centre on a has-been. Pat Hobby is a screenwriter
who was moderately successful during the silent era but who is now down on
his luck and has a drinking problem. His two distinctive features are greying
hair and bloodshot eyes. The latter contrast markedly with Stahr's expressive
gaze and they identify a recurring pattern to the Pat Hobby stories, whereby
he tries to read a situation and fails miserably. The stories usually end with
an ironic twist showing Pat's naivety or failure in some aspect of the Hollywood film business. In 'A Patriotic Short' Pat is called in for a 'polish job' to
make revisions to a script about General Lee. As if life in the present has
stopped for Pat, he keeps sliding into a reverie about meeting the US President in Hollywood and writes his consciousness of time passing into his script
through a film cliché: '*Insert: A calendar – with the years plainly marked and
the sheets blowing off in a cold wind, to show Fitzhugh Lee growing older and
older*' (italics in orignal).[87] Pat's total inability to work makes a direct contrast

with the versatility of Monroe Stahr's actions. Before the latter's illness is mentioned it looks as if he has unlimited success before him and this potential reflects an optimism on Fitzgerald's part about the cinema which was recorded by Sheilah Graham in her notes: 'I know for a fact that Scott felt that the day would come when another great figure – another Thalberg or Griffith – would succeed in again doing something fine with the movie medium. Scott, himself, wanted to be a movie director because of what he thought could be done'.[88]

Right up to his death Fitzgerald believed in the potential of Hollywood. His friend and colleague Budd Schulberg's *What Makes Sammy Run?* (1941), in contrast, satirizes Hollywood through a parodic version of a rags-to-riches success story. As we saw with Fitzgerald's more cinematic characters, Sammy Glick is given a visual 'signature' in the ostentatious new shoes he is constantly buying. Apart from reminding the reader of the title, the shoes represent Sammy's first purchasing power and in that sense lift him out of his childhood poverty on New York's Lower East Side. But shoes also signify movement here, Sammy's visible progression towards wealth.

Although the narrator Mannheim is a journalist by profession who tries Hollywood for a brief spell, his narrative is constructed with a sophisticated awareness of cinematic techniques. Although he personifies the traditional values threatened by Sammy and his like, Mannheim remains fixated on him throughout, and indeed Schulberg uses the representational techniques of the film business to depict Sammy's gradual penetration of that very business.[89] Once the action has moved from New York to Hollywood, for instance, Mannheim visits a night-club where his jaundiced perspective stresses cinematically how stereotyped the place and its customers are: 'It was a montage of hot music, drunken laughter, loud wisecracks and hostesses like lollypops in red, green and yellow wrappers'. As he looks round the place, the narrator gradually focuses more and more specifically: 'my angle narrowed from a full shot of the crowd, to a group shot of the ladies who floated through the semi-darkness on the loose, to a close-up of one particular hostess, large, but well-proportioned inside her tight evening gown'.[90] This hostess is talking to a blonde 'co-worker' and next to this blonde is sitting none other than Sammy Glick. The novel thus deploys characteristics of the medium Sammy set out to penetrate, showing him as a star of the commercial system. As the novel progresses from scene to scene, the gaps in the narrative raise ominous questions about *how* Sammy makes that progress. Instead we see only results. Thus, on the eve of Sammy's first production, the narrator freezes him for visual summary: 'there he stood in the doorway of his classy apartment, in his early twenties, in his expensive shoes, in his brand-new flashy jacket, in his brand-new Horatio Alger mind'.[91] Typically in the novel, Sammy is defined through his dress, through the appearance he has constructed for himself. We receive far more specific facial details of the characters Sammy meets and thereby get clear visual evidence of his impact on others. Sammy himself remains out of focus as a figure, or rather he remains just a figure donning guises, adopting different roles but with physical features unspecified except for hints of his age.

The effect of Schulberg's strategy here is to suggest that Sammy is a type-figure; one of Mannheim's earliest fears is that the USA is full of Sammy Glicks. It is also to suggest that there is nothing individuating about him. Even his speech idiom is rapid, street-wise and full of wisecracks. When Sammy forgets to play the appropriate role in Hollywood, he sounds like an actor in a gangster movie and this takes us further towards Schulberg's satirical purpose of showing Sammy to be the '*id* of our whole society'.[92] His life resembles a movie in that he develops real skill in adopting useful and appropriate roles. The novel synchronizes its conclusion with Sammy's 'happy ending' when he gets married. The wedding is a 'beautiful production' in which the bride's white skin and dress add to the 'unreality of the spectacle', but by this stage the charge of unreality has become irrelevant.[93] The novel progressively blurs any distinction between film and society, using the former to satirize the stereotyped and constructed nature of the American success story. Sammy seals his success at becoming a Hollywood producer by becoming the leading actor in his own production, literally so since he is performing to the newsreel cameras. Fitzgerald recognized the authenticity of Schulberg's satire and paid tribute to the scenic structure of the novel when he declared to Bennett Cerf that it was 'full of excellent little vignettes'.[94] One of Fitzgerald's last screen assignments was to collaborate with Schulberg on Walter Wanger's *Winter Carnival*. No script was produced but Schulberg later wrote their experiences into his 1951 novel *The Disenchanted*, in which Fitzgerald is presented as an alcoholic has-been. Ironically, Fitzgerald here played the leading role in his own decline.

Notes

1   F. Scott Fitzgerald, *My Lost City*, p. 148.
2   Matthew J. Bruccoli and Judith S. Baughman, eds., *Conversations with F. Scott Fitzgerald*, p. 51.
3   Aaron Latham, *Crazy Sundays*, p. 27. Chapter 14 of Edward Murray's *The Cinematic Imagination* gives a useful overview of Fitzgerald's relation to Hollywood.
4   The film *The Chorus Girl's Romance* was released later in 1920; see Turnbull, ed., *The Letters of F. Scott Fitzgerald*, p. 423. Fitzgerald felt that the publication in 1922 of Harry Leon Wilson's *Merton of the Movies* vindicated his suggestion.
5   Bruccoli and Baughman, eds., *Conversations with F. Scott Fitzgerald*, p. 7.
6   Bruccoli and Baughman, eds., *Conversations with F. Scott Fitzgerald*, pp. 51, 52–53.

7   The article was written for *Screenland* but was not published until 2003 because Fitzgerald missed his deadline. See F. Scott Fitzgerald, 'Fitzgerald and the Hollywood Hacks'.

8   F. Scott Fitzgerald, *Novels and Stories*, pp. 174, 175. Wheeler Winston Dixon's 1986 study *The Cinematic Vision of F. Scott Fitzgerald* is limited by not taking into account any works prior to *The Great Gatsby*.

9   Fitzgerald, *My Lost City*, p. 108. Fitzgerald draws a further analogy between his circle and the 'picture actors' in that both groups were 'in New York and not of it' (p. 110).

10 James R. Mellow, *Constructed Lives*, p. 170. *The Glimpses of the Moon* was released in 1923.

11 Turnbull, ed., *The Letters of F. Scott Fitzgerald*, p. 373.

12 Gloria's name may be a conflation of two starring roles: the personification of glamour (Gloria Swanson) and the lover (John Gilbert). According to Alexander Walker, Swanson personified the twenties' 'emphasis on material goods and fun living' (*Stardom*, p. 113).

13 Fitzgerald, *Novels and Stories*, p. 756.

14 Fitzgerald, *Novels and Stories*, p. 758.

15 Edwin T. Arnold, 'The Motion Picture as Metaphor', p. 44. Arnold has valuable comments to make on Fitzgerald's Hollywood stories 'Jacob's Ladder' and 'Magnetism' as well as on the novels.

16 Alan Margolies, '"Kissing, Shooting, and Sacrificing"'. For a detailed account of Fitzgerald's use of tropes from the cinema in his writings, see Somdatta Mandal, *Reflections, Refractions and Rejections*, pp. 96–123.

17 For details of Fitzgerald's film assignments, see Latham's *Crazy Sundays* (particularly useful in its extensive quotations from unpublished material), Alan Margolies' 'F. Scott Fitzgerald's Work in the Film Studios' and Matthew J. Bruccoli and J. E. Atkinson's 'F. Scott Fitzgerald's Hollywood Assignments'. Fitzgerald's published screenplays are *Infidelity* (in *Esquire*, December 1973), *Lipstick* (in the *Fitzgerald/Hemingway Annual* for 1978), *Three Comrades* (edited by Matthew J. Bruccoli, 1978), and *Babylon Revisited* (1993). A TV biopic *F. Scott Fitzgerald in Hollywood*, directed by Anthony Page, was released in 1976.

18 Latham, *Crazy Sundays*, p. 57.

19 F. Scott Fitzgerald, *Collected Short Stories*, pp. 83, 96.

20 *Collected Short Stories*, p. 454.

21 *Collected Short Stories*, p. 451.

22 *Collected Short Stories*, p. 567.

23 Sheilah Graham, *College Of One*, p. 167. The full lecture is reprinted on pp. 165–93.

24 For discussion of movie adaptations of Fitzgerald's works, see Ruth Perlmutter, 'Malcolm Lowry's Unpublished Filmscript of *Tender is the Night*'; Joanna E. Rapf, '*The Last Tycoon* or "A Nickel for the Movies"'; Stephen Matterson, 'A Life in the Pictures: Harold Pinter's *The Last Tycoon*'; and Frank E. Cunningham, 'F. Scott Fitzgerald and the Problem of Film Adaptation'.

25 *Collected Short Stories*, p. 628.

26 F. Scott Fitzgerald, *Babylon Revisited: The Screenplay*, p. 189. In the event, the screenplay was never used and the published version was found among Budd Schulberg's papers. In 1954 a different script was used for the film *The Last Time I Saw Paris*, which took its title from an Elliott Paul memoir.

27 Latham, *Crazy Sundays*, p. 248.

28 Turnbull, ed., *The Letters of F. Scott Fitzgerald*, p. 329.

29 Joseph Conrad, *The Nigger of the 'Narcissus'*, pp. xii, x.

30 Matthew J. Bruccoli, *Some Sort of Epic Grandeur*, p. 206. Doubleday lived near to Fitzgerald on Long Island at the time. For information on Conrad's talk, see Arnold T.

Schwab, 'Conrad's American Speeches'.

31 Matthew J. Bruccoli and Margaret M. Duggan, eds., *Correspondence of F. Scott Fitzgerald*, p. 168; Turnbull, ed., *The Letters of F. Scott Fitzgerald*, p. 378.

32 Mellow, *Constructed Lives*, pp. 184, 189. Another regular visitor was the writer Ring Lardner, who made his only substantial contribution to film in supplying the story for *The New Klondike* (1926).

33 Bruccoli, *Some Sort of Epic Grandeur*, pp. 208–209. The film starred Clara Bow, the 'It' Girl.

34 F. Scott Fitzgerald, *The Great Gatsby*, p. 54. In 1922 D. W. Griffith, whom Fitzgerald idolized, released *Orphans of the Storm*, a historical melodrama starring Dorothy and Lillian Gish.

35 North, *Camera Works*, chapter 4.

36 Fitzgerald, *The Great Gatsby*, p. 7.

37 Lawrence Jay Dessner, 'Photography in *The Great Gatsby*', p. 179.

38 Fitzgerald, *The Great Gatsby*, p. 7.

39 Clearly this suggests that Nick has become a cinematic *flâneur*, but Michael North also points out that by 1925 'flicker' had become a 'disparaging term for the movies' (*Camera Works*, p. 117).

40 Dixon, *The Cinematic Vision of F. Scott Fitzgerald*, p. 21.

41 Fitzgerald, *The Great Gatsby*, p. 125.

42 Scott F. Stoddart ('Redirecting Fitzgerald's "Gaze"') argues that Nick cinematically supports Gatsby's misogynistic gaze in the novel, whereas the 1974 film adaptation pushes him to the margin.

43 Fitzgerald, *The Great Gatsby*, p. 30.

44 Michael North states that Nick 'imagines actuality as if it were shakily projected on a screen always just before him' (*Camera Works*, p. 118).

45 Fitzgerald, *The Great Gatsby*, p. 6.

46 Dessner, 'Photography in *The Great Gatsby*', p. 177. Dessner argues that the novel presents 'photographic ways of seeing' while at the same time he leaves undeveloped passing allusions to film technique.

47 Richard Godden, *Fictions of Capital*, p. 78. Godden's chapter on *The Great Gatsby* remains an invaluable account of how scenic and narrative techniques articulate the commercial processes of that society.

48 Fitzgerald, *The Great Gatsby*, p. 27.

49 *The Great Gatsby*, p. 10.

50 *The Great Gatsby*, p. 138.

51 Joss Lutz Marsh, 'Fitzgerald, Gatsby and *The Last Tycoon*', p. 5. Marsh has further valuable points to offer, not least on Fitzgerald's assimilation of Valentino into Gatsby's portrait.

52 Dixon, *The Cinematic Vision of F. Scott Fitzgerald*, p. 23.

53 Fitzgerald, *The Great Gatsby*, p. 40.

54 *The Great Gatsby*, p. 68.

55 Maureen Turim, *Flashbacks in Film*, p. 33.

56 Fitzgerald, *The Great Gatsby*, p. 126.

57 Matthew J. Bruccoli and George Parker Anderson, *Tender is the Night: A Documentary Volume*, pp. 9, 57. Lew Kelly, Fitzgerald's director, seems to be modelled on Rex Ingram, the director of films such as *The Garden of Allah*, who had studios at La Turbie, as named in the novel.

58 Walker, *Stardom*, p. 43. Ruth Prigozy gives a detailed account of how Rosemary is a

composite of a number of film stars in her essay 'From Griffith's Girl to Daddy's Girl', pp. 189–221. Prigozy's commentary also offers valuable explanations of the traces of film subjects in Book I of the novel and on the symbolic relevance of Rosemary's film *Daddy's Girl*.

59 Walker, *Stardom*, pp. 8–9; F. Scott Fitzgerald, *Tender is the Night*, pp. 7–8.

60 Benjamin, *Illuminations*, p. 233.

61 Fitzgerald, *Tender is the Night*, p. 26.

62 Matthew Bruccoli points out that it was used instead of white, which was too reflective (Fitzgerald, *Tender is the Night*, p. 327).

63 Prigozy, 'From Griffith's Girl to Daddy's Girl', p. 216.

64 Bruccoli and Baughman, eds., *Conversations with F. Scott Fitzgerald*, p. 92.

65 Negri's 1925 film *A Woman of the World* opens on the Riviera. Fitzgerald knew and admired her acting.

66 Fitzgerald, *Tender is the Night*, p. 71.

67 Godden, *Fictions of Capital*, p. 122.

68 Fitzgerald, *Tender is the Night*, p. 110.

69 Bruccoli and Baughman, eds., *Conversations with F. Scott Fitzgerald*, p. 99.

70 There may be an allusion in this repeated line to Wallace McCutcheon's 1904 film about a peeping tom, *Pull Down the Curtains, Suzie*.

71 Fitzgerald, *Tender is the Night*, p. 220. This image probably alludes to the massive sets constructed for the MGM filming of *Ben-Hur* in Rome, before production shifted to the USA. The Fitzgeralds were in Rome during this filming in 1924 and joined the crew's parties. Valentino was considered for the part of Ben-Hur, which was actually played by Ramón Novarro.

72 The full text of this treatment is printed in Bruccoli, *Some Sort of Epic Grandeur*, pp. 608–22.

73 Latham discusses the treatment in detail *Crazy Sundays*, pp. 87–95.

74 Bruccoli, *Some Sort of Epic Grandeur*, p. 622.

75 F. Scott Fitzgerald, *The Love of the Last Tycoon*, p. lxviii.

76 Matthew J. Bruccoli, *The Last of the Novelists*, p. 40.

77 Fitzgerald, *The Last Tycoon*, p. 143. In another episode Fitzgerald was planning a 'very short transition or montage' to bring his characters together (p. 144).

78 On the Thalberg similarities, see *The Last Tycoon*, pp. xvii–xxiii. Fitzgerald met Thalberg in 1927 when working on *Lipstick* and in 1931 when working on a screen adaptation of *Red Headed Woman*.

79 Fitzgerald, *The Last Tycoon*, p. xxxii.

80 Dixon, *The Cinematic Vision of F. Scott Fitzgerald*, p. 93.

81 Dixon, *The Cinematic Vision of F. Scott Fitzgerald*, p. 87.

82 Fitzgerald, *The Last Tycoon*, pp. 15–16.

83 One of Fitzgerald's working titles was *Stahr: A Romance*.

84 Fitzgerald, *The Last Tycoon*, p. 32.

85 Gavriel Moses argues that Stahr is trying to construct a 'continuous, unified myth' out of 'disconnected fragments of feeling and reality' (*The Nickel was for the Movies*, pp. 186, 178).

86 Fitzgerald, *The Last Tycoon*, pp. 71, 80.

87 Fitzgerald, *Collected Short Stories*, p. 314.

88 Fitzgerald, *The Last Tycoon*, p. lvii. Fitzgerald was probably referring to this unspoken ambition when he wrote in a letter of 1940: 'My great dreams about this place are shattered' (Turnbull, ed., *The Letters of F. Scott Fitzgerald*, p. 448).

89 Chip Rhodes sees the novel as informed by masochism and relates it to Schulberg's
    support for the Screen Writers Guild (*Politics, Desire and the Hollywood Novel*, pp. 58–69).
90 Budd Schulberg, *What Makes Sammy Run?*, pp. 46–47. The character of Kit in this novel
    is based on the novelist-turned-screenwriter Tess Slesinger, who wrote scripts for *The
    Good Earth* and *A Tree Grows in Brooklyn* (Nancy Brooker-Bowers, *The Hollywood Novel*,
    p. 84). Schulberg describes the self-consciousness of Hollywood social life in his story 'A
    Table at Ciro's', collected in *Some Faces in the Crowd*, pp. 55–67.
91 Schulberg, *What Makes Sammy Run?*, p. 76.
92 Schulberg, *What Makes Sammy Run?*, p. 172.
93 Schulberg, *What Makes Sammy Run?*, p. 235.
94 Turnbull, ed., *The Letters of F. Scott Fitzgerald*, p. 625. Fitzgerald read the novel in
    December 1940 and declared it to be a 'grand book, utterly fearless and with a great deal
    of beauty side by side with the most bitter satire'. Schulberg for his part was approached
    about completing *The Last Tycoon*, as was John O'Hara.

6

William Faulkner: Perspective Experiments

L ike Hemingway, William Faulkner initially deploys quasi-cinematic methods to represent the processes of perception, but he also pursues experiments with the interplay between limited perspectives. Throughout the 1930s his novels make progressively more and more reference to film in their representational methods. Particularly since the 1970s, a considerable body of criticism has been built up on William Faulkner's relation to the cinema and most of his screenplays, even those for television, have now been published.[1] Claude-Edmonde Magny concludes his study *The Age of the American Novel* with a chapter discussing Faulkner's use of witnesses to establish point of view, reversal of chronology and other features of what he calls a 'film aesthetic'.[2] Edward Murray finds cinematic principles working behind Faulkner's use of cross-cutting (*The Sound and the Fury*) and flashbacks (*Light in August*);[3] Alan Spiegel focuses on *Sanctuary* as the textual embodiment of Hollywood in its subject, but also in its 'mode of expression: melodramatic, typological, hyperbolic'.[4] The most general explanation of the cinematic dimension to Faulkner has been given by Bruce Kawin, who argues that repetition and montage are central to his works.[5]

Faulkner became actively involved in screenwriting from 1931 and the following year he paid his first visit to Hollywood, registering astonishment at the impermanence and unreality of the place. Thereafter he had regular working spells throughout the 1930s and 1940s for MGM, Twentieth Century-Fox and Warner Brothers. The publication of his MGM screenplays demonstrates that by 1933 – the year before he started work on *Absalom, Absalom!* – Faulkner had already become adept in movie techniques such as the use of dissolves, double exposures, and close-ups. The evidence suggests that he was more successful at creating scenes and story-lines than writing dialogue.[6] In 1939 Faulkner attributed his studio work to mercenary greed: 'When I first went to the movies, I believed I saw there a small gold mine which I could work at will at need more or less for the rest of my active writing life […] I found pretty soon that I was not a movie writer'.[7] Money considerations apart, Faulkner remained fascinated by the cinema, an interest further developed by his long-standing friendship with the producer Howard

Hawks.[8] Surveying his activities in Hollywood, Faulkner's biographer Joseph
Blotner asks the question 'had Hollywood ever contaminated his work?'; but
that presupposes an intrinsic opposition between the two media.[9] In fact, like
Dreiser and other novelists discussed in this volume, Faulkner disliked the
way in which a writer's work was swallowed up the Hollywood system, but
revealed his enthusiasm for the film medium by incorporating cinematic
allusions and techniques in his fiction.[10] As Bruce Kawin has shown in his
extensive studies of Faulkner and film, writing fiction and working on
screenplays were complementary activities for him. It should also be remembered that in Hollywood Faulkner met and befriended a number of other
novelists-turned-screenwriters, figures such as Joel Sayre, Dashiell
Hammett (whom he had met earlier in New York) and Nathanael West.[11]

Although there are allusions to Hollywood in Faulkner's fiction, it is rare
for the movie capital to become a subject in its own right, but this is what
happens in the 1935 story 'Golden Land'. The narrative is minimal. Instead,
we are given glimpses of the place through the eyes of a Nebraskan real-estate
developer, who, like Nathanael West, sees Hollywood as a synthetic
construct with 'white villas halfhidden in imported olive groves or friezed by
the sombre spaced columns of cypress like the façades of eastern temples'. In
this setting the houses seem to have a curiously loose relation to the earth,
'bright beautiful and gay, without basements or foundations, lightly attached
to a few inches of light penetrable earth'.[12] In contrast with Faulkner's usual
Mississippi locations, as Bruce Kawin notes, the place is 'ungrounded physically and morally'.[13] The protagonist is an outsider, like Faulkner himself,
estranged from his family: his wife wears a 'paper mask' of makeup, his son
cross-dresses, and his daughter has been arrested in a hotel with a movie man
giving out parts. Although Faulkner uses his protagonist as a means of
visually recording Hollywood, he is not exempt from the collective sexual
masquerade of the place. Indeed his estrangement is so severe that he feels
himself poised on the cusp of a science-fiction scenario in which his 'race' is
about to be superseded by the beautiful but mindless young, 'precursors of a
new race not yet seen on earth'.[14]

The Early Writings

Critical commentary on Faulkner's relation to film has tended to concentrate
on his activities as a screenwriter in Hollywood after 1931, but Jeffrey Folks
has begun to revise this emphasis by demonstrating that Faulkner was a keen
movie-goer in the 1910s and that allusions to film occur from an early stage
in his writing. Thus he notes the following passage in *Mosquitoes* (1927), in
which a character makes the following comment on the yacht journey which

is taking place: 'This is kind of funny, ain't it? They are not going anywhere, and they don't do anything… kind of like a movie or something'.[15] This throwaway comparison actually sheds light on the novel's action, which consists of a series of scenes loosely linked by the voyage and by seascapes which resemble cinematic establishing shots and codas. Characters perform in an extended masquerade, striking postures for their mutual entertainment. Folk points out a general emphasis here on the visual, Faulkner's use of film stereotypes and even the inclusion of a character evidently modelled on Buster Keaton.[16] Similarly, D. M. Murray has cited numerous instances in Faulkner's fiction, especially in *The Hamlet* (1940), of allusions to slapstick humour from early film comedy.[17]

Well before he went to Hollywood, Faulkner was responding to the cinema in the visual construction of his narratives. Even in his 1925 New Orleans sketches film functions as an important point of reference. 'Mirrors of Chartres Street' is typical in taking the street, the place of public movement, as its main location. The narrator, typically for the series, is an anonymous *flâneur* whose sole purpose is to report chance urban sightings. In this sketch he sees a disabled man going into a movie-house to see 'one of those million-dollar pictures of dukes and adultery and champagne and lots of girls in mosquito netting and lamp shades'.[18] The sketch uses a scenic method of reportage to contrast the situation of its subject with the clichéd nature of the film he sees.

Faulkner's first novel about family inheritance and the complex relation between past and present, *Flags in the Dust* (written in 1927, shortened into *Sartoris*, 1932), is also the first to make sustained use of cinematic methods in its alternation between movement and stasis. Bayard Sartoris' obsession with the excitement of rapid motion is made possible by modern technology – the car and the aeroplane – and Faulkner constantly adjusts the point of view according to the pace of events. Bayard's sadistic desire to impress the Negro Simon by accelerating his car is represented as a loss of image definition: 'the roadside greenery was a tunnel rigid and streaming and unbroken'. Faulkner early on developed a skill at rendering movement in relation to a fixed point. In this scene the contrast is made with a wagon, which becomes an emblematic juxtaposition of old and new: 'the wagon was moving drowsily and peacefully along the road. It was drawn by two mules [...] The mules themselves didn't wake at all, but ambled sedately on with the empty wagon and overturned chairs, even when the car crashed into the shallow ditch and surged back onto the road again and thundered on without slowing'.[19] The perspective shifts outside the car to that of an imagined observer in the road near the wagon. The novel thus relies on visual witness for much of its effect, and specifically on Bayard for an acceleration of tempo through a racing horse, a car, and the plane in which finally he crashes to his death.

Flags in the Dust uses a principle of observation which is articulated through multiple cinematic devices: close-ups, pans, long shots, and above all perspective shifts. At one point a woman describes the behaviour of the character Belle with young men as being 'like a moving picture' and the comparison gives us a hint of how the perspective is being modulated.[20] Faulkner had already experimented with flashbacks in his unfinished novel *Elmer* and the novel opens with a scene from the past, then dissolves to the present.[21] Again, Faulkner uses freeze-frame effects (Bayard fox-hunting, for instance) whereby the point-of-view character himself becomes a brief spectacle to the reader/viewer. Although the novel is narrated in the third person Faulkner tends to limit the action to what can be seen by the main character in that episode. Thus, when Bayard and Aunt Jenny visit a local doctor, the effect is as if a camera were showing their shared point of view. The grotesque visual 'climax' to the visit comes with the emergence of the 'fattest man in Yocona county', Doc Peabody: 'he wore a shiny alpaca coat over waistcoat and trousers of baggy unpressed black broadcloth; above a plaited shirt the fatty rolls of his neck practically hid his low collar and a black string tie'.[22] The details of his personal image tie in comically with the novel's old/new contrasts since they reveal a doctor refusing any sort of professional dress and, in his sheer size, Peabody's overpowering of his younger medical colleague.

Domestic interiors are the key locations in this novel, in which rooms are constantly being opened up or closed. The Sartoris house is compared to a stage set on which actors are waiting to perform their roles and the novel concludes with a view from this same house: 'beyond the window evening was a windless lilac dream, foster-dam of quietude and peace'.[23] The fact that the final image is framed by a window reflects Faulkner's use of the house as a privileged site for memory, closely identified therefore with its inhabitants.

Where *Flags in the Dust* uses visual witness to embody its historical themes, *The Sound and the Fury* (1929) deploys visual perspectives for psychological purposes. Later in his career, Faulkner admitted that the novel was 'the homemade, the experimental, the first moving picture projector — warped lens, poor light, clumsy gears, and even a bad screen'.[24] Although this is a retrospective analogy, the 'warped lens' shows itself in Benjy's opening section, where his perspective resembles an animate camera, registering sights and sounds important to him without any conceptual apparatus for explaining them. Thus he fixates on certain objects like the bright red flag on the golf course linked subconsciously to his absent sister when a player calls 'caddie': 'it was red, flapping on the pasture. Then there was a bird slanting and titling on it. Luster threw. The flag flapped on the bright grass and the trees. I held to the fence'.[25] Benjy registers recurring images like the red flag here or the fence, which might give him access to his sister but at the same time functions as a barrier. His section resembles Robert Montgomery's experimental 1947 film *Lady in the Lake*, where the camera played the part of Chandler's private eye, but without the latter's deliberate movement. Like a camera, Benjy records the words of others and cuts backwards and forwards between different time periods. We never see him in this section, only see *from* him towards the actions of the other family members. Benjy demonstrates by default how visual data is interpreted to situate the perceiver within a perceptual field; when he records how a hill approaches and then recedes he is demonstrating a heightened, self-referential way of seeing the world. As Jeffrey Folks declares, Benjy lives in a 'silent world of exaggerated motion, in which images rush chaotically across the limited screen of his vision'.[26] This description helps to explain Benjy's estrangement from his own experience, which he registers largely as a spectator.

Both *The Sound and the Fury* and *As I Lay Dying* (1935) break their texts into segments giving radically different perspectives on the action. In the former there is at least the suggestion of the segments coming together when the novel shifts finally into an external third-person narrative mode, but in the latter this never happens. The narrator, who has been giving us visual and relational specificity, is suddenly and disturbingly removed from the text. Darl is the novel's scene-setter. Not only is he the first narrator, his sections are characterized by a unique visual precision. Consider the famous opening of the novel, which clearly exemplifies Faulkner's conviction that 'character must be told in motion':

> Jewel and I come up from the field, following the path in single file. Although I am fifteen feet ahead of him, anyone watching us from the cottonhouse can see Jewel's frayed and broken straw hat a full head above my own.
>   The path runs straight as a plumb-line, worn smooth by feet and baked brick-hard by July, between the green rows of laidby cotton, to the cottonhouse in the centre of the field, where it turns and circles the cottonhouse at four soft right angles and it goes on across the field again, worn so by feet in fading precision.[27]

Faulkner is striking a balance here between giving us the immediacy of the characters' movements and detailed visual attention which goes beyond the needs of that immediacy. Although Darl behaves and acts as a member of the Bundren family, his descriptions include a consciousness of hypothetical observers' perspectives. In effect, he constructs our observational role for us. Furthermore, his gaze logically extends physical movement. In the second paragraph Darl projects his gaze along the path-line, following its 'movement' around the cotton-house. There is an easy continuity from his physical walking to the movement of his point of view around the field.

By imagining an observer looking back towards his own visual vantage point Darl introduces the possibility of others' perspectives in the novel and begins to establish his credentials as a visual narrator. Take the following example, where Cash is looking up from his coffin-making towards his dying mother in the window: 'he looks up at the gaunt face framed by the window in the twilight. It is a composite picture of all time since he was a child'.[28] Cash is the observer but Darl is the composer of this image. Again and again in the narrative he freezes characters in emblematic postures which, as here, reveal more than their immediate present. Darl constantly shows an awareness of visual composition, of modulations of perspective demonstrated through close-ups (Cash's face after he has salvaged the coffin from the river), sights reflected through Dewey Dell's eyes, or the rapid montage of brief scenes when a barn fire breaks out. Darl's method of representation foregrounds seeing, indeed foregrounds eyes themselves, which are shown in the novel to be opaque, depthless or veiled organs, concealing as much as they reveal. What characters see and what they do, but not what they say, are brought out strikingly in Darl's sections, which at times resemble scenes from a silent film. When Addie finally dies, for instance, Dewey Dell draws the quilt up to her chin as if to give her dignity; Anse, on the other hand, stands contemplating the body, then attempts to smooth the quilt as if in imitation of Dewey Dell.

If the appearance of characters' actions is paramount, we rely particularly on Darl's visual precision because such clarity is traditionally tied to understanding. It therefore comes as a major shock in the novel for us to discover that Darl is an arsonist and that he is collapsing into insanity. His last section shows a fragmentation of perspective: the language splits between the narrative past in which Darl becomes 'othered' and the cinematic present in which Darl's family attenuate into their own empty vehicle: 'the wagon stands on the square, hitched, the mules motionless, the reins wrapped about the seatspring, the back of the wagon towards the courthouse'.[29]

Sanctuary: A Novel for the Eye

When *Sanctuary* was published in 1931 one reviewer commented: 'one is tempted to say that as a novelist Mr. Faulkner is a superb movie director [...] his technique is the technique of the cinema'.[30] Certainly, the novel's cinematic quality was quickly recognized by the Hollywood studios. In 1932 Paramount bought the film rights and their adaptation, *The Story of Temple Drake*, was released the following year, despite the overtly sexual subject of the novel.[31] Of this adaptation E. Pauline Dagenfelder has commented of the female protagonist Temple Drake: 'the film's alterations of the original [...] balance the dual aspects of Temple's personality and make her reformation plausible'.[32] Apart from the film adaptation, *Sanctuary* exists in two versions, that of 1929 and the final published text. As different critics have noted, one of the main differences between the two versions is the reduction of the role of the lawyer Horace Benbow, who originally acted as an intermediary between the reader and the grotesque and violent actions he described.

Inevitably, Benbow acted as a censoring or normalizing filter whereas the final printed version of the novel radically changes the mode of presentation towards the cinematic. Richard Gray has shrewdly described *Sanctuary* as a 'novel for the eye', a phrase borrowed for my local title here, in which all characters are engaged in spying on each other, collectively inducing the reader to share their view of the action as spectacle.[33] To modify this valuable insight, we could say that Faulkner no longer limits his perspective to that of Benbow, with complicating results for the reader. In the opening scene we are positioned in the vantage of Popeye, the sadist who later rapes Temple with a corn-cob. He is furtively watching the lawyer Benbow drink from a spring, who sees himself in the water: 'in the spring the drinking man leaned his face to the broken and myriad reflection of his own drinking. When he rose up he saw among them the shattered reflection of Popeye's straw hat, though he had heard no sound'.[34] As Edward Branigan has pointed out, 'a glance bristles with implications about space, time, and causality. A glance leaps across space: its direction orients us to something nearby and hence enables us to build spatial relationships within a scene'.[35]

In the original version of the novel, Benbow's thought processes dictate the rather leisurely pace of events, whereas by shifting narration to an impersonal voice Faulkner manages to capture the sudden transitions from image to image which give this novel its surreal quality. The language is not inflected by Benbow's thoughts; rather it directs us objectively to sights and actions within the two characters' field of vision. Things and characters appear and disappear suddenly, and it is the suddenness of this montage effect which generates much of the novel's drama.

The opening scene of the published text gives us, as Noel Polk has explained, two men's 'mutual vision of each other'.[36] However, this summarizes the end of the scene rather than the effect of the opening, which masterfully captures suspense. In filmic terms we start with a long shot, framed by the 'screen of bushes' hiding Popeye. Then we move to a close-up of Benbow's reflected face as he drinks, jumping startlingly to a sinister reflected medium shot of Popeye looking down at Benbow. Because Popeye is the degenerate agent in the subsequent rape action, the reader is implicated in his perspective even before he does anything. Similarly, during the action at the Frenchman place (the old house where the rape takes place) one of the main perspectives is that of Tommy, who is later shot. The reader is thus denied the space to maintain a detachment from a disturbing action but is instead drawn into a sequence of voyeuristic events in which the dividing line between the innocent and the guilty becomes hopelessly blurred. As in *As I Lay Dying*, the gaze is foregrounded and rendered grotesque by the novel's attention to eyes, which as often as not are described as opaque and depthless: Popeye's are like 'rubber knobs', for instance.[37] Tommy's eyes, on the other hand, glow in the dark, like the rat which Temple sees at the old house.

If a character's organs of sight are opaque, the character is perceived as an external image. This partly happens with the girl Temple, who is depicted through physical features and appurtenances (her red hair, hat, bag and so on); but there are sections of the novel giving us glimpses of her subjective life. This is never true for Popeye, who is completely externalized. As Alan Spiegel has noted, 'he *cannot* be explained'; he can only be apprehended as an image, that of a shortish thin man in a close-fitting black suit.[38] A number of critics have suggested that Popeye derives from late 1920s' gangster fiction, in his general style (laconic, quick-tempered) and in the nature of his role, which is played off against the female 'lead'.[39]

Temple Drake, repositioned in the final version of the novel in the centre of the action, is the focus of a collective local male gaze. In a sense she functions as the young 'star' of the action, but as such becomes the focus of male sexual sadism and jealousy. Typically she is seen in motion from her very first appearance in the text, where she is described as a 'speeding silhouette', and the verb which is most frequently used to describe her actions is 'whirl', suggestive of a sudden change of direction. Again and again she is described as 'running', even when she has fallen or is hallucinating leaving her body. This means that as a character she is defined through movement, albeit contradictory movement: when at the old Frenchman house she runs away and then runs back to the house. At moments of stasis like the following, Temple is 'fixed' in the voyeuristic gaze of a hidden male observer, in this case Tommy:

> Temple's head began to move. It turned slowly, as if she were following the passage of someone beyond the wall. It turned on to an excruciating degree, though no other muscle moved, like one of those papier-mache Easter toys filled with candy, and became motionless in that reverted position. Then it turned back, slowly [...] Then she faced forward and Tommy watched her take a tiny watch from the top of her stocking and look at it. With the watch in her hand she lifted her head and looked directly at him, her eyes calm and empty as two holes. After a while she looked down at the watch again and returned it to her stocking.[40]

Tommy is peeping in through a gap between sash and window frame, but the description elides this frame and gives Temple's movements in an affectless, neutral prose which externalizes her actions to the point at which she comes across as a mechanism. The slow-motion leaves an ambiguity in Temple's actions. And when she turns her face towards the observer, it is as if she looks into a camera, but does she actually see the hidden observer? Peter Lurie is in no doubt that she is 'complicit in the presentation, or *representation* of herself as an object of male voyeuristic pleasure' (emphasis in original).[41] Certainly Temple is self-conscious about her appearance, constantly attending to her clothes and make-up, hence the justification in Edith Wharton describing her as being 'like a cinema doll'.[42]

It is often difficult to keep track of who specifically is looking at Temple and in a sense that doesn't matter. As the novel progresses, she shifts from being the object of the sexual gaze to being the object of a doctor's gaze and finally, at the trial, to being the object of legal scrutiny. The situations change, but the gaze remains heavily gendered and prurient. When the lawyer Horace Benbow registers his horror at Temple's rape, this perception is figured as an expressionistic image maximizing her sexual passivity: 'she was bound naked on her back on a flat car moving at speed through a black tunnel, the blackness streaming in rigid threads overhead, a roar of iron wheels in her ears'.[43]

Faulkner's sequel to *Sanctuary* was planned as a 'story told in seven play-scenes, inside a novel'.[44] *Requiem for a Nun* (1951) presents an older, more sophisticated Temple who 'others' her earlier story into a distanced narrative in which she was playing the role of the 'foolish virgin'. The lawyer Gavin Stevens reappears to point his own commentary on Temple's experiences with Popeye, suggesting to her husband that she 'didn't even suffer, but on the contrary even liked it [...] like the episode in the old movie of the white girl held prisoner in the cave by the Bedouin prince'.[45] This cryptic comparison alludes to a film such as *The Sheikh* (1921) or its sequel *The Son of the Sheikh* (1926), in which the white female victim of a kidnapping becomes charged with sexual desire for her kidnapper.[46] The play or screenplay medium Faulkner uses for his dramatized scenes makes explicit the suggestions in *Sanctuary* that Temple is an actress, now clearly manipulating the men around her for sexual purposes.

The Cinematic Novels after *Sanctuary*

Critical opinion has varied as to which of Faulkner's novels is his most cinematic. In general preference has gone to his novels from the 1930s for their assimilation of filmic techniques, sometimes supported by specific allusions to the cinema. Of the opening scene to *Light in August* (1932) Doug Baldwin has stressed the 'delineated shifts in camera position that are juxtaposed for effect and [which] force a kind of "reseeing" of the same action from different angles'.[47] These scenes repeatedly focus the reader's visual attention on newcomers, the perspective being that of immobile observers on familiar ground gazing at strangers such as Joe Christmas. For Peter Lurie, the latter 'is defined by his position as the object of the gaze – of various characters, but more subtly and pervasively, of readers as well'.[48] The gaze in this novel is closely related to its evocation of estrangement: no one seems to know anyone else. This isolation reaches its culmination when Christmas walks the streets of the town at night: 'he went on, passing still between the homes of white people, from street lamp to street lamp, the heavy shadows of oak and maple leaves sliding like scraps of white velvet across his white shirt'.[49] Immediately before this passage we are told, ironically, that earlier the street would have been full of people going to the movies. The shared visual experience going on elsewhere only emphasizes Christmas's isolation. Faulkner posits a hypothetical observer in order to construct an image charged with implicit racial symbolism: Christmas may have a 'shadow' of Negro blood in his veins.

Unlike the shifts of perspective in *Light in August*, Faulkner's 1935 novel about aviators, *Pylon*, is largely presented through the eyes of a reporter. For Tom Dardis, this ensures its movie quality, since characters 'are always being seen from the outside'.[50] This means in effect that technique imitates subject since the spectacular flights of the aviators are described as just that – spectacle. The most striking episodes are those concerned with death: an in-flight collision between planes and the search by floodlight for the remains of another plane. As usual, Faulkner signals this theme through image when the reporter himself is being observed by his editor: 'the downfunnelled light from the desklamp struck the reporter across the hips; to the city editor sitting behind his desk the reporter loomed from the hips upward for an incredible distance to where the cadaverface hung against the dusty gloom of the city room's upper spaces'.[51] This striking visual perspective transforms the reporter into a macabre freak, scarcely human and certainly with no human relations. In effect he is transformed into a function.

From November 1935 to January 1936, with astonishing discipline, Faulkner worked on completing *Absalom, Absalom!* in the mornings and in the afternoons would go to the studios to collaborate with Joel Sayre on *The Road to Glory* for Howard Hawks at Twentieth Century-Fox. For Joseph R. Urgo, this novel marks a turning-point in Faulkner's career because for the first time 'perspectives are folded over one another to provide a single, recognizable text, or series of pictures, *by two of the narrators themselves*' (italics in original).[52] Urgo's argument is an important one in this context since he makes a convincing case that Faulkner appropriates the method of constructing a film narrative – the generation of a subject from an outline, the visualization of trial 'footage' and so on – for his own purposes in *Absalom,*

Absalom!. One of the main features of this process is that Quentin Compson repeatedly converts oral narrative into imagery, as in the following description triggered by his father's account of the Confederate soldiers in action and Thomas Sutpen's shipping of gravestones from Europe: 'It seemed to Quentin that he could actually see them: the ragged and starving troops without shoes, the gaunt powder-blackened faces looking backward over tattered shoulders, the glaring eyes in which burned some indomitable desperation of undefeat watching that dark interdict ocean across which a grim lightless solitary ship fled'.[53] The perspective shifts from Quentin's spectatorial gaze to that of the soldiers, ending with Sutpen's obsessed watching of the ocean. Urgo draws a distinction between Quentin's father's tendency to see things like photographs, i.e. as static images, and Quentin's own capacity to create visual continuity in the narrative. Faulkner's experience of film production earlier in the 1930s supplies a subtextual analogy for the composition of *Absalom, Absalom!*, whose text follows the 'progress of a story from property to synopsis to treatment to temporary screenplay [...] and then on to final screenplay'.[54]

The novel investigates the attempts by Thomas Sutpen to establish an estate and dynasty in Yoknapatawpha County. The compositional process described above reaches its climax of visualization in the confrontation between Sutpen's son Henry and Charles Bon, a mixed-blood relative. This scene, resembling what Bruce Kawin has described as 'mindscreen', is told through the present tense in a scene in which the mediating presence of a narrator is suspended so that we become, like Quentin earlier, 'viewers' of the action.[55] Sutpen discovers Bon at an army camp. The episode opens with a time jump – signalled in the text through a shift from roman to italic type – back to the last year of the Civil War. The young men are exhausted by the fighting, but their confrontation is over the personal issue of Bon marrying Sutpen's sister, an issue which will eventually lead Sutpen to kill the other. But that is still in the future. As the two men take their turns in the dialogue the point of view shifts to and fro between the speakers. When Sutpen refuses the marriage suit, the other reacts as follows:

> *Now it is Bon who watches Henry; he can see the whites of Henry's eyes again as he sits looking at Henry with that expression which might be called smiling. His hand vanishes beneath the blanket and reappears, holding his pistol by the barrel, the butt extended towards Henry.*
> *– Then do it now, he says.*
> *Henry looks at the pistol; now he is not only panting, he is trembling.* (italics in original)[56]

Speech plays only a relatively small part in this exchange, compared with the moment-by-moment changes of expression and physical gesture. The confrontation takes on a military dimension when Bon produces his pistol in a quasi-chivalrous gesture of defiance masked as surrender, a gesture suggestive of D. W. Griffith's films.[57] Shortly afterwards, the novel shifts back to its main method of narrative composition; the confrontation was, however, so important to the narrator Shreve that it had to be played out in his imagination with all the immediacy of a film scene.

If I Forget Thee, Jerusalem [The Wild Palms] and Hollywood Crime Fiction

At this point we make a brief diversion from Faulkner to consider two novels, both written by screenwriters, which deploy filmic methods to comment on the commercialism of Hollywood. The first of these was definitely familiar to Faulkner, the second may be considered by inference to have been familiar to him. Horace McCoy's *They Shoot Horses, Don't They?* (1935) was the first of a pair of novels examining the working of Hollywood and centres on Gloria, a would-be star, and Robert, a young man who dreams of becoming a movie director 'more important than Sergei Eisenstein'.[58] By the time McCoy wrote his first draft of the novel in 1933 he had been working in Hollywood for over twelve months, only that year securing a contract with Columbia as screenwriter. What is striking about his first novel is not only its oblique portrayal of Hollywood, which I shall consider in a moment, but its 'refiguring' of two 1933 musicals: *42nd Street* and *Gold Diggers of '33*. Charles Musser, whose term I use here, has demonstrated how McCoy appropriates and perverts aspects of both musicals in order to make a sardonic comment on the Depression and to skew the relation between actuality and the world of showbusiness.[59]

Not only does *They Shoot Horses* contain intertextual allusions to these musicals; on every page it bears testimony to McCoy's acquired skill at screenwriting. It consists of a rapid sequence of flashback scenes counterpointed against the narrative present situation of the protagonist being sentenced to death for murder.[60] The words of the trial judge cross-cut (in increasing type size) with the narrative sequence, which traces out through extended flashback the process whereby Robert finds himself in that position. The trial scene, or rather the *condemnation* scene, thus frames the action and determines its inevitability. McCoy constructs the narrative like a screenplay using Robert as the focalizer and the quasi-directorial organizer of scenes; in an opening section he dreams of working with von Sternberg, 'learning about composition and tempo and angles'.[61] The novel describes a dance marathon figured as a double analogy with a horse-race and with the jockeying for success in Hollywood. Robert's dream of becoming a director is a compensatory fantasy for his total lack of autonomy in the marathon, whose rules are set by others. The event is a spectacle orchestrated in such a way that behaviour becomes performance for the benefit of visiting stars and a wider audience. McCoy skilfully represents the process through visual imagery. As Charles Musser notes, the circularity of the narrative parallels the shape of the dance floor.[62] Also, the relation between the protagonists reads like a travesty of a Hollywood romance, in which the happy ending is replaced by a mercy killing: Robert shoots Gloria.

This killing is one feature of *They Shoot Horses* which justifies its description as a prototype *noir* narrative. Spectacle has its dark side in, for instance, the slippage of function from the pistol used to start and end the daily sessions and the weapon which kills the protagonists' patron in an unpredictable outburst of violence. She, like the protagonists themselves, is a victim of the event, a point which McCoy subtly articulates through the image of her eye: 'It was Mrs Layden, a single hole in the front of her forehead. John Maxwell was kneeling beside her, holding her head [...] then he placed the head gently on the floor, and stood up. Mrs Layden's head slowly turned sidewise and a little pool of blood that had collected in the crater of her eye spilled out on the floor'.[63] After the constant exhausting movement of the action this slow close-up powerfully figures the loss of life-blood as travesty tears.

James M. Cain, credited along with McCoy as one of the formative writers of *noir* fiction, also engages with Hollywood methods as well as themes in his early fiction. Cain worked in Hollywood from 1932 to 1948 and, as he acknowledges in his preface to *Double Indemnity* (1935), he learnt crucial lessons in narrative composition from the screenwriter Vincent Lawrence, specifically how to evoke and maintain interest in characters from the very first scene.[64] On Lawrence's death in 1946 Cain wrote a tribute in which he praised him for being the first 'to articulate the philosophy of the love story into [an] intellectual whole'.[65] Cain's career in Hollywood was patchy and on the whole unsuccessful. In his unpublished memoirs he recorded: 'at the time the picture business regarded the script as an inescapable, but loathsome evil, and approached it accordingly'.[66] On the other hand, this statement should be balanced against his thoughtful estimate in 'Camera Obscura' (1933), where he rejects popular perceptions that the studios were encouraging hack work. On the one hand he declares that 'the cinema itself to them [i.e. to writers] is Heaven', whereas Hollywood was hell because of all the disappointments and frustrations they suffered. Nevertheless, he records his education in movie techniques, especially in scene: 'all movie shots have to be brief and inter-cut with close-ups and angle shots, else you go insane from the monotony'.[67]

Here we get a clear indication of how Cain's technique was shaped by film practice: in his reliance on the composition of scenes and the creation of a rapid tempo through the brevity and juxtaposition of these scenes. The opening of *The Postman Always Rings Twice* (1934) quickly establishes the triangular situation that will produce the intrigue through a series of short scenes: the protagonist being thrown off a truck; his first appearance at the 'sandwich joint'; his conversation with the Greek owner; then the first view of the latter's wife, with a close-up on her pouting lips. This section concludes with a long shot of the kitchen (where the wife works) from the filling station, the protagonist's initial work-place.[68] Cain minimizes exposition and establishes the action through scene. He even uses point of view as an index of the narrator's impotence when he has to be carried into the final court scenes on a stretcher.

The Postman is thematically linked to film by Cora's unsuccessful screen test. *Serenade* (1938) is more explicit about both film and cinematic technique. Thus, when the narrator confronts the escort of his Mexican girlfriend-to-be, we are told: 'the room froze like a stop-camera shot'; and although the protagonist is a singer, he embodies Cain's own ambivalence about Hollywood. On the one hand he realizes that writing or talent was 'just something you buy'; on the other he gets engrossed in the technicalities of making successful films.[69] This commodification, together with the attempts by McCoy's and Cain's protagonists to create real-life scenarios for themselves, suggest links with Faulkner's 1939 novel *If I Forget Thee, Jerusalem* (originally published as *The Wild Palms*). At one point, as the two lovers are leaving Utah for Texas, they begin to see 'lunch rooms with broad strong Western girls got up out of Hollywood magazines (Hollywood which is no longer in Hollywood but is stippled by a billion feet burning coloured gas across the face of the American earth) to resemble Joan Crawford'.[70] In all three cases Hollywood is evoked as a system which standardizes and commodifies; here both personal and topographical difference is lost.

Already we can begin to see what lies behind Faulkner's use of a double plot in *If I Forget Thee*: of a doomed affair between Henry Wilbourne and Charlotte Rittenmeyer which results in the latter's death, and of convicts' relief work in a Mississippi flood. Faulkner counterpoints one action against the other in a way which has been compared to parallel montage in Griffith's *Intolerance* and which may have been further suggested by Eisenstein's practice and writings.[71] Indeed, Faulkner refers to the latter in his comparison of Utah mine tunnels with 'something out of an Eisenstein Dante'.[72] The novel's alternation between romance and flood casts a fatalistic pall over the former, which culminates in explicit comparison when Charlotte dies from a botched abortion. Death is the end result of both processes.

The collective action of the flood metaphorically renders the process of deprivation experienced in the Depression, shown as a loss of land, property and ultimately life. Early panning shots in the 'Old Man' sequence show how the flood erases the landscape itself, transforming it into a near-featureless expanse which subverts the convict's sense of time and place. A blow on the back of his head causes him to lose consciousness, represented as a fade to white in which bright light progressively fills his mental screen. Transitions become abrupt and surreal: 'now, instead of space, the skiff became abruptly surrounded by a welter of fleeing debris – planks, small buildings, the bodies of drowned yet antic animals, entire trees leaping and diving like porpoises above which the skiff seemed to hover'.[73] The experience of the flood is presented as one of visual disorientation and, apart from its allusions to the Mississippi flood of 1927, Michael Grimwood has suggested an imagistic debt to two films of 1937 – Pare Lorentz's *The River* and John Ford's *The Hurricane* – which helped Faulkner create an 'emblematic disaster-scape'.[74] The rapid sequence of images in the flood passages may well have been suggested by Faulkner's work in 1933 on the film *War Birds*, which contains what he called 'kaleidoscopic double exposure'. Bruce Kawin has glossed this phrase as an early reference to montage, before Faulkner had learnt the term.[75]

The two male protagonists are linked by a common desire for cinematic glamour. In the 'Old Man' sequence (the flood sections) a convict has been feeding his imagination on pulp fiction and dreams of rescuing a 'living Garbo', whereas the actual woman he helps could not be farther from this image. Similarly the affair between Harry and Charlotte is repeatedly figured by Harry, who supplies our angle of vision, as a cinematic romance. He compares Charlotte to Hollywood advertisements, commodifying his sexual experiences into a spectacle for his private gaze. As Richard Godden states, 'Harry is his own best audience. We know he has a propensity for mental home movies'.[76] This is shown in the way Harry figures memory as a mind-cinema played out against the screen of his eyelids. The latter are referred to again and again in the scene in which Charlotte dies. The operating theatre is lit by Klieg lights like a film set but these are extinguished when Harry finally gets to see her dead body. The performance is over and his eyelids become a screen from actuality, an effect further heightened after his trial by the 'bright silver curtain' of the rain which begins to fall.[77]

It is hardly surprising that *If I Should Forget Thee* should bear the textual signs of Faulkner's involvement in the film business for almost a decade. His care over scenic construction, alternation between long shots and close-ups, use of tableau images, and other devices testify to this presence.[78] Faulkner started the novel late in 1937 after a year's stint in Hollywood and his aware-ness of the work of Horace McCoy would have increased his perception of how the film medium could feed into the novel. Richard Godden has summa-rized the circumstantial evidence which makes it a strong possibility that

Faulkner knew McCoy, or at least his work, and a similar argument could be made for James M. Cain since *The Postman Always Rings Twice* became a bestseller which dramatically heightened his profile in Hollywood.[79] All three novels just discussed describe crimes of desire, desire fed by Hollywood.

Cinematic Public Narratives

In 1943 the Hollywood producer William Bacher and the director Henry Hathaway suggested to Faulkner the idea of a new treatment of the Unknown Warrior theme applying the Christ story. In the 1940s Faulkner worked on the project, intending to make it into a film for Warner Brothers, but it finally bore fruit in 1954 as the novel entitled *A Fable*. Its interest here lies in the evocation of large-scale spectacle, unusual in Faulkner's fiction, and suggesting the crowd scenes of Griffith's silent classic *Intolerance*. In the opening sequence a French urban crowd meets a troop of cavalry and by sheer mass begins to force it backwards. Faulkner sets up an implicitly high visual vantage point from which these movements are observed and skilfully alternates images of large-scale flow with specific close-ups on individuals within the mass. Within this flow there occur freezes, momentary close-ups, and aerial perspective shots from planes, all contributing to an effect of collective confrontation with militarism. At one point an officer thematizes these cinematic effects by denying grandeur to a queue of men: '*no*, the colonel thought, *not a cinema* [...] *They are like the parade outside a latrine*' (italics in original).[80] The general perspective of the opening chapters contradicts this sentiment by implicitly retaining the cinematic analogy.

Also in 1943 Faulkner published a story which uses film to engage with the bombing of Pearl Harbor. In 'Shall Not Perish' a young boy describes how his family visit the cinema one Saturday afternoon to see a Western that seemed to have been running for years. The most dramatic moment is 'when the horses all came plunging down the cliff and whirled around and came boiling up the gully until in just one more jump they would come clean out of the screen and go galloping among the little faces turned up to them like corn shucks scattered across a lot'.[81] At this point grandpa wakes up and starts shouting warnings to the audience. It seems that he is just responding to the film with the naivety demonstrated in early accounts of film viewing, but the story has a twist. The boy narrator, unlike the adults, understands how the Western is indeed jumping out of the frame and forming part of the grand epic narrative of America. The perceptual issue of viewer response thus becomes subsumed into a larger collective celebration of the nation.

Notes

1   Bruce Kawin's edition of *Faulkner's MGM Screenplays* (1982) publishes the scripts he
     wrote in 1932–33. His scripts for *The Road to Glory* (a collaboration with Joel Sayre of
     1936), *To Have and Have Not* (1944) and *The Big Sleep* (1946) were issued in 1981, 1980
     and 1971 respectively, the first edited by Matthew J. Bruccoli, the second by Bruce Kawin,
     the last in *Film Scripts One*, edited by George P. Garrett. Faulkner's scripts for *Battle Cry*,
     Stallion Road and *The De Gaulle Story* have all come out in separate volumes under the
     editorship of Louis Daniel Brodsky. Also under the latter's editorship, *Country Lover and
     Other Stories for the Screen* publishes story outlines for Warner Brothers written in the
     early 1940s. Faulkner's 1950s' television scripts with commentary can be found in William
     Furry, 'Faulkner in a Haystack: The Search for William Faulkner's Television Adapta-
     tions of *The Brooch* and *Shall Not Perish*', in Edwin T. Arnold, ed., *The Faulkner Journal*,
     pp. 119–215. Kawin gives a full filmography in *Faulkner and Film*, pp. 165–81. Gene D.
     Phillips' *Fiction, Film and Faulkner* (1988) surveys both Faulkner's screenwriting activi-
     ties and film adaptations of his novels. For a detailed study of one adaptation, see Regina
     K. Fadiman, *Faulkner's 'Intruder in the Dust'*.
2   Magny, *The Age of the American Novel*, pp. 178–223. This chapter is one of the weakest in
     Magny's study because of his refusal to demonstrate except in the most general terms
     Faulkner's cinematic dimension.
3   Murray, *The Cinematic Imagination*, pp. 154–67.
4   Spiegel, *Fiction and the Camera Eye*, p. 156.
5   Kawin, *Faulkner and Film*, p. 13; 'The Montage Element in Faulkner's Fiction', in Evans
     Harrington and Ann J. Abadie, eds., *Faulkner, Modernism, and Film*, pp. 103–26. Kawin
     finds five kinds of montage in Faulkner: 'the oxymoron, dynamic unresolution, parallel
     plotting, rapid shifts in time and space, and multiple narration' ('The Montage Element',
     p. 109).
6   See Phillips, *Fiction, Film, and Faulkner*, pp. 32–33. Faulkner owned a copy of the MGM
     employee Barrett Kiesling's *Talking Pictures: How They Are Made, How to Appreciate
     Them* (1937), but his copy was inscribed by the author in 1948 (Blotner, *William Faulkner's
     Library*, p. 39).
7   William Faulkner, *Selected Letters*, p. 110. In an interview of 1947 Faulkner stated: 'I'm a
     movie picture doctor. When they find a section of a script they don't like I rewrite it and
     continue to rewrite it until they are satisfied [...] I don't write scripts. I don't know enough
     about it' (M. Thomas Inge, ed., *Conversations with William Faulkner*, p. 70). Similarly in
     a 1956 interview he declared: 'I don't take writing for the movies seriously' (Cynthia
     Grenier, 'The Art of Fiction', p. 173). Neither statement would imply that Faulkner
     didn't take film itself seriously. For a summary account of Faulkner in Hollywood, see Ian
     Hamilton, *Writers in Hollywood*, pp. 191–209. Richard Fine stresses Faulkner's personal
     disquiet with Hollywood in *West of Eden*, pp. 124, 126.
8   See Bruce Kawin, 'Hawks on Faulkner'. Hawks records how Faulkner disliked a Norma
     Shearer film and, after Hawks's challenge, himself wrote a ghost story (p. 5).
9   Joseph Blotner, 'Faulkner in Hollywood', in W. R. Robinson, ed., *Man and the Movies*, p.
     300. He finds that Faulkner approached screenwriting as a job of work (p. 294). Blotner's
     survey remains one of the most thorough.
10   Even this generalization needs to be qualified. Faulkner was realist enough to recognize
     that his screenwriting was for 'certain key scenes and situations and part of the dialogue'
     rather than a whole work, and in a 1958 interview admitted that he enjoyed making his
     main films (Inge, *Conversations with William Faulkner*, pp. 50, 162).

11 Faulkner collaborated with Sayre on *The Road to Glory* (see Tom Dardis, *Some Time in the Sun*, p. 93). He went on hunting trips with West. Dardis's account of Faulkner in Hollywood remains one of the most balanced (*Some Time in the Sun*, pp. 73–133). Joel Sayre was also a close friend of the novelist John O'Hara who first came to Hollywood in 1934 and who helped compose scripts for Paramount and Twentieth Century-Fox.

12 William Faulkner, *Collected Stories*, pp. 701–702, 719. Faulkner's title makes a multiple pun on the promise of the USA to immigrants, the dream of wealth, and the sunny climate of California. 'Golden Land' has not been filmed but was adapted in 1988 for the US public television series *Tales from the Hollywood Hills* along with stories by John O'Hara, Budd Schulberg and others.

13 Bruce F. Kawin, 'Sharecropping in the Golden Land', in Doreen Fowler and Ann J. Abadie, eds., *Faulkner and Popular Culture*, p. 201.

14 *Collected Stories*, p. 721.

15 William Faulkner, *Mosquitoes*, p. 59.

16 Jeffrey J. Folks, 'William Faulkner and the Silent Film', pp. 173–75.

17 D. M. Murray, 'Faulkner, the Silent Comedies, and the Animated Cartoons'. Murray's demonstration of pinwheel images, comic distortion, freezes, etc. puts into perspective Faulkner's much-quoted statement that when he went to Hollywood he only knew about Mickey Mouse and newsreels. 'Mickey Mouse' should be taken as a self-derogatory reference to silent film comedy or cartoons.

18 William Faulkner, *New Orleans Sketches*, p. 54.

19 William Faulkner, *Flags in the Dust*, pp. 105–106.

20 *Flags in the Dust*, p. 167.

21 For commentary on *Elmer*, see Joseph Blotner, *Faulkner: A Biography*, Vol. I, pp. 455, 459.

22 *Flags in the Dust*, p. 86.

23 *Flags in the Dust*, p. 370. The passage alludes to Keats' 'Ode on a Grecian Urn', l. 2: 'Thou foster-child of Silence and slow Time'.

24 Quoted in Blotner, *Faulkner: A Biography*, p. 1216. The letter is undated, probably from around the end of the Second World War.

25 William Faulkner, *The Sound and the Fury*, p. 3. Even in such a short passage Benjy's habit of repetition emerges. The time jumps in his section are abrupt and quasi-cinematic, but could not be described as flashbacks because that term would imply a distinction between past and present, whereas Benjy's perceptions work on a more rudimentary opposition between presence and absence. Apart from Benjy's registration of sights, Bruce Kawin finds three kinds of montage in the novel: juxtaposition without explanation, extended oxymorons, and sections from past and present undercut by the stream of consciousness (*Faulkner and Film*, pp. 18–19).

26 Folks, 'William Faulkner and the Silent Film', p. 175. It is an inconsistency when Benjy says 'I cried' because this suggests subjective response, whereas throughout his section Benjy's reactions (moaning, crying, etc.) are verbalized by others.

27 William Faulkner, *Novels 1930–1935*, p. 3. The assertion of the need for motion was made by Faulkner to an aspiring writer, Joan Williams, in 1951 (Faulkner, *Selected Letters*, p. 323).

28 *Novels 1930–1935*, p. 32. Doug Baldwin overstates this issue by declaring that in this novel 'scenes are described in focal length' ('Putting Images into Words: Elements of the "Cinematic" in William Faulkner's Prose', in Arnold, ed., *The Faulkner Journal*, pp. 35–64; p. 47). The visuality of the different sections of *As I Lay Dying* varies considerably from narrator to narrator. Nevertheless Baldwin's essay remains one of the most useful pieces of commentary on this aspect of Faulkner's prose.

29 *Novels 1930–1935*, p. 172.

30 Edwin Seaver, 'A Chamber of Horrors', New York *Sun* (13 February 1931), quoted in Blotner, *Faulkner: A Biography*, p. 767.

31 For critical commentary on the film, see Kawin, *Faulkner and Film*, p. 33 (the film simplifies the novel); Phillips, *Fiction, Film, and Faulkner*, pp. 69–74 (on changes including the moral regeneration of Temple Drake; D. Matthew Ramsey, '"Lifting the Fog": Faulkners, Reputations, and *The Story of Temple Drake*', in Arnold, ed., *The Faulkner Journal*, pp. 7–34 (on publicity promotion of film, hints of lesbianism in the actress Miriam Hopkins, etc.).

32 E. Pauline Dagenfelder, 'The Four Faces of Temple Drake', p. 550.

33 Richard Gray, '*Sanctuary*, "Night Bird" and Film Noir'.

34 *Novels 1930–1935*, p. 181.

35 Edward Branigan, *Narrative Comprehension and Film*, p. 53.

36 Noel Polk, 'Afterword', in William Faulkner, *Sanctuary: The Original Text*, p. 303. Peter Lurie reads the relation of Popeye to Benbow as an allegorization of popular culture and high art (*Vision's Immanence*, pp. 28–38).

37 Popeye's very name plays on eyes. Although Joseph Blotner has linked the name to that of a Memphis gangster (*Faulkner: A Biography*, pp. 607–608), it should be noted that the Popeye comic strip began in 1929, the very year that Faulkner was writing this novel.

38 Spiegel, *Fiction and the Camera Eye*, p. 154.

39 Cf. Lurie, *Vision's Immanence*, pp. 26–27, 34. Popeye's last words to his executioner ('Fix my hair, Jack') may be an allusion to Rico in W. R. Burnett's *Little Caesar* (1929), who is inordinately vain of his hair and thus is compared with Rudolph Valentino. Popeye, however, is an unchanging image. He literally *is* his tight black suit, whereas Rico changes dress according to his rise through underworld society. The genesis and film adaptation of *Little Caesar* is detailed in Max Decharne's *Hardboiled Hollywood*, pp. 32–49. Faulkner was also familiar with Dashiell Hammett's fiction and his library included copies of *The Maltese Falcon* and *The Thin Man*. In comparing *The Maltese Falcon* with John Huston's 1941 film, Leslie H. Abramson points out the cinematic effect of Hammett's external descriptions: 'by choosing the unintrusive third person point of view, Hammett necessarily limited himself to visual clues regarding Spade's thoughts' ('Two Birds of a Feather', p. 309). Faulkner achieves a similar effect in Popeye, except that the reader's search for clues is as often as not blocked by Popeye's inexpressiveness. Hammett had a number of screenwriting assignments in Hollywood from 1930 onwards, his main success being *The Thin Man* (1934) and its sequel. He and Faulkner became friends in this period. Hammett's cinema stories include 'On the Way' (1932) and 'The Little Pig' (1934).

40 *Novels 1930–1935*, p. 226. This scene is one of many which justify Judith Sensibar's claim that *Sanctuary* is a novel 'where everyone sees or is seen in frames': 'Faulkner's Real and Imaginary Photos of Desire', in Fowler and Abadie, eds., *Faulkner and Popular Culture*, p. 132. David Madden also examines images frozen in photographs in 'Photographs and the 1929 Version of *Sanctuary*', in the same volume, pp. 93–109.

41 Lurie, *Vision's Immanence*, p. 39.

42 Unpublished letter quoted in Lurie, *Vision's Immanence*, p. 192.

43 *Novels 1930–1935*, p. 333. Bruce Kawin claims that Faulkner's own adaptation of *Absalom, Absalom!*, *Revolt in the Earth* (1942), shows the influence of German silent film (*Faulkner's MGM Screenplays*, p. 264).

44 Blotner, *Faulkner: A Biography*, p. 1322. For Blotner, Faulkner's positive experience of working with MGM director Clarence Brown in 1949 while filming on location in Oxford (Mississippi) gave him a crucial impetus for composing *Requiem* initially as a play (p. 1311).

45 William Faulkner, *Requiem for a Nun*, pp. 69–70.

46 This is essentially the shift in female character which Faulkner describes in his story outline *Night Bird* and his film script *The College Widow* from the early 1930s; see Kawin, *Faulkner's MGM Screenplays*, pp. 29–53.

47 Doug Baldwin, 'Putting Images into Words', in Arnold, ed., *The Faulkner Journal,*, pp. 47–48.

48 Lurie, *Vision's Immanence*, p. 69.

49 *Novels 1930–1935*, p. 482. Peter Lurie rightly notes that Christmas is represented as a 'shadowy, vague entity', often compared to a ghost (*Vision's Immanence*, p. 79).

50 Dardis, *Some Time in the Sun*, pp. 92–93.

51 *Novels 1930–1935*, p. 802. The compound words probably signal a debt to Dos Passos. The reporter's consciousness of cinema emerges in his comment on a woman that she had 'Harlowcoloured hair that they would pay her money for in Hollywood' (p. 804).

52 Joseph R. Urgo, '*Absalom, Absalom!*: The Movie', p. 59.

53 William Faulkner, *Novels 1936–1940*, p. 157. This image may have been suggested by the scenes of exhausted and wounded soldiers in the last part of *The Road to Glory*.

54 Urgo, '*Absalom, Absalom!*: The Movie', pp. 62–64, 68. Peter Lurie also describes Quentin Compson's position in the novel as similar to that of a 'film viewer' (*Vision's Immanence*, p. 120).

55 Kawin finds in Faulkner's 1933 film script *War Birds* the 'most elaborate and experimental use of mindscreens (cinematic analogues to first-person narratives) in *any* of Faulkner's scripts' (*Faulkner's MGM Screenplays*, p. 274). He seems to have in mind sequences such as those when John Sartoris alternately writes entries in his diary and visualizes scenes from the past. In a similar manner, the confrontation scene from *Absalom, Absalom!* emerges from a laborious process of narrative reconstruction.

56 *Novels 1936–1940*, p. 294.

57 Bruce Kawin asserts that Faulkner admired *The Birth of a Nation* (*Faulkner and Film*, p. 70). Peter Lurie relates Rosa Coldfield's narration to a cinematic practice affected by Griffith's films (*Vision's Immanence*, pp. 116–17). Faulkner could have seen the dramatization of Thomas W. Dixon's *The Clansman* (the source text for *Birth of a Nation*) in Oxford in 1908 and he owned a copy of the novel (Blotner, *Faulkner: A Biography*, pp. 115–16; *William Faulkner's Library*, p. 27).

58 Horace McCoy, *4 Novels*, p. 40. McCoy's other Hollywood novel was *I Should Have Stayed Home* (1938), which describes how behaviour becomes a commodity to circulate in the fan magazines and gossip columns. Faulkner owned a copy of McCoy's novel as well as Dashiell Hammett's *The Maltese Falcon* and *The Thin Man*, all evidence of his interest in Hollywood and crime fiction (Blotner, *William Faulkner's Library*, pp. 35, 41).

59 Charles Musser, 'The Devil's Parody: Horace McCoy's Appropriation and Refiguration of Two Hollywood Musicals', in Robert Stam and Alessandro Raengo, eds., *A Companion to Literature and Film*, pp. 229–57. Musser locates the centre of McCoy's novel as follows: 'the contrasts between the backstage world constructed by the "dream factory" and the brutal realism of the dance marathon is the fulcrum around which McCoy builds his critique of Hollywood' (p. 245). The marathon is a crude exercise in social Darwinism in that quite literally only the fittest survive.

60 For commentary on the 1969 film adaptation's use of flash-forwards and flashbacks, see Paul Warshow, 'The Unreal McCoy', in Peary and Shatzkin, eds., *The Modern American Novel and the Movies*, p. 35.

61 McCoy, *4 Novels*, p. 7.

62 Musser, 'The Devil's Parody', in Robert Stam and Alessandro Raengo, eds., *A Companion*

to Literature and Film, p. 246.

63 McCoy, *4 Novels*, p. 72.

64 Author's preface to *Double Indemnity*, *The Five Great Novels of James M. Cain*, pp. 236–40. *Double Indemnity* was published in magazine form in 1935, in book form in 1943.

65 James M. Cain, *60 Years of Journalism*, p. 210. Lawrence scripted over twenty films throughout the 1930s and collaborated with Horace McCoy on the script of *Gentleman Jim* (1942).

66 Roy Hoopes, *Cain*, p. 221. Hoopes supplies a complete filmography for Cain on pp. 650–53.

67 Cain, *60 Years of Journalism*, pp. 190, 194.

68 Lawrence even suggested the title for Cain's first novel (*The Five Great Novels of James M. Cain*, p. 239).

69 *The Five Great Novels of James M. Cain*, pp. 86, 158.

70 *Novels 1936–1940*, p. 636. Faulkner had to rewrite the script for *Today We Live* (1933) to create a part for Crawford (Kawin, *Faulkner's MGM Screenplays*, p. 101).

71 Doug Baldwin draws the Griffith comparison ('Putting Images into Words', in Arnold, ed., *The Faulkner Journal*, p. 57).

72 *Novels 1936–1940*, p. 621. The comparison suggests an underground hell and possibly alludes to Eisenstein's *Strike*.

73 *Novels 1936–1940*, p. 601.

74 Michael Grimwood, *Heart in Conflict*, pp. 118–20. Grimwood's argument is based on specific parallels between the films and novel rather than on any explicit reference to the films by Faulkner.

75 Kawin, *Faulkner and Film*, pp. 87–88. Kawin suggests a possible parallel between D. W. Griffith's *Intolerance* (1916) and Faulkner's novel in their uses of counterpointed action (p. 125).

76 Richard Godden, *Fictions of Labor*, p. 217. Peter Lurie makes the same point, seeing Harry's memory as a 'kind of film viewing' (*Vision's Immanence*, p. 158). Lurie draws other filmic comparisons, e.g. reading the scene between Charlotte and her husband as a 'set piece of melodrama' (p. 147).

77 The image resembles the description of film viewing in the last scene of 'Dry September' (1931), where the movie-house is described as being 'like a miniature fairyland with its lighted lobby'. When the film starts, 'the screen glowed silver, and soon life began to unfold' (*Collected Stories of William Faulkner*, p. 181).

78 Doug Baldwin specifically ties scenes such as Charlotte's drawing story to silent film ('Putting Images into Words', in Arnold, ed., *The Faulkner Journal*, p. 58). There is a further biographical factor in the novel articulating Faulkner's depression after the ending of his affair with Meta Carpenter, Howard Hawks' secretary. Comparing her memoir with the novel, Anne Goodwyn Jones has concluded that Carpenter 'sees herself through the lens of a movie camera' and that both figures perceived their affair as 'mediated by cultural images and plots' ('"The Kotex Age": Women, Popular Culture, and *The Wild Palms*', in Fowler and Abadie, eds., *Faulkner and Popular Culture*, p. 149).

79 Godden, *Fictions of Labor*, p. 200. He argues that McCoy helped Faulkner 'focus his own ideas on the "prison" of a commodity-based society' (p. 202). In 1943 Faulkner worked on the film script for Cain's novel *Mildred Pierce*.

80 William Faulkner, *Novels 1942–1954*, p. 720.

81 *Collected Stories of William Faulkner*, p. 113. Faulkner adapted 'Shall Not Perish' for television; it was broadcast in 1954.

7

John Dos Passos and the Art of Montage

We have seen instances in the previous chapter of William Faulkner using montage. We now need to turn to the leading theorist of montage – the Soviet film-maker Sergei Eisenstein – and to a novelist who from the beginning of his career saw film as helping his aim of social investigation: John Dos Passos. Although Eisenstein will figure in this chapter as a leading practitioner and theorist of montage, he himself admitted that this form of construction had been suggested to him by the methods of D. W. Griffith, the 'most thrilling figure against this background' as he called him.[1] As many critics have noted, Griffith pioneered a method of cutting between sequences which became one of the hallmarks of modernist fiction and which Michael Rogin has summarized as follows:

> by cutting back and forth, Griffith juxtaposed events separated in time (the flash-back) and space (the cutback) and collapsed the distinctions between images in the head and events in the world. By speeding up, reversing, and stopping time, he brought the past into the present [...] By juxtaposing events widely separated in space, he overcame the barriers of distance [...] Griffith created an art of simultaneities and juxtapositions rather than traditions and continuities.[2]

It is this fracturing of narrative sequence which we will encounter again and again in the present chapter and in subsequent chapters in which juxtaposition features prominently. Not surprisingly, *The Birth of a Nation* (1915) was the main film which stuck in John Dos Passos' memory as having made an unusually strong impression in his youth.

Dos Passos not only made sustained attempts to incorporate cinematic elements in his most famous fiction, *Manhattan Transfer* and the *U.S.A.* trilogy; he also saw film as a unique force for cultural change in the modern era. In 1925 he noted that 'the movies have made the theatre of the transparent fourth wall unnecessary and obsolete, just as photography has made obsolete a certain sort of painting. The camera and screen can transport the audience into circumstances, in the ordinary sense, real'.[3] Dos Passos suspected that the new media of film and radio would sooner or later doom the theatre to extinction and he summarized such developments as marking a broad change in US culture: 'from being a wordminded people we are becoming an eyeminded people'.[4] The signs were the startling experiments in the visual arts, the development of advertising, and above all the emergence of the cinema. As a painter, Dos Passos was later to recall how Cubism encouraged a kind of representation analogous to that in film: 'The artist must record the fleeting world the way the motion picture recorded it. By contrast, juxtaposition, montage, he could build drama into his narrative'.[5]

Dos Passos' ambition to be the chronicler of the modern age meant that, however much he was concerned with appearances, he was never satisfied to remain there. In his famous essay 'The Writer as Technician', prepared for the 1935 American Writers' Congress, he declared: 'I feel that American writers who want to do the most valuable kind of work will find themselves trying to discover the deep currents of historical change under the surface of opinions, orthodoxies, heresies, gossip and the journalistic garbage of the day'.[6] Dos Passos was drawn to an art of surface appearance which would reveal what was going on beneath that surface.

Dos Passos was concerned with new ways of seeing, new practices of consumption, and the general role of the media in society. Hence it is not surprising that in the 1960s he became interested in the writings of Marshall McLuhan, who, he admitted, did 'open up all sorts of things'.[7] In particular, he must have been drawn to McLuhan's argument in *Understanding Media* (1964) that the different media interact and that film-viewing draws on 'literacy', i.e. on the skills necessary for reading texts. Thus, 'film both in its reel form and in its scenario or script form, is completely involved with book culture'.[8] McLuhan also discusses Chaplin, who, as we have seen, was an important symbolic figure for the modernists; McLuhan stresses Chaplin's skill at exploiting the film medium to protest against the mechanical world.

Dos Passos' earliest comments on the cinema date from the late 1910s. Looking back in later life on 1919, he recalled: 'whenever you went to the movies you saw Charlie Chaplin at his best'; but his first important experience of film took place the preceding year.[9] While at military camp in 1918 he enjoyed seeing films every night for entertainment but remained unimpressed by the anti-German propaganda film he had to sit through. Referring to himself in the third person for his diary, he records: 'What he saw was a village in an over picturesque country with local colour plastered on very thick, donkey carts, dog carts, milk carts with much shell fire and Germans rushing about with cans of kerosene setting things on fire – Germans whom the brave Americans chase out of towns, thereby saving crowds of young girls in peasant costume a la musical comedy'.[10] Evaluating the film's incapacity to blend together incongruous genres, Dos Passos plicitly refuses the spectacle offered and detaches himself from the men ound him who are moved to hostile anger against the Germans.

This episode was so important to Dos Passos that he wrote it into his novel *Three Soldiers* (1921), in which film supplies the young protagonists with images against which to measure their experience, 'long movie reels of heroism' contrasting forcibly with the squalor of actual warfare. In the scene where the soldiers are shown the propaganda film there is no sign of the detachment Dos Passos recorded in his diary. Now all the soldiers, the main observer included, react as 'one organism' and the description of the film contains no reference to genre: 'the movie had begun again, unfolding scenes of soldiers in spiked helmets marching into Belgian cities full of little milk carts drawn by dogs and old women in peasant costumes […] [Andrews the observer gets drawn into the mounting hostility] as the troops were pictured advancing, bayonetting [*sic*] the civilians in wide Dutch pants, the old women with starched caps, the soldiers packed into the Y.M.C.A. hut shouted oaths at them'.[11] Paul Fussell has pointed out that this cinematic dream owes everything to *The Birth of a Nation* and similar melodramas.[12] Where the diary account includes compositional aspects, this description stays focused through the group perspective of the viewers who simply read it in terms of victim and victimizer. In that respect the film forms a part of the military machine to which the young recruits will be sacrificed. It also forms part of Dos Passos' subject rather than of his method. For this crucial development in his writing we must look to *Manhattan Transfer*.

Manhattan Transfer

Manhattan Transfer (1927) was designed as a portrait of the city of New York. Dos Passos uses a decentred method of description through brief narrative fragments in which it no longer makes sense to speak of protagonists. In their reviews of the novel Sinclair Lewis and D. H. Lawrence both drew analogies with film. Lewis commented that 'it is, indeed, the technique of the movie, in its flashes, its cut-backs, its speed'; and Lawrence declared: 'it is like a movie-picture with an intricacy of different stories and no close-ups and no writing in between. Mr. Dos Passos leaves out the writing in between'.[13] Lawrence found the action of *Manhattan Transfer* largely determined by a rapid tempo and this tempo made him think of a film.[14] Looking back on his career in 1967, Dos Passos confirmed the analogy in his account of how he came to construct the novel: 'I started a rapportage on New York'. Then he realized that he could not use a method with a protagonist: 'there was more to the life of a great city than you could cram into any one hero's career. The narrative must stand up off the page. Fragmentation. Contrast. Montage.

The result was *Manhattan Transfer*.[15] Michael Spindler has seen the presence of D. W. Griffith in this application of montage: 'in *Manhattan Transfer* [Dos Passos] emulated *The Birth of a Nation's* dynamic quality by his own repeated shifting of scenes and rapid episodic narration, thus building up an impression of the flux of city life through the accumulation of many different shots'.[16] Apart from a directly cinematic model, Dos Passos had another fictional precedent on which he could draw.

Dos Passos had one supreme example before him of modernist treatment of the city in fiction: that of James Joyce. When he first read *A Portrait of the Artist* Dos Passos was so impressed that he was afraid he might start imitating it and in later life he admitted that Joyce was a major influence on his writing.[17] The way in which Joyce depicts the criss-crossing of Dublin by his characters in *Ulysses* helped Dos Passos achieve a similar mosaic-like structure for *Manhattan Transfer*; the captions for the Aeolus section could have suggested Dos Passos' choice of titles; and there are many detailed similarities between both novels in what the characters register as they move around their cities. Alan Spiegel has taken Joyce as symptomatic of a shift away from nineteenth-century descriptive methods towards the practice of modernism in the ways in which the visual field is represented. This is a difference, he argues, between a 'unified, unobstructed, continuous field of vision and a blockaded, truncated, and discontinuous field', a difference in short 'between scenography and cinematography'.[18] For him, Joyce demonstrates a constant estrangement or alienation in his observers and even breaks up the behaviour of his characters into a 'discontinuous series of visualized fragments'.[19]

This fragmentation is demonstrated strikingly in the Wandering Rocks episode of *Ulysses* where we are given a series of short segments placing characters in different parts of the city. Take the instance of Father Conmee, who opens that section: 'Father Conmee began to walk along the North Strand road and was saluted by Mr William Gallagher who stood in the doorway of his shop. Father Conmee saluted Mr William Gallagher and perceived the odours that came from bacon-flitches and ample cools of butter. He passed Grogan's the tobacconist against which newsboards leaned and told of a dreadful catastrophe in New York'.[20] Joyce constantly situates his characters in relation to different landmarks or streets of the city. On the one hand he is concerned to give the sights (and here the smells) of Dublin; on the other his use of names suggests at least the potential knowability of his characters, who are constantly encountering acquaintances. Lastly, the city is a place to be read through its shop or news signs.

If we compare Joyce's method with that of Dos Passos striking differences emerge. The following lines describe two new acquaintances walking together after a drinking spree:

Arm in arm they careened up Pearl Street under the drenching rain. Bars yawned bright to them at the corners of rainseething streets. Yellow light off mirrors and brass rails and gilt frames round pictures of pink naked women was looped and slopped into whiskyglasses guzzled fiery with tipped back head, oozed bright through the blood, popped bubbly out of ears and eyes, dripped spluttering off fingertips. The raindark houses heaved on either side, streetlamps swayed like lanterns carried in a parade.[21]

The most noticeable absence in this passage is that of names. Joyce identifies his characters by name and title as if to imply that their position within Dublin was relatively stable, whereas throughout *Manhattan Transfer* Dos Passos shows his characters in motion, arriving and departing, succeeding or failing, but always on the move. His choice of the name of a railway station for the title of the novel strikes the keynote of transit.[22] As Leo Charney has pointed out, Dos Passos' choice of an external setting is also important because 'the fragmentation of modern life communicated itself in the experience of the urban street, traversed by vision, motion, and perception'.[23] Joyce's stylistic marker of non-hyphenated compound adjectives (also used by Faulkner) is followed in the Dos Passos quotation above and throughout *Manhattan Transfer*, usually to convey a nuance of appearance.[24] Here another difference from Joyce emerges. Dos Passos usually gives priority in his descriptions to the city context, imagistically suggesting that the latter must have priority over his characters. New York is a city of desire fed by its solicitations. Here the bars themselves seem to invite the men inside, and once they are inside alcoholic and sexual consumption blur together in a drunken haze.

Eisenstein praised Joyce for 'unfolding the display of events simultaneously with the particular manner in which these events pass through the consciousness and feelings, the associations and emotions of one of his chief characters'.[25] We shall consider shortly how important Eisenstein was in the development of Dos Passos' method for his *U.S.A.* trilogy, but his account of Joyce already applies to the structure of *Manhattan Transfer*. Through local focalization in the passage quoted above, Dos Passos gives us the sights the two men encounter and then, through a syntax which minimizes the disruption of punctuation, as it were takes the reader inside the bars, then inside the men's bodies as they drink. Dos Passos thus, like Joyce, adjusts the point of view constantly, depending on the requirements of the local scene. He may wish to convey an individual angle or he may spread the point of view across a group of spectators, as happens in the first description of a city fire. We start at street level with the arrival of the fire engine, then the focus rises to the signs of the fire and its victims: 'People watched silent staring at the upper windows where shadows moved and occasional light flickered'.[26] Dos Passos' exclusion of sound encourages the reader to identify with the crowd's struggle to see, and at the same time gives us a graphic illustration of New York as spectacle.

Dos Passos presents New York as a city of signs as well as sights. Throughout the novel characters are constantly being solicited by advertising images and slogans – as well as by what he calls the 'visual attack of the showwindows of Fifth Avenue stores' – which offer their commodity as a key to success.[27] The first example of this process occurs in the last part of the opening chapter. Here a 'small bearded bandylegged man in a derby' walking along a street in one of the poorer parts of New York concentrates all his attention on an advertising card with its 'highbrowed cleanshaven distinguished face with arched eyebrows and a bushy neatly trimmed mustache, the face of a man who had money in the bank, poised prosperously above a crisp wing collar and an ample dark cravat. Under it in copybook writing was the signature King C. Gillette'.[28] This image seems to promise a whole change of features as a means to achieving prosperity, the erasure of Old World signs as a necessary step to becoming an American. The image has a name, but the immigrant does not.

In this episode Dos Passos establishes that, much more so than Joyce's Dublin, New York is an aggressive, soliciting environment which repeatedly attempts to create desires in the city-dwellers. The process links, indeed blends together, social and sexual appetite through the mediation of newspapers, advertising, and the cinema. Two commentators have found a gender dimension to this process, which focuses particularly on the figure of the actress Ellen Thatcher. Carol Shloss argues that the latter's sense of becoming a photograph amounts to being 'caught in, or have accepted, someone else's image of what one should be'.[29] Similarly Janet Casey rightly describes Ellen Thatcher as the entrapped victim of the masculine gaze: her 'depiction as an actress heightens her symbolic import as representative of the broader cultural dynamic whereby women are contained through their very visibility'.[30] Hyper-conscious of being the object of a male sexual gaze, she makes a career out of her attractiveness. At one point she assesses her own mirror-image. Here her self-alienation has become so severe that she literally loses a conviction of her own reality: 'She kept winding up a hypothetical dollself and setting it in various positions. Tiny gestures ensued, acted out on various model stages'. She has internalized the role of a male director and becomes so estranged from herself that she feels as though she is turning to porcelain, i.e. turning into a literal ornament, sitting with an equally dehumanized companion: 'his wooden face of a marionette waggled senselessly in front of her'.[31]

So far we have been considering the nature of visibility in *Manhattan Transfer*, the different ways in which appearances are constructed and assessed. We need now to turn to the cinematic aspect to which Dos Passos attached great importance, namely the use of montage. For Eisenstein, 'montage is the idea that arises from the collision of independent shots – shots even opposite to one another'. As many critics have noted, apparent conflict lay behind his notion of film editing, but according to Eisenstein the true art of cinematography, including montage, lay in 'every fragment being an organic part of an organically conceived whole'.[32] More importantly for the connections between this theorizing and novelistic practice, Eisenstein saw the spectator of montage as a co-creator of visual meaning.[33] Dos Passos almost goes to Joycean extremes in weaving together the texture of *Manhattan Transfer* through the repetition of visual motifs such as fire and nickel, the latter connoting minimal spending power and the purchase of sights (the nickelodeon). These recurrences imply that no one's experience is unique to himself or herself. One example of montage will help to make this clear. A character called Joe Harland enters a bar one afternoon. After a short break in the text we are told: 'After the rain outdoors the plastery backstage smell was pungent in their nostrils. Ellen hung the wet raincoat on the back of the door and put her umbrella in a corner of the dressing room where a little puddle began to spread from it'.[34] In the next sentence it is revealed that Ellen is with Stan, an alcoholic who enters 'staggering'. Because there remains the visual break in the text, we could hardly argue that Dos Passos is suturing these segments together. We register a continuity of action but a change of character. Indeed it is sometimes slightly unclear who is doing what in the novel and this effect is strategic because Dos Passos repeatedly drama-tizes overlaps in his characters' fortunes.

This example does not show conflict between segments in Eisenstein's sense, however. For that we could consider the opening shots of *Manhattan Transfer*:

1. An establishing shot of a ferry boat arriving where the focus moves from the sky down to the rubbish in the water.
2. A nurse holding a newly born baby in a basket.
3. An old man playing a violin on the ferry.
4. Bud Korpening, a new arrival, asks the old man for directions.

The apparent discontinuity between segments gives the reader/viewer a cue to speculate on their links. Without compromising their visual specificity as metonyms of city life, Dos Passos invites us to consider whether one image could be an analogue of the other. Thus, the people arrive in a crowd through a heavily mechanized process. The baby too could be considered an arrival, even an interchangeable one when Dos Passos glances at the possibility of babies being given to the wrong parents. As we move to the third shot, the ironies multiply in that his time it is an old man who arrives. These juxtapositions question the nature of beginnings in the novel and indeed the fragmentation of the narrative makes it impossible to fit the segments into a clear paradigm of success or failure. Characters such as Congo drop out of the narrative and reappear prosperous, while others fail. Montage in *Manhattan Transfer* is thus used to demonstrate the local ignorance of characters about their own fortunes and a collective domination by the impulse to acquire money.

Dos Passos' methods were followed by Nathan Asch, whose 1930 novel *Pay Day* is also set in New York. The action of this novel takes place over a single day and focuses on the efforts by Jim the protagonist to pick up a young woman and take her to the movies. Like Dos Passos, Asch stresses throughout the tempo of city life, the chance encounters in the street or subway, and the hopes of sexual success produced by the city. Unlike Dos Passos, however, Asch demonstrates a total discontinuity between the movie Jim sees and his own experience. The film assembles a montage of national activities, spaced out on the page as in the following sequence, which takes place around lunch-time on a composite day:

A five mast schooner sailed away.

A cop bawled out speeders he had stopped on a country road.

Interior of Grand Central Terminal in New York, with thousands hurrying, trains entering and leaving.

A shipload of bananas was being unloaded. – Crated automobiles were loaded into a ship.

Down the Mississippi rolled an old fashioned back-wheeler excursion boat. Scenes on deck with couples spooning. An orchestra played dance music.[35]

The movie assembles different images of the nation in which characters perform representative tasks; old contrasts with new, city with country, and sea with land. The effect resembles a Whitmanesque panorama with near and aerial views presenting a kind of national reportage. If the city is the protagonist in *Manhattan Transfer*, here it is the nation, but to the bewilderment of the audience. One viewer complains: 'It hasn't got a story. It hasn't got a plot'; and this could stand as a comment on the novel too, which consists of small events and chance meetings.[36] Characters expect a conventional entertainment and instead are given a documentary montage which contextualizes the novel itself, even including a movie-house queue in its images.

Asch met Dos Passos through the *New Masses* group and must have been familiar with the latter's modernist experiments, himself producing an effect of radical textual discontinuity in *Pay Day*. Before we see how Dos Passos refines this method in the *U.S.A.* trilogy we need first to consider two inter-mediary factors which affected his writings: his contact with Blaise Cendrars and his encounters with the Soviet film-makers.

Blaise Cendrars and Cinematographic Writing

What Philippe Soupault was to William Carlos Williams, the Swiss French poet Blaise Cendrars was to Dos Passos.[37] In 1931 he published his transla-tion of Cendrars' poem *Panama* and used his foreword to present a roll-call of modernist experimentation in the arts.[38] Dos Passos' admiration for Cendrars has a more specific relevance, however, because the latter rational-ized his enthusiasm for film into a belief that the cinema was the quintessentially modern medium. He assisted Abel Gance in making the film *J'Accuse* in 1918 and the following year published his 'L'A.B.C. du Cinema', in which he asserted: 'nous nous acheminons vers une nouvelle synthèse de l'esprit humain, vers une nouvelle humanité [...] Leur langage sera le cinéma' ['we are on the road to a new synthesis of the human spirit, toward a new humanity [...] Their language will be that of the cinema'].[39] For Cendrars the cinema was the medium which could best give expression to the tempo of modern life and to his conviction in this essay that 'tout change'. The essay's title jokingly warns the reader to start learning afresh, to start learning a new pictorial alphabet whose signs of cut-back and close-up have been suggested by D. W. Griffith, 'le premier metteur en scène du monde'.[40] Like Vachel Lindsay, H. D., and other commentators on silent film, Cendrars saw this new pictorial language as a kind of updated hieroglyphic. In 1936 he published *Hollywood la mecque du cinéma* [*Hollywood the Mecca of Cinema*], in which he described the movie capital as 'un spectacle spontane' ['a spontaneous spectacle'] with its own pace, mystery, and system of sex-appeal.[41]

Eric Robertson has argued that Cendrars' work with Gance increased the cinematic structure to his writing, producing an effect of rhythmic montage, and even more importantly Cendrars helped to establish the genre of the *ciné-roman* with his 1919 novel *La Fin du monde filmée par l'Ange Notre-Dame* [*The End of the World Filmed by the Angel of Notre-Dame*], in which he uses a method of numbered scenes and present-tense narration comparable to that of a screenplay.[42] One section of the narrative is entitled 'Cinéma accélère et cinéma ralenti' and the novel concludes by going into reverse back to the scene where God is sitting in his office from which the action springs. Cendrars' 1923 novel *La Perle fiévreuse* [*The Feverish Pearl*] is even more explicit in its cinematic technique, numbering shots more stringently and using the terminology of panning, close-ups, half-iris, and so on. The beginning of the action proper is introduced by the warning – '*Ca, c'est du cinéma (comment on découpe une scénario.)* – that the text will be cut up like that of a screenplay.[43] Cendrars' practice is more explicit than Dos Passos'. Nevertheless, even by the time *Manhattan Transfer* was published in 1925 Dos Passos would have had plenty of opportunity to encounter Cendrars' experiments with cinematic form.

Dos Passos meets Soviet Film-Makers

In 1928 Dos Passos visited the Soviet Union and there met Eisenstein, Pudovkin and other film-makers. That same year he reported to his close friend e. e. cummings: 'the most interesting and lively people I met in Leningrad and Moscow were the movie directors'.[44] Most importantly, he met Eisenstein and discussed montage with him, writing to cummings that he was using this technique himself.[45] It is impossible to overstate the importance of Eisenstein in relation to twentieth-century US fiction. His name will recur in Chapter 7 in relation to such figures as Theodore Dreiser and Upton Sinclair, and indeed one of his earliest enterprises was a theatrical adaptation of a Jack London story.[46] In later years Dos Passos looked back on his meeting with Eisenstein as one of the most important of his life. In his 1961 essay 'Contemporary Chronicles' he recalled: 'Somewhere along the line I had been impressed by Eisenstein's documentary films like the Cruiser Potemkin. Eisenstein used to say that his master in montage was Griffith of the *Birth of a Nation* fame. Montage was the word used in those days to describe the juxtaposition of contrasting scenes in motion pictures. I took to montage to try to make the narrative stand off the page'.[47] Dos Passos is careful not to state that he only encountered montage in his discussions with Eisenstein and in interview further elaborated on their meeting: 'At the time I did *Manhattan Transfer*, I'm not sure whether I had seen Eisenstein's films. The idea of montage had an influence on the development of this sort of writing. I may have seen *Potemkin*. Then, of course, I must have seen *The Birth of a Nation*, which was the first attempt at montage'.[48] Dos Passos took care to stress that he was interested in the technique rather than the subject-matter of these film-makers, but he admitted how important this technique was to be for *U.S.A.*: 'by that time I was really taken with the idea of montage […] My hope was to achieve the objective approach of a Fielding, or a Flaubert, particularly as one sees in Flaubert's letters, which are remarkable'.[49] The meeting with Eisenstein therefore seems to have sharpened Dos Passos' interest in the cinema and encouraged him towards this stated goal of narrative objectivity already exemplified in Flaubert, a novelist who figures repeatedly in critical accounts of cinematic fiction.[50]

Dos Passos' admiration for Eisenstein was shared by the left-wing American writer Joseph Freeman, who devoted a whole chapter of his 1936 memoir *An American Testament* to the Soviet film-maker. He recalls clippings from New York about *Potemkin*, 'the first Soviet movie to make any impression in America'.[51] Just as Dos Passos praised Eisenstein's synthesizing intelligence, so Freeman recorded that Eisenstein saw himself as a 'scientific engineer whose field happened to be cinema', a stance entirely congenial to Dos Passos' notion of the writer as technician in the same decade. Eisenstein's experiment with the 'play without a hero' in which 'he was able to transfer attention away from the individual and to focus it on the entire group involved in the action' is also strikingly similar to Dos Passos' dispersal of action in *Manhattan Transfer*.[52]

The other Soviet film-maker of direct relevance to Dos Passos' practice was Dziga Vertov, who pioneered a new, experimental form of newsreel in the Kino-Eye movement. Carol Shloss has made out a circumstantial but convincing case that Vertov influenced the Camera Eye sections of *U.S.A.* 'From Vertov', she declares, Dos Passos 'took the idea of the interval, the thought that the space between fragments could invite participation, that the film-maker/writer/technician's job was to edit, to provide the juxtaposition of information that, when assembled in the viewing/reading, would lead to a recognition of the importance of each unit within the whole'.[53] Vertov asserted a quasi-mechanical role for the camera, declaring in 1923: 'I am a kino-eye, I am a mechanical eye. I, a machine, show you the world as only I see it'.[54] By animating his camera Vertov creates a startling, paradoxical effect, leaving the reader uncertain how technological is the process he describes. Certainly, as Carol Shloss noted, Vertov was at pains to show that his camera was not an eye or the eye's extension, but his aim was to go beyond the limits of individual vision. For that reason he saw his purpose as being to probe behind appearances, stating in 1929: 'Kino-eye is the documentary cinematic decoding of both the visible world and that which is invisible to the naked eye'.[55] Vertov uses the figure of decoding; Dos Passos in 'The Writer as Technician' writes of going beneath the social and cultural phenomena of the times, but the aim of both men was similar. Writing in 1936 about the impact of George Grosz, Dos Passos explains the need to break down habits of perception and assemble new entities: 'Experiments in the visual arts (the invention of new ways of seeing things), are made because, due to the way the apparatus that makes up the mind is made, old processes and patterns have continually to be broken up in order to make it possible to perceive the new aspects and arrangements of evolving consciousness'.[56] Transpose this account on to visual narratives and Dos Passos' sequence of deconstruction followed by re-assembly stands as a valuable summary of his own practice, as well as of the practice of Eisenstein and Vertov. Vertov in his 1934 diary acknowledged Dos Passos' application of his ideas: 'I am accused of corrupting Dos Passos by having infected him with kino-eye. Otherwise he might have become a good writer, some say. Others object and say that if it were not for kino-eye, we wouldn't have heard of Dos Passos'. And then Vertov gives his own explanation of the latter's cinematic fiction: 'Dos Passos' work involves a translation from film-vision into literary language. The terminology and construction are those of kino-eye'.[57]

U.S.A.: Montage, Camera Eye, Newsreels, Stardom

When the U.S.A. trilogy was published in 1938 Delmore Schwartz noted that Dos Passos had 'put the book together as a motion-picture director composes his film, by a procedure of cutting, arranging, and interposing parts'.[58] Dos Passos' own retrospective statement that he was consciously applying the notion of montage at this point in his career sheds light on his use of juxtaposition throughout and his presentation of narratives without discursive commentary. Donald Pizer and Barry Maine have both given valuable commentaries on Dos Passos' juxtapositions. Maine has noted the recurrent use of white space in the text, which he compares to cinematic cuts, and he further argues that the disconnectedness within the text reflects characters' recurring sense of lacking connection with their own history. Finally, Maine argues that in the trilogy Dos Passos uses a broadly film-like method which is 'presentational, not assertive'.[59] By this, Maine is referring to the absence of inferential commentary within the narratives and also the relative lack of thought sequences within characters' consciousnesses. In that sense, as Claude-Edmonde Magny has argued, U.S.A. is the supreme example of the 'impersonal novel'. Dos Passos' emphasis on the 'physical aspects of existence' in his characters gives them a general externality which Magny identifies with film.[60] These subsequent judgements coincide in part with the opinions of some reviewers. The English novelist Compton Mackenzie found the experience of reading Nineteen Nineteen similar to that of seeing a 'good film' and Delmore Schwartz compared the trilogy to a documentary film, with many reservations about its success, however.[61]

Dos Passos constructed the Camera Eye sections of his trilogy, he explained, 'as a safety valve for my own subjective feelings', and subsequent critical discussion has centred around how, if at all, these sections could be read as cinematic.[62] There is first of all the question of their title. As Donald Pizer has noted, this title implies a double concept of vision: 'the camera is a symbol of impersonal and "objective" depiction. But it is also possible to look through the "eye" or lens of the camera to see within the camera itself'.[63] In other words, 'camera' could signify either objectivity or its opposite. In an attempt to explore the first of these possibilities, Stephen Hock has retrospectively read René Bazin's theories into the sections, arguing that they work by synthesis.[64] Hock notes that each Camera Eye has material in parenthesis which helps to clarify and support the trilogy's main themes, but his application of Bazinian notions of cinematic objectivity would have been anathema to Dos Passos the modernist, as it was to the editors of the Paris journal *transition*. In June 1927 the latter declared: 'realism in America has reached its point of saturation. We are no longer interested in the photography of events'.[65] Nor was Dos Passos, in any straightforward sense. His use of different modes in *U.S.A.* – particularly of Camera Eye, Newsreel and biography – problematizes the very exercise of narrative presentation based on a notion of objectivity.

Examining some of the drafts for the Camera Eye sections, Carol Shloss has made out a convincing case that they echo Dziga Vertov's Kino-Eye principles in including the relation between planes, foreshortening, relations between movements and between light and shade, and varying speed of 'recording'.[66] Of the two senses of 'camera' proposed by Donald Pizer above, she tends towards the objective meaning, seeing these sections as moving well beyond the limits of an individual's vision. On the other hand, Michael North has argued that the Camera Eye sections are far less visual than they profess to be and that Dos Passos actually evokes subjectivity in separating sight from the other senses.[67] Thus we have rival arguments for objectivity and subjectivity. In fact, the Camera Eye sections enact a negotiation between these extremes.

The earliest discussions of the Camera Eye sections tended to centre on their autobiographical dimension.[68] Certainly they are linked through experiences shared by the unnamed young man (a Whitmanesque personification of the USA) and the author. There is a clear progression from childhood to mature observation. Thus Camera Eye (3) centres on a young boy travelling by train: 'O qu'il a des yeux beaux said the lady in the seat opposite but She said that was no way to talk to children and the little boy felt all hot and sticky but it was dusk and the lamp shaped like half a melon was coming on dim red and the train rumbled and suddenly I've been asleep and it's black dark and the blue tassel bobs on the edge of the dark shade shaped like a melon and everywhere there are pointed curved shadows'.[69] Every Camera Eye section gives an impression of flow by limiting punctuation to the spatial arrangement of lines. At times this flow seems to resemble the stream of consciousness and Dos Passos probably was aiming, as Eisenstein saw in Joyce, at running internal and external experience together. But this short passage makes it clear that he is also shifting round perspectives. The theme of this Camera Eye is, not surprisingly, sight. We start with the subject's eyes being under observation by another. Only after the intervention of another adult (presumably the boy's mother) does he start registering sights and other sense impressions. The time of day is dusk, but the time of the boy's life is childhood; thus his incapacity to distinguish objects clearly reflects on his limited understanding.

The sequence continues with the boy's eyes shifting outside the train; close-up details are replaced by longer shots of an industrial landscape: 'but you're peeking out of the window into the black rumbling dark suddenly ranked with squat chimneys and you're scared of the black smoke and the puffs of flame that flare and fade out of the squat chimneys
Potteries dearie they work there all night Who works there all night?'. The gap in the text clearly suggests the space of the observer's query as he tries to understand the distant alien sights. As he tries to understand, the boy's subjective status shifts from person seen (him), through observing consciousness (I) to the second-person designation as if he is watching himself. Here the main dynamic of the Camera Eye emerges. The protagonist's attempts to understand his experiences are often expressed through shifts in seeing, like the movement of his gaze here from interior to external scene. Different kinds of seeing reflect different phases in the shifting relation between the young man and the USA.

The presence of the Newsreels which frame the narrative sections of *U.S.A.* reflects Dos Passos' new-found awareness of the increasing role of the media in American life. Reporting on the 1932 Republican Convention in Chicago for the *New Republic*, Dos Passos found his attention constantly being diverted from the politicians to the technicians who were working the lights and generally directing the 'rumble and chaos' in ways which strongly reminded him of a circus. This experience pointed a moral which was all the more important because the political parties did not seem to have realized it: 'we do not appreciate yet how enormously the whole technique and machinery of politics has been changed by the mechanics of communication. The architecture of stadiums, klieg lights, radio and the imminent danger of fairly perfected television are as important a factor in future political life as committees, votes, resolutions, theories, vested interests'.[70]

This account anticipates Dos Passos' view in 1935 of the writer as embattled within the different modes of cultural production: 'newspapers, advertising offices, moving picture studios, political propaganda agencies, produce the collective type of writing where individual work is indistinguishable in the industrial effort'.[71] This statement helps to explain the special significance in *U.S.A.* of J. Ward Moorehouse, the journalist turned PR specialist whose role is to link advertising with politics, in short to produce desired images. Here is Dos Passos again reflecting on the 1932 convention:

history, or the mass mind [...] is becoming more and more involved with the apparatus of spotlights, radio, talking pictures, newsprint, so that the image-making faculty, instead of being the concern of the individual mind, is becoming a social business. The control of the radio waves is externalising thought and feeling to a hair-raising degree. A man in his shirt-sleeves handling a battery of spots can give the effect of a great wave of mass emotion in a convention hall. The possibilities of control of the mass are terrifying.[72]

Here Dos Passos unconsciously predicts the activities of Joseph Goebbels in Nazi Germany and also anticipates the means used to establish a fascist dicta-torship in Sinclair Lewis' 1935 novel *It Can't Happen Here*, in which the demagogue consolidates his power by buying up newspapers and constructing a network of television transmitters.[73]

Dos Passos' stated purpose in using the Newsreels was to 'give an inkling of the common mind of the epoch' and to 'give the clamour, the sound of daily life'.[74] It was, in other words, a contextualizing function, but one which has been criticized for misleading the reader by Michael North, who argues that the Newsreels are based on a method of collage, not montage, and that they were conceived in terms of sound.[75] North is absolutely correct about Dos Passos' method of constructing the Newsreels, which was to cut and paste or copy lines from contemporary newspapers.[76] However, the title 'Newsreel' does invite us to read these sections analogically, and here we need to consider the historical characteristics of the newsreel form. Raymond Fielding offers the following summary: 'the newsreel was a nine- or ten-minute collection of more-or-less newsworthy footage, comprising eight or nine items, each subject separated abruptly from the others by a title, all of them backed up by a noisy musical score and a high-speed, invisible narrator'.[77] Fielding makes it clear that the newsreel was a hybrid form, having a score and voice-over, as well as introductory title cards. In other words, it was to be consumed through reading and listening as well as viewing. One other factor should be borne in mind before we consider specific Newsreels in *U.S.A.*: Eisenstein's notion of montage. During a discussion of the ideogram, Eisenstein stresses that a shot is a 'cell' of montage and asks: 'By what, then, is montage characterized and, conse-quently, its cell – the shot?' His answer is categorical: 'By collision. By the conflict of two pieces in opposition to each other. By conflict. By collision'.[78] We shall now see how Dos Passos attempts to reproduce effects of the newsreels and to apply Eisenstein's principle of conflict in his writing.

The opening Newsreel of *The 42nd Parallel* (1930), the first volume of the trilogy, thematizes conflict through references to wars in South Africa and the Philippines, but really as a prelude to US appropriation of the twentieth century itself. Thus, a senator is quoted as declaring that 'the twentieth century will be American'. Dos Passos establishes the global theme to which his Newsreels will return constantly, namely the emergence of the United States as a leading political and military player on the world stage. Bearing this in mind, we can now turn to Newsreel 38 from *Nineteen Nineteen* (1932), which opens as follows:

> *C'est la lutte finale*
> *Groupons-nous et demain*
> *L'Internationale*
> *Sera le genre humain*
> FUSILLADE IN THE DIET
> Y.M.C.A. WORKERS ARRESTED FOR STEALING FUNDS
> declares wisdom of people alone can guide the nation in such an enterprise
> SAYS U.S. MUST HAVE WORLD'S GREATEST FLEET
> when I was in Italy a little limping group of wounded Italian soldiers sought an interview with me [...][79]

It is immediately obvious that Dos Passos is using different type and the spatial arrangement of items to maximize their disjunction. We have the socialist anthem quoted as an articulation of a collectivity but every item in the ensuing Newsreel pulls that notion apart, amassing instances of conflict both social and military. The part-quoted paragraph demonstrates a strategy which Dos Passos uses repeatedly in his Newsreel: the erasure of the subject and therefore the origin of different utterances. The first statement here seems to express a democratic faith in the people, but the following one (rendered in capitals, which is one way of suggesting volume) makes a crude claim to military might. This is one of many instances of 'collision' in the Newsreels whereby one voice contradicts another, or acts contradict stated aims. Dos Passos thus converts the discontinuity within the newsreel form into an ironic means of demonstrating again and again America's self-interest.

The Newsreels incorporate fragments of popular songs, fashion shows and other events on the margin of news, but here again Dos Passos was simply following common practice. Raymond Fielding quotes a spokesman for the film industry as stating that the 'newsreels have no social obligations beyond those of the amusement industry and theatres they are supposed to serve'.[80] A newsreel was therefore conceived as being an adjunct to entertainment, just as Dos Passos makes his Newsreels a kind of para-narrative, supplementing the main stories.

As the media become progressively more important in his trilogy, it is appropriate for Dos Passos to make one of his last narratives that of Margo Dowling's rise to film stardom, a narrative flanked by the biography of

Valentino. During the composition of *The Big Money* Dos Passos himself gained first-hand knowledge of Hollywood. In 1934 he was offered a writing assignment by Paramount which he took up to work with Joseph Von Sternberg on *The Devil is a Woman*, which was released in 1935 and which starred Marlene Dietrich in one of her *femme fatale* roles.[81] This experience clearly supplied Dos Passos with material for his own narrative, as we shall see.

Margo begins her career in the trilogy as an actress, but her real opportunity comes when she is taken to a photographer's studio. This is a foretaste of the cinema and of the sexual themes inseparable from film success: 'When Sam Margolies [the photographer] turned the floodlights on her, the skylight went blue, like on the stage. Then when he got to posing her in the Spanish shawl and made her take her things off and let her undies down so that she had nothing on but the shawl above the waist, she noticed that Mr A had let his cigar go out and was watching intently'.[82] Dos Passos makes it explicit that Margo is performing sexually to the male gaze; the anonymity of the observer here simply confirms his typicality. Critics have speculated about which films Dos Passos was referring to in Margo's sections but it seems more likely that he was composing a thinly disguised version of the power relationship between Von Sternberg and Dietrich (she has the same initials and a similar background in the theatre), in which the director had qualities suggestive of Svengali.[83] Shortly after this photo session Margo goes to Hollywood where she meets up with Margolies again, by now a successful film director. He now takes her in hand, organizes a screen test, and her film career is launched.

Dos Passos does not moralize this story as the exploitation of Margo's innocence. She remains unfazed by the constant sexual overtures to her. Instead, her story is a collaboration between her director and herself, made all the easier by the fact that Margolies shows real skill in bringing out her theatrical talent. Margo sees herself in mirrors constantly, as if she has become her own object of visual attention, and the results of her screen test are presented as a sequence of grotesquely enlarged self-images: 'nobody said anything as they looked at Margo's big gray and white face, grinning, turning, smirking, mouth opening and closing, head tossing, eyes rolling. It made Margo feel quite sick looking at it, though she loved still photographs of herself. She couldn't get used to its being so big'.[84] Margo is positioned here at a point of transition, where she is about to learn new and bigger images of herself. The last term of the quotation identifies the theme of the last novel in the trilogy: making it big, thinking big. Margo is herself her own most appreciative observer and for that reason Eleanor Widmer has found her a welcome relief from Dos Passos' conventional images of women: 'here conception and technique are united – the movie star plays herself, the screen image, and the personification of the American Dream simultaneously'.[85] Like J. Ward Moorehouse and a host of other characters, Margo deploys her skills with costume and behaviour towards the goal of personal success.

Dos Passos' experiences of Hollywood fed into one of his post-war novels, *Most Likely to Succeed* (1954). The protagonist Jed Morris is a thinly disguised version of Dos Passos' friend, the left-wing screenwriter John Howard Lawson. Despite his ambition to make a progressive epic modelled on *The Birth of a Nation*, Morris gets swallowed up in the Hollywood system, probably articulating in retrospect a fear which swayed Dos Passos' decision not to stay in the movie capital.

Edward Dahlberg

Dos Passos' attitude to the machine developed in sophistication during the 1920s. From *Three Soldiers* through to the beginning of the *U.S.A.* trilogy the machine started as a catch-all trope for technological and social processes threatening the individual and gradually became part of a complex recognition by Dos Passos that all American citizens were caught up in the processes of cultural production, including the cinema and the business of publishing. The machine by this point had partly become a fact of American life and this perception was shared by Edward Dahlberg, seen by some as a disciple of Dos Passos, whose first novel, *Bottom Dogs* (1929), was reviewed with Dos Passos' work. [86] The reason for this connection lay partly in Dahlberg's choice of social subjects – itinerants in search of job opportunities – and partly in the sensuous immediacy of his descriptions. A third connection was the two writers' interest in film. In *Ariel in Caliban* (1929) Dahlberg praised German expressionist film: 'The German UFA cinema productions are exploiting in full measure modern decorative art and cubist architecture both of which have arisen out of the social and economic conditions of a nature thoroughly mechanized'.[87] The final word in this passage is crucial. Like Dos Passos, Dahlberg saw mechanization as a process extending into all areas of experience. And again like Dos Passos, he saw the sites of this change as being particularly the cities. Hence, in the same essay he declares: 'everything is artifice and machinery'; and bemoans the fact that virtually no American writer has even attempted to do for the American city what Joyce had done for Dublin in *Ulysses*.[88]

In his early novels Dahlberg draws on film analogies to characterize, but not ridicule, his characters' style of behaviour, even of thought. In *Bottom Dogs* a character's slow walk is described as follows: 'he wandered hazily, slowly, his legs jerking forward automatically, as if his motions had been arrested and slowed down eight times by a moving-picture camera'.[89] In the hands of Nathanael West, this image would be pushed towards caricature, but Dahlberg is more concerned to help the reader visualize the character

Lorry's strange walk, as if it implies an ambivalence of purpose. *From Flushing to Calvary* (1932) describes an environment in which the cinema has become much more important for employment and for creating desires. The very first episode shows the protagonist Jerry Calefonia trying (unsuccessfully) to pick up a woman in a movie house; and later he is cheated in an arcade peep show. More importantly, his manner has unconscious cinematic aspects: his smile is 'like a badly projected film against a white sheet' and his thoughts flick through his mind 'newsreel-wise'.[90] Through these analogies Dahlberg implies that his characters' subjective life cannot be separated from their environment and also suggests a way of seeing them. Different aspects of their behaviour are separated out for the reader/viewer's scrutiny and Dahlberg follows a similar method when evoking New York, where the cinema signs have become part of the city's appearance: 'The moving-picture electric advertising signs flowed a sleazy nedick's chemise orange through the mist [...] Gotham gold-striped legs passed up and down. Baby highheels clicked with the precision of typewriter keys against the stone. Some linoleum tigerlilies gleamed from the window of the florist next door'.[91] Dahlberg captures the visual dynamics of the city through a serial sequence of images of artifice.

As with Dos Passos, Dahlberg's interest in the cinema did not imply a positive reaction to Hollywood. When he went to the movie capital full of expectations he was asked to 'search for a narrative for Tom Mix's horse'.[92] In *From Flushing to Calvary* the experience of his protagonist is equally absurd. The latter attends a scenario school and starts devising movie plots, including an adaptation of Wilde's *Ballad of Reading Gaol*. But he too comes up against the fashion for Westerns: 'Lorry tried to show the main reader how Universal could work *Reading Gaol* into a cowboy film'.[93] Not surprisingly, he has no success. Dos Passos' own experience of Hollywood was similarly brief, if less bizarre. Although he received a writing credit for *The Devil is a Woman*, Dos Passos became disillusioned by the endless revisions to the script, being more fascinated by the people of Hollywood who, he told e. e. cummings, were all 'on the make' but at the same time had the 'frank innocent viciousness of little children left down in study hall on a rainy afternoon'.[94] As frequently happened with American novelists, Dos Passos' dislike of Hollywood in no sense diminished his enthusiasm for the film medium.

Notes

1   Eisenstein, *Film Form*, p. 204.
2   Michael Rogin, ' "The Sword Became a Flaming Vision"', p. 157.
3   John Dos Passos, *The Major Nonfictional Prose*, p. 77.

4   Dos Passos, *The Major Nonfictional Prose*, p. 173.

5   Dos Passos, *The Major Nonfictional Prose*, p. 272.

6   Dos Passos, *The Major Nonfictional Prose*, p. 171.

7   *The Major Nonfictional Prose*, p. 278. The sentence begins with a proviso: 'I am not at all satisfied with McLuhan'.

8   Marshall McLuhan, *Understanding Media*, p. 286. McLuhan saw film as standing behind modernist experimentation in the novel: the stream of consciousness method was 'really managed by the transfer of film technique to the printed page, where, in a deep sense it really originated' (p. 295).

9   John Dos Passos, 'The Workman and His Tools', in *Occasions and Protests*, p. 5.

10 John Dos Passos, *Travel Books and Other Writings*, p. 755.

11 John Dos Passos, *Novels 1920–1925*, pp. 107–108.

12 Paul Fussell, *The Great War and Modern Memory*, p. 221. Dan Fuselli is used by Dos Passos as symptomatic movie-goer, whose consciousness is packed with film images of glamorous heroism in battle.

13 Barry Maine, ed., *Dos Passos: The Critical Heritage*, pp. 69, 75.

14 Michael Spindler has similarly argued that *Manhattan Transfer* is organized on the principle of unity from fragmentation, a principle deriving from the cinema ('John Dos Passos and the Visual Arts', p. 400).

15 John Dos Passos, 'What Makes a Novelist', in *Major Nonfictional Prose*, p. 272. Gretchen Foster notes the relevance to *Manhattan Transfer* of the experimental New York documentary film *Mannahatta* (1921), made by the painter Charles Sheeler and photographer Paul Strand. Dos Passos confirmed that he had seen the film, but exactly when remains uncertain ('John Dos Passos' Use of Film Technique', pp. 188–89).

16 Spindler, 'John Dos Passos and the Visual Arts', p. 401.

17 John Dos Passos, *The Fourteenth Chronicle* , p. 193; Spiegel, *Fiction and the Camera Eye*, p. 177.

18 Spiegel, *Fiction and the Camera Eye*, p. 65.

19 Spiegel, *Fiction and the Camera Eye*, pp. 66, 96.

20 James Joyce, *Ulysses*, p. 212.

21 Dos Passos, *Novels 1920–1925*, p. 563.

22 Cecelia Tichi comments in relation to William Carlos Williams and his contemporaries that 'much of twentieth-century life for poet and populace alike was experienced in passing glimpses from the train, from the elevated, from the automobile' (*Shifting Gears*, p. 247). Train-journey narratives figure in William Carlos Williams' *In the Money* (1940).

23 Leo Charney, *Empty Moments*, p. 52. Charney's study provides a valuable discussion of how Walter Benjamin's commentaries on film related to modernism.

24 Dos Passos' term 'raindark' is a clear Joycean allusion to the Homeric epithet 'winedark' as applied to the sea and then taken through different permutations in *Ulysses*.

25 Eisenstein, *Film Form*, pp. 184–85. Eisenstein met Joyce in 1930 and recorded that Joyce was 'intensely interested in my plans for the inner film-monologue' (*Film Form*, p. 104). Joyce for his part considered that Eisenstein was virtually the only man capable of making a film of *Ulysses*. The American poet and novelist Louis Zukofsky also worked up a number of cinematic treatments of *Ulysses* and submitted them to Joyce.

26 Dos Passos, *Novels 1920–1925*, p. 490.

27 Dos Passos, *The Major Nonfictional Prose*, p. 174.

28 Dos Passos, *Novels 1920–1925*, p. 488.

29 Carol Shloss, *In Visible Light*, p. 148. Shloss makes the valid point that there is currency of photographs in *Manhattan Transfer* but then rashly claims that Dos Passos saw the

photograph as a 'model for his narrative art' (p. 144). This is to ignore the dynamics of cinematic narrative and also Dos Passos' own admission in 1934 that American writers rest content with superficial images: 'we do the snapshot, the silhouette, the true-to-life spittin' image very well, but that is as different from the real invention of a personality out of the tangle of functions, sense reactions, memories, habits that are observable in the people we know, as a photograph is different from the person photographed' ('The Business of a Novelist', in *The Major Nonfictional Prose*, p. 160).

30 Janet Gallignani Casey, *Dos Passos and the Ideology of the Feminine*, p. 119.

31 Dos Passos, *Novels 1920–1925*, p. 811.

32 Eisenstein, *Film Form*, pp. 49, 92.

33 Cf. 'The spectator not only sees the represented elements of the finished work, but also experiences the dynamic process of the emergence and assembly of the image just as it was experienced by the author' (Eisenstein, *The Film Sense* [in *Film Form*; separately paginated], p. 32).

34 Dos Passos, *Novels 1920–1925*, p. 664.

35 Nathan Asch, *Pay Day*, p. 154. Asch's *The Office* (1925) was compared by a reviewer with *Manhattan Transfer* in its use of short sketches. In the 1930s Asch served as a scriptwriter for Paramount. Rita Barnard sees this novel as making a diagnosis of the passive spectatorial attitude induced by the modern city ('Modern American Fiction', pp. 42–43).

36 Asch, *Pay Day*, p. 172.

37 For valuable comment on the relation between these two writers, see William Dow, 'John Dos Passos, Blaise Cendrars, and the "Other" Modernism'.

38 Dos Passos, *The Major Nonfictional Prose*, p. 134. Dos Passos noted gloomily that the segmentation of texts in prose and poetry had degenerated into a 'parlour entertainment for high-school English classes'.

39 Blaise Cendrars, *La Perle fiévreuse*, p. 165. Cf. Shi, 'Transatlantic Visions', p. 586.

40 Cendrars, *La Perle fiévreuse*, p. 163.

41 Cendrars here simply narrows down his general view of America. Elsewhere he wrote: 'Pour un homme d'aujourd'hui, les Etats-Unis offrent un des plus beaux spectacles du monde' ['for a man of today, the United States offers one of the most beautiful spectacles in the world']; Cendrars, *La Perle fiévreuse*, p. 169.

42 Eric Robertson, 'Writing the Alphabet of Cinema: Blaise Cendrars', in Murphet and Rainford, eds., *Literature and Visual Technologies*, pp. 142–43, 148–49. Robertson argues that as early as *Panama* (the poem translated by Dos Passos) Cendrars was using a technique of cuts and montage signalled through references to guillotining in the poem: 'The slicing motion and clicking sound of the blade evokes the act of splicing and the cinematic cut that generates movement' (p. 140). *La Perle fiévreuse* (1921–22) was even more explicit in its analogies between narrative and cinema.

43 Cendrars, *La Perle fiévreuse*, p. 17.

44 Dos Passos, *The Fourteenth Chronicle*, p. 386.

45 Virginia Spencer Carr, *Dos Passos: A Life*, p. 244. At this meeting Eisenstein recommended the Japanese Kabuki theatre to Dos Passos and also expressed his misgivings about the coming of sound to the cinema. Dos Passos declared to cummings that he and Eisenstein 'agreed thoroughly about the importance of montage' (*The Fourteenth Chronicle*, p. 180).

46 *The Mexican* (1920–21) was an adaptation made for the First Workers' Theatre, where Eisenstein designed the sets.

47 Dos Passos, *The Major Nonfictional Prose*, p. 239. (Eisenstein's film was first shown in the USA in 1926 under the title *The Armoured Cruiser Potemkin*.) In *Film Form* Eisenstein

recorded that the impact of Griffith on Soviet film-makers was nothing less than a 'revelation' and paid tribute to the latter's pioneering of montage (pp. 201, 204). *The Birth of a Nation* is virtually the only film to be named in Dos Passos' *U.S.A.* and is one which has a powerful impact on the young couple who see it.

48 Dos Passos, *The Major Nonfictional Prose*, p. 247.

49 *The Major Nonfictional Prose*, p. 247.

50 The other writer who appears in the same context is Stephen Crane. Dos Passos had been an enthusiastic reader of Crane throughout his life and numbered *The Red Badge of Courage* among his favourite novels.

51 Joseph Freeman, *An American Testament*, p. 497. Charlie Chaplin described *Potemkin* as 'the best film in the world' and the reviewer for *Photoplay* claimed that it represented a 'primitive newsreel' though it contained sequences of great beauty (Richard Taylor, *The Battleship Potemkin: The Film Companion*, p. 117).

52 Freeman, *An American Testament*, p. 499.

53 Shloss, *In Visible Light*, pp. 158–59.

54 Annette Michelson, ed. *Kino-Eye*, p. 17.

55 Michelson, ed., *Kino-Eye*, p. 87.

56 John Dos Passos, 'Grosz Comes to America', in *The Major Nonfictional Prose*, p. 177.

57 Michelson, ed., *Kino-Eye*, p. 174.

58 Maine, ed., *Dos Passos: The Critical Heritage*, p. 184.

59 Barry Maine, 'Dos Passos and the Rhetoric of History', in Donald Pizer, ed., *John Dos Passos' U.S.A.: A Documentary Volume*, pp. 170, 172, 174. Donald Pizer's comments on juxtaposition can be found in his *Dos Passos' U.S.A.: A Critical Study*, p. 91. The latter is an invaluable study of the trilogy.

60 Magny, *The Age of the American Novel*, pp. 109, 119. Magny's comment on the impersonality of *U.S.A.* would apply equally well to an imitation of Dos Passos by the British novelist John Brunner. The latter's futuristic *Stand on Zanzibar* (1969) follows Dos Passos' method of sectionalizing his narrative in segments labelled 'Continuity', 'Tracking with Closeups', etc. Brunner acknowledged his debt to Dos Passos' *Midcentury* 'because it's the one in which […] his technique of documentary is most highly evolved' ('The Genesis of *Stand on Zanzibar* and Digressions', p. 36).

61 Maine, ed., *Dos Passos: The Critical Heritage*, pp. 109, 177. Schwartz reads the trilogy as an ultimate, self-fragmenting exercise in naturalism.

62 Dos Passos, *The Major Nonfictional Prose*, p. 247.

63 Pizer, *Dos Passos' U.S.A.: A Critical Study*, p. 56.

64 Stephen Hock, '"Stories Told Sideways Out of the Big Mouth"'.

65 'Suggestions for a New Magic', in Noel Riley Fitch, ed., *in transition*, p. 23.

66 Shloss, *In Visible Light*, pp. 160–61.

67 North, *Camera Works*, pp. 145–46.

68 See James N. Westerhoven, 'Autobiographical Elements in the Camera Eye'; Townsend Ludington, 'The Ordering of the Camera Eye in *U.S.A.*'; Donald Pizer, 'The Camera Eye in *U.S.A.*'.

69 John Dos Passos, *U.S.A.*, p. 36.

70 John Dos Passos, 'Washington and Chicago II', p. 179A.

71 Dos Passos, *The Major Nonfictional Prose*, p. 169.

72 Dos Passos, 'Washington and Chicago II', p. 179B.

73 Lewis includes a religious broadcaster based on Father Coughlin, who through his weekly programme on CBS denounced Roosevelt and the Jews for the social ills of America. Lewis' dictator introduces nation-wide TV broadcasting in 1937.

74 Dos Passos, *The Major Nonfictional Prose*, pp. 179, 283.

75 North, *Camera Works*, p. 143.

76 For more on the composition of the Newsreels, see Donald G. England, 'The Specific Sources of Newsreel I, *The 42nd Parallel*, in Pizer, ed., *John Dos Passos' U.S.A.: A Documentary Volume*, pp. 127–33.

77 Raymond Fielding, *The March of Time, 1935–1956*, p. 3. The first US newsreel was Pathé, which started in 1911. By the mid-1920s the five major US newsreel companies were Pathé, Fox Movietone, Universal, Hearst International, and Paramount. These dominated the world market.

78 Eisenstein, *Film Form*, p. 37.

79 Dos Passos, *U.S.A.*, p. 668.

80 Fielding, *The March of Time*, p. 6.

81 This film was praised for its lavish visual effects and was the last collaboration between Dietrich and Von Sternberg

82 *U.S.A.*, p. 999. In *The Devil is a Woman* Dietrich plays a Spanish costume role.

83 The scenario which Margolies composes for Margo has been compared to Von Sternberg's *Morocco* (1930), but there Dietrich again plays the *femme fatale* whereas in Margolies' scenario Margo is offered a straight romantic lead.

84 *U.S.A.*, p. 1056.

85 Eleanor Widmer, 'The Lost Girls of *U.S.A.*: Dos Passos' '30s Movie', in Pizer, ed., *John Dos Passos's U.S.A.: A Documentary Volume*, p. 280. Justin Edwards ('The Man with a Camera Eye') strikes a more moralistic note in seeing the transformation of Margo into a marketable product. Clara Juncker has taken Margot to be the last in a series of star figures in Dos Passos' writing and a character he uses to satirize the emptiness of the post-war generation's pursuit of illusion ('Dos Passos' Movie Star').

86 Edmund Wilson reviewed *Bottom Dogs* with *The 42nd Parallel*, and D. H. Lawrence with *Manhattan Transfer*: Maine, ed., *Dos Passos: The Critical Heritage*, pp. 84, 74.

87 Edward Dahlberg, *Bottom Dogs, From Flushing to Calvary, Those Who Perish, etc.*, p. 132. This is a multi-work volume which for convenience will be cited as the Dahlberg Omnibus.

88 Dahlberg Omnibus (*Ariel in Caliban*), p. 133.

89 Dahlberg Omnibus (*Bottom Dogs*), p. 206.

90 Dahlberg Omnibus (*From Flushing to Calvary*), pp. 333, 343.

91 Dahlberg Omnibus (*From Flushing to Calvary*), p. 429.

92 Edward Dahlberg, *The Confessions of Edward Dahlberg*, p. 114.

93 Dahlberg Omnibus (*From Flushing to Calvary*), p. 363.

94 Carr, *Dos Passos: A Life*, p. 331.

8

Dreiser, Eisenstein and Upton Sinclair

Dreiser on Film

In addition to sharing Dos Passos' conviction that film should inform representations of society in his novels, Theodore Dreiser's interest in the cinema had a long history, as has been partly acknowledged by three critics.[1] In 1928 Dreiser published an article about Mack Sennett in which he records that he had been an enthusiastic viewer of his films since 1910.[2] In 1938 Dreiser wrote to Sergei Eisenstein, whom he had met in Moscow ten years earlier, declaring: 'ever since the inception of the moving picture technique, I have looked on it as an artistic medium far surpassing for most expressive purposes, writing, painting and the other arts, and I have hoped that my own work could be satisfactorily translated into it'.[3]

The first signs of this interest begin to show themselves in Dreiser's writings of the 1910s, although it is important to recognize that even earlier, around the turn of the century, he had expressed a related fascination with photography, writing articles on Alfred Stieglitz and the Camera Club of New York.[4] In a letter of 1914 to H. L. Mencken (by then a close friend), he discussed the scene divisions in 'The Born Thief', a script he had submitted to Pathé for consideration, and the following year he told Mencken that he had been approached about becoming scenario director for Mirror Films, 'a new and somewhat imposing film corporation'.[5] Dreiser was so enthusiastic about this idea that he asked Mencken to suggest a subject for his first production. At the same time he was recording in his diaries films of note which he had seen. In 1917 he praised Clara Kimball Young's performance in *Magda* and in 1920 expressed his admiration for D. W. Griffith's *The Idol Dancer*: 'the best film I have seen in a long time. Shows what may be done'.[6] Despite this praise, Dreiser later objected to seeing Griffith as a 'great creative director'.[7]

1920 was important for Dreiser's pursuit of film projects. In that year he moved to Hollywood with his wife-to-be Helen Richardson, who was looking for an acting job. After a series of minor roles as an extra she secured supporting roles in *The Flame of Youth* (1920) and Rudolph Valentino's first film *The Four Horsemen of the Apocalypse* (1921).[8] Although he was at first enthusiastic about her venture, Dreiser's sexual jealousy quickly got the better of him and Richardson's acting career was cut rudely short. At the same time, Dreiser was himself busy with movie projects throughout 1920. He sketched out 'Lady Bountiful, Jr.', a 'film adaptation of a proposed novel' on the theme of disinheritance for which there was a chance of support by Mary Pickford; and he wrote further screenplays, including 'The Choice' on a young woman falsely convicted on a vice charge and 'The Door of the Trap' about a girl falsely convicted of theft.[9] He seems to have approached these tasks as hack work for the studios, not to be taken seriously.[10]

Never one to lose an opportunity to capitalize on potentially publishable material, Dreiser drew on Helen Richardson's reports of life at the studios in a four-part article for the film journal *Shadowland*, which appeared under the umbrella title of 'Hollywood: Its Morals and Manners' in 1921–22.[11] In these pieces he took a sociological approach, commenting on the difficulties of getting into the business and stressing the prime importance of dress and make-up, a factor which links the cinema retrospectively with Dreiser's 1900 novel *Sister Carrie*. Perhaps with one eye on Helen Richardson, Dreiser concentrates on the predicament of the young woman who sooner or later will fall sexual prey to those in a position to advance her fortunes. In the second essay, 'The Commonplace Tale with a Thousand Endings', Dreiser outlines the case of one Cerise (i.e. 'cherry', a sexual innocent) 'all aflame with what it means to be a star or within the ranks of those who may reasonably aspire to stellar honours'.[12] He offers the reader a generic story of the would-be star and then invites us to complete it after stressing the mercenary nature of the film business, mercenary in the sexual sense that Cerise will never get on unless she supplies the quid for the directors' quo. In placing this emphasis Dreiser was (probably unconsciously) echoing the warnings in early Hollywood fiction against what John Springer has called the negative myth of 'Hollywood the Destroyer'.[13]

At the time of writing these articles Dreiser was trying to work out his attitude towards the cinema, no easy matter for him because he had to weigh up factors as diverse as the commercial exploitation of actresses, the studios' treatment of writers, and the prurient appeal of films masked by Puritanism. No doubt with the 1918 prosecution of his novel *The 'Genius'* for supposed obscenity on his mind, Dreiser wrote to the journalist Charles Boni in 1921 to attack the hypocrisy of the average 'decent' American, whose interest in the movies was far from aesthetic: 'He still forms, daily, outside some fourth rate moving picture palace block-long queues wherein he waits patiently, for hours, if need be, in order to be permitted to see Blossom Springtime or Cerise Fudge illustrate, or so he thinks, the honour, virtue, heroism, self-sacrifice, charity, etc., of American manhood and womanhood. His real, yet self denied purpose, is to view Cerise and as many of her ilk as may be, in a state of smirking nudity'.[14]

However much Dreiser railed against the commercialism and shoddiness of Hollywood, he never lost faith in the possibilities of the film medium, in 1920 looking to it to lift American culture out of its doldrums. That year he explained to a correspondent:

> Despite many defects I think the movies show more of an advance than do our current books and plays. As I see most books and plays they are somewhat more sensibly interpreted in the films than on the stage or between the cheap paper covers. Some moving picture directors appear to have more brains and taste than the authors whose work they interpret. Yet this is not a clean bill of health for the movies by any means. They have a long way to go. Yet they do give some evidence of being on their way. The trouble with the movies as they stand and apparently must remain is that they are a composite of minds and borrowed ideas. But even so they are in the main truer to fact than the current books and plays from which they are taken.[15]

Dreiser does not share Fitzgerald's apocalyptic gloom that the movies will supersede the novel; however, he is clearly trying to work out the relation between the two media. Note how the sentences follow an 'on-the-one-hand, on-the-other-hand' sequence. Much later, in 1936, as the mass media proliferated, Dreiser began to take a gloomier view of the future for the novel, declaring 'I have a feeling that the novel is dying not only because of multiplicity but because of the movies, the radio and what is sure to be, television'.[16]

There does not seem to have been any point in Dreiser's career at which he finally sorted out his view of the cinema. In an article of 1932, 'The Real Sins of Hollywood', he returned to his assertion that film had more in common with the novel than the theatre: 'I believe that motion pictures offer great possibilities as a medium of art. The pictorial effects on the screen are real, while those on the stage, especially outdoor scenery, are artificial. The camera can interpret as well as create by moving rapidly to any idea or place in the world. In that respect a movie is more like a novel than is the limited legitimate drama'.[17] So much for the theory. The bulk of his article, however, addresses the commercial side of Hollywood. Citing his own trouble with Paramount over the adaptation of *An American Tragedy* – of which more later – he attacks Hollywood for dumbing down films to make them popular, discusses cases in which adaptations have ruined masterpieces, and takes the star system to task for type-casting. Quixotically, he proposes that each outstanding actor should be reserved 'for at least one superior production a year'.[18] There is no sign that Dreiser's suggestion was acted on.

Dreiser's attitude to the cinema seems to have been similar to that of his long-standing friend, H. L. Mencken. Although Mencken included aspects of the cinema in his attacks on American popular taste, it was the sensation-alizing of Hollywood that he particularly ridiculed. A 1927 interview in *Photoplay* promised 'The Low-down on Hollywood', but in fact gave a serious meditation on the problems facing the studios: 'the movie folks are on the hooks of a sad dilemma', he declared. 'In order to meet the immense cost of making a gaudy modern film they have to make it appeal to a gigantic audience. And in order to appeal to a gigantic audience they have to keep it within a narrow range of ideas and emotions, fatal to genuine ingenuity. Soon or late the movies will have to split into two halves. There will be movies for the mob, and there will be movies for the relatively civilized minority'.[19] Like Dreiser, Mencken criticized popular cinema and the cult of stardom (he described the world of cinema-going as 'Moronia'), but respected the new possibilities in the medium itself.[20]

The main event of the 1920s concerning Dreiser's interest in film was his visit to Russia in 1927–28 when he met the film-maker Sergei Eisenstein. Dreiser had been invited as a literary celebrity to attend the anniversary celebrations of the Russian Revolution and went armed with letters of intro-duction from the American Communist writer Joseph Freeman. Dreiser set off to meet Eisenstein with the best of dispositions towards Soviet films, 'in my humble opinion most of them far superior to our American or Hollywood product'.[21] Throughout his stay in the Soviet Union Dreiser had misgivings over the extent of government regulation and the cinema was no exception, although he did recognize the value of subsidies. The main focus in the two men's discussion centred on the notion of drama. Here is Dreiser summa-rizing Eisenstein:

> His theory was that what is best and greatest in the movies is, first, no plot, no dramatic stories, but pictures which are more nearly poems; and second, no professional actors but rather people direct from the streets or places where the pictures are to be taken [...] This method is entirely possible because at no time in connection with his work does he plan extensive or dramatic scenes but rather chooses to portray the ordinary daily life of the world about him, its natural drama.[22]

Although Dreiser was impressed by the products of this theory of demotic naturalism, praising Eisenstein's film of village development *The General Line*, he nevertheless decided that Eisenstein was undervaluing less 'utili-tarian' films such as *The Cabinet of Dr. Caligari* and countered his notion of drama with the following: 'I said to Eisenstein that I still considered the drama of the individual to come first – his personal trials, terrors, and delights – since only through the individual could the mass and its dreams be sensed and interpreted. But with this he would not agree'.[23] We shall see in the discussion of film adaptations of *An American Tragedy* that the differences between the two men were not as stark as Dreiser's account suggests. In his diary he records how he pointed out to Eisenstein the existence of documentaries such as *Nanook of the North* (1922) and Westerns such as *The Iron Horse* (1924) and *The Covered Wagon* (1923).[24] Despite their disagreements, Dreiser was very impressed by Eisenstein's 'intellectual fire' and his capacity to seize on diverse material which could be applied to the cinema.

Dreiser's meeting with Eisenstein was not his sole encounter with Soviet cinema during his visit. He subsequently went to the Sovkino studios in Leningrad where he was shown a film of rural life in Russia among others. Of this he noted: 'a really beautiful picture – the best cinema photography I have ever seen. I want to have it shown in America'.[25] On his second visit to the same studios he saw Pudovkin's *Storm over Asia* ('the photography is good and the general technique very good') and Olga Preobranzhenskaya's *Women of Ryazan*, which made him rise to new heights of enthusiasm. 'The second picture is a gem', he recorded. 'I have never seen more beautiful photography. The story is compelling, the characters and scenes very realistic'. In his diary he recorded the plot in detail and concluded that its only flaw was a scene showing the government's intervention in the community: 'Except for the little incident of the Soviet children's home in the picture, it is artistically perfect. The sweep of the grain fields rippling in the sunlight, the villagers in their picturesque costumes, the village streets, make lovely pictures. And like every serious picture of Sovkino, it has its social purpose'.[26] The visual authenticity of scenes and the question of social purpose we shall see again as figuring in *An American Tragedy*, whose filming will be discussed later. Indeed, coming so soon after the publication of the novel in 1925, Dreiser's comments on Soviet film help to clarify the principles underlying his own work.

The cinema remained a constant concern for Dreiser throughout the 1930s. Partly this was shown in his recurrent suspicions of plagiarism. Had MGM stolen the plot of *Wonder of Women* (1929) from *The 'Genius'*? Had Warner Brothers taken *Second Choice* (1930) from a short story of his? Had Universal stolen from *Jennie Gerhardt* for their own *Back Street* (1932)?[27] The questions multiplied to the point of paranoia, perhaps reflecting an underlying fear of failure on Dreiser's part, especially after he lost the Nobel Prize to Sinclair Lewis in 1930. Nevertheless, Dreiser's appetite for cinematic schemes continued unabated. In 1930 he suggested a film for Paramount 'based on the activities of Jesuits in opening up the country' and in 1934 came up with ideas of scripts for Lillian Gish and others.[28] That same year he was discussing an adaptation of *A Gallery of Women*.[29] In all these cases Dreiser shows an anxiety to protect the artistic value and integrity of his works, as well as his financial interests. Hence his complaint to Eisenstein in 1938 that he was disgusted with the US movie industry 'because of their cheap commercialism and toadying to the lowest and most insignificant tastes'.[30]

The other strand to Dreiser's cinematic activities was his continued engagement with social subjects. He contributed a prologue to a 1933 newsreel compilation on Tom Mooney, who had wrongly been accused of a bombing in 1916.[31] The following year he enrolled Sherwood Anderson, John Dos Passos and Carl Van Vechten in producing a series of radical film scenarios but the scheme came to nothing.[32] One of the few projects to have a tangible result started in 1932 when Dreiser began gathering material towards a screenplay on the 1906–1907 revolt by Kentucky tobacco producers against the tobacco trust. Like Upton Sinclair with his *Que Viva Mexico!*, Dreiser wanted to make it an independent production to avoid the studios' preference for love stories. Taking with him the New York playwright Hy Kraft 'to verify the background and locale', Dreiser visited key locations and interviewed any locals who could remember the conflict.[33] Dreiser subsequently wrote up the scenario from his notes in 1933 and took pride in the fact that it would be the product of serious research. Writing to a Russian correspondent in 1934 who was evidently confusing this project (to be called *Tobacco*) with Erskine Caldwell's *Tobacco Road*, Dreiser explained: 'my scenario relates to what amounted to a tobacco revolt on the part of several thousand tobacco farmers, which occurred in eastern Kentucky and western Virginia some twenty-five years ago. My scenario is the result of personal investigation, not only of the history of the case, but of the actual conditions in Kentucky and Virginia at that time'.[34] Dreiser planned *Tobacco* to dramatize events within a certain phase of American commercial development. In his foreword he wrote: 'It will involve not only what is common in American life – the aggressive and dynamic plans and actions of a certain group of American industrial leaders, practical and of course ruthless in their approach to the lesser individual and his life – but what is rarer: the sudden and very dynamic reaction of these same minor and oppressed individuals who, finding themselves inequitably treated, proceed to fight and in such a way as to involve them in civil war'.[35]

Although Dreiser expressed interest in a Russian production, in the event this film was never made, but in the early 1960s Dreiser's papers were offered to the Mississippi novelist Borden Deal, who published a novel based on them in 1965 with the title *The Tobacco Men*. Deal's narrative follows conventional realism without ever exploring the filmic potential of the story – with one exception. When the organizer of local opposition to the trust hears of the first attempt at intimidation by the Trust he suddenly visualizes it:

Dr. Amos saw the whole scene as vividly as if he had been present. The quiet crossroads settlement, not a light showing, sleeping in the peaceful night. On the road the muffled sound of hoofbeats as the small party of men came closer. Perhaps a dog had barked a warning of the approach of strangers; but the settlement slept on, secure in the peaceful knowledge that no one could mean them harm. Perhaps the men on the horses had paused and clustered before launching the animals into the midnight charge. The sudden drum of hoofbeats as the horses raced at full gallop through the intersection, people rousing in their sleep at the unexpected sound; then the fusillade of shots, sharp and deadly in the stillness, the hail of bullets shattering glass, thunking into wood. An instant's terror, old wartime fears aroused; but in a minute it was over, the sounds of the horses receding into the distance.[36]

For a rare moment in this novel the reader is positioned as an imaginary witness to a scene which depends on its secrecy (i.e. on the *absence* of witnesses) for its effect. We are placed outside but near the settlement, at a fixed point which can be passed by the riders, and thus we register it not just as an attack but as an echo of the none-too-distant Civil War.

Scene and Image in *An American Tragedy*: America's Visual Culture

Although it predates Dreiser's interest in the cinema, *Sister Carrie* (1900) is an important precursor work in its examination of appearance. When Carrie arrives in Chicago at the beginning of the novel she is drawn immediately to one of the most eye-catching signs of the modern metropolis – its department stores. Throughout the novel clothes offer a means of constituting social selves, something which Carrie dimly senses: 'Not only did Carrie feel the drag of desire for all which was new and pleasing in apparel for women, but she noticed too, with a touch at the heart, the fine ladies who elbowed and ignored her, brushing past in utter disregard of her presence, themselves eagerly enlisted in the materials which the store contained'.[37]

In her discussion of turn-of-the-century consumerist fiction, Rachel Bowlby has suggested that the transformation of merchandise into spectacle anticipates the cinema in the way in which spectacle suppresses the mechanisms of production.[38] The comparison applies well to Dreiser's novel, which shows Carrie both as potential consumer and as worker or producer. It is impossible to overstate the importance of clothes – the outward sign of the social self – in this novel, in which status is measured in terms of appearance. The nearest Dreiser comes to giving us a seduction scene is focused through a close-up on the traveller Drouet's hand closing over Carrie's: 'He pressed her hand gently and she tried to withdraw it. At this he held it fast, and she no longer protested. Then he slipped the greenbacks he had into her palm.'[39] The moment is sexually charged, but is not encoded as Victorian melodrama where seduction would involve loss. Instead, Drouet is enabling Carrie, offering her the means of purchasing clothes and therefore of constructing a new self. As Bowlby notes, clothes signify possibilities, but also risk, since the materially constituted self turns out to be unstable. Carrie herself becomes an image, a celebrity 'for others to emulate and envy'.[40] Years before the term was used ('star' in the context of the movies became current in the mid-1910s), Carrie becomes a 'star' of society and of the theatre, which, for Tim Armstrong, is a direct result of Dreiser's use of electric lighting and eye-play.[41] Throughout *Sister Carrie* allusions to the theatre and acting are used to denote the performatory dimension to the self and the notion of society as spectacle, especially in locations such as Broadway.

An American Tragedy develops the methods of *Sister Carrie* in a more cinematographic direction: indeed, part of the later novel was written while Dreiser was staying in Hollywood.[42] This helps to explain why the cinema should be written into the novel as a new source of entertainment. The protagonist Clyde Griffiths spends his first money on the movies and, ironically, his mother later uses the cinema as a means of appealing for her son's life. One of the first critics to recognize that the novel itself has a cinematic dimension was the novelist Robert Penn Warren, who asserted that, apart from its verbal style, 'there is the language of unfolding scenes [...] the language of the imagery of enactment, with all its primitive massiveness – the movie in our heads, with all the entailed questions of psychological veracity and subtlety, of symbolic densities and rhythmic complexities'.[43] In most examples of cinematographic fiction considered in this study the film analogy encourages economy of expression, but not in Dreiser's case. As Eisenstein wryly noted when adapting it for the screen, Dreiser's text was verbose in the extreme. His use of image, therefore, does not replace narrative commentary but rather highlights moments of drama within a large unfolding action.

Dreiser explained the structure of *An American Tragedy* as consisting of three phases: a presentation of social miseries, Clyde's confrontation with a 'much more fortunate world', and the resulting effects on his temperament.[44] The relation between Books 1 and 2 therefore is one of contrast, thesis and antithesis. The novel opens with a description of Clyde's family making its way across Kansas City to take up a spot for a religious meeting. The human figures are dwarfed by the huge city blocks, the signs of modernity scarcely relevant to them, and they move *across* the traffic as if at odds with the main direction of contemporary city life. The young Clyde walks with his eyes downcast and this is a crucial symbolic detail because it suggests that he has not yet come alive as an independent being. Ellen Moers has rightly drawn attention to this aspect of the narrative, arguing that 'at every important twist of the narrative Dreiser gives us a "closeup" of Clyde's face; and in that face it is the eyes that speak better than the mouth the tale of Clyde's desire'.[45]

An American Tragedy is a tale which measures the vitality of its protagonist in visual terms and which from a very early stage alerts the reader to scrutinize appearances. Clyde comes gradually to consciousness as he lifts his gaze to look beyond the restricted space of his parents' life. Ironically, the mission where they live is called 'The Door of Hope' but it offers no material possibilities at all. It is only when Clyde has moved away from his family that hope begins to emerge. Books 1 and 2 are full of doors which open to Clyde, disclosing new sights like the 'moving panorama' of a hotel lobby: 'It was all so lavish. Under his feet was a checkered black-and-white marble floor. Above him a coppered and stained and gilded ceiling [...] And between the columns which ranged away toward three separate entrances, one right, one left and one directly forward toward Dalrymple Avenue – were lamps, statuary, rugs, palms, chairs, divans, tete-a-tetes – a prodigal display'.[46] It is as if Clyde has entered an elaborate stage or film set. Notice how the columns give perspective, opening up routes before the young man, and of course the overwhelming impression is one of wealth. In Sister Carrie we saw how desire was fed by the city department stores. Now it is fed by more diverse locations, but all linked though the notion of spectacle. The key term in the passage just quoted is 'display'. Things are arranged for the comforts of the hotel customers and a repeated rhythm in An American Tragedy is of such scenes tantalizing Clyde by their difficulty of access. Every location in the first two books of An American Tragedy is assessed by Clyde in terms of its material wealth and promise.

Carrie Meeber is seduced by the need for a new coat. Clyde too is drawn to clothes for the possibilities they open up. Here, as in his first novel, Dreiser links clothes to theatre, luxury, and sexuality in such a way that one becomes an aspect of the other. Take the early example of Hortense, a coquettish poseur who observes herself in mirrors while posturing to her male audience. The gendering of the novel's overall point of view, for the first two books at any rate, is clearly masculine since all young women are assessed sexually in terms of figure, style and features. Hortense is no exception. She dresses up strikingly to go to the theatre with Clyde, an erotic display of intimacy which he quickly internalizes as mental cinema: 'At night, in his bed at home, he would lie and think of her – her face – the expressions of her mouth and eyes, the lines of her figure, the motions of her body in walking or dancing – and she would flicker before him as upon a screen'.[47] Film offers him a means of visualizing imaginary erotic encounters with Hortense in which she is performing only for Clyde. Unfortunately, she has other admirers and she too draws on film in composing her appearance. In one scene 'on her left cheek, just below her small rouged mouth, she had pasted a minute square of black court plaster in imitation of some picture beauty she had seen'.[48]

In Book 2 of *An American Tragedy* two changes occur in Clyde's visualization of himself and others. For Ellen Moers he is 'reduced to a look and a shadow', though this puts it too baldly and suggests that Clyde is becoming desubstantialized.[49] As we saw in *Sister Carrie*, the material constitution of a character's self can be notoriously unstable. Clyde's desire at this point is to acquire the wealth to buy expensive clothes which in turn will secure his visual status in local society, but the closer he approaches this goal the more he comes to resemble someone else: his cousin Gilbert. In that sense he becomes a 'shadow' since he is constantly being mistaken for his rich relative.

The killing of Roberta arises from a fracturing of Clyde's social life whereby Roberta's pregnancy makes it impossible for him to jettison her in favour of the dizzy social heights offered by Sondra. Once again clothes signal a clear visual distinction. When Clyde first sees Roberta, she is wearing a rather shabby dress, whereas Sondra is associated with whiteness, bright colours and crystal. As Roberta becomes increasingly defined by her pregnancy, in Clyde's eyes a biological confirmation of her socio–economic stasis, Sondra comes to resemble a fairy played off against Roberta's transformation into a 'spectre'.

As these two figures polarize in Clyde's imagination and Roberta's killing approaches, Dreiser begins to make increasing use of montage in his narrative. Initially this is done through a dialogue between the rival voices of desire and conscience; then images come to oppose one another, as in the following juxtaposition between flying birds and Clyde's emerging plan:

(Those five birds winging toward that patch of trees over there – below that hill.)
It certainly would not do to go direct to Big Bittern from Utica for a boat ride – just one day – seventy miles. That would not sound right to her, or to anyone.[50]

The birds give us an image of free, direct movement which contrasts proleptically with Clyde's mapping out of their journey to the lake. We still have an implicit dialogue of images, now between external nature and Clyde's plan of action. As the moment of the killing draws ever nearer, he seems gradually to lose contact with this outside world. At the point of killing we are given a shot/reverse-shot where we look at Clyde through Roberta's eyes: 'in the meantime his eyes – the pupils of the same growing momentarily larger and more lurid; his face and body and hands tense and contracted [suggesting] the imminence of trance or spasm'.[51] The drama focuses on Clyde's psychology, not the fate of his victim. As the point of view swings round to his, he pushes Roberta with a camera so that the very instrument used by tourists to preserve moments of pleasure turns into a fatal instrument. Visually the reader/viewer is embedded in the scene, which is rendered with powerful immediacy without, however, losing its essential ambiguity.

In his essay 'Life, Art and America' Dreiser waxes indignant against the puritanism of American life which criminalizes sexual activity and which condemns media such as theatre and cinema as leading to vice: 'the theatre was an institution which led to crime, the saloon a centre of low, even bestial vices. The existence of such a thing as an erring or fallen woman, let alone a house of prostitution, was a crime, scarcely a fact to be considered. There were forms and social appearances which we were taught to wear, quite as one wears a suit of clothes'.[52] We have seen how important clothes are in Dreiser's novels as signs of the wearer's prosperity. Here he presents them as metaphors of social concealment, the material embodiment of a refusal to face – or we should say to *see* – undesirable aspects of American society. Long before the machine of the law swings into action, the novel demonstrates how social taboos, especially that against sexual behaviour, leads characters into secrecy, deception and the construction of alibis. In short, long before any actual crime has been committed, characters behave in a quasi-criminal way to avoid the social gaze. It has become a truism in discussion of *An American Tragedy* that Clyde is a product of social conditions and we will see that this was one of the novel's main sources of interest for Eisenstein, but it has not been adequately recognized how these conditions are enacted through a collective surveillance which Clyde struggles to avoid.

The investigation of Roberta's death and subsequent trial represent institutional attempts to expose what happened and to construct the narrative and imagery of these events in such a way that the double standards and hypocrisy go unchallenged. We can see a sign of what is to come in the juxtaposition between the ending of Book II, where Clyde has become de-individualized into a 'youth making his way through a dark, uninhabited wood' (implying his estrangement from society) and the opening of Book III. In the latter we start with an aerial panorama of the district where Roberta drowns, gradually closing up on a town and finally the county courthouse. The building embodies the institution which will dominate the final section of the novel, in which Clyde shifts from being an agent in his own right to an object of investigation. In Book II he resembles a shadow-image of his rich cousin; in Book III he becomes an image which has to be constructed painstakingly from the glimpses of others. The trial confirms that he has become the object of the collective gaze, figured technologically as he is filmed going into court. The novel begins with doors opening to Clyde and concludes with his entry into the death-chamber. Unconsciously, Clyde figures himself as a star performer; one of the lawyers in his trial compliments a colleague for his 'excellent stage play'. Here, the visualized final scene makes a final indictment of American society, as Eisenstein realized in his adaptation of the novel for the screen.

Eisenstein's Adaptation of *An American Tragedy*

The story of the first adaptations of *An American Tragedy* is a familiar one.[53] Paramount invited Eisenstein to write a screenplay based on the novel, which he did with enthusiasm. This script was applauded by Dreiser but rejected by Paramount, who released a movie adaptation in 1931 by Joseph von Sternberg, which outraged Dreiser so much that he took Universal to court, a suit which he lost. It is not the business of this study to consider adaptations of fiction, but this case is exceptional because it sheds light on tensions within *An American Tragedy* and also because of the unusual intellectual rapport between Dreiser and Eisenstein, despite their disagreement over the collective and individual dimensions to drama.

An American Tragedy actually suggests that this opposition was more apparent than real. Despite his stated commitment to individualism, Dreiser repeatedly shows how Clyde realizes his individual potential by adopting the guises – literally the dress – of different socio-economic groups. The uniform of the hotel bell-hop is an important early example: his progress is shown visually by his entry into a group within which he is indistinguishable from the others. Ultimately, it emerges that Clyde's clothes become one factor giving him away to the law because he seems too well-dressed for the role of tourist he simulates prior to Roberta's death. In an important historical analysis of the novel, Walter Benn Michaels has identified a central, unresolved tension between the individual and the social group which approaches paradox in Dreiser's depiction of middle-class mobility. Clyde's hotel uniform for Michaels is one example of many social uniforms since 'for Dreiser, the uniform makes difference possible […] and in making difference possible it makes possible new areas of what he will call "personal" experience'.[54] It is a nice irony of the novel that Clyde should find advancement through working in a factory which mass-produces an item of clothing – collars – thereby promising its customers the possibility of uniform appearance.[55] Dreiser reveals this tension between the individual and the group in the numerous occasions when he seizes on a character's appearance to categorize them according to this or that social type.

It was this typifying strategy which fascinated Eisenstein in the project of adapting the novel. During his discussions about the adaptation with the head of Paramount, the latter asked Eisenstein whether Clyde was guilty or not. Eisenstein replied promptly in the negative, whereupon B. P. Schulberg concluded: 'then your script is a monstrous challenge to American society'.[56] For Eisenstein, the real tragedy lay in Clyde's 'clash with American realities', hence, he recorded, 'it was imperative for us to stress the *actual* and *formal* innocence of Clyde at the very moment when the crime was perpetrated'.[57] By his own account, Eisenstein was trying to show how Clyde falls victim to external forces ranging from the market-place to the local political factors at play in his trial. He later recalled: 'What interested me here was depicting the society and the morals that impelled Clyde to do everything he did, and then, in the hullabaloo of the pre-election fever, in the interests of getting the prosecutor re-elected, Clyde is broken'.[58]

Eisenstein's formulation in the passive voice reflects a perception of Clyde's drama which was written into every phase of his screenplay. Take, for example, the following description of the Kansas City hotel where Clyde finds work: 'Across a yard into which the hotel garbage is being thrown and where coal is being unladen for the heating of the building – through the door where dirty linen is being checked into a van and by sculleries where dishes are being washed, Clyde passes into the office of Mr. Squires'.[59] Where Dreiser presents the lobby, i.e. the most glamorous part of the hotel, Eisenstein takes us behind the scenes to remind us that the hotel is a nexus of different forms of unglamorous commerce. The latter are virtually all suppressed in Dreiser's novel, which concentrates (through Clyde's point of view) on frontages. In other words, Eisenstein keeps reminding us of economic factors by making them more explicit than they often are in the novel. Thus, he designs a stark cut from Clyde's shabby room to the luxury of his relatives' house and also, without confining the scene to the purely romantic, Eisenstein shows how liberating the love between Clyde and Roberta can be: 'when they stop their kisses for a moment, behold, the ceiling of her little room has opened to the heavens and so have the walls'.[60] At different points in his screenplay Eisenstein shapes his scenes according to the psychological state of Clyde. Here the intimacy between the couple gives them the illusion of having broken through their physical and economic circumstances, opening up the space of life for them.

This does not mean that Eisenstein is suppressing material factors in favour of romance, since almost immediately afterwards he describes a scene in close-up in which hands are fixing clothing. As the camera panned out, it would have been revealed that the hands were Sondra's and the clothes Clyde's. Hands always denote agency and so, even though it is a small event being shown, Eisenstein is raising questions about Clyde's autonomy, and the same is even more true when the idea of killing Roberta comes into his mind. Here it is expressed by an external 'whisper' which plays on Clyde's mind and introduces a visual disparity between his actions and their background; rapid movement within a slow scene and vice versa. As the idea gains hold, every voice in Clyde's environment seems to be shouting 'kill!'. Eisenstein carefully stresses how this impulse grows out of society, not out of innate wickedness, deflecting Clyde's guilt well before the death actually occurs. Eisenstein is also making use of the relatively new medium of sound here in applying Dreiser's old-fashioned moral debate ('kill'/'don't kill') within Clyde.[61]

Two other shifts of emphasis consolidate Eisenstein's reading of Dreiser. Firstly, he fills out Roberta as a visual image by showing her suffering through facial expression, zombie-like movement, and so on. This is not enough, however. Roberta actually states to Clyde the social taboo she fears she is breaking: 'I can't be alone with a child on my hands, and no husband!'[62] Eisenstein makes it impossible for the viewer to forget the social issues embedded in the story, just as he deploys montage between scenes with Roberta and scenes featuring Sondra to foreground their economic differences.[63] Roberta's death is described by Dreiser in strategically blurred detail which leaves an important margin of ambiguity over whether Clyde actually did kill her. Eisenstein's script does everything it can to remove this ambiguity. When Clyde's expression fills with misery Roberta crawls to him and holds one of his hands. Then one accident leads to another:

> Clyde opens his eyes suddenly and sees near him her anxious, tender face. With an involuntary movement of revulsion he pulls back his hand and jumps up quickly. As he does so the camera, *quite accidentally*, strikes her in the face.
> Roberta's lip is cut; she cries and falls back in the stern of the boat.
> '*I'm sorry, Roberta, I didn't mean to,*' and he makes a *natural* movement towards her. Roberta is afraid. She tries to get up, *loses her balance*, and the boat oversets. [italics added][64]

Eisenstein takes care to show this action as a small sequence of misunderstandings in which accident replaces deliberate intent. There is a clear line to the action, but it is one motivated by the extreme stress of both characters. It was crucial to Eisenstein's purposes that Clyde should not emerge as a murderer and that the event should be the outcome of social circumstances. Dreiser welcomed this interpretation and, when the script was turned down, he wrote to Eisenstein to enquire into the possibility of making the film in Russia.[65]

Despite the fact that B. P. Schulberg described Eisenstein's script as the 'best scenario that Paramount had ever had', it was rejected, apparently because they preferred a 'simple, tight whodunit about a murder' and a boy-meets-girl story.[66] They seem to have found this in Sternberg's script, which, however, reduced Dreiser to fury because it grossly simplified the drama, although the film was reviewed by Pare Lorentz as a 'splendid production'.[67] Dreiser insisted that Clyde was a 'creature of circumstances, not a scheming, sex-starved "drugstore cowboy"'; and he felt that the proposed action moved too quickly to the drowning, which as a result became the 'act of a temporarily crazed youth, instead of the planned culmination of a series of inescapable circumstances'.[68] The court decision against Dreiser had implications for the ending of the film in pronouncing that 'the great majority of people composing the audience [...] will be more interested that justice prevail than that the inevitability of Clyde's end clearly appear'.[69] By stopping the action at the court's verdict on Clyde, the Sternberg version simplified and curtailed the film's attention to the American legal system, which therefore emerged unscathed. This was not a question of conservative censorship but rather, as Richard Maltby has shown, the result of a general situation in which the studios had to consolidate the status of films as entertainment by containing signs of subversion or social criticism. Thus, the problem with *An American Tragedy* lay in the fact that 'both its detailed actions and its thematic concerns were inappropriate to an affirmative medium'.[70]

Upton Sinclair

It is ironic that the two most famous projects which Eisenstein pursued with American novelists should have been abortive. The plan to film *An American Tragedy* produced a completed screenplay; Eisenstein's enterprise with Upton Sinclair to make the film *Que Viva Mexico!* resulted in a shorter film released under the title *Thunder Over Mexico* in 1933.[71] Before we consider this project further, we should note that Sinclair's interest in film dates back at least to his involvement in an adaptation of his novel *The Jungle* in 1914.[72] Indeed, as early as 1906, when the novel was first published, Sinclair was using a range of proto-cinematic techniques to present the reader with his famous reportage on the Lithuanian community of Chicago and that city's stockyards. The novel opens with an account of Jurgis Rutkus' wedding celebrations, recorded in the present tense as if the festivities are taken out of time by the participants in rituals which remind them of the old country: the procession of the women bringing vast bowls of food, the dances and the first violinist who abandons himself to his music: 'he stamps with his feet, he tosses his head, he sways and swings to and fro'.[73] The wedding over, the real business of the novel begins, which is to give a picture of conditions in contrast to the 'lies' of commercial signs around the city. Sinclair uses perspective shots and a sunset panorama of the city in which the only colour arises from industry: 'it was a study in colours now, this smoke; in the sunset light it was black and brown and gray and purple. All the sordid suggestions of the place were gone – in the twilight it was a vision of power'.[74] Again and again Sinclair shows how industrial process swallows up human operatives through expressionistic scenes like the one quoted. His repeated strategy is to take the reader-as- newcomer on a series of tours through the stockyards, slaughterhouses and fertilizer works (the last described like a Dantesque labyrinth).

Sinclair must present authentic visual images of conditions ready for reform. By the late 1910s he was considering ways in which he could use films for socialist purposes, including a scenario with Chaplin, but his early fiction already shows signs of this documentary approach through its representational methods. The 1914 film of *The Jungle* was unevenly successful, but its distribution was severely hampered by pressure from big business.[75] *Potemkin* made a particularly deep impression on Sinclair and by 1927 he had started correspondence with Eisenstein. After the decision had been taken to drop Eisenstein's script for *An American Tragedy*, Sinclair wrote to him, declaring: 'I am much disappointed by the news that you are not going ahead with the picture. I looked forward to it as the most interesting one I had ever seen or heard of'.[76] Once the scheme to make *Que Viva Mexico!* got under way, Eisenstein and his crew went to different Mexican locations to start shooting while Sinclair stayed in the USA to organize the financial backing. He took no part in the actual making of the film and the project ground to a virtual halt for a complex set of reasons including poor planning, Eisenstein's cavalier attitude to expenses, and political tensions with the Soviet authorities (Sinclair even had to write to Stalin to reassure him that Eisenstein was a loyal Russian).

The *Que Viva Mexico!* project has been interpreted as one which caused the film critics of the American left to reassess their attitude to Hollywood and it also helped to consolidate Eisenstein's status in the USA.[77] Early in proceedings Sinclair expressed the following conviction: 'I believe this picture is going to be the greatest sensation the art world has ever had'. And despite endless financial problems and personality clashes, he paid his tribute to Eisenstein in an introduction to the first release print of *Thunder Over Mexico* in which he declared that the film would be a 'new revelation of the arts of composition and photography. Every scene has been studied with the loving care of a great painter; the very trees on the hilltops have posed, the clouds in the sky have acted'.[78] Eisenstein had planned the film to be a 'symphony' of six stories, but *Thunder Over Mexico* only showed one. Despite this stark reduction, Sinclair's admiration for Eisenstein continued undiminished.

Shortly after the *Que Viva Mexico!* project, Sinclair published his only work to deal with the movie business. *Upton Sinclair Presents William Fox* (1933) is a study of the movie tycoon from his birth up to his financial difficulties at the time of publication. Sinclair extended his muckraking exposés into the complex and shadowy world of American finance, although the book really straddles two genres: the biography of the immigrant who rose from poverty to success and wealth, and commercial reportage. It thus presents the light and dark sides of the American Dream: a story of individual achievement and a much longer account of credit conspiracy which results in Fox's loss of control over his companies. In short, Sinclair presents the financial negotiations which lie behind every single film but which remain unknown to the vast majority of any cinema audience.

In order to make his 'presentation' (the same term used by Dreiser in Book III of *An American Tragedy*) Sinclair dons the persona of a movie producer and on the flyleaf of his book promises the reader the following attractions:

A FEATURE PICTURE OF WALL STREET AND HIGH FINANCE

In Twenty-nine Reels with Prologue and Epilogue

A Melodrama of Fortune, Conflict and Triumph. Packed with Thrills and Heart Throbs. East Side Boy Conquers Fame and Power. The Masters of Millions Envy His Triumph and Plot His Downfall. The Octopus Battles the Fox. The Duel of a Century! The Sensation of a Lifetime!

Never in Screen History has there been a Feature so Stupendous as this.[79]

In order to transpose his largely personal or confidential subject-matter into the public domain, Sinclair boosts his own narrative as if it is a production by Fox's own medium. He advertises it as a drama between the wily manoeuvres of an individual (the fox) and the sinister forces of a banking trust, figured here and throughout the book as an octopus, an echo of Frank Norris's 1901 novel about the railroad trust in the South-West.

Pursuing the cinematic analogy, Sinclair designates each chapter a 'reel' and opens his account with a 'close-up' of William Fox in his study, which includes details of his dress: 'under his coat is a white sweater; and in an article published in *Fortune*, the magazine which caters to bankers and magnates, I read that William Fox was accustomed to appear at directors' meetings of his companies wearing a sweater, also white socks; whereas Mr. Harold Leonard Stuart of Halsey Stuart & Co., the investment banker who helped to oust Fox, invariably appears at directors' meetings wearing a carnation in his buttonhole'.[80] This detail is loaded with symbolism because it immediately sets up a contrast between the relative informality of Fox (the future victim of the financial 'hunt') and the formal dress of his opponent. Sinclair thus sets up a polarity between individual and group action which will recur throughout his book. The visual image is rare, however. Sinclair's account is primarily a narrative one and the cinematic analogy is used as an ironic frame to his text, in which revelations of the banking octopus are given in a calculatedly unsensational way.

Throughout his career Sinclair was aware of the cinema as business and as supporting business interests. In the magazine *Screenland* for 1922 he declared: 'the movies are made for children, and for grown people who have remained at the mental age of children'.[81] During the 1930s he wrote a fictional account of a naïve young man from the Mid-West trying to make his fortunes in Hollywood. 'The Golden Scenario' (unpublished until after Sinclair's death) was his own version of Harry Leon Wilson's 1922 satire *Merton of the Movies* and describes the experiences of Danny Dane, a 'true child of the movies'. Arriving near Hollywood by train, he sees a film crew in action and to his astonishment discovers that the 'star' is a girl from his home town. Most of Sinclair's narrative bounces Danny's wide-eyed innocence off the disillusioned cynicism of 'Lily Lowe'. When she marries a film writer it is revealed that he was already married. The moment of revelation moves Danny to tears but at the same time delights him because 'this was the Golden Scenario, and he was in it!'[82] Danny's naivety is shown in his incorrigible tendency to imagine his own experiences in filmic terms and to believe promises of success in Hollywood (Dreiser's *American Tragedy* is cited in the adverts as an instance of what could happen). When he finally submits his scenario it is swallowed up in the system, cut and reshaped until it has become unrecognizable; and of course Danny does not receive a cent.

Sinclair was well aware of the political dimension to film. In 1919 he recorded seeing an article in *Moving Picture World* about the film *Bolshevism on Trial*, which called on readers to support the anti-socialist cause, citing Sinclair as one of socialism's apologues.[83] In the year following the publication of his William Fox book Sinclair experienced at first hand the use of film to block his 1934 campaign to become governor of California. Louis B. Mayer, head of MGM and high official in the local Republican party, headed the studios' opposition to Sinclair. Irving Thalberg (the prototype of Fitzgerald's Monroe Stahr in *The Last Tycoon*) ordered an MGM producer and camera crew from Hearst Metrotone News to take footage of bogus interviews with dishevelled Sinclair 'supporters' (played by actors), which was then spliced into local newsreels, giving the impression that California was going to be swamped by thousands of hoboes flocking to Sinclair's utopia.[84] Ironically, this event only strengthened Sinclair's conviction of the educational potential in film, even though this was being used negatively. In 1936 he declared: 'hitherto the movies have maintained that they could not do any kind of "educational" work; their audiences demanded entertainment, and they could have nothing to do with "propaganda". But now, you see, that pretence has been cast aside. They have made propaganda, and they have won a great victory with it'.[85]

Notes

1   Murray, *The Cinematic Imagination*, pp. 116–32; Laurence E. Hussman, 'Dreiser's (Bad) Luck in Hollywood', pp. 14–16; Haberski, *It's Only a Movie!*, pp. 63–80.

2   'The Best Motion Picture Interview Ever Written', in Anthony Slide, ed., *They Also Wrote*

for the Fan Magazines, pp. 40–58. Mack Sennett (1880–1960) was one of the most prolific producers and directors, especially in the silent film era, and a formative figure in slapstick comedy.

3   Robert H. Elias, ed., *Letters of Theodore Dreiser: A Selection*, p. 789.

4   See 'A Photographic Talk with Edison' (1898), 'A Master of Photography' (on Stieglitz) collected in Dreiser, *Selected Magazine Articles*, vol. I, pp. 111–19, 248–53. For commentary on Stieglitz's impact on Dreiser, see Ellen Moers, *Two Dreisers*, pp. 10–13; and Shloss, *In Visible Light*, pp. 96–101. Shloss argues that Stieglitz's photographs helped persuade Dreiser that poverty could be a fit subject for art (p. 101).

5   Elias, ed., *Letters of Theodore Dreiser*, pp. 176–77; Thomas P. Riggio, ed., *Dreiser–Mencken Letters*, vol. I, p. 201.

6   Theodore Dreiser, *The American Diaries*, pp. 214, 323. *Magda* (since lost) dramatized the story of a strong-willed singer who defies her father's wishes in pursuing her career and lover. Griffith's *The Idol Dancer*, starring Richard Barhelmess and Clarine Seymour, presented the drama of a group of characters thrown together on a South Sea island.

7   Elias, ed., *Letters of Theodore Dreiser*, p. 642.

8   At some point, presumably after she gained sufficient film experience, Helen Richardson wrote a screenplay for *Sister Carrie*, now in the Dreiser papers at the University of Pennsylvania Library.

9   Dreiser, *The American Diaries*, pp. 307–308, 326, 329.

10   Jerome Loving, *The Last Titan*, p. 289.

11   They were published as follows: 'I. The Struggle on the Threshold of Moving Pictures', *Shadowland*, 5 (November 1921), pp. 37, 61–63; 'II. The Commonplace Tale with a Thousand Endings', 5 (December 1921), pp. 51, 61; 'III. The Beginner's Thousand-to-One Chance', 5 (January 1922), pp. 43, 67; 'IV. The Extra's Fight to Exist', 5 (February 1922), pp. 53, 66. I–III are reprinted in Slide, ed., *They Also Wrote for the Fan Magazines*, pp. 21–40. In February 1921 Dreiser's plan was for a slightly different sequence of five articles: 'Hollywood Now' [actually published in *McCall's*, 48 (September 1921), pp. 8, 18, 54]; 'The Overcrowded Entryway'; 'The Room at the Top'; 'A Group of Directors' ['a study of the queer fish']; and 'A Group of Stars' ['a picture of seven or eight of the biggest fish at close range'] (Elias, ed., *Letters of Theodore Dreiser*, p. 353).

12   Slide, ed., *They Also Wrote for the Fan Magazines*, p. 33.

13   John Parris Springer, *Hollywood Fictions*, pp. 41–46.

14   W. A. Swanberg, *Dreiser*, p. 251.

15   Elias, ed., *Letters of Theodore Dreiser*, pp. 331–32.

16   Elias, ed., *Letters of Theodore Dreiser*, p. 778. Television (also mentioned in Fitzgerald's *Tender is the Night*) was slower to be developed in the USA than in Germany or Britain. Experimental transmissions were made in 1936 and commercial transmissions in 1939, when the first mass-produced TV sets went on sale. Among the subjects for the first transmissions were short films, film stills, and coverage of the 1940 Republican convention in Philadelphia.

17   Theodore Dreiser, 'The Real Sins of Hollywood', in Geduld, ed., *Authors on Film*, p. 206.

18   Dreiser, 'The Real Sins', in Geduld, ed., *Authors on Film*, p. 215.

19   H. L. Mencken, 'The Low-Down on Hollywood', in S. T. Joshi, ed., *Mencken's America*, p. 177. Mencken married the Hollywood screenwriter Sarah Haardt and during the 1930s encouraged the young Italian-American writer John Fante when he was starting his career as novelist and screenwriter. Mencken numbered Anita Loos among his friends and it is said that an episode with Mencken inspired Loos's novel *Gentlemen Prefer Blondes*. Mencken particularly applauded German cinema and in his 'Low-Down' interview

declared that F. W. Murnau was setting a lead for others to follow (p. 177).

20 Even here, Mencken's statements were contradictory. Although he saw potential in the cinematic medium, he also complained when film moved away from the linearity of the theatre to experiment with montage. The result, he declared, was a 'maddening chaos of discrete fragments' ('Appendix from Moronia', in *Prejudices: Sixth Series*, p. 291).

21 Theodore Dreiser, *Dreiser Looks at Russia*, p. 204. This volume was composed immediately after his visit. During the visit itself Dreiser's secretary Ruth Kennell took detailed notes for his diary, later publishing an expanded version as *Theodore Dreiser and the Soviet Union, 1927–1945: A First-Hand Chronicle* (1969). Dreiser's *Russian Diary* was published in 1996.

22 *Dreiser Looks at Russia*, p. 207.

23 *Dreiser Looks at Russia*, p. 208. Dreiser attached considerable importance to Robert Wiene's classic film. In 1933 he told a correspondent: 'Never doubt that I believe the cinema is a new and powerful art form. I have always thought so, and have seen proofs of it from the very beginning. Consider *The Cabinet of Dr. Caligari*' (Elias, ed., *Letters of Theodore Dreiser*, p. 642).

24 Theodore Dreiser, *Dreiser's Russian Diary*, p. 102. The other films Dreiser mentioned were *Grass: A Nation's Battle for Life* (1925) and *Chang* (1927).

25 *Dreiser's Russian Diary*, p. 153.

26 *Dreiser's Russian Diary*, pp. 160, 161.

27 Swanberg, *Dreiser*, pp. 367, 421.

28 Swanberg, *Dreiser*, pp. 366, 412.

29 In a letter Dreiser wrote: 'I feel that the *Gallery of Women* script would make a standard Hollywood picture, but no more. The happy-ending story which encloses the dramatic story is all right as a device, but there is no novelty about it' (Elias, ed., *Letters of Theodore Dreiser*, p. 674).

30 Elias, ed., *Letters of Theodore Dreiser*, p. 789.

31 William Alexander, *Film on the Left*, p. 31. Tom Mooney's case became a *cause célèbre* in the 1930s. Dreiser was active in the campaign for his release from prison and enlisted the assistance of Upton Sinclair, Carl Sandburg, Sherwood Anderson, and Sinclair Lewis, among others.

32 Swanberg, *Dreiser*, p. 413.

33 Hy Kraft, 'Foreword' to Borden Deal, *The Tobacco Men*, p. 12.

34 Elias, ed., *Letters of Theodore Dreiser*, pp. 677–78.

35 Quoted in Kraft, 'Foreword' to Deal, *The Tobacco Men*, p. 12. Dreiser's notes and scenario for *Tobacco* are in the University of Pennsylvania library. The project and scenario are discussed by Richard A. Fine in 'Theodore Dreiser's "Revolt"'. He notes that the 'spectacular sweep of the script [is] reminiscent of D.W. Griffith's *The Birth of a Nation*' (p. 122).

36 Deal, *The Tobacco Men*, p. 333.

37 Dreiser, *Sister Carrie*, p. 17.

38 Rachel Bowlby, *Just Looking*, p. 6.

39 Dreiser, *Sister Carrie*, p. 47.

40 Bowlby, *Just Looking*, pp. 60, 62.

41 'Dreiser's novel looks forward to the Hollywood-star system, when the electric image began to rule the world' (Armstrong, *Modernism, Technology and the Body*, p. 26).

42 A little more than Book I was drafted in Hollywood in 1920; Loving, *The Last Titan*, p. 290.

43 Robert Penn Warren, 'Homage to *An American Tragedy*', pp. 24–25.

44 Elias, ed., *Letters of Theodore Dreiser*, p. 528.

45 Moers, *Two Dreisers*, p. 232.

46 Theodore Dreiser, *An American Tragedy*, p. 32.

47 *An American Tragedy*, p. 101.

48 *An American Tragedy*, p. 125.

49 Moers, *Two Dreisers*, p. 236.

50 *An American Tragedy*, p. 476.

51 *An American Tragedy*, p. 492.

52 Theodore Dreiser, *Hey, Rub-A-Dub-Dub!*, p. 261. This book was published in the year that Dreiser began *An American Tragedy* (1920). Later in the same essay he criticizes the hypocrisy of a film made to expose the white slave trade which actually gave graphic detail on the business it was supposedly attacking.

53 For a discussion of the different adaptations of Dreiser's novels, see Laurence E. Hussman, 'Squandered Possibilities'.

54 Walter Benn Michaels, 'An American Tragedy, or the Promise of American Life', p. 83.

55 The 1951 film *A Place in the Sun* changed the factory product to swimsuits and introduced it through a massive hoarding on which the model resembles a film star, thereby strengthening the overlap between commodity and sexual consumption.

56 Eisenstein, *Film Form*, p. 96.

57 Eisenstein, *Film Form*, p. 98.

58 Eisenstein, *Immoral Memories*, p. 156.

59 Ivor Montagu, *With Eisenstein in Hollywood*, p. 220.

60 Montagu, *With Eisenstein in Hollywood*, p. 259.

61 Keith Cohen discusses such elaborations in 'Eisenstein's Subversive Adaptation', in which he argues that the latter was drawing out the potential in Dreiser's fragmented prose, visual imagery, and thought-sequences (Cohen, pp. 240–45).

62 Montagu, *With Eisenstein in Hollywood*, p. 280. Other changes of emphasis are discussed by Bernice Kliman in '*An American Tragedy*: Novel, Scenario, and Film', pp. 260–62.

63 Apart from showing social differences, this kind of montage is much more psychological and thus a significant step away from his earlier conception of montage as scenic opposition, which fragments and objectifies characters, as we see in Dos Passos' *Manhattan Transfer*.

64 Montagu, *With Eisenstein in Hollywood*, p. 295.

65 Letter to Eisenstein of 1 September 1931, in Eisenstein, *Notes of a Film Director*, p. 105.

66 Montagu, *With Eisenstein in Hollywood*, p. 120; Eisenstein, *Film Form*, p. 96. Eisenstein told Upton Sinclair that when he mentioned Dreiser's novel to another screenwriter at Paramount, the latter said: 'Oh, that is the story about the guy who got hot nuts, screwed a girl and drowned her' (Harry M. Geduld and Ronald Gottesman, eds., *Sergei Eisenstein and Upton Sinclair*, p. 135).

67 Pare Lorentz, *Lorentz on Film*, p. 78. Lorentz declared: 'Sternberg is at his best with the courtroom crowds. With superb timing, he takes his camera from the stony faces of the dazed farm couple whose child went to the bottom of the lake outside to the hot-dog vendors, the sex-story publishers, and the insane townspeople drooling with blood-lust from the stimulation of an illicit love affair and a murder' (pp. 77–78).

68 Elias, ed., *Letters of Theodore Dreiser*, pp. 510, 511. Kliman also notes Sternberg's use of old-fashioned devices such as titles ('*An American Tragedy*: Novel, Scenario, and Film', p. 264). The film critic Harry Potamkin argued that Sternberg had suppressed both milieu and therefore social process in his version, reducing Dreiser's characters to mere 'digits' ('Novel into Film: A Case Study of Current Practice', in Lewis Jacobs, ed., *The Compound*

Cinema, pp. 186–96).

69 Swanberg, *Dreiser*, p. 377.

70 Richard Maltby, "'To Prevent the Prevalent Type of Book'", p. 564.

71 It has been argued that *Thunder Over Mexico* influenced Malcolm Lowry's 1947 novel *Under the Volcano* (Lionel Rolfe, *Literary L.A.*, p. 21).

72 Geduld and Gottesman, eds., *Sergei Eisenstein and Upton Sinclair*, p. 17. This volume tells the story of *Que Viva Mexico!* through the primary documents (letters, agreements, telegrams) of the participants.

73 Upton Sinclair, *The Jungle*, p. 9. Sinclair started going to the cinema in New York around 1904–1905, so it is possible that films had their impact on the technique of *The Jungle* (*Upton Sinclair Presents William Fox*, p. 32).

74 Sinclair, *The Jungle*, p. 31.

75 The critic Clement Wood declared enthusiastically: 'innumerable scenes are gripping and powerful'. A revised version of the film was released by the Labour Film Service in 1922 with limited impact: see Philip S. Foner, 'Upton Sinclair's *The Jungle*: The Movie'.

76 Geduld and Gottesman, eds., *Sergei Eisenstein and Upton Sinclair*, p. 19.

77 See Chris Robe, 'Eisenstein in America'.

78 Geduld and Gottesman, eds., *Sergei Eisenstein and Upton Sinclair*, p. 110; Upton Sinclair, 'Introduction to "Hacienda"', in Geduld and Gottesman, eds., *Sergei Eisenstein and Upton Sinclair*, p. 376. This introduction was dropped in subsequent viewings. In an interview later in 1933 Sinclair stated that in the film 'everything is of newsreel character' (p. 411). In his memoirs of the project Sinclair presents Eisenstein as a self-engrossed genius who shot endless miles of film in Mexico while the money-raising went on in the USA: 'the most marvellous material: pictures of golden sunlight and black shadows; dream-scenes of primitive splendour; gorgeous pageants, like old tapestries come to life; compositions in which the very clouds in the sky were trained to perform!' (*American Outpost*, p. 270).

79 *Upton Sinclair Presents William Fox*, p. v.

80 *Upton Sinclair Presents William Fox*, pp. 1–2.

81 Upton Sinclair, 'Big Business and Its Movies', in Coodley, ed., *The Land of Orange Groves and Jails*, p. 98.

82 Upton Sinclair, 'The Golden Scenario', in Coodley, ed., *The Land of Orange Groves and Jails*, pp. 110, 128.

83 Upton Sinclair, *The Brass Check*, p. 73. The film was based on Thomas Dixon's 1909 novel *Comrades*, itself a parody of Sinclair's utopian Helicon Home Colony (see Slide, *American Racist*, pp. 134–40).

84 See Greg Mitchell, *The Campaign of the Century*. Dorothy Parker (at the time working for MGM along with her husband Alan Campbell) was one of the few screenwriters to speak up in support of Sinclair.

85 Upton Sinclair, 'The Movies and Political Propaganda', in Stephen J. Ross, ed., *Movies and American Society*, p. 161.

9

Documentary of the 1930s

In the cases of Dreiser and Sinclair we saw examples of fiction embedding their action in reports on social conditions, in other words of fiction approaching documentary. It has been an abiding dream of the cinema that it could depict reality directly. A 1902 advertisement for the kinetoscope claimed that it could give 'apparently life itself' in its directness and breadth.[1] Documentaries, it seemed, had finally achieved this ultimate objectivity. The term 'documentary' was first applied in 1926 to *Moana*, a film about a Polynesian family, and by 1930 had taken on its current sense of a generic marker. The fact that it was applied to an ethnographic film has an important symbolism because, as Eliot Weinberger has shown, it reflects ethnographers' belief that they are invisible and can therefore produce their report without disrupting the communities under observation. Their ideal is 'either a dream of invisibility, or worse, the practice of the surveillance camera'.[2] If we broaden this category of film to include social reportage, we can see that Weinberger is raising an issue which will recur throughout this chapter. Whether the subjects of film are Polynesians or American migrant workers, for the investigative writer or film-maker the problem remains of how to report on their lives without disrupting their living habits and also without presenting them as alien to the viewer/reader.

In his pioneering study *Documentary Expression in Thirties America* (1973) William Stott has shown that the documentary impulse was fuelled by a desire to discover America. Although this desire had its roots in the 1890s, it came into its own during the 1930s under the impact of the Depression. Peter Humm has demonstrated how the trope of the camera and documentary methods generally inform a whole range of 1930s' American fiction, especially private eye novels.[3] By the time of the 1935 American Writers Congress documentary had become so established that Joseph North, editor of *New Masses*, could present reportage as *the* literature of the age. He defined this new mode as follows: 'Reportage is three-dimensional reporting. The writer not only condenses reality, he helps the reader feel the fact. The finest writers of reportage are artists in the fullest sense of the term. They do their editorialising through their imagery'.[4] North argued that already American documentary had established its own tradition and credibility, citing as formative examples John Reed (described in Dos Passos' *U.S.A.* as the 'best American writer of his time'), Stephen Crane, Agnes Smedley and Dos Passos.[5] The works which North singled out for special praise were polemical but also a hybrid product. 'Boundary lines are being trampled all the time', he noted later in his talk, suggesting that a work of reportage could include narrative as well as documentary descriptions. As film became championed by the Left it was not surprising that Soviet films should be compared to Hollywood productions, to the detriment of the latter.[6] We shall see how photography and film either became incorporated into documentaries or suggested analogues for their descriptions.

Eudora Welty

The development in reportage most relevant to the present context was experimentation in juxtaposing photographic and verbal texts or in attempting to apply in words the techniques of the cinema. Although she is not normally associated with reportage, Eudora Welty presents an interesting example of a writer cross-applying photographic and cinematic methods in her fiction. She began her career photographing subjects in Mississippi for the Works Progress Administration (WPA) and in her preface to *One Time, One Place* (her 1971 retrospective collection of photographs) she recorded a lesson learnt from photography: 'the camera I focused in front of me may have been a shy person's protection [...] It was an eye, though – not quite mine, but a quicker and an unblinking one – and it couldn't see pain where it looked, or give any, though neither could it catch effervescence, colour, transience, kindness, or what was not there'.[7] Welty engages in a delicate balancing act here, weighing up the pros and cons of the camera: its clarity as against the subtler nuances of experience. Her ambivalence forms part of a wider debate running through the 1920s and 1930s over whether the camera was an extension of the eye or its technological substitute. Despite Welty's misgivings, her early photography furnished her with a set of tropes for discussing fiction; for instance, point of view is conceived as a 'sort of burning-glass' or lens.[8]

For Welty, the act of photographing became analogous for epiphanic moments of revelation in which a character suddenly becomes visually evident:

> I learned quickly enough when to click the shutter, but what I was becoming aware of more closely was a story-teller's truth: the thing to wait on, to reach there in time for, is the moment in which people reveal themselves [...] The human

face and the human body are eloquent in themselves, and a snapshot is a moment's glimpse (as a story may be a long look, a growing contemplation) into what never stops moving, never ceases to express for itself something out of our common feeling.[9]

The capture of expressive features was a crucial factor in photo-reportage. In Dos Passos' fictionalized account of the preparations for the film *The Spanish Earth*, he has his parodic Hemingway-figure insist 'Faces [...] what we want is faces. Faces of old peasants working in the fields, of muledrivers and tavern-keepers, vineyard workers turned into infantrymen'.[10] In Welty's account, the camera becomes an enabling instrument which can capture those rare moments where an individual's identity is fleetingly revealed, and Louise Westling has argued that, unlike James Agee or Richard Wright, Welty was far less concerned with situating her photographic subjects within the material context of poverty than with conveying this elusive selfhood.[11] The camera for her was not just a means of recording but an embodiment of her desire to know, to reconcile vision with the inner life.[12]

Years before her work for the WPA, Welty came under the influence of a different visual medium. In her autobiography *One Writer's Beginnings* (1984) she recorded how 'all children in those small-town, unhurried days had a vast inner life going on in the movies'.[13] Apart from Chaplin, Keaton and others who introduced her to the 'antic pantomime' of comedy, she recalled the special impact of *The Cabinet of Dr Caligari*, which made a startling (and frightening) change from the weekly fare of comedies and westerns. In interview Welty admitted that she had always been a keen movie-goer, once even trying to write a screenplay. It was the close relation of film to the short story that particularly engaged her: 'the use of flashbacks and memory, of a dream sequence – things you couldn't show on a stage, that you can show in a fluid form of a film which can move back and forward, and back and forth in time, and can speed up life, can slow it down, just the way you do in a short story. It can elide, and it can compound, and it can exaggerate. It can do all the things you do as a short story writer to bring out what you are trying to do. And I think as a short story writer I feel that I must have absorbed things'.[14]

This was a recognized influence earlier and broader than that of documentary photography. Drawing on such statements and the allusions to film in her works, Leslie Kaplansky has demonstrated how Welty evokes a 'cinematic rhythm' in her stories.[15] Although she tends to avoid the strategies of reportage in her fiction, she characteristically opens her stories with an image which is gradually investigated. Thus 'The Whistle' presents a moonlit view of a farmstead. We then move inside to the couple's bedroom where dying firelight gives us a faint but distinct image of the couple. The man is deeply asleep but his wife is staring upwards in silence. As the fire dies, the room gets colder and the wife's discomfort increases; indeed, there is a strong suggestion that her immediate physical state makes a comment on their relationship. There is, however, another issue here which will recur throughout this chapter: that of privacy. Welty has given us unique visual access to a scene of intimacy, which reveals the isolation of the central character. She writes this issue into 'A Piece of News', in which a woman is drying herself after a rainstorm. As she goes through small private acts, she suddenly imagines she is being watched: 'Then a look of fear. She stared about… What eye in the world did she feel looking in on her?'[16] Her husband's? Even that seems frightening. It is as if Welty's subject has sensed the scrutiny of the 'camera eye' and the brief narrative comments on the women seem intended to minimize this impression of voyeuristic intrusion.

Tom Kromer and the Present Tense

One aim of documentary is to convey authentic immediacy in its descriptions. Anglophone literature tends to use the narrative past tense, but the present tense is used in Samuel Ornitz's 1923 novel about New York's East Side, *Allrightniks Row: 'Haunch, Paunch and Jowl'*. Here the young Jewish narrator Meyer Hirsch uses an impressionistic technique to convey his animated perception of the changes taking place around him. For him, the present is the actual and his narrative attempts to capture a film-like authenticity of the immediate, which carries an implicit rejection of the past.[17] Writers such as Faulkner and Dos Passos also tried experimenting with present-tense narration. We can see this in the opening of *U.S.A.*: 'the young man walks fast by himself through the crowd that thins into the night streets […] eyes greedy for warm curve of faces, answering flicker of eyes, the set of a head, the lift of a shoulder, the way hands spread and clench'.[18] We have a generic image and an unnamed individual searching for visual signs of contact with others; like so many of Dos Passos' characters he is a transient. The present tense is normally used in screenplays and indeed this scene resembles the opening of a film. Everything focuses on the visualized present moment.

Compare this image with the opening of another novel published in 1935: 'It is night. I am walking along this dark street, when my foot hits a stick. I reach down and pick it up. I finger it. It is a good stick, a heavy stick. One sock from it would lay a man out. It wouldn't kill him, but it would lay him out.'[19] These lines come from Tom Kromer's *Waiting for Nothing*, a novel about Depression America told throughout in the present tense. Unlike the opening of *U.S.A.*, it is also narrated in the first person and these first lines immediately suggest a tension between the haves and the have-nots. Where

Dos Passos invites the reader into a situation of potential communication, Kromer implicates us in planned physical violence. Dos Passos imagines the eyes of others looking back at his protagonist; Kromer's narrator is using his eyes like a camera. Further, by evoking his protagonist through the present tense, Kromer denies something which emerges immediately in Dos Passos: purpose.

Waiting, for Kromer, becomes a condition of being which could only be expressed through a continuous present. This has nothing to do with Gertrude Stein's use of the present tense to give a quasi-filmic effect of constantly restarting a description, but Kromer's style is actually more cinematic in effect. *Waiting for Nothing* is a monochrome narrative whose narrator scrutinizes people and situations entirely in terms of strategy, asking himself whether he can get money or food. Take the following scene in which he has briefly paired up with another transient and managed to get some food from a local bakery: 'He pushes his papers to one side and spreads this stuff out on the table. We are both excited. Our eyes glisten. Our mouths water. Never have I seen a prettier sight than these doughnuts and rolls, and in the centre, standing out proudly above all, this coconut pie'.[20] The narrator constantly gives us an impression of watching himself, but here the shared reaction enables Kromer to focus the scene on the observers' faces before gradually closing up on the central object: the coconut pie.

Unfortunately this passage reveals a contradiction at the heart of Kromer's method. By using the present tense and by trying to close up the gap between author and narrator, Kromer tries to insist on the authenticity of his narrative. But inevitably a gap repeatedly opens up between the supposed hardships endured by the narrator, which reduce him to a virtually animal-like existence, and the skill with which he controls image, the pacing of events, and the visual perspective. This very skill turns out to be his enemy. Indeed, William Stott has taken him to task for an exercise of bad faith: 'the "Tom Kromer" of the book is a craftily simple version of the Tom Kromer who wrote it: the former doesn't know where his next meal is coming from, but the latter knew to tell it like *A Farewell to Arms*'.[21] The ending of the novel is narrated with characteristic care as Kromer's character just lies on a bed in a mission wondering whether he will die like another bum in the room; in other words, will it be an ending? In contrast, Dos Passos closes *U.S.A.* by returning to the present tense with more images of his unnamed transient trying to thumb lifts along a road. This too is an open, problematic ending, but one with more possibility than Kromer's apparent cul-de-sac.

The Spanish Earth: Dos Passos and Hemingway

Kromer's experiment has clear cinematic aspects. As we have seen, *U.S.A.* also deploys cinematic strategies. Throughout his career Dos Passos recognized the proximity of literature to film. In the mid-1930s he was involved in the Film and Photo League and its offshoot Nykino. More importantly, he was closely involved in two documentary films produced to support the democratic front in the Spanish Civil War: *Spain in Flames* (1937), for which he wrote a commentary, and *The Spanish Earth*. However, Dos Passos' relation to the American Left, which broadly championed documentary, was not straightforward. The formal complexities of *U.S.A.* for Juan A. Suarez suggest a rejection of 'straight realism, the aesthetic of immediate impact and intelligibility practised by 1930s left documentary' in favour of a 'blend of realism and modernist experimentation'.[22] There was thus an important gap between Dos Passos and the practice of the Left, which came to a head in *The Spanish Earth*.

The Spanish Civil War was *the* international cause of the 1930s and *The Spanish Earth* (1937) was the most famous film made of that conflict, famous because of the participation of Hemingway and Dos Passos. The involvement of US novelists in such projects clearly reflects their recognition of the political power of film, which was seen throughout the decade as a key medium of reportage. From 1935 onwards that the involvement of writers in film becomes most visible. In that year the Nykino (New York Kino) group broke away from the Comintern-funded Workers Film and Photo League. It included among its members Pare Lorentz, who was to play a major role in Steinbeck's career, and Leo Hurwitz, who with Dos Passos added the subtitles to Paul Strand's documentary film of a Mexican fishing village.[23] The Dutch documentary film-maker Joris Ivens was invited to join Nykino by the New Film Alliance which included on its board Langston Hughes, Dos Passos and the playwright Clifford Odets. When Nykino became Frontier Films in 1937 it in turn included the following writers on its board: Dos Passos again, Waldo Frank, Josephine Herbst, Irwin Shaw, and Muriel Rukeyser.[24] I include these details because it was clearly important to the credibility of these organizations that they should name famous writers on their boards.

With the outbreak of war in Spain it became a matter of political urgency to produce documentaries to support the republican side. Because of his long-standing affection for Spanish culture Dos Passos agreed to collaborate with his friend Jose Robles on a film. Dos Passos collaborated with the freelance photographer Bill Field to produce a short film called *Spain and the Fight for Freedom*, for which Dos Passos (possibly with the help of Archibald MacLeish) supplied the narration. In the meantime Hemingway collaborated with the Spanish novelist Prudencio de Pereda to produce a different documentary called *Spain in Flames*, which was subsequently attacked in some quarters for being Soviet propaganda.[25] It was at this point that the project to make *The Spanish Earth* originated, and here it is important to recognize the role of Joris Ivens, which went far beyond that of a film-maker. Ivens was a Comintern agent arranging the production of this film behind the scenes and organizing the Contemporary Historians group set up specifically for this film, whose chairman was the writer Archibald MacLeish and whose board carried the names of Dos Passos, Hemingway, Dorothy Parker, and Dashiell Hammett. According to Stephen Koch, this organization seems to have been set up on orders from Moscow as a smoke-screen behind which the real filming was done.[26] Before Dos Passos and Hemingway even reached Spain, Ivens had shot most of the footage for *The Spanish Earth*. Thus we have the strange example of an ostensible collaboration in which neither writer actually played an important role. The film was apparently designed as a propaganda exercise whose aim was to enlist Hemingway on the left and to discredit Dos Passos.[27]

Once he had arrived in Spain, supposedly to start work on *The Spanish Earth*, Dos Passos discovered that his friend Jose Robles had disappeared; only later did he discover that Robles had been secretly executed.[28] Understandably, this distracted him from the film project, at which point Hemingway stepped in and claimed the film as his own. The only substantial engagement with the film itself by either writer seems to have been a dispute over the relative merits of certain kinds of shots. Hemingway was convinced that there should be battle scenes and rashly led the film crew into combat areas. Dos Passos for his part became convinced that the villages were the real heart of Spain and persuaded Ivens to shoot some footage of a local land reclamation project.[29]

When the film was completed, the job of its narration was offered to Orson Welles by MacLeish, but Welles found the script too 'pompous and complicated' in places and it was finally done by Hemingway.[30] Dos Passos was studiously excluded from its first viewing at the New York Writers Congress, where Hemingway introduced it with a short address titled 'Fascism is a Lie'.[31] Similarly, in his later account of how the film was made, Ivens reduced Dos Passos' role to that of translator and described Hemingway's participation in glowing terms as that of a student learning the craft of documentary.[32] The film was subsequently shown in the White House and in a number of homes in Hollywood (Fitzgerald was among the guests who saw it at Fredric Marsh's). The film was well reviewed in the *New Republic*, where Otis Ferguson declared: 'Much of the carrying power in the understatement should be credited to Ernest Hemingway's commentary'.[33]

This commentary was published in book form in 1938 with a fulsome introduction by Jasper Wood, who claimed that the text was Hemingway's 'greatest contribution to society' and that 'never before has such a dramatic use of the face been incorporated into a picture'.[34] The text, with new illustrations, is divided according to reels. The first establishes the significance of the title by presenting the hardships of the villagers of Fuenteduena, ironically the very place Dos Passos felt should be highlighted. Having established peacetime labour, the script moves on to combat: 'the troops are called together. The company is assembled to elect representatives to attend the big meeting for celebrating the uniting of all militia regiments into the new brigades of the People's Army'.[35] Here we approach the ideological core of the film and script. The Spanish loyalists are shown to be workers jolted out of their peacetime occupations by the enemy. A simple and stark opposition is set up between the people and the professional soldiers confronting them, who represent the forces of tyranny. Thus in the final reel a battle is shown where 'the cameras need much luck to go'. The symbolism of the event is made clear: 'this the moment that all the rest of war prepares for, when six men go forward into death to walk across a stretch of land and by their presence on it prove – this land is ours'.[36] The six set out, become five, then four and finally three, at which point the road is saved. It is a small victory but presented as the result of understated heroism. One of the aspects of this film which confirms its propagandistic nature is the near-total exclusion of its wider context – the international brigades, the involvement of Communist and fascist forces; in short, the exclusion of anything that would detract from the main image of valiant peasants struggling against the forces of tyranny.

Hemingway published two short stories which drew on his *Spanish Earth* experience, both centring on the member of a film crew in battle. In 'Night before Battle' the point-of-view character surveys the battle field from a high vantage point which is too distant to film from except for the explosions: 'It was not too far to get the pine studded hillside, the lake and the outline of stone farm buildings that disappeared in the sudden smashes of stone dust from the hits by high explosive shells [...] But at eight hundred to a thousand yards the tanks looked like small mud-coloured beetles in the trees and spitting tiny flashes and the men behind them were toy men who lay flat'.[37] The perspective here is doubly professional. The battle is assessed by an observer who is at once a film specialist and an expert in strategy. Inevitably the distant view has an ironic reductive effect, a very far cry from the Popular Front perspective in *The Spanish Earth*.

Similarly 'Under the Ridge' opens with a broad long shot within which movement is taking place in opposite directions:

There was the tank reserve, the tanks covered with branches chopped from olive trees. To their left were the staff cars, mud-daubed and branch-covered, and between the two a long line of men carrying stretchers wound down through the gap to where, on the flat at the foot of the ridge, ambulances were loading. Commissary mules loaded with sacks of bread and kegs of wine, and a train of ammunition mules, led by their drivers, were coming up the gap in the ridge, and the men with empty stretchers were walking slowly up the trail with the mules.[38]

The ordering of visual data here ironically suggests that technology has become immobilized and that combat is taking place at a slower, pre-mechanized pace. Once again there is no suggestion of triumph, rather the opposite in the line of casualties. In the scenes from both stories visual clarity is kept quite distinct from filming; indeed, in neither story do we witness film shots. But the presence of the film camera has sharpened up the clarity of these scenes which open both stories. This clarity is then undermined by the arguments about strategy, commitment and courage which form the body of the narratives. The fields of the observers' vision establishes the subject matter for characters to debate and so both stories demonstrate a more complex and ambivalent perspective on the war than does the film.

Erskine Caldwell and the Photo-Text

During the 1930s a new documentary genre emerged which combined prose narrative or commentary with photographs. One of the most famous examples was *You Have Seen Their Faces* (1937), a collaboration between the Southern novelist Erskine Caldwell and the *Fortune* photographer Margaret Bourke-White. Caldwell approached reportage through journalism, from which he subsequently claimed he had learned his skills as a writer. When starting his career as a writer he secured a post with the *Atlanta Journal*, for which he wrote articles and also book reviews.[39] Caldwell served spells as a screenwriter for MGM in Hollywood but remained unimpressed with his experience. On one assignment he was brought in to replace William Faulkner –the worse for drink – in scripting a film by Tod Browning set in the bayous. This was shelved and he was offered a different assignment writing short scripts for a series called *Crime Does Not Pay* adapted from the FBI files.[40]

Caldwell seems never to have revised his poor opinion of Hollywood. He turned to the project which was to result in *You Have Seen Their Faces* to authenticate the 'cyclorama of Southern life' he had already begun in works such as *God's Little Acre* (1933) and *Tobacco Road* (1934).[41] Caldwell explains his purpose as follows: 'I had become determined to vindicate my writings about the South and I had formed a clear idea about the kind of book I wanted to prepare. For one thing, it was to be a factual study of people in the cotton states living in economic stress and it was my intention to show that my fiction was as realistic as life itself in the contemporary South. And, to be completely authentic, as I was well aware, the book would have to be thoroughly documented with photographs taken on the scene by a perceptive photographer'.[42] He found the latter in Margaret Bourke-White, who had started her career by taking industrial photographs, and the fruit of their collaboration was published under the accusatory title of *You Have Seen Their Faces* in 1937.

The volume is devoted to visibility, to forcing the reader to confront the visual evidence of Southern poverty.[43] The photographs come accompanied by brief legends quoting the subjects and similarly each prose passage by Caldwell is framed by longer quotations from subjects. Despite this strategy, the subjects appear not to have their own voices. Caldwell summarizes their speech at one or two points but these are exceptions to a general rule. Correspondingly the subjects are rarely seen in motion.[44] The scenes are static, sometimes powerfully suggesting the exhaustion of the subjects, and often being skilfully composed images carrying their own irony. For instance, the photograph captioned 'BELMONT, FLORIDA' shows two African American children, one standing and looking off left and the other, evidently disabled, in a rocker looking up towards the ceiling. These two figures are seen against a background of news-pages, which make up a collage of advertisements for the latest motor-cars. Nothing could be starker than this contrast between the poverty of the subjects and the commercial promises of mobility. A second strategy followed by Bourke-White in some of her external shots – and this resembles Pare Lorentz's practice in his documentary films – is to exploit the space of the frame to dwarf the human figures against a huge sky or landscape. We shall see Steinbeck evoking similar effects in the opening of *The Grapes of Wrath*.

In her postscript to *You Have Seen Their Faces* Bourke-White explains the care they took over choosing the moment for photographs. Caldwell would converse with subjects to distract their attention: 'It might be an hour before their faces or gestures gave us what we were trying to express, but the instant it occurred the scene was imprisoned on a sheet of film before they knew what had happened'.[45] Bourke-White gives an impression of attempted self-effacement, exactly what Steinbeck was aiming for in his early reportage. He found great power in the photographs of Bourke-White and Dorothea Lange, and chose one of the latter's studies of a mother breast-feeding her child for the cover of his 1936 pamphlet on share-croppers, *Their Blood Is Strong*.

James Agee: Screenwriter, Documentarist and Film Reviewer

In the figure of James Agee, one of the most famous documentary authors of this period, we find a combined interest in film, photography, fiction and reportage. His interest in film started so early that one of his first essays was a polemic on behalf of the cinema published in his high school magazine.[46] Throughout the late 1920s and early 1930s we find him commenting enthusiastically on films such as Murnau's *The Last Laugh* ('the perfect moving picture') and Eisenstein's *Potemkin*. But Agee's interest did not stop with viewing. In 1927 he told his friend Dwight Macdonald that he had a 'wild desire to direct *Ethan Frome* [by Edith Wharton]' and also that he would like to experiment in portraying a 'state of mind by the method of photographing commonplace things'.[47] In 1937 when he applied for a Guggenheim Fellowship, Agee listed his ongoing projects as including newsreel ('clips from newsreels, arranged for strongest possible satire, significance and comedy, with general elliptic commentary and sound'), 'a new form of movie roughly equivalent to the lyric poem', 'two forms of history of the movies', and 'moving picture notes and scenarios'. On the last, he wrote: 'much can be done […] even without a camera and money, in words. I am at least as interested in moving pictures as in writing'.[48] The declaration of a dual interest in the two media and how they might cross-match is unambiguous.

Agee privileged film among the different aspects of modernist experimentation. Seizing the opportunity of reviewing Gertrude Stein's *Geographical History of America* in 1936 as a pretext for attacking the Left's suspicion of artistic innovation, he argued that Russian movies had a unique power to engage the viewer's imagination, since 'a man who cannot by mischance grasp a problem intellectually is grasped by it if it is presented through the subtler, more forceful, and more primitive logic of movement, timing, space, and light'.[49]

Two scenarios published by Agee in the 1930s demonstrate this interest clearly and also make it clear that he was not only concerned with film as a medium of reportage. 'Notes for a Moving Picture: The House' (1937) presents a surreal portrait of a Victorian household in a modern industrial city. The opening establishes the city setting through a sinking shot which gradually reveals its chimneys and railway yards. The aerial view tends towards abstraction in composing the light and dark areas of the scene. As we follow the viewpoint down to street level, Agee gives us three measured shots (central, left and right), apparently of a deserted place. At this point human figures enter the scenario, which becomes progressively more surreal. First we see a legless army veteran reduced to selling pencils; then come two nuns, one a 'doped and dangerous homosexualist', the other demonized with 'two pale fangs'; finally a procession of scouts filmed as a group, followed by a

rapid montage of violence: 'swift intimate detail of childish feet grinding
faces of Negroes, Jews; a heel twisting out the lenses of horn-rimmed spectacles; a little hand grabbing at an open book and ripping out leaves'. As the
sequence of hands and what are held in those hands accelerates, Agee finally
reveals a 'swastikaed armband'.[50] In this sequence the first visual impression
is undermined by its succeeding details, precise close-up images suggesting
that the USA is a place of repression, violence and conflict. The street thus
becomes a metaphor of the nation and a potential site for this conflict.

The major part of Agee's scenario is devoted to a well-to-do family living
an outdated Victorian existence in a huge house. Here the Freudian imagery
becomes unmistakable as suggestive of repressed energy or lassitude: thus we
learn of one 'heavy, fly-blown woman', 'pressed next her heart she carries a
discoloured and exhausted phallus from whose glans, pulling a long hole in
the flesh, droops a wide wedding ring'.[51] The decorum of the family's procession from house to car is again undermined by such details of their
appearance which render in pictorial terms their social or sexual situations.
The family is evidently rich and so presumably members of the ruling elite of
the city; but they are presented as self-mystified anachronisms, grotesque
puppets miming out a defunct lifestyle.[52] At the end Agee shows an old woman
inside a collapsing house, apparently on the verge of the ultimate ending –
death. This scenario seems to draw on the methods of German expressionist
cinema. Agee was an admirer of Sternberg and Pabst as well as Murnau.

The second scenario which Agee published in the 1930s was an adaptation
of Part Six of André Malraux's 1934 novel *Man's Fate* (*La Condition
humaine*).[53] According to Claude-Edmonde Magny, the novel itself uses a
cinematic scenic method to depict the Communist uprising in Shanghai. It
'presents us with a series of interrelated scenes [...] always described from
the point of view of one or another of the characters [...] the camera is always
in the consciousness of a particular person'.[54] By the sixth section the
uprising has failed and one of its leaders, Kyo, has been captured and taken
to a city prison. The opening image in the novel establishes the local theme
of captivity: 'The door through which he had just passed opened on to a
corridor similar to the one he was leaving; right and left, up to the ceiling,
enormous wooden bars. Within the wooden cages, men. In the centre, the
warder seated before a small table, on which lay a whip: a short handle, a flat
thong, broad as a hand, thick as a finger – a weapon'.[55] Maurois focalizes most
of this section through Kyo until he later commits suicide with a cyanide
capsule. The description carefully follows the visual logic of the newcomer,
as his eyes take initial bearings from the entrance and then range round the
enormous cages, finally coming to rest in a close-up of the object carrying the
greatest physical threat.

For his scenario Agee drew on at least three recent films. From Jesse

Lasky's *Zoo in Budapest* (1933) he took the atmospheric use of mist and an image of captivity (most of the film takes place in a zoo). From John Ford's *The Informer* (an IRA drama of 1935) he again took the use of fog and possibly the use of the camera as narrator, for which the film was praised. Finally and most close to his subject, he acknowledged a debt to Alexander Dovschenko's 1929 film about the 1918 Bolshevik uprising in Kiev, *Arsenal*, a film which caused consternation with its sequences of apparently unrelated images. The twin motifs running through these films are rebellion and captivity; in *Arsenal* the rebels are besieged in the eponymous munitions plant.

Unlike Malraux, Agee does not limit himself to what is focalized by the characters.[56] To open his adaptation, he constructs a montage sequence of a ship's wake fading into a view of Shanghai harbour, followed in turn by the blowing of a locomotive whistle, a commentating voice explaining that the Communist captives are awaiting execution, the striking of a clock bell, and a shot of the door to the prison yard. In this way, and with great economy, Agee evokes Kyo's abandonment (his friends have fled the city) and suggests the working of a process with machine-like inevitability. Within the prison Agee scans the distorted postures of the prisoners wounded and injured, and – as he stresses in his outline – 'thrown down here like straws'.[57] The scenario is frankly partisan in its recording of the visual details of these bodies because this is exactly the sort of information not registered by the guards. Malraux understates the pathos of Kyo's suicide by quietly shifting the point of view to another prisoner as he dies. Agee, in contrast, transforms Kyo into a central figure in whom focus the different voices of the prisoners. His imminent death is shown through a progressive close-up against a background chant: 'As the A note is struck, Kyo's hand, close, intimately and silently efficient, extracts the cyanide from his belt buckle and holds it on the palm unemotionally but sensuously as a jewel, then, the A held, Kyo's face, very close, transfigured in a serene, cold exalted smile. The note enlarges to the end of its beat and quits abruptly on dead silence: the face grows brighter and stiller'.[58] On the one hand, Agee attempts to take us into Kyo's subjective life and to humanize the prisoners; on the other, his notes stress that he wanted the film to be grainy like a war newsreel. The resemblance would have been ironic, because his main concern is to show scenes which would never have appeared in a newsreel.

Agee's most famous single work from this period is his study with the photographer Walker Evans of Southern sharecroppers, *Let Us Now Praise Famous Men* (1941). This classic of reportage grew partly out of Agee's abiding interest in the cinema. As early as his Harvard days he had seen films by Robert Flaherty, famous for his documentary *Nanook of the North* (1921). Flaherty's films were produced through collaboration with the local communities he visited and we shall see how the issue of intervention is central to

Agee's own account.[59] So strong was the impact of Flaherty's films that Agee planned to make experimental films of the Boston area, though the plan came to nothing.[60] Two other films appear in the notes at the end of *Let Us Now Praise Famous Men*. The first, Karl Brown's *Stark Love* (1927), is close to Agee's own subject in being a semi-documentary on North Carolina hill folk. To depict a romance between a young couple, Brown chose two locals who were not professional actors, thereby blurring the line between his subjects and the representational process.[61] The second film was Alexander Dovschenko's *Frontier* (1935), which made a deep and lasting impression on Agee for its brilliant directing.[62]

Both the latter films clearly caught Agee's imagination because they challenged orthodoxies in their methods. As William Stott has stated, in *Let Us Now* 'Agee felt the way to shake his readers into awareness was to cheat his expectations by violating as many canons of documentary reportage as possible'.[63] The signs are everywhere, from extended catalogues risking tedium to disruptions from Agee as reporter/narrator, down to the attack on Margaret Bourke-White at the end of the book.[64] Among the many violations which Stott noted, he states that the book 'used the case-study method, but not to simplify the tenant families. It insisted that its subjects, rather than being average or representative types, were each unique'.[65] In his insistence on the actuality of the families and their homes, Agee makes his famous statement that he would like to avoid words for a more immediate medium: 'If I could do it, I'd do no writing at all here. It would be photographs; the rest would be fragments of cloth, bits of cotton, lumps of earth, records of speech, pieces of wood [etc.]'.[66] We should not read this too literally. What Agee is striving for here is a means that would do justice to the physical actuality of the sharecroppers' lives, hence his use of lists like the enumeration of items found under the main house. These objects are the metonyms of the family's life, the objects which the reader can scrutinize with the minimum intrusion into that family's life. By fantasizing an objectivist method through things Agee draws the reader's attention to the medium of reportage itself, thereby denying his text any transparency.

A preliminary step in constructing *Let Us Now* thus involves Agee's denial of his own special expertise and, more importantly for our present context, also an assertion of the proximity between verbal and photographic texts. He insists on the urgency of 'discerning' the immediate world of actuality and continues: 'This is why the camera seems to me, next to unassisted and weaponless consciousness, the central instrument of our time'.[67] Agee here validates his own collaboration with Walker Evans (who shared his enthusiasm for the cinema) and anticipates scenes in their book which he has constructed cinematically, for, apart from the risk of families attenuating into 'cases' which Stott notes, there was also the problem of intervention. How could Evans and Agee visit the families and stay in their homes without disrupting the very lives they were there to observe? Agee negotiates his way through this delicate problem in his text.

It is when Agee describes his first encounters with the families that he draws on cinematic methods. Take the example in 'At the Forks', which alternates between visualizing three figures sitting on a porch and representing what they are seeing. Despite, or rather because of the fact that the two men and one woman are sitting in silence, all the drama of the encounter is packed into the gaze. Agee gives us first the outsider's view – facial appearance, dress, etc. – then he starts his interview, but as this interview gets under way he focuses the reader's attention on the interviewees' unwavering stare: 'None of them relieved me for an instant of their eyes; at the intersection of those three tones of force I was transfixed as between spearheads as I talked'. The effect here is as if the three figures were filmed while the conversation went on below the level of audibility. Everything is happening through the eyes, not through speech. Even though they seem to relax a little, 'the qualities of their eyes did not in the least alter, nor anything visible or audible about them', because they continue to suspect that Agee is a spy.[68]

Agee never loses an awareness of his subjects' privacy. Thus in section III he gives another carefully paced awakening. This time the visual vantage point is located within a room in which others are sleeping. Agee's tact towards the intimacy of the scene is shown in his self-effacement, again into a recording agency concentrating on the exterior. As the darkness lifts the observer begins to distinguish objects, but the main signs of life at this point are sounds: the birds 'whistle, and beat metals with light hammers; and a dog comes casually though somewhat stiffly round the corner of the house, and smoke sprowls up from chimneys: and the light still whitens'.[69] Agee disperses the point of view among the members of the family as they awaken, draining off the privilege of his own initial viewpoint and rendering himself as an observer among other observers.

This same issue of privacy is addressed by Agee when he introduces us to the Gudger household. First he establishes the spatial layout of the garden plot, smokehouse, henroost and other features of their holding. Then Agee describes the exit of the mother and her children:

> slowly they diminished along the hill path, she, and her daughter, and her three sons, in leisured enfilade beneath the light. The mother first, her daughter next behind, her eldest son, her straggler, whimpering [...] At length, well up the hill, their talking shrank and became inaudible, and at that point will give safe warning on the hill of their return. Their slanted bodies slowly straightened, one by one, along the brim, and turned into the east, a slow frieze, and sank beneath the brim in order of their height, masts foundered in a horizon.[70]

This description probably owes much to the first writer named in Agee's notes – Faulkner.[71] This kind of Indian-file movement along a path opens *As I Lay Dying* and Agee shares Faulkner's care over movement and distance. The syntax draws out the slowness of the figures' movement, stating the effect first and then enumerating the subjects as the observer's eye ranges along them from front to back. Once they cross the brim of the hill the angle of their figures alters and they gradually disappear laterally. There is implicit social information conveyed through Agee's description about the observation of a family hierarchy in their order, but there is a further point to Agee's method.

The visual authenticity of this account is achieved through perspective effects measured against an unmoving observer, namely Agee himself. And notice the gloss on the figures' audibility, which will be a 'warning' on their return – a warning because the Gudgers have left their house empty and open to the investigative gaze of the narrator. The intensity of this moment of availability is expressed by Agee through a visual trope: 'upon this house the whole of heaven is drawn into one lens'.[72] No sooner has Agee identified himself with the all-seeing eye of God than he reduces his gaze to that of an adolescent probing through his own family's rooms. Agee is well aware of the voyeuristic, even sexual nature of his investigation – the house is described as a naked body sleeping before him – and so disclaims any putative objectivity. As happens at many points in the book, the reader is reminded of Agee's physical presence.[73] Instead he draws on Faulkner to give such precise descriptions of the rooms that they appear geometrical. Internal investigation is followed by slow pans and rising shots of the house frontage. Agee replaces the issue of the observer's objectivity with a quality of language. Again and again he tries to empty words of their connotations, to emulate a camera which is 'incapable of recording anything but absolute, dry truth': and at one point reflects with exasperation: 'your medium, unfortunately, is not a still or moving camera, but words'.[74]

Given Agee's repeated allusions to film, it is not surprising that one of the codas of *Let Us Now Praise Famous Men* should be 'Shady Grove: Two Images', which, he explains, are not words. The first of these is an Alabama graveyard recorded during an afternoon of absolute stillness and silence. Although Agee calls this an 'image', there is a dynamism to the scene. Having established the setting, his viewpoint then ranges along the rows of graves in a series of close-ups: 'On one of these there is a china dish on whose cover delicate hands lie crossed, cuffs at their wrists, and the nails distinct. /On another a large fluted vase stands full of dead flowers, with an inch of rusty water at the bottom'.[75] And so the items mount up, but instead of allowing a generalization about commemorative objects to emerge, Agee maintains such a detailed level of specificity that the reader is left with a startling sense of variety within this custom. The first description of this pair concerns death; the second new life. On a porch a young mother breast-feeds her baby boy. Once again the image has a general stasis but, within that, considerable movement. As he feeds, the baby's hands move, his mouth moves backwards and forwards, all small movements measured in close-up against the unchanging posture and gaze of his mother. We shall meet this concluding image again in the coda to *The Grapes of Wrath*.

During the 1940s Agee concentrated his activities in film reviewing for *Time* and *The Nation*. He later moved to Hollywood to work on film scripts with John Huston, most famously co-writing *The African Queen* (1951) and also adapting two Stephen Crane stories.[76] Film remained a central interest of Agee's right up to his death in 1955. His unfinished autobiographical novel *A Death in the Family* opens with detailed scene-by-scene memories of the Chaplin movies he had seen in childhood.[77] Chaplin was such an important figure in Agee's career that in 1947 the latter wrote a post-nuclear screenplay for him, which has only recently been unearthed and published.[78] *The Tramp's New World* combined a homage to Chaplin with an attempt to replace what Agee saw as a bland and anodyne account of the atom bomb in the 1947 documentary film *The Beginning or the End*. His screenplay comments explicitly on documentary practice in its opening scene in a movie theatre, in which a news film similar to *The March of Time* gives a 'concentrated image of the state of the world' immediately before the dropping of an atomic bomb.[79] The Tramp is the survivor-figure of the narrative, at first discovering the flattened-out traces of urban civilization and then forming a close relationship with a young girl he encounters. Agee drew on accounts of the flourishing plant life in Hiroshima to produce a surreal imagistic representation of reversion to the wilderness: 'Next shot: a show-window of Abercrombie & Fitch's; the paraphernalia of expensive big-game hunting, already half-strangled with moving vines. Swing camera left to door as Tramp emerges casually slashing out of his way, with a machete, an arm-thick vine'.[80] Agee sets up a dialogue on the nature of humanity by cutting between the actions of the Tramp and those of scientists which have survived in underground laboratories. The ending of the screenplay shows the Tramp escaping the clutches of the scientists, walking down an endless road into the sunset 'growing ever more spry in its sense of freedom and a little twilight of fun ahead'.[81] Although there is an ambiguous openness to this ending, Agee made no bones about parodying the USA, which in his screenplay is re-named Obnoxia.

Notes

1   Denzin, *The Cinematic Society*, p. 16.
2   Eliot Weinberger, 'The Camera People', pp. 12, 8.
3   Peter Humm, 'Camera Eye/Private Eye', in Brian Docherty, ed., *American Crime Fiction*, pp. 23–38.
4   Joseph North, 'Reportage', in Henry Hart, ed., *American Writers Congress*, p. 121.
5   Agnes Smedley (1892–1950) had been making a name for herself since 1928 through her reports on developments in China.
6   For example, in the pages of *New Masses* Robert Forsythe contrasted Frank Borzage's film about a young couple in the Depression, *Little Man, What Now?* (1934), with Pudovkin's adaptation of Gorky's *Mother*, finding the latter full of 'vitality and warmth and deep emotional content' (Robert Forsythe, 'Hollywood – and Gorky' (1934), in Joseph North, ed., *New Masses*, pp. 230–33).
7   Eudora Welty, *The Eye of the Story*, p. 353.
8   Welty, *The Eye of the Story*, pp. 14–15.
9   Welty, *The Eye of the Story*, p. 354.
10 John Dos Passos, *Century's Ebb*, p. 42.
11 Louise Westling, 'The Loving Observer of *One Time, One Place*'.
12 Shloss, *In Visible Light*, p. 263.
13 Eudora Welty, *Stories, Essays, and Memoir*, p. 880.
14 Peggy Whitman Prenshaw, ed., *Conversations with Eudora Welty*, p. 169.
15 Leslie A. Kaplansky, 'Cinematic Rhythms in the Short Fiction of Eudora Welty'. This essay concentrates mainly on slow-motion effects and cutting techniques.
16 Welty, *Stories, Essays, and Memoir*, p. 17.
17 For instance, Ornitz's narrator describes a smoky goulash restaurant as follows: 'My impression is of a misty sea with bobbing heads as buoys and waving hands as sails; laden schooners, waiters, carrying remarkable numbers of dishes in both arms, cruise through the aisle-channels' (Samuel Ornitz, *Allrightniks Row*, p. 195). These sense-impressions are loosely linked by ellipses, as happens in Henry Miller's Paris novels, and are presented as a series of 'Periods' in the narrator's life. The novel's orchestration of visual scenes anticipates Ornitz's career change in 1928 when he moved to Hollywood to write screenplays for the major studios. He collaborated with Dos Passos in investigating the conditions of the Harlan County miners. For commentary on Ornitz's Hollywood career, see Gabriel Miller, 'Samuel Ornitz', in Randall Clark, ed., *American Screenwriters: Second Series*, pp. 273–77.
18 Dos Passos, *U.S.A.*, p. 5.
19 Tom Kromer, *Waiting for Nothing*, p. 5.
20 Kromer, *Waiting for Nothing*, p. 68.
21 William Stott, *Documentary Expression*, p. 198. For further commentary on Kromer, see Hugh Crawford, 'On the Fritz'.
22 Juan A. Suarez, 'John Dos Passos' *U.S.A.*', pp. 62–3. This essay contains valuable details of Dos Passos' film activities in the 1930s.
23 Alexander, *Film on the Left*, p. 74. In 1935 Strand had visited the Soviet Union and met with Eisenstein.
24 Alexander, *Film on the Left*, pp. 113, 146.
25 Carr, *Dos Passos: A Life*, p. 364.
26 Stephen Koch, *The Breaking Point*, p. 62 and passim. Koch's information on Comintern activities is taken from Hans Schoot's biography of Ivens and from FBI files on former

Communist agents.

27 Dos Passos was to be discredited in line with Stalin's directive that socialist realism should replace modernism in the arts. Whether by accident or design, his name was used without his permission to support the American Committee for Leon Trotsky. Despite the evidence to the contrary, some critics still seem convinced that Hemingway had major input into the film; see John Garrick's 'Hemingway and *The Spanish Earth*' (in Oliver, ed., *A Moving Picture Feast*, pp. 76–90), in which he argues that Hemingway went to Spain from professional motives rather than from political commitment.

28 The first sign that Robles was dead came to Dos Passos from the novelist Josephine Herbst who conveyed to him the Comintern smear that Robels had been killed as a fascist spy. Herbst was present at some of the filming of *The Spanish Earth* and recorded her own memories of the civil war in *The Starched Blue Sky of Spain* (1991). Dos Passos' thinly disguised account of Spain comes in *Century's Ebb* (1975).

29 Carr, *Dos Passos: A Life*, pp. 369–72.

30 Jeffrey Meyers, *Hemingway: A Biography*, p. 313. MacLeish and Ivens liked Welles's reading; Fredric March and Lillian Hellman found it too polished.

31 Koch describes this speech as a 'pack of Popular Front platitudes rehashed in Hemingwayese' (*The Breaking Point*, p. 224).

32 Joris Ivens, *The Camera and I*, pp. 113–14.

33 Meyers, *Hemingway: A Biography*, p. 316.

34 Ernest Hemingway, *The Spanish Earth*, pp. 9, 13. Dos Passos was acknowledged for his help in creating Contemporary Historians, but not for participating in the film. The book concluded with an essay by Hemingway called 'The Heat and the Cold' in which he elaborates on the proposition that 'what you see in motion on the screen is not what you remember' (p. 55). Richard Allan Davison has shown that Hemingway was profoundly dissatisfied with the published volume *The Spanish Earth* ('The Publication of Hemingway's *The Spanish Earth*').

35 Hemingway, *The Spanish Earth*, p. 27.

36 Hemingway, *The Spanish Earth*, p. 51.

37 Hemingway, 'Night before Battle', in *Complete Short Stories*, p. 438.

38 Hemingway, 'Under the Ridge', in *Complete Short Stories*, p. 460. Hemingway also wrote a story called 'Landscape with Figures' around 1938 dealing with a film crew in the Spanish Civil War.

39 One of the books he reviewed was Anita Loos's *Gentlemen Prefer Blondes*, suggested by his fellow reviewer Margaret Mitchell.

40 Erskine Caldwell, *Call It Experience*, pp. 102–103. MGM called Caldwell back for a further spell of screenwriting to collaborate with Harry Behn on a story about logging.

41 Caldwell, *Call It Experience*, p. 156. A cyclorama was a huge circular painting, usually depicting historical and military scenes. One of the most famous cycloramas in the USA was housed in Atlanta and depicted the Battle of Atlanta of 1864. This was probably the local origin of Caldwell's analogy.

42 Caldwell, *With All My Might*, p. 145.

43 It is the volume's regionalism that gives it much of its force. In contrast, Caldwell and Bourke-White's later collaboration, *Say, is this the U.S.A.* (1941) presents contemporary American life as a huge spectacle, a kind of nation-wide theatre, which the reporters can enjoy through tours around the country by train.

44 In the summer of 1932 Bourke-White made a second visit to the Soviet Union where she shot several film sequences. She subsequently tried to place these in Hollywood, but without success.

45 Erskine Caldwell and Margaret Bourke-White, *You Have Seen Their Faces*, p. 51.
46 James Agee, 'The Moving Picture'. Discussed in Laurence Bergreen, *James Agee: A Life*, pp. 37–38.
47 Bergreen, *James Agee: A Life*, pp. 37, 48, 49. Macdonald, a friend from Agee's Harvard years, went on to become a leading film critic. His reviews are collected in Dwight Macdonald, *On Movies* (1981), which contains his memoir essay 'Agee and the Movies' (pp. 3–14).
48 James Agee, *Collected Short Prose*, pp. 131–32, 139, 147.
49 James Agee, 'Art for What's Sake', *New Masses*, p. 50.
50 Agee, *Collected Short Prose*, p. 154.
51 Agee, *Collected Short Prose*, p. 157.
52 The scenario was first published in a 1937 anthology of proletarian literature, *New Letters in America*, edited by Horace Gregory and Eleanor Clark.
53 'Man's Fate' was published in Jay Leyda's *Films* (1939). Leyda had studied under Eisenstein, whose works he subsequently translated, at the Moscow Film Institute. After his return to the USA in 1936 he became the assistant film curator at the New York Museum of Modern Art. Leyda and Agee were regular correspondents in the 1940s.
54 Magny, *The Age of the American Novel*, p. 85. For Magny this technique reflects Malraux's existential commitment to individual engaged vision. Malraux himself approached Eisenstein about the possibility of collaborating on a film adaptation of his novel.
55 André Maurois, *Man's Fate*, p. 205.
56 In that sense Agee's adaptation might be even more cinematic than Malraux's narrative since, as Bruce Morissette argues, cinematic viewpoint does not have to follow the same rules as point of view in fiction and therefore does not have to be tied to an individual consciousness (*Novel and Film: Essays in Two Genres*, pp. 42–43).
57 Agee, *Collected Short Prose*, p. 206.
58 Agee, *Collected Short Prose*, p. 215.
59 Flaherty went on to produce a domestic documentary, *The Land* (1942), made for the US Department of Agriculture.
60 Bergreen, *James Agee: A Life*, p. 63.
61 Brown had earlier served as assistant to Billy Bitzer, D. W. Griffith's cameraman, and had helped create some of the special effects for *Intolerance*.
62 Agee, *Film Writing and Selected Journalism*, p. 295.
63 Stott, *Documentary Expression*, p. 265.
64 Carol Shloss explains this attack as arising from a perception that Bourke-White was pandering to middle-class images of poverty in her readers (*In Visible Light*, pp. 183–87).
65 Stott, *Documentary Expression*, p. 291.
66 Agee, *Let Us Now Praise Famous Men*, p. 28.
67 Agee, *Let Us Now Praise Famous Men*, p. 20.
68 Agee, *Let Us Now Praise Famous Men*, p. 45.
69 Agee, *Let Us Now Praise Famous Men*, p. 88.
70 Agee, *Let Us Now Praise Famous Men*, p. 128.
71 'Detail of gesture, landscape, costume, air, action, mystery throughout the writings of William Faulkner' (Agee, *Let Us Now Praise Famous Men*, p. 381).
72 Agee, *Let Us Now Praise Famous Men*, p. 128.
73 And therefore Carol Shloss's claim that Agee tries to strike the posture of a disembodied camera is only rarely valid (*In Visible Light*, p. 193).
74 Agee, *Let Us Now Praise Famous Men*, pp. 206, 207.
75 Agee, *Let Us Now Praise Famous Men*, p. 369.

76 *The Blue Hotel*, written in 1948–49, was never made into a film. *The Bride Comes to Yellow Sky* was written in 1951–52 and the subsequent film released in 1952. Both scripts are published in *Agee on Film: Five Film Scripts* (1960).

77 Chaplin was such an important figure to Agee that he reviewed *Monsieur Verdoux* (1947) no less than four times in defiance of Chaplin's declining popularity. *A Death in the Family* was published in 1957, edited by David McDowell.

78 John Wranovics' *Chaplin and Agee* (2005) publishes the full text of Agee's screenplay together with a detailed account of Agee's respect for Chaplin, the latter's fall from grace in the USA, and Agee's Hollywood activities.

79 Wranovics, *Chaplin and Agee*, p. 164.

80 Wranovics, *Chaplin and Agee*, p. 178.

81 Wranovics, *Chaplin and Agee*, p. 208.

10

John Steinbeck: Extensions of Documentary

Steinbeck before *The Grapes of Wrath*

The flourishing of documentary gives us a context within which to situate the most famous works of John Steinbeck. Indeed there is some evidence that he planned *The Grapes of Wrath* to be a photo-text and, if so, he was picking up on a two-media kind of reportage which was becoming popular in the 1930s.[1] Agee and Evans did most of their work for *Let Us Now Praise Famous Men* in 1936, the same year in which Steinbeck produced his articles on the migrant workers of California, which were to lead ultimately to *The Grapes of Wrath*.[2] He was invited to write these pieces by the editor of the *San Francisco News* and they were later published in pamphlet form with photographs by Dorothea Lange under the title *Their Blood is Strong*.[3] It has been argued convincingly by Carol Shloss that these essays followed in tracks well laid out by the reports on migrant workers' camps by Paul Taylor and Lange, and for the most part they simply rehearse facts and figures.[4] One exception, however, is the second article in the series, which takes the reader on a guided tour of one of these camps. Steinbeck acts on the reader's assumed need to see by transforming himself into a verbal camera while keeping up a running commentary. First he locates the typical camp near a water source, then he gives us the long shot: 'from a distance it looks like a city dump, and well it may, for the city dumps are the sources for the material of which it is built. You can see a litter of dirty rags and scrap iron, of houses built of weeds, of flattened cans or of paper. It is only on close approach that it can be seen that these are homes'.[5] Steinbeck shrewdly implies that the reader's conception of such a camp is formed by notions of normality, within which rubbish and home would be mutually exclusive categories, but the visual movement of this opening gradually breaks down this opposition. As we approach, we register texture and then shape, only finally interpreting the significance of the latter.

A major issue that recurs in this chapter has been the fantasy of the investigator's invisibility in reportage and a number of critics have commented on Steinbeck's insistence that his identity be concealed when in 1938 he visited other migrant camps with Tom Collins, a worker for the Resettlement Administration. Early signs of that self-elision can be found in Steinbeck's cumbersome formulation 'it can be seen' to depersonalize his report. In his account of the camp Steinbeck directs our attention insistently outwards away from his camera eye, in the process suppressing the question of how the migrants responded to the intrusion of the investigator. Having taken us towards a home, Steinbeck leads us inside and only after establishing the physical actuality of their dwelling does he introduce the migrants themselves. Where the opening has a clear cinematic dynamic, the subsequent descriptions resemble a series of snapshots loosely linked by the indicator 'here'. Thus Steinbeck tries to convey the inertia that hardship is inducing in one family: 'the dullness shows in the faces of this family, and in addition there is a sullenness that makes them taciturn'.[6] Once again we encounter the faces of the poor as the most expressive image in the report. Steinbeck obviously wants to keep his descriptions immediate and clear, but the result – as witnessed by his use of serial statements ('this the middle of the squatters' camp', 'he sits on the ground', and so on) – is that the migrants are flattened out into visual data on a par with their environment.

It was in this period that Pare Lorentz began his film-making and we shall see that Lorentz not only became a personal friend of Steinbeck's but also suggested ways in which *The Grapes of Wrath* could be constructed. In 1935 Lorentz joined the Nykino group, becoming known as the 'Erskine Caldwell of the movies'.[7] After the Resettlement Administration was established in 1935 Lorentz was named as their film consultant and when Roosevelt established the US Film Service in 1938 it was with Lorentz as director. He established himself through two documentary films: *The Plow that Broke the Plains* (1936) and *The River* (1938).

The Plow (as it is usually named) 'embodied a concept of epic implications: capitalism's anarchic rape of the land'.[8] It had the broad historic sweep that we shall find in Steinbeck's novel and more importantly Lorentz made the land itself the protagonist. The narration opens with the words 'this is a record of land... / of soil, rather than people', but of course it is a record of the impact of the land on the fortunes of its inhabitants.[9] First the film shows the coming of the cattle herds, then the railways and settlers. A montage of the first harvesting machines gives way to an ominous shot of gathering clouds and the warning 'settler, plow at your peril!'[10] Lorentz's initial contrasts are established between movement and stasis: between the activity of settlement and cultivation, and the sudden paralysis as the land begins to fail. Then, with the coming of the First World War, we enter a sequence in which lines of tanks repeatedly alternate with rows of tractors, ostensibly reflecting the historical drive to produce more wheat. At the end of this section Lorentz underscores the symmetry between warfare and industrial farming by having tanks move across the screen from left to right, immediately followed by tractors moving in the opposite direction. The effect is to transpose the imagery of conflict on to the land and to suggest an attack on the landscape itself by big business.[11]

Lorentz makes no bones about apportioning responsibility for the destruction of the land to the forces of big business, which are figured as a line of harvesters moving repeatedly across the screen over which he superimposes shots of posters promising migrants free land. Once again, rapid movement gives way to immobility. As the land fails, the camera pans over close or medium shots of abandoned homesteads, pieces of machinery, and dead animals. The deceptive calm of these shots is totally lost as storm clouds gather and break. Against the noise of the wind we hear the following: 'baked out – blown out – and broke! / Year in, year out, uncomplaining they fought / the worst drought in history… / their stock choked to death on the barren land… / their homes were nightmares of swirling dust / night and day'.[12] This is the same trigger which Steinbeck was to use as the opening of *The Grapes of Wrath*. Lorentz anticipates his novel by counterpointing lines of migrants' cars moving along the road with images of domestic items and spaces abandoned. Interestingly, in these shots the men are shown inactive, pointlessly whittling sticks, while the women unpack gear for their camps. The coda to Lorentz's film shows the new land improvement schemes and the building of federal housing areas, predictably since the film was made to support Roosevelt's agencies.

Although the narration for *The Plow that Broke the Plains* is relatively spare, the film is a formally complex work at times; in the episode where the promotional posters are shown these have to be read against the background image. In the case of *The River* Lorentz used a narration in a free verse form which had originally been intended to stand alone as an article in *McCall's*. Not only was it more substantial; it was so well received that Lorentz published it in book form with stills from his film. The popularity of the narration can be related to the film's subject. This time 'the Mississippi is Lorentz's epic hero', presented as an image of the nation itself.[13] The film opens in the northern mountains at the river's source and then the poetry of names begins as Lorentz lists all the tributary rivers feeding into the Mississippi:

> Down the Yellowstone, the Milk, the White and Cheyenne;
> The Cannonball, the Musselshell, the James and the Sioux;
> Down the Judith, the Grand, the Osage, and the Platte,
> The Skunk, the Salt, the Black, and Minnesota…[14]

And so the list goes on. Like Whitman before him, Lorentz enumerates names as a means of evoking the whole nation. Indeed in film and book a relief map shows the whole drainage area of the Mississippi with the caption 'The Body of the Nation'. More than that, Lorentz presents the Mississippi as the supreme highway of America in a way which anticipates Steinbeck's depiction of Route 66, with the difference that Lorentz's river is above all a trade route, a place for national areas to converge and then at its mouth expand outwards towards the world.

The point of the early scenes is first to establish the natural plenty of the USA, then to show national strengths, and only after that to depict the recurring problem of flooding.[15] In both films Lorentz was particularly concerned to convey the scale of his subject, which he did by supplying statistics and also by exploiting the space of the screen, in *The River* showing the water level no more than a third of the way up the frame. Here Lorentz implicitly criticizes the traces of the frontier mentality – which assumes that the cure for a problem is to move on – by insisting on the scale of waste. The following lines in the book face a still of a sharecropper staring out across a dry, barren landscape:

Year in, year out, the water comes down
From a thousand hillsides, washing the top off the Valley.
For fifty years we dug for cotton and moved West when the land gave out.
For fifty years we plowed for corn, and moved on when the land gave out [...]
And four hundred million tons of top soil,
Four hundred million tons of our most valuable natural resource have been washed into the Gulf of Mexico every year.[16]

Unlike *The Plow*, this film shows the battle between humanity and the elements. It reaches a grand symbolic climax in panning along power lines to highlight the film's main theme: human power to control the environment.

Steinbeck met Lorentz in February 1938 shortly before he left to report on the floods in Vissalia. He had already begun work on *The Grapes of Wrath*, but subsequently, perhaps under the influence of the meeting and seeing Lorentz's films, completely revised his manuscript. The two men quickly became close friends and Steinbeck admitted: 'he's about the *only* man I would do a picture with'.[17] Lorentz took Steinbeck to Hollywood to try get United Artists interested in adapting *In Dubious Battle*, which Lorentz was convinced was one of Steinbeck's best books and for which he planned to co-write the script with Steinbeck.[18] He also arranged for Steinbeck to see *The Plow that Broke the Plains* and *The River*; Steinbeck later admitted that the latter film had played a part in the chapter of *The Grapes* where he names the towns along Route 66.[19] Steinbeck was enthusiastic about Lorentz's radio play *Ecce Homo!*, whose use of the Battle Hymn of the Republic may have suggested the title for Steinbeck's novel to his wife Carol.[20] In the course of their meetings Lorentz explained his theories of documentary to Steinbeck, which very likely had an impact on the latter's composition of *The Grapes*.[21] In January 1939 Steinbeck wrote to Lorentz saying 'if I could be of any service in your work, I'd like to be. I am quite selfish about this. I want to learn the medium or something about it and I want to study it under you.'[22] By this date Steinbeck had completed the manuscript of *The Grapes of Wrath* but it would be absurd to deny that his interest in film dated from a period prior to 1939.

Lorentz's montage in *The River* was designed to sum up the nation. In a similar spirit, the novelist Thomas Wolfe started a cinematic text to express the USA. Despite his refusal of an invitation to write screenplays when he visited Hollywood in 1935, according to John Lane Idol, this visit gave him a 'renewed appreciation of cinematic techniques', which bore fruit in his unfinished montage sequence *The Hound of Darkness*.[23] Wolfe's plan was to present images of the USA starting with an opening panoramic shot in which the point of view ranges around national space. Like other documentary writers of this period, Wolfe attempts to present a summative visual image of the USA: 'the spectator to this giant panorama sees at once and instantly the whole dimension of the nation, spread out in the essential lineaments of a gigantic map'. This panorama is the establishing shot, which then closes up in phases ('the vision nears and deepens' is the repeated guide-phrase) on to scenes from different states.[24] Wolfe's transitions are cinematic in using fades and dissolves or the images of leaves to facilitate movement from one activity to the other; and he shares the common documentary impulse of the 1930s in attempting an inclusive, anonymous point of view which will actualize the USA visually. His use of panorama, cinematic transitions and his projection of the scale of his subject link his project with Steinbeck's epic novel.

The Grapes of Wrath

When Steinbeck saw the 1940 film of *The Grapes of Wrath* he expressed his pleasure at the fact that Darryl F. Zanuck had produced a 'hard, straight picture in which the actors are submerged so completely that it looks and feels like a documentary film'.[25] His satisfaction implies that he had conceived his novel, if not on documentary lines, at least with a strong documentary emphasis, and towards this end he designed two types of chapters. The single most striking formal characteristic of *The Grapes of Wrath* is its alternation between chapters dealing with the Joad family and those dealing with contextual material. Clearly the latter were designed to give the larger picture, but to this end they demonstrate a considerable range of visual techniques: a depiction of the reclaiming of deserted houses by cats and bats when there is no longer any actual human presence (11), roadside montage and reversed points of view on the migrants (15), generic views of fruit-picking (27), or panoramic and accelerated sequences of the masses in search of work (21). By Steinbeck's own account, the interchapters were conceived at an early stage of the composition of the novel and before he saw Lorentz's *The River* (though he does not mention *The Plow*), and one model which he confirmed for this structure was that of Dos Passos' *U.S.A.*, which, as we have seen, was itself cinematic in conception.[26]

Dos Passos thus offered Steinbeck a means of moving to and fro between a specific narrative and analogous or contextualizing material.[27] In addition, Dos Passos probably alerted Steinbeck to the imagery of the roadside which comes out powerfully in Chapter 15:

> Along 66 the hamburger stands – Al & Susy's Place – Carl's Lunch – Joe & Minnie – Will's Eats. Board-and-bat shacks. Two gasoline pumps in front, a screen door, a long bar, stools, and a foot rail. Near the door three slot machines, showing through glass the wealth in nickels three bars will bring. And beside them, the nickel phonograph with records piled up like pies [...] The walls decorated with posters, bathing girls, blondes with big breasts and slender hips and waxen faces, in white bathing suits, and holding a bottle of Coca-Cola [...] The signs on cards, picked out in shining mica: Pies Like Mother Used to Make. Credit Makes Enemies, Let's Be Friends.[28]

The visual particularity in this description clearly exemplifies Steinbeck's incremental method of 'piling detail on detail until a picture and an experience emerge'.[29] The ordering of these details follows the visual sequence of someone arriving, entering and then scanning the interior along the bar to the slot machines, up to the walls, and finally back to the cards at bar level. As Dos Passos demonstrated in *Manhattan Transfer*, advertisements and signs generally make promises to the gazing consumer. Put a nickel in the machine and you might get rich; buy a Coke and you might get a bathing beauty.[30] Not only does a picture of the interior emerge; Steinbeck also ironically demonstrates through deadpan juxtaposition the blatant contradictions between the signs in the final quoted examples. Some profer a bogus intimacy; others (the more overt or honest) warn of hostility between consumer and seller. Ultimately *The Grapes of Wrath* is about conflict and the signs enumerated both demonstrate and partly explain the cause of this conflict. The Coke poster is more glamorous than the handbills promising work to the migrants, but both are making promises that cannot be fulfilled.

If Dos Passos alerted Steinbeck to the visual signs of American commerce, Pare Lorentz indicated ways in which the scale of rural disruption could be represented. William Howarth, one of the very few critics to address the importance of Lorentz, has argued that Steinbeck's fiction 'emulated Lorentz's narrative principles, shifting from foreground to background, cutting from panorama to close-up, providing choric and lyric commentary in the expository chapters'.[31] *The Grapes of Wrath* begins and ends with cataclysms, with a dust storm and a flood, and Lorentz's *The Plow* could have suggested the first and *The River* the second. Steinbeck's famous opening resembles a nature documentary in which the narration explains the pattern of events. However, as the description progresses, there is a gradual lapse of colour to grey (the land) and red (the sun); and once the storm starts distinctions between the land and the air become totally lost. Steinbeck evokes the huge spaces of the American landscape by weaving in the presence of the farmers, tiny figures dwarfed by the dust storm. This is one of the last images in *The Plow that Broke the Plains* and Steinbeck may be playing on the ambiguity of an ending (of the rain, of the order of Nature) being presented as a beginning. The dust in this chapter not only immobilizes the farmers; they also lose their sight as the world seems to descend into an extended twilight. Steinbeck's evocation of the dynamics of space, to Lorentz's disappointment, was lost in Ford's film adaptation. Lorentz complained that the screenwriter (Nunnally Johnson) 'needed to think in terms of skies and brown land and, most of all, wind'.[32] In fact, the film does evoke space in its transitional sequences, either to suggest distance through perspective shots along roads or by dwarfing human figures in the bottom of the frame, but these sequences tend to be brief.

Exactly the same process occurs in the penultimate chapter when the rains come. This time Steinbeck shows the grey twilight to be the prelude to an invasion from below, as the flood waters gradually rise.[33] Here, as in the opening chapter, natural events are tied to the bemused observers within the scene and both episodes are linked through an unobtrusive but important image: the green shoots in the ground. In the first chapter they die; at the end they might be read as promising rebirth, though any signs of optimism in the novel's ending must remain problematic.

Steinbeck has confirmed that he drew on Lorentz in Chapter 12 where he names all the towns along Route 66. In *The River* Lorentz had presented the Mississippi as the main artery running through the national organism of the American landscape. In *The Grapes of Wrath* Steinbeck similarly designates 66 as the 'mother road', implying that all the towns are its biological offshoots. His application of Lorentz's poetry of place-names, however, is offset by two ironies. Firstly Route 66 was constructed as a commercial route – remember that the very first image in the Joad chapters is of a huge red truck – and secondly the changed circumstances of the Depression have transformed 66 into a means of flight (the word is repeated throughout the chapter). Within the organic metaphor, then, it is as if the migrant farmers represent the collective blood of the nation, draining wastefully away.

The interchapters to *The Grapes of Wrath* do much more than simply add new information. They constantly invite the reader/viewer to take up a new perspective on the novel's subject. For instance, the famous land turtle chapter (3) suggests a natural analogue for the migrants' dogged progress westward and also sets up a very low vantage-point almost at road level. Or again Chapter 11 describes an abandoned farm-house, evoking its pathos from the fact that no one is observing it. A more complex and emotive instance comes in Chapter 5 where Steinbeck gives concrete embodiment to the process of dispossession in the tractors. In Lorentz's *The Plow* we saw how lines of tractors were identified with tanks attacking the landscape itself. Steinbeck pursues a similar tack by making his tractors mechanical travesties of living creatures seen from a distance as scavengers. When the focus suddenly closes up on the driver the image begins to resemble science fiction: 'The man sitting in the iron seat did not look like a man; gloved, goggled, rubber dust mask over nose and mouth, he was a part of the monster, a robot in the seat'.[34] It was scarcely necessary, but Steinbeck glosses his appearance as a muffling of the senses, a blocking especially of his organs of sight and speech. The novel constantly modifies its own imagery according to local situations and the image of the driver recapitulates the farmsteaders' reaction to the dust storm in the opening chapter. The difference is that now the driver has become the alienated agent of the big landowners. Despite the implication of control in his role, he is shown – again through image – to be an extension of his machine, which is used to push houses off their foundations. In the equivalent scene of the 1940 John Ford film the tractors drive into the screen towards the viewer's vantage point as if they are running over us.

Scenic Composition in *The Grapes of Wrath*

During the late 1930s when Steinbeck was turning his hand to reportage, he tried out an experiment which anticipates part of *The Grapes of Wrath*. *Of Mice and Men* (1937), his short narrative of itinerant farm hands, was conceived as a 'play-novelette', a 'play written in the physical technique of the novel'. It was designed to limit the action to a sequence of scenes, but using descriptive methods from the novel to 'make for a better visual picture for the reader'.[35] This is the crucial point. Although Steinbeck explained his novel in terms of a theatre analogy, a better comparison, or at least an equally productive one, would be with the cinema. *Of Mice and Men* uses a number of exterior scenes which would be near-impossible to present on the stage. The opening shot, for example, establishes a natural context within which the two protagonists George and Lennie (the massively built 'natural' of the novel) are introduced. From the very start Steinbeck uses setting to comment on his characters, especially at the point at which the novelette's sexual drama begins.

Steinbeck evokes a world of farmhands which is almost entirely male. When George and Lennie first hear that one of the workers has a young wife, it occurs in the men's bunk-house, a place of male camaraderie and a refuge from the beating sun. Notice how the first appearance of Curley's wife is a visual shock: 'Both men glanced up, for the rectangle of sunshine in the doorway was cut off. A girl was standing there looking in. She had full, rouged lips and wide-spaced eyes, heavily made up. Her finger-nails were red. Her hair hung in little rolled clusters like sausages. She wore a cotton house dress and red mules, on the insteps of which were little bouquets of red ostrich feathers'.[36] Curley's wife is seen first as a shadow, someone who blocks the light of the sun, and who is thus implicitly contrasted with nature. Steinbeck leaves us in no doubt about this by foregrounding her make-up as her main gender marker in the description. She is literally red from head to foot, making a startling contrast with the drab hues of the men's appearance. More than this, Steinbeck crudely exploits the conventional connotations of redness to present the girl as a brazen temptress who initiates a sexual melodrama that will lead ultimately to her death and that of Lennie. And all of this without any narrative comment. The suggestions all emerge through the narrative's imagery.

Steinbeck applies a similar method in *The Grapes of Wrath*, where the limiting of commentary to the interchapters gives greater visual immediacy to the Joad chapters and also suggests the migrants' isolation. The famous opening description of the dust storms evokes not just a radical disturbance to the order of Nature, but also a confusion of vision. The point of view here is larger than that of any individual within the scene and Tom Joad enters the narrative initially as a generic figure already in transit. From the very beginning Steinbeck establishes a quasi-documentary perspective on events – a perspective of informed visual witness. Although the interchapters temporarily suspend the Joad narrative, Steinbeck takes care that continuity should be maintained through suture-like linking passages at the beginning and end of each of the Joad chapters. He is, as it were, stitching together his narrative over the gaps created by the interchapters, but never with the intention of an effect of seamlessness which characterizes suture in film criticism.[37] On the contrary, Steinbeck never allows us to forget the interchapters, which determine our view of the main narrative. As Vivian Sobchack has noted, the Joads' 'family unit is not metaphorical in function; it is, instead, illustrative. Its importance in the novel is not in its mythic cohesion and endurance, but in its realistic specificity'.[38]

In his documentary film *The Forgotten Village* Steinbeck explains that from two possible approaches – the 'generalized method' and the specific – he chose the second: 'our story centred on one family in one small village. We wished our audience to know this family very well, and incidentally to like it, as we did'.[39] This could stand equally well as a comment on his novel. Steinbeck draws us into the Joads by initially exploiting the point of view of Tom rejoining his family from prison. Through him, the narrative makes extensive use of the family gaze, the subtle exchange of looks between different members which helps to re-bond them prior to setting off on their travels. For example, in the reunion between Tom and Ma Tom bites his lip with emotion so hard that it starts bleeding. This is a visual sign recognized by the reader through Ma's point of view. Since the Joads in general speak laconically, it is crucial that such visual hints of their subjective life be given in order to engage the reader from the start. Thus, in the silent mime in Chapter 10 where Ma alone puts her keepsakes into the stove, the visual focus alternates between her face and the objects being thrown away, giving the reader privileged access to a moving private moment.

Steinbeck's general visual focus from the first chapter on through succeeding interchapters gives an added dimension to the action. Just as Frank Norris evokes the huge open spaces of the landscapes in *The Octopus* and *McTeague*, Steinbeck uses perspective shots along roads partly to convey the sheer distance the migrants have to travel and at one point to suggest their rite of passage into California as they cross the 'ramparts' of the Arizona mountains. One of the most charged moments in the early section of the novel is the Joads' departure from their home. To render the pathos of this event Steinbeck visually transforms the farm as the family gazes on it one evening:

> The film of evening light made the red earth lucent, so that its dimensions were deepened, so that a stone, a post, a building had greater depth and more solidity than in the daytime light. [Objects become over-individualized and even the earth seems to glow.] The front of the grey, paintless house, facing the west, was luminous as the moon is. The grey dusty truck, in the yard before the door, stood out magically in this light, in the overdrawn perspective of a stereopticon.[40]

Steinbeck repeatedly uses references to the sun as a visual time marker, specifically exploiting the traditional associations of sunset as an ending to colour departures and leave-taking. Steinbeck highlights this aspect of scale on the morning the Joads are about to set out: 'They saw the shed take shape against the light, and they saw the lanterns pale until they no longer cast their circles of yellow light. The stars went out, few by few, towards the west. And still the family stood about like dream-walkers, their eyes focused panoramically, seeing no detail, but the whole dawn, the whole land, the whole texture of the country at once'.[41] Proximate domestic objects give us the measure of distance here. Indeed, the scene is like a dissolve away from their home (signifying the past) towards the land in the west where their future lies. In contrast, the Joads' first view of California takes place in morning light shining westwards down the valley before them and casting a golden glow over everything. Here the scene visually encapsulates the migrants' hopes as idyllic images of promise stretching into the distance.

Once the Joads join the other migrants on the road, Steinbeck begins to make regular use of firelight and candle- or lamplight in the visual composition of scenes. When characters gather round a candle, as they do after Grandpa's death, or around a fire at the migrants' camps, the light composes the scene, drawing the travellers into circles of shared suffering or endeavour against the hostile forces of the night. The one section which makes a startling exception to this practice is the Weedpatch camp where everything is seen clearly. Once again we have a symbolic time marker: a father and son were 'facing to the east and their faces were lighted by dawn. The image of the mountain and the light coming over it were reflected in their eyes'.[42] This scene is focalized through Tom and clearly suggests new hope. Without allegorizing the image too heavily (although Steinbeck's allusions to *The Pilgrim's Progress* encourage us to do so), the mountain of difficulty is being surmounted by the light of a new beginning. Not only is the Weedpatch camp described more vividly; its inmates regain pride in their appearance. In other words they are taking over control of their own visibility. Brightly lit images of cooking, washing, and dancing therefore reflect a shift in the behaviour of the inmates. Unfortunately, the imperative of finding work to survive means that the Joads' stay will only be temporary.

Where the film adaptation of the novel concludes with a progressive image of the workers ascending a hill range, Steinbeck's own final scene is the tactful filmic (but probably still unfilmable) scene of Rose of Sharon giving her breast to an old man. Steinbeck carefully avoids any hint of voyeurism by concentrating on mothering gestures and Rose's enigmatic smile: 'Her hand moved behind his head and supported it. Her fingers moved gently in his hair. She looked up and across the barn, and her lips came together and smiled mysteriously'.[43] The visual vantage point is notional because we know no one else is present in the barn, but the implicit direction of Rose's gaze away from the 'camera' reassures the observer that her privacy is intact. This marks an important difference from Steinbeck's source image, the Dorothea Lange photograph which he used for the cover of his pamphlet *Their Blood Is Strong*. The scene with Rose represents a kinetic variation on this image whereby the subject looks away from the visual vantage point. Apart from her enigmatic expression, the scene reflects its origin in continuing to present the reader with reportage; in other words it still reports on conditions, without giving any but the most tenuous hints of how the migrants can better their lot.

At the beginning of this chapter we saw how the investigative gaze in documentaries sometimes comes disturbingly close to that of the supervisory authorities; supervision literally means 'looking over'. Investigation approaches surveillance. This was the issue grappled with so strenuously by James Agee and this also lay behind Steinbeck's evocation of the family gaze in *The Grapes of Wrath*. However, this novel grows darker, literally and metaphorically, as the migrants come into conflict with the malign authorities who try to control and exploit the migrants within the novel and who tried to discredit Steinbeck after its publication.

In the course of her discussion of Steinbeck's relation to photographic documentary Carol Shloss relates the gaze to the politics of the novel in the following way. Considering scenes from *In Dubious Battle* (Steinbeck's 1936 novel about fruit-pickers' unrest) and *The Grapes of Wrath* in which sheriffs use spotlights on the workers, she argues that 'authority stands invisibly behind the light, using it to survey and then to control those who are caught in its beams. Light is not truth, but simply the agency of a supervisory power'. It is also an image suggestive of the writer's power to see without being seen. Disturbingly, the ability to visualize and thereby define becomes implicated in the power themes of this novel. Shloss continues: 'the power to control and the power to define are analogous, for the legitimation crisis of Steinbeck's book is the struggle of an inarticulate people to [...] evade the illegitimate control of others, to refuse the definitions of themselves and of life's possibilities put forward by those in authority'.[44]

Shloss's argument is an important one because it helps to explain how visibility itself becomes a political issue in *The Grapes of Wrath*. It is, for instance, a crowning irony that Tom Joad should be put under scrutiny by another as soon as he is released from prison. The truck driver who gives him a lift cannot keep his eyes off Tom's new clothes, which are his main giveaway. This sets a keynote of the novel in that the migrants are assessed visually as customers for food, petrol, and so on; and then are later examined by border guards (like the one who shines his flashlight on Grandma) for signs of illness.

The most dramatic confrontations take place in California, which proves to be a place of maximum surveillance. In one camp the arrest of a 'troublemaker' is authorized visually when a deputy is asked 'ever see this guy before?' and from this point on Tom gradually turns into a fugitive, an extreme personification of the migrants' general predicament since they are repeatedly described as a 'people in flight'. The camp for fruit-pickers which the Joads reach in Chapter 26 is crucial in this process. By then we have become used to swaggering deputies in uniform, but in this camp surveil-lance also involves the Joads being itemized on official lists. The camp – strikingly, after the comfort of the federal Weedpatch camp – resembles nothing so much as a prison with fences and guards, where it is even forbidden to go for a walk. More importantly, the action now takes place predominantly at night:

> [Tom] could see the high wire gate in the starlight.
> A figure stirred beside the road. A voice said: 'Hello – who is it?'
> Tom stopped and stood still. 'Who are you?'
> A man stood up and walked near. Tom could see the gun in his hand. Then a flashlight played on his face. 'Where you think you're going?'
> 'Well, I thought I'd take a walk. Any law against it?'[45]

The power play here is enacted through light reinforced by arms. Tom does not have to name himself since the answer to the guard's question is a category, not an individual. Tom must reveal himself as an 'inmate' and demonstrate that he poses no threat to the guard, who would remain only semi-visible throughout this scene. This meeting acts as an immediate prelude to the killing of Casy, after which Tom has to go into hiding. The ultimate consequence of this withdrawal is that Ma can only meet him in total darkness.[46] It seems that Tom can only stay at large by living like an animal and by avoiding the light of day.

Steinbeck's Later Films

As soon as he had finished the manuscript of *The Grapes of Wrath* in April 1939 Steinbeck went to Chicago to work with Pare Lorentz on a hospital documentary, *The Fight for Life*.[47] It was during this period that he conceived the idea for a documentary film of his own called *The Forgotten Village*, which was completed the following year. A member of Lorentz's team suggested the project, but Steinbeck chose the subject, which centred on the coming of modern medicine to a backward area of Mexico. As in his novel, he used a representative family and dramatized the clash between the old and the new as a conflict between generations. As in Lorentz's *The Plow*, Steinbeck establishes the family's dependence on the land, specifically on corn, but uses this to introduce the second and major issue of health. At market day, the boy Paco falls ill and dies, despite the attempts by the wise woman of the village to drive out his spirits. This death is offset by the birth of another boy, which occasions celebrations in the village. But then more children fall ill. This problem sets up the role of the elder son Juan who acts as a mediator between old and new (he asks his teacher to help) and between the local community and the wider nation. When the village elders refuse to send a petition for medical help, he sets off to the city himself and returns with a team of doctors. The last sections of the film show the villagers' hostility to the visitors, whom they drive away, but not before Juan's sister can receive treatment.

Jackson Benson has described the film as an 'essay in perception', but the action is less abstract than this sounds.[48] Steinbeck excels at showing the dynamics of family and village hierarchies, especially in dramatizing the community's resistance to change, even after they have been shown a film to demonstrate the benefits of medical care. In one scene the 'wise woman' strikes Juan in the face and accuses him of betrayal: 'And you, traitor to your own people, why do you deal with strangers?'[49] The fact that Juan does so ultimately saves the village from poisoning from a contaminated well and also motivates the ending, as he leaves the village for a city education. As his mentor, the visiting doctor explains, 'from the government schools, the boys and girls from the villages will carry knowledge back to their own people, Juan Diego'.[50] *The Forgotten Village* could be taken as Steinbeck's homage to Lorentz. It uses an individual narrative for documentary purposes; it uses some of Lorentz's imagery (railway and power lines as signs of modernity); and Steinbeck even published a phototext of the film the year after its completion as Lorentz had done with *The River*. The film's assertion of faith in government action echoes the special status of the federal camps in *The Grapes of Wrath* and also Lorentz's New Deal optimism in his earlier documentaries.

In order to make *The Forgotten Village* Steinbeck had turned down a lucrative offer from Darryl F. Zanuck of Twentieth Century Fox to write a screenplay. Later in the 1940s he returned to Zanuck to work with his close friend Elia Kazan on what was to become *Viva Zapata!* (1952), a film based on the life of the Mexican revolutionary. Throughout this period Steinbeck was involved in a number of different film projects, but that on Zapata was his only full screenplay.[51] Kazan had the original idea for the film, which must have appealed to Steinbeck's interest in Mexico, but when they were composing the script Kazan fed Steinbeck suggestions which he then filled out. Kazan recalled: 'I had worked up a frame of action for the whole script, and I would ask for lines of dialogue from John, which he'd provide one at a time. I'd type, then go on to the next line we needed'.[52] Steinbeck's editor Robert E. Morsberger has explained that, although the novelist drew on a biography of Zapata, he also interviewed Mexican locals. There was thus an element of documentary in *Viva Zapata!*, although Steinbeck's exposition is dramatic, through scenes, rather than relying on narrative commentary.

Viva Zapata! has strong thematic links with *The Grapes of Wrath*. It deals with the seizure of peasants' land by big estates which convert the crop from corn to sugar. Zapata was a difficult subject, Steinbeck admitted, because, like Christ, 'his life is an idea'.[53] Like Casy in the novel, he speaks to a collectivist ideology which will survive his death. The film also sheds more retrospective light on the method of the novel. In both cases, Steinbeck was representing action 'in microcosm', using selective scenes to evoke a wider picture. Similarly, Steinbeck studiously avoided the obvious drama of showing a town being burned by the military, rendering it obliquely as a reflection in the eyes of Zapata and others, just as in *The Grapes of Wrath* he deployed images which would include the observers' reactions to events.[54]

The main economic factor underpinning the action of both works was of course rural poverty and the following sequence shows a visual expansion of image and subject alike. We start with a close-up: '*Close Shot – Bowl, showing hands breaking eggs in the bowl. Another hand puts a sponge into the egg mixture and the* CAMERA RISES *with the sponge and we see an* INDIAN *sponging the eggs into the coat of a* HORSE *tied to the outside of a box stall.* CAMERA PULLS BACK *and we see that we are in magnificent stables [...] Along one wall are luxurious carriages*'.[55] In Steinbeck's original treatment, there is no drama in the scene. It is merely witnessed by Zapata with pleasure because of his love of horses. The script, however, uses the image with skilful economy to evoke central tensions in the action. At first the close-up could be of preparing food. Then a second person enters the image and it is revealed that an Indian is using the eggs as horse dressing. In *Viva Zapata!* the Aztecs are the peon underclass equivalent to the Okies in the novel. The film image at this point shifts into an emblem of servitude and extravagance. *The Grapes of Wrath* showed few images of wealth and those always at a distance. Here the stark contrast between rich and poor emerges with immediacy and irony: the next scene shows a little boy about to be punished for stealing horse food. The themes and methods of these late projects reflect a continuity with the social concerns of Steinbeck's most famous novel and further confirm the skill at filmic composition he began to acquire in the late 1930s.

Notes

1   Joseph R. Millichap, *Steinbeck and Film*, pp. 28–29. D. G. Kehl has attempted to address the critical neglect of Steinbeck's pictorialism by arguing that *The Grapes of Wrath* owed a direct debt to photo-volumes such as Archibald MacLeish's *Land of the Free* (1938) and Dorothea Lange and Paul Taylor's *An American Exodus* (1939) ('Steinbeck's "String of Pictures" in *The Grapes of Wrath*'). Unfortunately Kehl's argument is vitiated by his limitation of pictorialism to human features, the fact that Steinbeck had completed *The Grapes* earlier than he supposes, and his admission that some of Steinbeck's portraits may

be composites from a number of different photographs. However, his general point stands that Steinbeck was consciously writing within the documentary reportage of the period.

2 See Jackson J. Benson, 'The Background to the Composition of *The Grapes of Wrath*'.

3 For full details on these articles, see Charles Wollenberg's introduction to the 1988 reprint of *The Harvest Gypsies*, pp. v–xvii.

4 Shloss, *In Visible Light*, pp. 213–14.

5 John Steinbeck, *America and Americans*, p. 78. This collection only includes the one essay from the series, under the title 'The Harvest Gypsies: Squatters' Camps'. This entry to a migrants' camp is incorporated into one of the scenes in the film of *The Grapes of Wrath*.

6 Steinbeck, *America and Americans*, p. 80.

7 Alexander, *Film on the Left*, p. 96. Lorentz himself applied exactly this phrase to Rowland Brown in 1934, whose gangster film *Blood* Lorentz thought had the 'same gusto and shocking humour' (Lorentz, 'The Screen', p. 46).

8 Alexander, *Film on the Left*, p. 98.

9 Lorentz, 'The Screen', p. 45.

10 Pare Lorentz, *FDR's Moviemaker*, p. 47. This line is followed by a further warning ('two hundred miles from water, two hundred miles from town') not in the printed text. One of the most famous examples of montage in this period was the 1936 film *San Francisco*, scripted by Anita Loos, whose action begins as a quasi-documentary report on the 1906 earthquake.

11 Reportedly Lorentz wanted to include a scene in which men in top hats would drive the tractors in the ploughing (Alexander, *Film on the Left*, p. 99).

12 Lorentz, *FDR's Moviemaker*, pp. 48, 50. Lorentz spaces out his commentary on the page like free verse.

13 Alexander, *Film on the Left*, p. 140.

14 Pare Lorentz, *The River*, [p. 6]. The volume is unpaginated.

15 David Bordwell and Kristin Thompson, *Film Art*, pp. 143–44.

16 Lorentz, *The River*, [p. 39].

17 John Steinbeck, *Working Days*, p. 17.

18 It was, Lorentz wrote, a 'complete tragedy in which the land holders, the land users, and the land workers all lost' (*FDR's Moviemaker*, p. 108). Lorentz got as far in his planning as getting James Cagney and Paul Muni to agree to act in the film.

19 Jackson J. Benson, *The True Adventures of John Steinbeck, Writer*, p. 399. However, Benson also suggests that *The River* 'may have provided the rhythm, the sense of epic motion' for Steinbeck's novel (p. 400).

20 Lorentz had probably sent Steinbeck a sound recording of *Ecce Homo* (*FDR's Moviemaker*, pp. 120–21). He later invited Steinbeck to collaborate with him on *Ecce Homo*.

21 Benson, *The True Adventures of John Steinbeck, Writer*, p. 399.

22 Lorentz, *FDR's Moviemaker*, p. 122.

23 John Lane Idol, *A Thomas Wolfe Companion*, p. 16. I am grateful to Anne Zahlan for bringing this work to my attention. *The Hound of Darkness* was composed in 1935 and published by the Thomas Wolfe Society in 1986.

24 Thomas Wolfe, *The Hound of Darkness*, pp. 3–5. For further discussion of this work, see Idol, *A Thomas Wolfe Companion*, pp. 83–85.

25 Benson, *The True Adventures of John Steinbeck, Writer*, pp. 410–11.

26 Benson, *The True Adventures of John Steinbeck, Writer*, p. 399.

27 For comment on this relation, see Barry G. Maine, 'Steinbeck's Debt to Dos Passos'.

28 John Steinbeck, *The Grapes of Wrath*, p. 159. Apart from the ironies in this passage, Stein-beck may also have been imitating the Works Progress Administration documentary accounts of American highways.

29 Steinbeck, *Working Days*, p. 25.

30 Just as happens in Dos Passos' novel, Steinbeck plays on the double status of nickel as an industrial material and as a coin, on commodity and purchasing power.

31 William Howarth, 'The Mother of Literature', p. 91.

32 Lorentz, *Lorentz on Film*, p. 184. He also complained that the opening scenes 'did not give you the feeling of the land' (p. 184). Vivian Sobchack has extended this criticism to argue that the film de-emphasizes the land by concentrating spatially on the Joads ('*The Grapes of Wrath* (1940)', p. 602).

33 William Howarth finds signs in Steinbeck's sentence structure of his trying to imitate the motion of the streams in Lorentz's *The River* ('The Mother of Literature', p. 92).

34 Steinbeck, *The Grapes of Wrath*, p. 37.

35 Steinbeck, *America and Americans*, p. 155. The other works which Steinbeck composed within the same genre were *The Moon is Down* (1942), *The Pearl* (1948), and *Burning Bright* (1950).

36 Steinbeck, *Of Mice and Men*, p. 47.

37 For a discussion of suture in film, see Stephen Heath, *Questions of Cinema*, chapter 3.

38 Sobchack, 'The Grapes of Wrath (1940)', p. 601.

39 Steinbeck, *The Forgotten Village*, p. 5.

40 Steinbeck, *The Grapes of Wrath*, p. 104.

41 Steinbeck, *The Grapes of Wrath*, p. 118.

42 Steinbeck, *The Grapes of Wrath*, p. 304.

43 Steinbeck, *The Grapes of Wrath*, p. 476.

44 Shloss, *In Visible Light*, p. 219.

45 Steinbeck, *The Grapes of Wrath*, p. 397.

46 Vivian Sobchack has taken the 1940 film of *The Grapes of Wrath* to task for making an excessive use of chiaroscuro which 'evokes the vague outlines of night and dream rather than the harsh specificity of daylight and Depression America' ('*The Grapes of Wrath* (1940)', p. 611). The lighting of the novel is in fact more complex than this contrast suggests.

47 That same year Joris Ivens tried to get Steinbeck interested in doing the narrative for his documentary film *Power and the Land* (Robert L. Snyder, *Pare Lorentz*, p.127. Snyder's study gives full details of the production and reception of Lorentz's documentaries).

48 Benson, *The True Adventures of John Steinbeck, Writer*, p. 457. On the basis of the child-birth scene the New York Board of Censors decided that the film was 'indecent'.

49 Steinbeck, *The Forgotten Village*, p. 126.

50 Steinbeck, *The Forgotten Village*, p. 140.

51 For details of Steinbeck's film projects, see 'Steinbeck's Screenplays and Productions' in John Steinbeck, *Zapata*, pp. 339–65; Roy Simmonds also gives useful commentary on the cinematic dimension to *The Pearl* (1948) in *John Steinbeck: The War Years*, pp. 256–59. *Zapata* contains Steinbeck's original narrative (summaries of parts of Zapata's life, Mexican customs, drafts of scenes, and suggestions of how they might be filmed) as well as the script of *Viva Zapata!*. Following the controversy attached to the film's politics, Steinbeck subsequently suggested to Kazan that they revise the script and re-release *Viva Zapata!* but that plan came to nothing.

52 Elia Kazan, *A Life*, pp. 396–97.

53 Steinbeck, *Zapata*, p. 140.

54 In this respect Steinbeck was following Lorentz's practice. Joris Ivens praised the latter's inclusion of locals' reactions to the floods in *The River* (*The Camera and I*, p. 122).
55 Steinbeck, *Zapata*, p. 244. The editor Robert Morsberger comments on this scene at p. 209.

11

Taking Possession of the Images:
African American Writers and the Cinema

The Birth of a Nation and Beyond

During his campaign for the governorship of California in 1934 Upton Sinclair was partly defeated by bogus newsreels showing unkempt migrants heading for that state. He was, in other words, defeated by images over which he had no control. And when the migrants in *The Grapes of Wrath* are called 'Okies' they are being framed by an abusive label, which Steinbeck's visual techniques are designed to counter. African American writers at the beginning of the twentieth century were even more severely disadvantaged by the fact that they were operating within a culture in which they were already colonized by hostile stereotypes. Their self-images were not their own, nor did their situation improve with the coming of the cinema. Thomas Cripps has shown in his 1977 study *Slow Fade to Black* that, after a brief period of relatively free imaging in early films, from the mid-1910s into the twenties the cinema 'continued to draw on old Southern stereotypes of Negroes as happy, lazy workers on the plantation'.[1] This situation lasted at least up to the Second World War. As late as 1943, answering his question 'Is Hollywood Fair to Negroes?', Langston Hughes declared: 'for a generation now, the Negro has been maligned, caricatured, and lied about on the American screen, and pictured to the whole world [...] as being nothing more than a funny-looking, dull-witted but comic servant'.[2] Such a state of affairs meant that African American writers were inevitably forced into an oppositional stance towards abusive and humiliating images of their own group, either through disturbing the category of blackness or through appropriating the cultural gaze. As bell hooks has written, 'spaces of agency exist for black people, wherein we can both interrogate the gaze of the Other but also look back, and at one another, naming what we see'.[3] This means in turn that the gaze, important throughout this study, becomes particularly charged with implications of identity formation in African American contexts.

This predicament worsened with the release in 1915 of D. W. Griffith's film *The Birth of a Nation*. This event at one and the same time triggered widespread protest and also speeded up African American film activity. In 1915 the National Association for the Advancement of Colored People (NAACP) distributed a pamphlet called *Fighting a Vicious Film* and that same year organized a scenario committee, which briefly included W. E. B. DuBois, who attacked the film in the pages of the NAACP journal *The Crisis*.[4] Booker T. Washington worked on a film designed as a counter to Griffith but died before it could be completed.

The writer James Weldon Johnson joined the protest against Griffith's film in the *New York Age* in 1915. The grounds of his protest are important in that he draws his readers' attention, via comments on Thomas Dixon's novel *The Clansman* (see Introduction), to the disturbing power of the new film medium: '*The Clansman* did us much injury as a book [...] It did us more injury as a play [...] Made into a moving picture play it can do us incalculable harm. Every minute detail of the story is vividly portrayed before the eyes of the spectators [...] [summarizing the attempted rape of a small white girl by the Negro Gus] Can you imagine the effect of such a scene upon the millions who seldom read a book, who seldom witness a drama, but who constantly go to the "movies"?'[5] While Johnson and DuBois attacked Dixon and Griffith for *The Birth of a Nation*, Thomas Dixon made a rejoinder to them in his last novel, *The Flaming Sword* (1939), in which he evoked the imminent death of civilization from a conspiracy between Communists and the black liberation movement.[6]

One result of this perception of the power of film was a pressure exerted on African American film-makers to ensure that all their race images were positive counters to such negative images. In a 1924 promotional statement for Eugene O'Neill's play *All God's Chillun' Got Wings*, W. E. B. DuBois noted that 'the Negro today fears any attempt of the artist to paint Negroes. He is not satisfied unless everything is perfect and proper and beautiful [...] lest his human foibles and shortcomings be seized by his enemies for the purposes of the ancient and hateful propaganda'.[7] *The Birth of a Nation* for years remained a major reference point in African American discussion of film. When told by a board of censors in 1925 that one of his films might cause racial tension, the novelist Oscar Micheaux retorted that 'there has been but one picture that incited coloured people to riot, and that still does, that picture is *The Birth of a Nation*'.[8] More recently, in his 1976 consideration of racism in the American cinema *The Devil Finds Work*, James Baldwin reflected that, however much it is disguised, the film was 'really an elaborate justification of mass murder'.[9]

Oscar Micheaux, Novelist and Film-maker

One of the earliest African American film-makers was the novelist Oscar Micheaux, who appears to have been catapulted into the film business by an approach from George Johnson of the Lincoln Motion Picture Company to adapt his own novel *The Homesteader*.[10] Negotiations fell through because the company felt that the novel was 'too advanced' for its time, so Micheaux proceeded to set up his own company and produce his own adaptation. The result was billed as 'Oscar Micheaux's Mammoth Photo-play' to capitalize on its unusual length. From 1918 onwards Micheaux pursued a double career as novelist and film-maker. Indeed he saw the one as dependent on the other.

In a 1919 essay 'The Negro and the Photo-Play' he declared: 'the Negro will break into the movies, in the way he wishes to see himself portrayed when members of the race open the way, and only through race people'. In other words, African Americans must rely on themselves and not the white studios. He continued by insisting on the double need for realism and for race novelists to create potential subjects: 'the Negro nor any other race can ever be thoroughly appreciated until he appears in plays that deal in some way with Negro life as lived by Negroes in that age or period, or day [...] before we expect to see ourselves featured on the silver screen as we live, hope, act and think today, men and women must write original stories of Negro life'.[11]

The emergence of race cinema coincides approximately with that of African American fiction – novels by Paul Laurence Dunbar or Charles Chesnutt, for example – and the debate over subject treatment in which Micheaux found himself embroiled throughout his career has a direct relevance to novelistic as well as cinematic representation. There are signs that Micheaux saw his own fiction as feeding directly into film production. In 1920 he promised his public that *The Brand of Cain* would be his next film, which he had just finished in book form.[12] Similarly, he tried to get leading figures of the African American community actively involved in his film-making. Not only did Micheaux adapt Charles Chesnutt's *The House Behind the Cedars* (1925); he also invited Chesnutt to write a screenplay for *The Conjure Woman* (1926).[13] As early as 1920 he referred in a letter to Chesnutt, James Weldon Johnson and W. E. B. DuBois, claiming: 'two or more of these men have stated their desire to attempt writing for us'.[14] Despite financial setbacks and a steady rise in hostility from the African American press, Micheaux went on to make over forty films and to publish seven novels.[15]

Micheaux repeatedly declared his debt to Booker T. Washington in his commitment to the cause of individual betterment in his narratives. When adapting Chesnutt's *The House Behind the Cedars* he told the writer that he wanted to alter the ending to make it more upbeat because he wanted to 'send them [the audience] out of the theatre with the story lingering in their minds, with a feeling that all good must triumph in the end'.[16] Endings were one thing, treatment another. One reviewer of Micheaux's *The Brute* insisted that every effort should be made in race films that 'the Negro is given high ideals and types which he can emulate and of which he can feel justly proud'.[17] In response to such criticisms, in 1925 Micheaux made a declaration of principle attached to his film *Birthright*, in which he projected his work as a microcosm and declared that uplift could only come from realism:

> the completed picture is a miniature replica of life, and all the varied forces which help to make life so complex [...] I have always tried to make my photoplays present the truth, to lay before the race a cross section of its own life, to view the coloured heart from close range [...] It is only by presenting those portions of the race portrayed in my pictures, in the light and background of their true state, that we can raise our people to greater heights.[18]

The Homesteader (1917) was the first novel which Micheaux adapted for the screen and is a narrative depicting the triumph over adversity by its African American protagonist Jean-Baptiste. The novel reveals its awareness of the cinema through a comment on a different ethnic type – the Native American – who has also fallen victim to stereotyping through ignorance. Micheaux contrasts the latter's actual behaviour with 'all the roles in which he is characterized in the movies and dramas as the great primitive hero, brave and courageous'.[19] This is exactly the quality attributed to Jean-Baptiste by his white lover Agnes, who implicitly stereotypes him, albeit not in an abusive way. The novel sets up a triangular relationship between the protagonist, his desired partner (Agnes) and the black woman he marries (Orlean). Unable to cope with the hardships of pioneer life and caught between the rival claims of Jean-Baptiste and her egotistical father, Orlean collapses into madness and commits suicide, thus clearing the way for the protagonist's final union with Agnes, whose mother is revealed to have been 'of Ethiopian extraction'. The novel is set mainly in the western prairies where towns and settlements are coming into being, in other words where there is no fixed spatial separation between groups as there was in Chicago, the novel's other location. Space thus underpins Micheaux's optimistic sense of possibility, his confidence that the protagonist can acquire land and make his livelihood through sheer hard work.

The novel follows conventions of screen melodrama in its use of sudden scene shifts, hidden identities (all the main characters are migrants) revealed through devices such as misplaced documents, and also italicized lines which punctuate the action, sometimes highlighting suspense ('*something was going to happen*'[20]) and in general functioning like the title cards in silent films. More importantly, Micheaux embeds the action in characters' appearance, thereby highlighting the visual throughout the novel. Characters carry their history encrypted in their features and one impetus in the novel is the drive to reveal, for example, the 'mystery' of Agnes' eyes. Usually preceding dialogue, characters' gestures and in particular their look become their most expressive features. Often an exchange of looks can 'say' far more than speech. When her father appears after a long absence Orlean 'understood what he carried behind his masklike face'. He approaches her sick-bed: 'she was frightened when he was near and saw his face and what it held. Hatred was there and she shuddered audibly'.[21] Micheaux skilfully modifies the focalization in the novel from Jean-Baptiste's dynamic, mobile gaze to a fixed vantage point, as here. Approaching the bed, the father becomes a figure of threat and the scene is typical of *The Homesteader* in tying its drama to moments of revelation.

The apportioning of roles here is conventionally melodramatic. Agnes is the sentimental heroine, weeping at appropriate cruxes; Jean-Baptiste the proud hero striking appropriate postures of defiance in adversity; and Orlean the distraught means of retribution. When she discovers that her father is a promiscuous hypocrite she stabs him in his bed, inverting the scene structure we were examining in the previous paragraph. The moment of his dying is drawn out through retarded movement and through the direction of his gaze towards his daughter: 'he struggled upward while she stood over him with that same white expression upon her face [...] he turned his dying eyes toward her. Regarded her blindly for a moment, and then, dropped limply back from where he had risen, dead. In that moment she regained her sanity. She regarded him a moment wildly, and then she closed her eyes to shut out the awful thing she had done and screamed long and wildly'.[22] In later African American fiction skin colour becomes an important factor in the action. Here 'white' is scarcely literal and certainly not used as an ethnic marker; rather, it is a sign within the melodramatic code of emotional extremity. Orlean gazes at the spectacle of her father's collapse, which cannot be presented as simply liberating. It is after all patricide. Just as the father loses his sight, so Orlean attempts to symbolically blind herself by closing her eyes on her own deed. But the melodramatic code must work its way through the action. The only way Orlean can really blind herself is through suicide. After that necessary purgation, Jean-Baptiste's domestic idyll with Agnes can conclude the novel.

In *The Homesteader* and throughout his career Micheaux was concerned to question racial stereotyping. Despite all his efforts and the changes which took place during the thirties, as late as 1946 in his preface to *The Story of Dorothy Stanfield* Micheaux complained that 'for two years or more, due to his agitation for better and more dignified roles, except for a menial task now and then, in which he is required to roll his eyes, say all the lines in dialect, and in short, be stupid and funny, he [the Negro] has been practically barred from the screen!'[23]

Zora Neale Hurston and the Dimensions to the Gaze

Zora Neale Hurston also concerned herself with stereotypes – those of folklore – but she found that the discipline of anthropology gave her an essential detachment. Introducing her 1935 collection *Mules and Men*, she explained that to understand the meaning of Brer Rabbit and similar tales she had to experience a double distancing from the familiar: 'it was only when I was off in college, away from my native surroundings, that I could see myself like somebody else'. She figures this folklore as a tight-fitting garment and continues: 'then I had to have the spy-glass of Anthropology to look through at that'.[24] 'Spy-glass' suggests both a technological facility analogous to a camera and also inevitably an element of covert surveillance. Nevertheless, commentators on Hurston's anthropological research have described her enterprise as one of enabling, of giving voice to her subjects and rescuing them from the colonizing gaze.[25] Although Hurston does not mention the cinema as contributing to this process, in her retrospective essay 'What White Publishers Won't Print' (1950) she turns the colonizing concept of folkways against whites, accusing them of perpetuating a superstition that 'all non-Anglo-Saxons are uncomplicated stereotypes'.[26] Her anthropological enterprise was to rectify that projection by recording the complexities of African American rural life. One of the physical means given to Hurston was a movie camera supplied as part of her work contract for her patron Charlotte Osgood Mason and in many parts of *Mules and Men* Hurston transforms herself into a recording agent, though she remained constantly on the alert for signs of observer interference. She was well aware of the racial and cultural implications in her fieldwork. In 1940, for example, she was filming church practices in South Carolina and reflected wryly in a letter that she was only paving the way for other (white) cameramen to 'take the sound pictures'.[27] The dimensions to the gaze are explored in Hurston's most famous novel.

As many critics have noted, Janie in Hurston's 1937 novel *Their Eyes Were Watching God* evolves from the object of a group gaze – both male and female – into a character with a full subjective life. Karen Jacobs, for one, notes that as Janie gains autonomy 'she initiates a reversal of subject/object relations, significantly through the subjective prerogative of the gaze'.[28] This process is punctuated through a series of visual cruxes, which revolve around the twinned issues of what Janie sees and how she is seen by others. The first such moment occurs when she describes peering at a photograph and engaging with her own image last: 'there wasn't nobody left except a real dark little girl with long hair standing by Eleanore [...] Ah couldn't recognize dat dark chile as me'.[29] Invisible to her childhood self, Janie here begins to learn an externalized self-image significantly defined through her long hair. The latter becomes a visual sign of her selfhood, suppressed when Janie's first husband forces her to wear a head-cloth.

Just as Janie learns to see herself through the means of a photograph, so she reifies her husband Jody as a concrete image, again like a family photograph, which falls off a shelf inside her. However, she can only achieve autonomy by observing herself in motion: 'Then one day she sat and watched the shadow of herself going about tending store going about tending store and prostrating itself before Jody, while all the time she herself sat under a shady tree with the wind blowing through her hair and her clothes'.[30] The first images considered above resemble stills. Now it is as if Janie is watching her domestic behaviour on a mind-screen on which her projected self has lost substance and authenticity. It is an important symbolic detail that in her evolving relationship with Tea Cake Janie learns to travel and that one of their recreations is to go to the movies in Orlando. Her new-found mobility reflects an opening up and sophistication of Janie's visual field; typically the second half of the novel contains open landscapes stretching towards distant horizons.

Hurston represents self-awareness and the working of memory through visual images. Her 1942 autobiography *Dust Tracks on a Road* contains a series of 'vision pictures', anticipatory scenes of how she was to develop; and in *Their Eyes* Janie's Nanny remembers the past through similar 'mind-pictures' whereby earlier episodes are recalled through visualization. For Karen Jacobs, Janie's development towards visionary awareness at the end of *Their Eyes* reflects Hurston's ambivalence towards African American culture in that it represents a retreat from black embodiment, an Emersonian fantasy of 'pure' vision.[31] This account engages vigorously with the hierarchies of the novel but understates the circular frame to the narrative, which opens with Janie's return to the community after burying her husband. In that sense the ending has only limited finality and Janie's cherishing of her husband's memory is once again expressed as a projection on to an internal screen: 'The kiss of his memory made pictures of love and light against the wall'.[32] By this stage Janie's room has become the embodiment of her own psychological space; the earlier tension between inner and outer no longer operates in this scene.

There is relatively little evidence available on Hurston's interest in the cinema, but thanks to Elizabeth Binggeli's research into the Hollywood studio archives we now know that *Their Eyes* was reviewed by Warner Brothers, *Dust Tracks on a Road* by different studios, and *Seraph on the Suwanee* (1948) by both MGM and Warner Brothers.[33] Robert Haas has argued convincingly that the depiction of rabies in *Their Eyes* was shaped by the 1936 MGM movie *The Story of Louis Pasteur*, in its insistence on the need for modern medicine rather than folk remedies.[34]

Hurston was hired by Paramount as a story consultant between October

1941 and January 1942. She told a correspondent that 'this job here at the studio is not the end of things for me. It is a means'.[35] We should not, however, interpret this as a dismissal of Hollywood because the following year (1942) Hurston told Carl Van Vechten: 'I have a tiny wedge in Hollywood and have hopes of breaking that old silly rule about Negroes not writing about white people. In fact, I have a sort of commitment from a producer at RKO that he will help me to do it. I am working on the story'.[36] It is possible that Hurston hoped *Seraph on the Suwanee* would enable her to break into the Hollywood market but in the event the novel was rejected by the studios.

Movie-making and Movie-going

We saw in Chapter 9 how documentaries of the Left frequently took their lead from the Soviet Union and in 1932 Langston Hughes, Dorothy West and a group of other African Americans were invited to the Soviet Union to participate in the making of a film about conditions in the USA to be called *Black and White* and to be set in Birmingham, Alabama. When he saw the scenario Hughes was aghast: 'It was so interwoven with major and minor impossibilities and improbabilities that it would have seemed like a burlesque on the screen', he later recalled.[37] After meetings with Eisenstein and Pudovkin, and after the script was revised, the project was cancelled because Stalin did not want to compromise his relationship with the USA, from which he was seeking diplomatic recognition.[38] Hughes reflected on his experiences in one of his dispatches home in which his dislike of Hollywood was confirmed: 'in Hollywood,' he wrote, 'the production of films is frankly a business for the making of money. In Moscow the production of films is quite frankly an art for the advancement of certain ideas of social betterment'.[39] Despite his reservations about Hollywood, Hughes attempted unsuccessfully to place a burlesque with Paramount and in 1939 collaborated with Clarence Muse on the movie *Way Down South*.[40] In common with many American writers, Hughes' dislike for Hollywood did not extend to the film medium itself and shortly after the Harlem riot and the bombing of Ethiopia in the mid-1930s he wrote a sardonic scenario in free verse entitled 'Air Raid over Harlem'.[41]

Because it involves a confrontation with sometimes threatening and abusive images, African American accounts of visits to movie houses involve far more than entertainment. In an autobiographical sketch 'Remembrance' the novelist Dorothy West recalled going to see one of the adaptations of *Uncle Tom's Cabin* when she was a young child. The first thing that struck her was the stark racial difference between characters: 'the white people looked happy and the black people looked sad. The white people looked rich and the black people looked poor'. Then, as her mother started crying when she saw Tom being beaten by a white man, the young Dorothy tries to soothe her, saying 'Don't cry. It's not real. It's make-believe'. In retrospect the mature Dorothy realizes that the scenes cannot be dismissed so easily; they form part of her cultural imagery and she reflects: 'I was not yet ready to bear the burden of my heritage'.[42]

One of the earliest accounts of movie-going in Harlem appears in Claude McKay's 1928 novel *Home to Harlem*, where the West Indian protagonist takes his lover as part of their 'atmosphere of dreams':

> They went to the Negro Picture Theatre and held each other's hand, gazing in raptures at the crude pictures. It was odd that all these cinematic pictures about the blacks were a broad burlesque of their home and love life. These coloured screen actors were all dressed up in expensive evening clothes, with automobiles, and menials, to imitate white society people. They laughed at themselves in such roles and the laughter was good on the screen. They pranced and grinned like good-nigger servants, who knew that 'master' and 'missus', intent on being amused, are watching their antics from an upper window. It was quite a little funny and the audience enjoyed it. Maybe that was the stuff the Black Belt wanted.[43]

Jake's perspective divides between the pleasure of the moment and a critical perception of how black burlesque is tacitly complicit with racism. By ridiculing themselves as comic imitations of whites the actors – and by implication the audience – are internalizing the gaze of whites in a position of power. The mimicry is thus simultaneously set up and comically dismissed, with the effect that white superiority goes unquestioned. What appears on the surface to be entertainment in fact demonstrates what W. E. B. DuBois described in *The Souls of Black Folk* as the African American's 'double-consciousness, this sense of always looking at one's self through the eyes of others, of measuring one's soul by the tape of a world that looks on in amused contempt and pity'.[44] We will encounter further internalizations of the white gaze in Richard Wright's *Native Son*.

Movie-going need not, however, be a negative experience. In Jessie Redmon Fauset's 1928 novel *Plum Bun*, Angela Murray, the light-skinned protagonist, decides to move from Philadelphia to New York to pursue her artistic ambitions. She both changes her name and decides to pass as white, and these changes even affect the way she experiences film: 'she found herself studying the screen with a strained and ardent intensity, losing the slightly patronizing scepticism which had once been hers with regard to the adventures of those shadowy heroes and heroines'.[45] Her earlier detachment may have reflected her perception of limited possibilities, whereas now she experiences a sense of freedom in going to white movie houses. Angela reinvents her subjectivity as spectator, not only here but also in Harlem, which she relishes as a temporary visitor. We are told that she is 'visual minded' in her pursuit of art as well as a new identity for herself.

Less liberating is the experience of Jay, the dark-skinned protagonist of Rudolph Fisher's story 'High Yaller', whose title refers to the beautiful light-skinned African American girl he sets his romantic sights on. After the preliminary negotiations of dancing together in Harlem, the couple set out to see New York and Fisher sets the last scene of his story in a movie house. This time the visit is not one of entertainment, but rather an opportunity for recall: 'from a point in the wide, deep balcony's dimness, Jay followed the quick-shifting scenes; not those on the screen at which he stared, but others, flashing out from his mind'.[46] The actual film seems to be a naïve story of 'two chubby infants', which hardly keeps Jay's attention at all. Instead, the physical comfort of the movie house facilitates a 'replay' of Jay's memories whereby film techniques are internalized into a means for recapturing the noise and tempo of New York life.

Jay's memory sequence consists of a rapid montage of paragraph scenes captioned 'Coney Island ... An ice-cream parlour ... The subway ... Finally a back room in the police station'. The first of this series establishes the evocation of action through participles followed by a sudden reversal: 'Coney Island. He and Evelyn arm in arm, inconsequent, hilarious, eating sticky popcorn out of the same bag, dipping in at the same time, gaily disputing the last piece. Their laughter suddenly chilled by an intentionally audible remark: "Look at that white girl with a nigger". A half-dozen lowering rowdies. Evelyn urging him away. People staring'.[47] The film Jay is half-watching evokes a child-like innocence which is denied him at Coney Island. His shared pleasure is rudely interrupted by a provocative statement which separates himself and Evelyn into different racial categories. This separation is further compounded when he is refused ice-cream and when he is beaten by the police for going with a 'white' girl. Jay is caught in the double-bind of being unable to re-identify Evelyn without tacit complicity in the whites' racism and as a result senses himself becoming converted into a spectacle for passers-by. But there is a further twist to the story's concluding scene. The balcony where Jay sits apparently offers him a place for recalling earlier events – until he sees Evelyn sitting nearby with a white boy! The pleasure Jay thought he was sharing with her now backfires into an image of personal and racial betrayal. Is Evelyn engaged in passing? The story doesn't say. It merely cuts off its narrative at the moment of ironic visual recognition.

In his history of American race cinema Thomas Cripps argues that, despite Oscar Micheaux's achievements, by the late 1920s 'blacks simply did not see *themselves* on the screen'.[48] This would explain the young Dorothy

West's non-recognition of *Uncle Tom's Cabin*. In the other cases just examined movie-going involves the observer in registering a complex relation between image and reality. The presumption that the one mirrors the other can be a serious error, as happens in Dorothy West's story 'Odyssey of an Egg'. Here a young black man enjoys the simple, hard-boiled message projected in a gangster movie: 'you had to be tough to get on in this world'.[49] The film offers Porky Tynes an image and a style for coping with poverty and the insignificance of his life in the city. However, just when he has perfected his swagger, his role is disrupted by an old woman asking him to help her home. None too willingly, Porky obliges, lets her into her apartment, where-upon she falls dead at his feet! This shock is offset when Porky discovers a wad of banknotes, which he pockets, and returns to the movie house to watch (again?) the feature film. Now he figures himself as a gang leader: 'this was the way the big shots did it. Self-identification made him shiver with joy'.[50] There seems to be an odd congruence between Porky's wish-fulfilment and his actual experience, but when he returns to the apartment he is arrested by a detective, who has been pursuing the old woman for passing counterfeit money. Thus yet another reversal problematizes the relation between image and actuality. Porky's dream of power, stimulated and then renewed by the movie, is dashed by a twist which only confirms his social entrapment.

So far we have been considering a range of responses to essentially the same conventional act of going to the movies, but supposing a character encounters a film by accident; supposing he enters an auditorium through a door clearly signed 'exit' on to a balcony not from street level. This is precisely what happens in Richard Wright's short novel *The Man Who Lived Underground* (written 1941). Taking refuge down a sewer, the protagonist encounters society in reversed terms: from inside not outside, in the cinema from above not below. The fact that his accidental visit to the cinema is one of his first experiences suggests that Wright was using the episode to make a comment on society, for it is the audience that catches his protagonist's atten-tion, not the film. Wright uses the balcony as vantage-point for social observation, transforming into an advantage a location which would have been reserved in segregated movie houses for African Americans.[51] Estranged from the situation as if he is scarcely a member of that society, he exclaims to himself: 'these people were laughing at their lives, he thought with amaze-ment. They were shouting and yelling at the animated shadows of themselves'.[52] His astonishment comes, however, at a price. The only way the protagonist can register this scene in the way he does is by himself becoming an invisible vantage point. Seeing the humans around him as ghosts is only possible because he himself is unseen, has himself become a ghostly presence.

Imprisonment by Images: Richard Wright

In his account of the composition of *Native Son* (1940) Wright explains that 'the environment supplies the instrumentalities through which the organism expresses itself'.[53] Leaving aside the awkwardly behaviourist terminology, Wright here expresses a conviction that the environment inflects behaviour, a conviction which he had already written into his earlier novel *Lawd Today!* (written 1934–36, published 1963). Here the media textually precede any description of rooming blocks and the landscape of Chicago. By opening the novel with a radio announcer's voice Wright opens up a cultural environment which situates the individual as consumer and patriot (the action takes place on Lincoln's birthday). We start with the young black protagonist waking up to the sound of the radio, as the announcer invites every listener to look out of their window to see the stars and stripes. In his dream, however, Jake fails to see and finds himself running up an endless flight of stairs. Annoyed at being woken up, he attempts to recapture his dream but 'the dream steps were drowned in a vast blackness, like a slow movie fadeout'.[54] Already Wright has established the penetration of Jake's psyche by the movies, his exclusion from national celebrations, and his futile attempts to follow the American Dream. The steps of advancement lead nowhere; there is no goal in sight.

Wright takes great care to detail the solicitations levelled at Jake by circulars and advertisements, often giving their complete text. Like Dos Passos on New York, he evokes Chicago as a city of signs, all promising success and achievement – but at a price. The most eye-catching signs which Jake encounters on his way to work are seven movie posters giving a serial summary of the film they are advertising. As if to signal their impact on Jake, Wright shifts his prose into an extended stream-of-consciousness sentence. The first poster is read as follows:

> A bluehelmeted aviator in a bloodred monoplane darting shooting speeding zooming careening out of a bank of snowwhite clouds in hot pursuit of two green monoplanes and just above the cockpit of the red plane the hero's head could be seen and his eyes were blazing deathly hate and his lips were skinned back over his teeth in a horrible avenging grin and the faces of the two aviators in the fleeing planes were desperate despairing hopeless and at the side of the hero sat a golden-haired blueeyed girl operating a machinegun spewing fire and death and the girl's hair was blown straight back in the wind and her eyes were widened in fear [...][55]

Jake reads the poster imagery from action to facial expression and finally to the heroine. In every respect the film contrasts with his own situation. The hero flies, but Jake is bound to monotonous immobility in his job at the post office; the hero fights against clearly visualized enemies to get his girl, while Jake has to struggle against an amorphous poverty. There is an irony in the film which Jake misses in his craving for excitement. The enemies are encoded as 'desperate foreigners' (the Yellow Peril features briefly) and the heroine as a white girl identified by her clichéd racial features (blue eyes, golden hair). The appeal of the film lies in its apparent depiction of decisive individual action and its presentation of the heroine as the sexual 'prize', but Jake remains unaware of how his enthusiasm shows tacit complicity with a racist system he encounters every day of his waking life. Perhaps for this reason, Jake's dissatisfaction with his lot is articulated as sexual desire for a figure he cannot quite visualize beyond thinking of her as '*the* woman'.

Lawd Today! was a trial run of some of the themes Wright further developed in *Native Son*, not least the importance of the cinema. In his essay 'How "Bigger" Was Born' he explained how film helped to capture his paramount effect of immediacy: 'For the most part the novel is rendered in the present; I wanted the reader to feel that Bigger's story was unfolding *now*, like a play upon the stage or a movie unfolding upon the screen [...] Wherever possible, I told of Bigger's life in close-up, slow-motion, giving the feel of the grain in the passing of time'.[56] Wright had in mind a primarily white readership, whose detachment he was aiming to break down by closing up the distance between reader and Bigger.

Film operates in *Native Son* both as theme and technique, as part of Bigger's environment and as a means of expressing his relation to that environment. Indeed Ross Pudaloff has argued that 'every critical episode in *Native Son* [...] is framed, perceived, and mirrored in and through the images provided by mass culture.'[57] One of the first things Bigger does in the novel is go to the movies with his friend Jack. In her ground-breaking study of the cinema and the African American community, *Migrating to the Movies* (2005), Jacqueline Stewart argues that movie-going helped the 'creation of literal and symbolic spaces in which African Americans reconstructed their individuality and collective identities in response to the cinema's move towards classical narrative integration, and in the wake of migration's fragmenting effects'.[58] This contrast can be seen clearly in *Lawd Today!* in the disparity between the resolution of the action film narrative and the disjunctions of Jake's own life. In *Native Son* the cinema acts as a 'medium of absorption and distraction' in distracting Bigger from his planned robbery and in opening up sexual desire for white women on the screen.[59] Furthermore, the Regal Theatre (opened 1928), which Bigger and Jack attend, was a local landmark in African American neighbourhoods with its oriental décor and enormous size. In addition to its other attractions, it offered Bigger the space and privacy of darkness totally lacking at home. Hence the symbolism of the two boys masturbating as the viewing starts, a scene which was heavily revised by demand from the Book of the Month Club.

In the original version of Wright's text, now restored in the Library of America edition, the boys watch a newsreel and then *Trader Horn*. The first of these offers not news but images of white girls at leisure in their bathing costumes, including Mary Dalton, Bigger's employer-to-be. The revisions imposed on Wright were aimed at erasing any sign of Mary's sexual activity, both before her killing and in scenes like these at the movies, whereas the newsreel is used 'to establish that the movies have constructed a Mary who is attractive because she is rich and sexually provocative'.[60] The newsreel closes up on Mary's legs and follows her to her lover, again tracking her legs. The film thus makes it possible for Bigger to identify with her lover and begin a fantasy of sexual contact, although Jack's rude reminder of Bigger's black body ('you'd be hanging from a tree like a bunch of bananas') blocks that identification.[61] The second film, *Trader Horn* (1931), describes how plucky white men on African safari rescue the daughter of a missionary from African 'killers'.[62] The impact of this film, with its images of African nudity, on Bigger is strikingly different from that of the newsreel. No sooner does it begin than he performs a mental 'dissolve' and shifts scene: 'he looked at *Trader Horn* and saw pictures of naked black men and women whirling in wild dances and heard drums beating and then gradually the African scene changed and was replaced by images in his own mind of white men and women dressed in black and white clothes, laughing, talking, drinking and dancing'.[63] Bigger displaces images of African 'primitives', routinely applied in racial abuse (and which will figure in public reactions to Bigger's arrest), in favour of the only images of success he knows – that of prosperous whites.

In his revisions of the cinema episode Wright replaced the newsreel with a film called *The Gay Woman* (echoing earlier film titles of the 1930s), 'in which, amid scenes of cocktail drinking, dancing, golfing, swimming, and spinning roulette wheels, a rich young woman kept clandestine appointments with her lover while her millionaire husband was busy in the offices of a vast paper mill'.[64] This time Bigger's attempted identification with the white lover is blocked by Jack's explicit comparison between himself and King Kong. At this point Wright inserts a third element, a different stereotype of a 'crazy man'. He is none other than a 'red' with a bomb, but the lover saves the day, the Communist is arrested, the wife returns to her husband. As Jack remarks, 'they got to kiss in the end'. This clichéd resolution could not contrast more strongly with the end of Bigger's story as he waits alone for his impending execution. Admittedly imposed on Wright, this version compli-cates Bigger's identifications – he assumes reds are a 'race of folks who live in Russia' – and seems to sacrifice psychology to supplying anticipations of the novel's action.[65]

Bigger's early visit to the cinema thus establishes important themes which the novel will go on to develop. However, as Wright himself acknowledged, film also informs the representative techniques of the novel, especially scenes of dramatic intensity. The opening sets the tone of *Native Son* in its alarm, a signal to us to pay particular attention to the unfolding action. The very first visual image we get of Bigger is that of a 'black boy standing in a narrow space between two iron beds, rubbing his eyes with the backs of his hands'.[66] This immediately establishes a claustrophobic impression of Bigger's home conditions. Once the drama of the rat commences, Wright shifts the point of view rapidly from shots of the mother, to Bigger stalking his prey, up to the climactic close-up: 'the rat's belly pulsed with fear. Bigger advanced a step and the rat emitted a long thin song of defiance, its black beady eyes glittering, its tiny forefeet pawing the air restlessly'.[67] A close-up can give immediacy; it also here suggests the confined space of the confrontation. Wright subsequently explained that he 'restricted the novel to what Bigger saw and felt' so that there should be no barrier between him and the reader.[68] Throughout most of Book One we see Bigger in company. It is therefore appropriate for Wright to use the method he establishes in the opening scene of alternating Bigger's point of view with others' views of him.

The ubiquity of the latter suggests that Bigger is constantly under surveillance, hence the symbolism of the poster depicting the State's Attorney Buckley. It is Orwellian (and cinematic) in its effect of arresting the gaze of the person 'under observation':

> the white face was fleshy but stern; one hand was uplifted and its index finger pointed straight out into the street at each passer-by. The poster showed one of those faces that looked straight at you when you looked at it and all the while you were walking and turning your head to look at it it kept looking unblinkingly back at you until you got so far from it you had to take your eyes away, and then it stopped, like a movie blackout.[69]

The film comparison gives us the necessary signal that this poster is neither two-dimensional nor inert. It projects its image outwards, creating a domain through the apparent extent of its gaze, and in that respect functions as an image of white power in the city; in every sense it is an arresting poster. And power is established visually through the gaze. *Native Son* is packed with innumerable references to eyes, to seeing and blindness, and we will see how this motif informs Bigger's first meeting with the Daltons.

The Daltons' house is not just spacious, but seems to be packed with white furnishings. Bigger's visual responses to the Daltons themselves are of a piece with his consciousness of entering a new domain. Mr Dalton is scarcely visualized at all because Bigger lowers his gaze to conform to the behaviour he assumes is expected. Then Mrs Dalton approaches: 'he saw coming slowly towards him a tall, thin, white woman, walking silently, her hands lifted delicately in the air and touching the walls to either side of her [...] Her face and hair were completely white; she seemed to him like a ghost'.[70] This is one of the most powerful moments of the novel since it is entirely visual, encoded within the novel's black/white polarity, and an image of objective visuality – Mrs Dalton is blind. Indeed she resembles an eerie embodiment of whiteness. Like an inverted image of witchcraft, she is followed by her 'familiar', a white cat. And then there is Mary, whom Bigger recognizes from the newsreel, with the difference that off-screen she seems positively dangerous. It is only when he is driving the car and has re-established visual distance from her that he can briefly relax. In the car window 'she looked like a doll in a shop window'.[71] Mary has become re-situated in a frame with an invisible (glass) barrier before him, whereas once events move towards her killing such barriers fall away and with them Bigger loses his bearings. One of the most biting ironies in the novel lies in the fact that the scripts of racialized behaviour offer Bigger more security than supposedly liberating divergences from those scripts, divergences which ultimately cost him his life.

Once it becomes clear that Bigger cannot perform the role of driver as he expected, the visualization of the novel changes. Images blur; the killing of Mary (and later that of Bessie) takes place in darkness, and also introduces a new element into the colour-coding of the novel. The action throughout is insistently depicted in terms of black and white. Whether the text is referring to newsprint or to racial groups, Wright builds up a remorseless sense of Bigger's visual environment being surcharged with images of division. Once the killing of Mary takes place, a third colour enters the narrative: the red glow of the furnace. Redness becomes a multiple sign, denoting death, blood, or the politically demonized Left. Bigger's mounting panic at not being able to escape the consequences of the killing is reflected in the recurrent location of investigative scenes in the furnace basement.

The death of Mary triggers a loss of reality in Bigger's consciousness. He constantly feels himself haunted by a 'white blur' and internalizes his hopelessness into nightmare. The after-image of Mary's severed head becomes a grotesque self-image in dream: 'he stood on a street corner in a red glare like that which came from the furnace and he had a big package in his arms [...] he wanted to know what was in the package and he stopped near an alley corner and unwrapped it and the paper fell away and he saw – it was his *own* head – his own head lying with black face and half-closed eyes and lips parted with white teeth showing'.[72] Wright is now applying a method similar to cinematic expressionism whereby Bigger's mental state determines the visualization of his surroundings. Here a number of displacements have occurred. Inside (the furnace room) has become outside; other has become self. Bigger hallucinates his own inevitable death as if his killing of Mary were tantamount to suicide. Bigger's encounter with death is further reinforced in his entry into skull-like abandoned buildings with Bessie.[73] In a further reversal snow blankets Chicago, literalizing its status as a white city. Visually the effect is like a film shifting into negative whereby dark bodies – especially the dark body of Bigger – are defined against a white ground. Even in the last stages of his pursuit Bigger visualizes the detached head of a policeman emerging from a skylight and 'moving like a figure on the screen in close-up slow motion'.[74] Here and throughout the novel, Bigger's sense of danger is reflected in the shifting pace of descriptions.

The variations in the novel's many cinematic allusions deny Bigger any stable position as spectator because they insistently 'other' him and his situation. Tantalized by the imagery in his early visit to the movie house, he dimly comes to realize that cinematic processes are constantly inflecting his perceptions of his own situation as it slides into nightmare after the first killing. If these perceptions suggest different cinematic scripts – romance, political melodrama, horror film – these scripts have been composed elsewhere; in other words, Bigger's helplessness is constantly being reconfirmed to him.

With Bigger's capture Wright shifts the visual focus of the novel back to realism, but realism with a satirical purpose. Even during his pursuit Bigger had been transformed into a news item and the same is true once he is in custody. Now, in every sense, he has become a case. Although Chicago prided itself on being a free northern city, all the racist signs of the South are transposed on to the urban scene: the threats of lynching, the fiery cross of the Ku Klux Klan, and the news accounts of the 'brutish' Bigger. In this Wright was drawing on the 1938 Robert Nixon murder case, which broke in Chicago while he was composing *Native Son*. News reports stereotyped Nixon as a 'jungle Negro' who is 'known to be ferocious and relentless in a fight'.[75] Exactly the same stereotypes operate in Bigger's trial and it is consistent with the novel's imagery that the last speaker in his trial should be Buckley (the poster has come alive) and that Buckley should use Mary's newsreel as 'evidence' of her rape by Bigger. The difference for the reader of course lies in the fact that we have witnessed the working of Bigger's subjective life; we have seen with his eyes and registered his sense of being trapped by circumstances. It is no coincidence that Wright greatly admired Dreiser's *Sister Carrie*. During the trial, however inevitable the outcome seems, it has become impossible for us to dehumanize Bigger into an animal or a racial inferior, as the prosecutor does.

Following the success of *Native Son*, Wright was approached by the Hollywood producer Harold Hecht who was interested in making a film adaptation, but negotiations fell through when Hecht revealed that he wanted to use an all-white cast![76] During the 1940s Wright was involved in a number of film projects: an invitation to write a screenplay of Booker T. Washington's life, a script on the Fisk Jubilee Singers to be called *Melody Unlimited*; and a collaboration on a film about an American Nazi.[77] In 1941 Wright co-published with Edwin Rosskam *12 Million Black Voices*, a work of photo-reportage on African Americans in the Depression. Rosskam assembled the photographs and Wright composed the text, which one reviewer compared to a 'cinematic soundtrack'. On the strength of this publication Wright then approached the documentary film-maker John Grierson about a post as a scriptwriter, but was turned down. At the end of the Second World War, under the impact of reading Parker Tyler's *The Hollywood Hallucination*, he bought himself a movie camera.[78] None of these projects bore fruit and Wright eventually made a film adaptation of *Native Son* in Argentina, which was released as *Sangre Negra* in 1951.[79] Even here, however, he was bitterly disappointed by the way the film was cut and the trial reduced to a visual spectacle.[80]

Notes

1   Cripps, *Slow Fade to Black*, p. 5.

2   Langston Hughes, *Collected Works, Volume 9*, p. 226.

3   bell hooks, *Black Looks*, p. 116.

4   Cripps, *Slow Fade to Black*, pp. 71–72. For a full account of black protest against *The Birth of a Nation* see Everett, *Returning the Gaze*, pp. 59–106.

5   James Weldon Johnson, 'Uncle Tom's Cabin and the Clansman', in *Selected Writings*, vol. 1, p. 12. Johnson also attacked the pseudo-historical pretensions of *The Birth of a Nation* in 'Perverted History', in *Selected Writings*, vol. 1, pp. 156–58. For commentary, see Laurence J. Oliver and Terri L. Walker, 'James Weldon Johnson's *New York Age* Essays'. This essay documents Johnson's attack on Woodrow Wilson, an admirer of the film, and on Griffith's falsification of Southern history.

6   For a discussion of this novel, see Lawrence J. Oliver's 'Writing from the Right during the "Red Decade"'. Among many other points, Oliver notes that Dixon took his title from DuBois' *Black Reconstruction in America*.

7   Quoted in Pearl Bowser, Jane Gaines and Charles Musser, eds., *Oscar Micheaux and his Circle*, p. 110.

8   Pearl Bowser and Louise Spence, *Writing himself into History*, p. 18. Micheaux's 1920 film *The Symbol of the Unconquered* was billed as 'A Story of the Ku Klux Klan' and attempted to reverse Griffith's imagery. For a discussion of Micheaux's 1919 film *Within Our Gates* as a rejoinder to Griffith, see Jane Gaines, '*The Birth of a Nation* and *Within Our Gates*: Two Tales of the American South', in Richard H. King and Helen Taylor, eds., *Dixie Debates*, pp. 177–92.

9   James Baldwin, *The Price Was Right*, p. 584. *The Birth of a Nation* is discussed on pp. 583–93.

10 For valuable commentary on the adaptations of Micheaux, novels by Paul Laurence Dunbar, Charles Chesnutt and others, see Charlene Regester, 'African-American Writers and Pre-1950 Cinema'.

11 Oscar Micheaux, 'The Negro and the Photo-Play', in Ross, ed., *Movies and American Society*, pp. 184–85.

12 Earl James Young, Jr, and Beverly J. Robinson, eds., *The Life and Work of Oscar Micheaux*, p. 67. The film materialized as *The Gunsaulus Mystery* (1921) but the novel was never published.

13 Young and Robinson, eds., *The Life and Work of Oscar Micheaux*, p. 83.

14 Bowser and Spence, *Writing himself into History*, p. 32. Statements like these should be viewed with caution. Micheaux was a very efficient self-publicist. Similarly, in 1926 the Micheaux Film Corporation announced plans to film Zora Neale Hurston's 'Vanity' (Bowser and Spence, *Writing himself into History*, p. 218).

15 For detailed commentary on press responses, see Charlene Regester, 'The African-American Press and Race Movies, 1909–1929', in Bowser, Gaines and Musser, eds., *Oscar Micheaux and his Circle*, pp. 34–49. For a detailed filmography of Micheaux, see Young and Robinson, eds., *The Life and Work of Oscar Micheaux*, Appendix B. Micheaux's novels were *The Conquest: The Story of a Negro Pioneer* (1913), *The Forged Note* (1915), *The Homesteader* (1917), *The Wind from Nowhere* (1943), *The Case of Mrs Wingate* (1945), *The Story of Dorothy Stanfield* (1946), and *The Masquerade* (1947). At time of writing (2006) only *The Conquest* and *The Homesteader* have been reprinted.

16 Bowser and Spence, *Writing himself into History*, p. 141.

17 Young and Robinson, eds., *The Life and Work of Oscar Micheaux*, p. 74.

18 Young and Robinson, eds., *The Life and Work of Oscar Micheaux*, pp. 117–18.

19 Oscar Micheaux, *The Homesteader*, p. 101.

20 *The Homesteader*, p. 55.

21 *The Homesteader*, p. 260.

22 *The Homesteader*, p. 521.

23 Young and Robinson, eds., *The Life and Work of Oscar Micheaux*, p. 138. Young and Robinson reprint the full text of this preface. These sentiments were echoed by, among others, James Weldon Johnson, who in *Black Manhattan* (1930) noted that, despite advances in the theatre, 'in no moving picture [...] has any Negro screen actor been permitted to portray as high a type as has been portrayed on the stage' (p. 230).

24 Zora Neale Hurston, *Mules and Men*, p. 1. In 1930 Hurston was accused of attacking African American writers (in an article she repudiated) for their ignorance of their own community (Everett, *Returning the Gaze*, pp. 184–85).

25 See, for example, Katherine Henninger, 'Zora Neale Hurston, Richard Wright, and the Postcolonial Gaze'. Karen Jacobs sees more ambivalence in Hurston, who, she argues, 'uneasily vacillates between speaking as and speaking for the given group, an insider and outsider, participant and observer' (*The Eye's Mind*, pp. 124–25).

26 Hurston, *I Love Myself*, p. 170. Her caricature of the Native American is surely drawn from Westerns: 'The American Indian is a contraption of copper wires in an eternal war-bonnet, with no equipment for laughter, expressionless face and that says "How" when spoken to' (*I Love Myself*, p. 170).

27 Carla Kaplan, *Zora Neale Hurston: A Life in Letters*, p. 456. For commentary on Hurston's films see Gloria J. Gibson, 'Cinematic Foremothers: Zora Neale Hurston and Eloyce King Patrick Gist', in Bowser, Gaines and Musser, eds., *Oscar Micheaux and his Circle*, pp. 195–209; and Elaine S. Charnov, 'The Performative Visual Anthropology Films of Zora Neale Hurston'.

28 Jacobs, *The Eye's Mind*, p. 131. Jacobs reads the novel as a 'triumph of participation over observation' (p. 127) and her whole chapter gives a valuably detailed account of the shifts in Janie's subjectivity.

29 Zora Neale Hurston, *Their Eyes Were Watching God*, p. 21.
30 *Their Eyes Were Watching God*, p. 119.
31 Jacobs, *The Eye's Mind*, pp. 142–44.
32 *Their Eyes Were Watching God*, p. 286.
33 Kaplan, *Zora Neale Hurston: A Life in Letters*, p. 435.
34 Robert Haas, '*The Story of Louis Pasteur* and the Making of Zora Neale Hurston's *Their Eyes Were Watching God*'.
35 Kaplan, *Zora Neale Hurston: A Life in Letters*, p. 463.
36 Kaplan, *Zora Neale Hurston: A Life in Letters*, p. 467.
37 Langston Hughes, *I Wonder As I Wander*, p. 76.
38 No reason was given for the cancellation. The American builder of the Dnieper Dam threatened to halt construction if the film went ahead. Dorothy West recorded this but Hughes never commented on the cancellation. For a summary account, see Cripps, *Slow Fade to Black*, pp. 212–14. Louise Thompson Patterson, another member of the American group in Moscow, has recorded how, on the announcement that the project was cancelled, the majority (including Hughes) signed a declaration that the film could not be made without an adequate scenario, while a minority group signed a different declaration accusing the Soviet Union of betraying American Negroes ('With Langston Hughes in the USSR').
39 Langston Hughes, 'Moscow and Me', in *Collected Works, Volume 9*, p. 58.
40 Arnold Rampersad, *The Life of Langston Hughes*, vol. 1, pp. 284–85, 366–67. For commentary on *Way Down South*, see Thomas Cripps, 'Langston Hughes and the Movies', in which he argues that Hughes fell victim to Hollywood practice and conventions (pp. 305–17). Very few African American broke into the Hollywood business. For a discussion of one success, see Phyllis Klotman, 'The Black Writer in Hollywood, Circa 1930'.
41 Robert Shulman describes this work as combining 'modernist disruptions of the text, surreal dreams and political juxtapositions, and the techniques of the Living Newspaper' (*The Power of Political Art*, p. 286). The Living Newspaper was organized in 1935 within the Federal Theater Project and contained, among other things, actors delivering the actual words of politicians.
42 Dorothy West, *The Richer, The Poorer*, pp. 202, 203.
43 Claude McKay, *Home to Harlem*, p. 219. It is quite likely that the burlesque described in the quotation was based on a story by Octavus Roy Cohen, self-styled African American humorist, whose stories were adapted for the screen throughout the 1920s and 1930s. His 1925 collection *Bigger and Blacker* describes the working of the Midnight Pictures Corporation (president, Orifice R. Latimer). Cohen was criticized by DuBois and others for recycling stereotypes in his comedies. In the late 1920s McKay found himself work reading novels for scripts at Ralph Ingram's Victorine Studios in Nice. In his autobiography, McKay describes the hostility of white Americans to his appointment and records his impressions of studio life: 'the movie establishment was like a realistic dream of my romantic idea of a great medieval domain' (*A Long Way from Home*, p. 273). Ingram had set up his studio in 1925 with the actress Alice Terry in a desire to get away from the Hollywood ethos. There is some evidence that he supplied Scott Fitzgerald with a model for Dick Diver in *Tender is the Night*.
44 W. E. B. DuBois, *Writings*, p. 364.
45 Jessie Redmon Fauset, *Plum Bun*, pp. 91–92. The classic 'passing' narrative is Nella Larsen's *Passing* (1929). For an excellent account of the complex shifts in visual perspective within that novel, see Lori Harrison-Kahan's 'Her "Nig": Returning the Gaze of Nella Larsen's *Passing*'.

46 Margaret Perry, ed., *The Short Fiction of Rudolph Fisher*, p. 69.

47 Perry, ed., *The Short Fiction of Rudolph Fisher*, p. 70.

48 Cripps, *Slow Fade to Black*, p. 189.

49 West, *The Richer, the Poorer*, p. 109.

50 West, *The Richer, the Poorer*, p. 113.

51 One of the most famous inter-war novels about Harlem, Carl Van Vechten's *Nigger Heaven* (1926), took its title from the slang expression for a theatre gallery, deriving from the practice of segregation. At one point in that novel an aspiring African American novelist reflects bitterly: 'Nigger Heaven! That's what Harlem is. We sit in our places in the gallery of this New York theatre and watch the white world sitting down below in the good seats in the orchestra' (p. 149). With the rise of Harlem chic, African Americans complained repeatedly of becoming a spectacle for white entertainment, but the indignation here arises from the sheer unconsciousness on the whites' part of the existence of the gallery.

52 Richard Wright, *Eight Men*, p. 38.

53 Richard Wright, 'How "Bigger" Was Born', in *Early Works*, p. 862.

54 Wright, *Early Works*, p. 6.

55 Wright, *Early Works*, p. 52. Wright's use of compound adjectives may have been suggested by Dos Passos' *Manhattan Transfer*.

56 Wright, *Early Works*, p. 878.

57 Ross Pudaloff, 'Celebrity as Identity', p. 156.

58 Jacqueline Stewart, *Migrating to the Movies*, p. 94.

59 Stewart, *Migrating to the Movies*, p. 98.

60 Shulman, *The Power of Political Art*, p. 146.

61 Wright, *Early Works*, p. 474; Stewart, *Migrating to the Movies*, p. 105.

62 The film has been recognized as a precursor to *King Kong* (1933).

63 Wright, *Early Works*, p. 476.

64 Richard Wright, *Native Son*, p. 69.

65 Wright, *Native Son*, p. 71.

66 Wright, *Early Works*, p. 447.

67 Wright, *Early Works*, p. 449.

68 Wright, *Early Works*, p. 879.

69 Wright, *Early Works*, p. 456.

70 Wright, *Early Works*, p. 488.

71 Wright, *Early Works*, p. 503.

72 Wright, *Early Works*, p. 599.

73 The buildings have 'black windows, like blind eyes' (p. 606), an image Wright took from Poe's 'Fall of the House of Usher' which further blurs the visual distinction between inside and outside, self and environment.

74 Wright, *Early Works*, p. 690.

75 Charles Leavelle, 'Brick Slayer is Likened to Jungle Beast', *Chicago Sunday Tribune* (5 June 1938), Part 1 p. 6. Coincidentally Nixon himself had a film connection, having acted as an extra in the 1937 films *Slave Ship* and *Souls at Sea*. This news report compares Nixon's murders with the killings by the orang-utan in Poe's 'The Murders in the Rue Morgue'.

76 Elizabeth Binggeli has shown from Warner Brothers records that the studios turned down *Native Son* partly from their uncertainty over what should replace the older stereotyped images of African Americans ('Burbanking Bigger').

77 Thomas Cripps, '*Native Son* in the Movies'.

78 Hazel Rowley, *Richard Wright*, pp. 262, 318.
79 The film was made by the French director Pierre Chenal with Wright himself playing the role of Bigger. The CIA made attempts to interfere with the making of the film, which was only shown in the USA in a cut version and to poor reviews (Rowley, *Richard Wright*, pp. 392–95). For further commentary, see John Pyros, 'Richard Wright: A Black Novelist's Experience in Film'.
80 Peter Brunette, 'Two Wrights, One Wrong', in Peary and Shatzkin, eds., *The Modern American Novel and the Movies*, pp. 136–37.

12

Into the Night Life:
Henry Miller and Anaïs Nin

In the chapters on Dos Passos, Dreiser, Steinbeck and documentary the emphasis has tended to fall on exteriorities, on a naturalistic use of film to help writers in articulating their perceptions of America. At the same time, in the cases of Fitzgerald, Richard Wright and others, we have also seen how film complicates such perceptions by creating fantasies which repeatedly collide with actuality. We turn now to writers – primarily Henry Miller and Anaïs Nin – who were fascinated by the new possibilities film offered of expressing the inner world of dream. In 1936 Walter Benjamin expressed a conviction which was implicitly shared by both writers, namely that 'the camera introduces us to unconscious optics as does psychoanalysis to unconscious impulses'.[1]

Henry Miller's imagination was shaped by the films he saw in New York and, after 1930, in Paris. At the end of the thirties he claimed to have seen 'practically all the important films produced by Russia, Germany, France and America'.[2] He was astonished by Buñuel's *Un Chien Andalou* (1928) and, when exploring the district near Reamur-Sebastopol, he exclaimed to a friend: 'there are Caligari doorways'.[3] He waxed enthusiastic about Marlene Dietrich in *The Blue Angel* (1930) ('what carnality', he exclaimed) and, as his biographer Robert Ferguson has written, 'films became the mirrors in which he could trace mythological reflections of himself and the events of his own life'.[4] Miller's fascination with the cinema was so strong that he hoped for a job with the French avant-garde film-maker Germaine Du Lac and in 1932 started planning a book on film in collaboration with his then lover Anaïs Nin. From the same period Miller's biographer Jay Martin has suggested that Miller's narrative persona in *Tropic of Capricorn* (1936) was influenced by the Werner Krauss film *The Man Without A Name* (1920), whose protagonist suffers from amnesia and gives himself a new name.[5]

From the start Miller recorded his hostility to Hollywood commercialism, but did find a saving grace occasionally in works such as *Lost Horizon* (1937: 'the first *significant* film out of Hollywood'). His special praise went to those works which engaged the viewer's active imagination or which operated on different levels of experience. Thus, he was fascinated by the way in which Buñuel's *L'Age d'Or* (1930) was 'composed of a succession of images without sequence the significance of which must be sought for below the threshold of consciousness'; and in an essay of 1931 he paid tribute to Buñuel's capacity to reveal the 'complete and bloody machinery of sex' lying beneath what we call love.[6] As we shall see, Miller tried out his own experiments in prose image sequences. He devoted a whole essay to *Ecstasy* (1932), in which he praised the use of slow motion and other techniques; 'each time I go [to see the film],' he exclaimed, 'I discover new marvels in it'.[7] Perhaps under the impetus of this enthusiasm, Miller told Anaïs Nin in 1933 that his film book would include a section on stars, his purpose being to 'reveal their appeal, their inner symbolism for the public, in terms of this death nonsense'.[8]

Miller's tribute to the French film actor Raimu became the occasion of his most sustained statement on Hollywood. Once again he attacked the 'democratic disease' of the USA which reduced 'everything unique to the level of the herd'. Here Miller makes one of his most challenging judgements: 'the real key to the American sense of grandeur lies in the glorification of catastrophes. Nature is the hero, not man! If it is not an earthquake it is a hurricane or a landslide or a flood, dramatic incidents which have their human counterpart in battle scenes, prison riots, and so on'. Projecting his own values (his privileging of individualism, political non-participation, etc.) onto the medium, Miller obliquely describes himself through the national character: 'the American *is* a different animal, and he is primarily a non-political, non-cultural animal. In his most Utopian dreams he is most truly himself'.[9] Despite his efforts to be even-handed in his comparisons, Miller tilts his argument against Hollywood by enumerating the number of times American films fail in casting, realism, and other aspects.[10]

At the end of his stay in Paris Miller became involved in two film projects, both of which came to nothing. In 1942 he considered collaborating with Marcel Friedman in writing a screenplay adaptation of Jacob Wassermann's 1929 novel *The Maurizius Case*.[11] And in 1944 Parker Tyler commissioned Miller to write a preface to his study *The Hollywood Hallucination*, but in the event Miller's piece was rejected by the publishers, probably because it had only an oblique relevance to Tyler's book.[12] Although Miller declares grandly at the beginning of the preface 'it was always my intention to write a book about Hollywood', he only discusses it in very general terms, limiting himself to two aspects.[13] Firstly, he attacks the production code supporting a supposedly 'democratic art' as flattening out difference. Secondly, he extrapolates newsreel commentary as the voice of Hollywood itself, blandly boosting all subjects, and reflects: 'Is this the Voice which even the Czar of Hollywood is powerless to prevail against?'[14] Parker Tyler's study presented Hollywood, six years before Hortense Powdermaker popularized the phrase, as a dream factory.[15] Tyler strengthened both Miller's conviction that film was closely linked to dream and also his distaste for the mechanical, commercialized processes he identified with Hollywood. When he actually visited Hollywood during his travels for *The Air-Conditioned Nightmare* (1945), Miller was extremely selective in his comment, ridiculing a soiree but also recognizing the surreal dimension to the place. Looking at the night lights of Los Angeles, he recorded, was like looking into an ominous future: 'the city resembled something out of Fritz Lang's feeble imagination'.[16]

In the *Tropics* Miller first gave successful expression to his persona of a consciousness at large. Drawing on the model of Whitman's visual catalogues, Miller attempts to take visionary possession of the cities of New York and Paris. He saw Whitman as the supreme poet of the body and the very embodiment of America; hence his assertion that 'Whitman is a beginning'.[17] In particular Miller was fascinated by Whitman's construction of visionary panoramas of his country in which the observing poet gathers all national types and occupations into himself. In his poems the USA becomes a huge spatial area around which his eye can range, sometimes sweeping across tracts of country. Seeing thus becomes for Whitman a way of mediating the variety of American national life. Miller, in contrast, casts himself as the personification of an anti-America, a lonely seer who gathers the migrant poor together into an increasingly apocalyptic image sequence: 'I saw them hobbling along like twisted gnomes or falling backwards in the epileptic frenzy, the mouth twitching, the saliva pouring from the lips, the limbs writhing; I saw the walls giving way and the pest pouring out like a winged fluid'.[18] Where Whitman enacts identification through visual recognition, Miller sets up an implicit distance from the figures he is describing by making them into a physically grotesque spectacle designed to counter national images of success as physical well-being.

Miller drew on the practice of the Hungarian photographer Brassaï to concentrate the visual focus in his fiction. Where he describes Brassaï as 'an eye, a living eye', in *Tropic of Capricorn* he fantasizes about becoming the eye of New York: 'Above all I was an eye, a huge searchlight which scoured far and wide [...] This eye so wide awake seemed to have made all my other faculties dormant; all my powers were used up in the effort to see, to take in the drama of the world'.[19] Miller's claim to be a hyper-conscious recording instrument sounds strained in the context of New York. It was Paris above all which fired his imagination. Thus, in his essay on Brassaï ('The Eye of Paris') he looks into the latter's eyes only to see himself and then appropriates Brassaï's role to record a montage of Paris images: 'What a procession passes before my eyes! What a throng of men and women! [...] I see the old hats [...] I see the corners of walls eroded by time and weather [...] I see the old tin urinals'.[20] Miller contrasts the age of the spectacle before him with the animated present immediacy of recovered perception. 'Through me Paris will live again', he reflects. In this novel Miller opposes speech to sight, figuring his wife as a ventriloquist working her dummy and then as a disembodied mouth: 'The lips were finely parted, smoothed down with a thick paste of dark blood: I watched them open and close with the utmost fascination [...] They were always close-up, as in the movie stills, so that I knew every crevice, every pore'.[21] Here the movie analogy helps Miller to neutralize, or rather 'gag', his wife. She is described as a 'vamp' exercising her power through speech, whereas Miller's detailed focus on the appearance of her organ of speech at once blanks out her words and transforms her mouth into a bizarre visual spectacle. It is only through such transformations that the narrator can retain control of his own record.

Tropic of Cancer (1934) makes explicit Miller's incorporation of visual technologies into the processes of perception. Here he registers his sense of the city through an internalized camera which 'pans' round Paris from a high vantage point above the railway. This establishing shot indicates at once reverie and visual perception: 'Indigo sky, swept clear of fleecy clouds, gaunt trees infinitely extended, their black boughs gesticulating like a sleepwalker'.[22] The background colouring reminds us that Miller was a painter. More importantly, it enables him to set up a mobile image of thought whose branches extend outwards into the Paris scene.

Miller finds Paris, unlike New York, to be liberating in that its street life fills his whole field of vision. Miller the *flâneur* relishes night scenes because he can more easily order the sequence of his perceptions: 'wandering along the Seine at night, wandering and wandering, and going mad with the beauty of it, the trees leaning to, the broken images in the water, the rush of the current under the bloody lights of the bridges, the women sleeping in doorways, sleeping on newspapers, sleeping in the rain'. As Miller moves from the river to the inhabitants, the former becomes a metaphor of flow and change which fragments the city's images. At this point the description is generic and one which shifts through different spatial relations: *in* doorways, *on* newspapers, *in* the rain. And then Miller introduces a Dickensian figure, a woman with a broken umbrella who always sleeps in the Place St Sulpice: 'every night she slept there on a bench under her torn umbrella, the ribs hanging down, her dress turning green, her bony fingers and the odour of decay oozing from her body'.[23] Just for a moment it becomes impossible to distinguish woman from umbrella and is as if we are watching a human body decay before our eyes. Miller's choice of title is strategic in the sense that he gradually accumulates more and more images of decay and death. Because most of these are nocturnal it is easier for Miller to give the images a surreal distorted dimension, as if perceived in dream. Characters are defined through grotesque features: bulging eyes, yellow whiskers, swollen glands.

Two interests converged in the visual composition of Miller's narratives: film and dream. In 1932 he started keeping a dream-book (he called it his 'dream-cinema') and in *The World of Sex* he declared: 'It is our dream life which offers a key to the possibilities in store for us'. For this reason he stated that in his own books he had 'endeavoured to plot the inner pattern, follow the potential being'.[24] This belief in the closeness of film to dream, shared by Miller and Anaïs Nin, is reflected in a letter Nin wrote to Miller in 1932: 'We won't write a book on movies, but maybe a book of dreams'.[25]

Miller's first attempt at a dream narrative occurs in *Tropic of Cancer*, a dream significantly triggered while he is at the cinema. The imagistic link between waking and dreaming is the 'artificial eye' of the exit sign:

> Standing in the courtyard with a glass eye; only half the world is intelligible. The stones are wet and mossy and in the crevices are black toads. A big door bars the entrance to the cellar; the steps are slippery and soiled with bat dung. The door bulges and sags, the hinges are falling off, but there is an enamelled sign on it, in perfect condition, which says 'Be sure to close the door.' Why close the door?

The description internalizes one of Miller's favourite Parisian scenes, the run-down courtyard, and also captures the absent logic of dream through a paratactic sequence of images. Once Miller pauses to ask questions or comment in any way other than adding visual data, the immediacy of the narrative becomes compromised. The shifts in the dreamer's perspective are appropriately left implicit as objects undergo surreal transformations. Once through the threshold, Miller enters a place of knowledge:

> A woman is sitting on a dais above an immense carven desk; she has a snake around her neck. The entire room is lined with books and strange fish swimming in coloured globes. There are maps and charts on the wall [...][26]

Does the snake demonize the woman? We cannot be sure. At any rate she comes to embody the knowledge hinted at in the maps and books. The room begins to revolve and geography slides off the walls on to the woman's body, which becomes a terrain to be explored by the dreamer.

Black Spring (1936) is Miller's dream-book. Here his interests in Surrealist art and film, his recollections of his childhood, and his desire to celebrate his own subjectivity all converge in narrative which collapses together different time-levels. He declares: 'I am a man without a past and without a future. *I am* – that is all'.[27] Miller's evocation of an extended present makes each scene equally immediate at the moment of narration. When he states 'in my dreams I come back to the 14th Ward [of New York] as a paranoiac returns to his obsessions' he is at once affirming a belief in the artistic validity of obsessions and also strengthening his projections of scenes through juxtaposition.[28] In her examination of the differences between written and cinematic autobiography Elizabeth Bruss draws a distinction which sheds helpful light on shifts within *Black Spring* and Miller's other novels. She notes how one speaking 'I' can shade easily into another whereas 'the spectator in film is always out of frame, creating an impassable barrier between the person seeing and person seen'.[29] Paradoxically, the more insistently Miller uses the first-person pronoun, the more disparate become the guises and roles adopted by the narrator. In *Black Spring* and the *Tropics* the narrator will typically approach vantage points, such as a hotel window, from which to observe the city scene. At the point at which he focuses the reader's attention totally on things seen, he shifts from an 'I' to an eye, a shift which Miller makes explicit in *Tropic of Capricorn*. Miller was well aware of the framing of his visual sequences. He relishes street descriptions because as observer he is embedded within the field of vision. However, when he introduces the formulaic 'I see... I see' he raises his descriptions towards the visionary.

The central dream sequence of *Black Spring*, 'Into the Night Life', opens as follows:

> Over the foot of the bed is the shadow of the cross. There are chains binding me to the bed. The chains are clanking loudly, the anchor is being lowered. Suddenly I feel a hand on my shoulder. Someone is shaking me vigorously. I look up and it is an old hag in a dirty wrapper. She goes to the dresser and opening a drawer she puts away a revolver.[30]

We start with the dreamer registering inertia as bondage, as being 'anchored' (through an actualized metaphor) to the bed. The only active figure here is one of the many female embodiments of threat, sexual and otherwise, which recur throughout Miller's writings.

At one point in *Black Spring* Miller imagines the 'complete destruction of anagogic dream interpretation' but, despite this attempted refusal to be confined by any single interpretive system, his chapter contains different forms of dream-work.[31] The transformation of scenes and figures, the shifts from enclosed spaces to open expanses, and even word-play are all consistent with dream-narratives. For Miller the ground of the real is never stable. Miller paces his scenes with cinematic care, slowing down the sequence to give long perspective views or suspending sound to maximize the horror of seeing a stream of coffins pour from a factory outlet. This chapter is subtitled 'A Coney Island of the Mind' to signal a growing awareness of how flimsy surface phenomena are. Sidewalks collapse, house walls bulge open, and human figures seem masked as if lacking substance. Broadly speaking – but this can only be an approximate summary – Miller takes us towards a heightened realization of death.

It would be inconsistent with the local convention of this narrative to reach a summarizing conclusion. Instead Miller closes with an image of origin: the mind-vortex which produces these visions. Here he is reflecting his allegiance to Surrealist practice in suggesting the need to let these scenes flow forth. In the opening we saw an image of bondage; towards the end we have an image of liberation as a menagerie is set free. Even this progression risks sounding too orderly. What is more important to note is Miller's use of montage as he 'cuts' from scene to scene. Towards the end of the chapter he revives the Indian wars, no doubt drawing on the Western films he had seen:

> Once more the tomahawk gleams, scalps fly, and out of the river-bed there rolls a bright billowy cloud of blood. From the mountain sides, from the great caves, from the swamps and Everglades pours a flood of blood-flecked men.

By evoking the whole landscape of the nation Miller briefly gains an effect of spectacle reminiscent of D. W. Griffith, except that he is reviving those killed by the dominant culture in the USA. His local identification with the dead motivates the next 'shot' which describes the dismemberment of the dreamer:

> My scalp is cut away, the grey meat hangs over my ears in shreds; my feet are burnt away, my sides pierced with arrows. In a pen against a broken fence I lie with my bowels beside me; all mangled and gory the beautiful white temple that was stretched with skin and muscle.[32]

This passage demonstrates that in dream narratives not only do place and dimension mutate unpredictably, but also that the gaze carries unusual complexities. To apply Elizabeth Bruss again, this kind of visual description might seem impersonal because the vantage point is 'out of frame'.[33] But strictly speaking we have a narrating 'I' watching a second self, his projection as the dreamer. In the passage just quoted the dreamer is even watching a third self, the externalized body turned inside out by fantastic injuries. Literally dis-embodied, the dreamer/observer then transforms his body into an ornate spectacle: 'I am full of raw gems that bleed with icy brilliance'.[34] Miller may be throwing out an implicit allusion to his own narrative productivity here. At any rate the visual description is moving well away from realism and from the body towards images of radiance and special value.

Miller was attempting here to realize a method he valued in the films of Buñuel, namely the production of an image sequence which operates just below the level of consciousness. For instance, the sequence starts with a religious icon. Then Miller casts himself in a Christ-like role of victim and martyr (he discovers a large hole in his side) but this is gradually displaced by Miller's preferred role as witness, recording the repeated rituals of death at the end. He was well aware of how scene should support theme. Sitting in the Paris rush hour, he reflects: 'For him who is obliged to dream with eyes wide open all movement is in reverse, all action broken into kaleidoscopic fragments'.[35] Even here, the comment is based on visual technologies suggesting a film running backwards and imagery made relative and arbitrary by rotation.

Anaïs Nin and Djuna Barnes

Miller's attempts to apply Surrealist film techniques in prose were greatly helped by his friendship with Anaïs Nin and it is helpful to approach Nin through another American writer who, Nin repeatedly acknowledged, had set a new standard for the novel. When Djuna Barnes' *Nightwood* was first published in 1936, Nin was so moved by it that she wrote to Barnes to express her admiration for the latter's capacity to reveal life's 'most poetic, its most symbolic and human significance'.[36] Nin later explained the importance of Barnes as helping her to move away from the restrictions of realism: 'She is so marvellous because she was the one who knew that we could not describe the nocturnal world without the poetic metaphor'.[37]

There is, however, a second equally important reason for relating Barnes to Nin. The former was well aware of the rise of the cinema during the 1910s and, as we shall see, wrote this awareness of film into *Nightwood*. Thus in drawing on Barnes' novel to help her articulate connections between dream and film Nin was unconsciously applying a text in which the influence of film was already inscribed. From 1913 to 1931 Barnes interviewed a number of dancers, artists and singers – in 1925 even D. W. Griffith himself – many of whom went on to perform in the movies. For instance she interviewed John Bunny, the star of Vitagraph silent films, who told her: 'actors are merely public toys, playthings for the people to handle and grow tired of'.[38] Bunny was one of the most articulate commentators for her, especially in his sense of the star's persona and also of the imaginative appeal of film; he saw no threat to the stage here, arguing instead that 'moving pictures give you only two sides of a room, and out of your own imagination you supply the roof and the other sides'.[39]

Barnes's interviews reflect her awareness of the shared spectatorship demanded by the cinema, whereas in her most famous novel she expresses cinematic spectatorship as an internalized individual process. Barnes's close friend, the poet Emily Holmes Coleman, straddled the individual and the group in her 1930 novel of post-partum psychosis *The Shutter of Snow*.[40] Set in a psychiatric clinic in the mid-1920s, the novel describes the inmates' experience of film-going. The protagonist Marthe constantly shifts her attention between two spectacles: the film and the rest of the audience. Whereas her eyes become 'extended' to take in her new experience, with the other inmates 'many white faces turned eyes inward'. The movie hall becomes an analogue of their sealed minds: 'From the windows, high and darkened by the sacks of brown despair, poured down upon their drooling mouths a mist, heavy with wind-conceived duress'.[41] This symbolically suggestive description contrasts strikingly with the vivid clarity with which Marthe sees the film: 'She looked fast at the screen and a house was burning, clever lapping frames licking the fragile frame'. Disaster is averted when our hero rushes back into the house and rescues his loved one: 'The hero made a staggering dash into the burning house and staggered forth again, his love upon his shoulders hanging limp'.[42] Unlike the movie hall, the house does not contain the characters. Instead the film presents a scene of salvation (or delivery, remembering the origin of Marthe's illness) which anticipates the protagonist's own departure from the clinic. Here clear visual perception becomes an analogue of returning mental health.

Barnes's *Nightwood* also plays elaborately on interiors and indeed the character Robin Vote is compared at times to a film actress, frozen in tableau like Marlene Dietrich and in general presented as a 'blank screen' on which her observers can project their desires. *Nightwood* traces out the shifting relations between four characters; at the centre of this group stands Robin Vote, who first marries Felix Volkbein, a Jewish banker, and then moves into relationships with two women. The characters, like Jay Gatsby, construct identities for themselves by purchasing the necessary clothes and 'props'. Typically then we apprehend characters' appearance and setting before their person, and this reflects Barnes's sense of scenic construction. Not only do her characters appear to be acting out roles and poses, but also – as Andrew Field has pointed out – Barnes 'constantly inclined towards the framed scene rather than the flowing story in her writing'.[43] Her rootless characters drop in and out of the narrative, whose continuity is broken by shifts from one vivid scene to another. Thus the novel opens with Felix being born in a baroque canopied bed; later Robin's lover Nora Flood discovers Doctor O'Connor (the commentator of *Nightwood*, a disgraced gynaecologist) lying in bed, his face 'framed in the golden semi-circle of a wig with large pendent curls that touched his shoulders [...] He was heavily rouged and his lashes painted'.[44] In short, he is made up for an encounter with someone else, which is thwarted by Nora's arrival.

In these instances characters have composed their own appearances, but the first time we encounter Robin, the scene is more complex. It occurs in an anonymous place of transit, a typical Paris hotel. The doctor and then behind him Felix see Robin through the bedroom door frozen in tableau. Their eyes – focalization is scrupulously paced here – gradually move from bed to plants, then to bedding, only to finish with details of Robin's dress and limbs:

> On a bed, surrounded by a confusion of potted plants, exotic palms and cut flowers, faintly over-sung by the notes of unseen birds [...] half flung off the support of the cushions from which, in a moment of threatened consciousness she had turned her head, lay the young woman, heavy and dishevelled. Her legs, in white flannel trousers, were spread as in a dance, the thick-lacquered pumps looking too lively for the arrested step. Her hands, long and beautiful, lay on either side of her face.[45]

It is striking that the main identifying feature in this woman, her face, is elided in the description with the result that she comes across as a figure, a posed outline whose dress contradicts her immobility. The image resembles a film still. Indeed, Barnes makes it explicit that Robin is posing within a 'set' composed by someone else. Within the cinematic analogy, Robin's lack of autonomy is expressed as direction by an unnamed other. Part voyeurism, Felix's observation is also that of a one-man audience as he sees the showman Doctor O'Connor play out a Svengali-like role, passing his hands over Robin's face. This act only increases our conviction that Robin will be 'played' by others.

Even in her lover's dream Robin is viewed as spectacle, as 'a "picture" forever arranged': 'Nora dreamed that she was standing at the top of a house'. The house as usual is heavily furnished. 'Nora looked down into the body of the house, as if from a scaffold, where now Robin had entered the dream, lying among a company below'. Then a spotlight falls on Robin from off frame: 'A disc of light, which seemed to come from someone or thing standing behind her and which was yet a shadow, shed a faintly luminous glow upon the upturned still face of Robin'.[46] The term 'scaffold' suggests the structure of a film set and recalls John Bunny's statement about film reality quoted earlier. It also carries sombre connotations of death and looks forward to Nora's later dream of witnessing a struggle between her grandfather and dead grandmother ('whom I loved more than anyone') over the latter's death. Once again in the first dream Robin is immobile and passive under the dreamer's gaze. Only at one point does she return this gaze and that is when Nora sees Robin with another woman one night: 'by the intensity of their double regard, Robin's eyes and hers met. So they gazed at each other. As if that light had power to bring what was dreaded into the zone of their catastrophe, Nora saw the body of another woman swim up into the statue's obscurity'.[47] Laura Winkiel comments here that 'Robin looks straight into the camera, breaking the rule against the camera's direct look' and in turn 'Nora is struck by the violence of the cinematic gaze which undoes her'.[48] It is only a temporary effect that Nora's focalization becomes disrupted here. At no point in the novel is Robin given a subject position. Instead she is repeatedly objectified in the gaze of others. Barnes's preference for nocturnal scenes enables her to control the lighting effects as she does here and as she does in the novel's final climax when Robin sinks down on all fours in front of a candle-lit altar. Here Nora acts as spectator to Robin and the terrified dog within the scene, which is being confronted by Robin.

Barnes's cinematic representations, especially of dreams, were what impressed Anaïs Nin because she herself was experimenting in the 1930s with dream narratives. In her theoretical statements on the novel she constantly returned to the interconnections between dream and film. Looking back on her career in the 1960s, Nin singled out film for special emphasis. She found a 'mutual influence' between these media, stating: 'the novel will have come closer to the film. It will have less space-filling descriptions and reduce dialogue to essential talk [...] the films have brought us back to the importance of the image and the study of dreams'.[49] And in *The Novel of the Future* (1968) she recorded: 'It was not the writers but the film-makers who opened the way to the language of images which is the language of the unconscious'.[50] As we saw with Miller, Nin combined interests in film, Surrealism and dream, which for her came together in the language of the image. One difference lies in the extent to which Nin incorporates cinematic terminology in her discussion of her own writings. Distinguishing her own practice from that of the realists, she notes that dreams (and therefore her own fiction) have no frames; she developed a strategy of 'placing the "camera" within women and elucidating women's feelings'; and in general she insisted: 'the only objectivity we can reach is achieved, first of all, by an examination of our *self* as lens, as camera, as recorder, as mirror'.[51]

During her early years in Paris Nin attended screenings at the Cinémathèque club of the first Surrealist films, screenings attended by Buñuel and Dalí. On another occasion, after seeing *Metropolis*, she recorded in her diary: 'I felt last night that it is only in *film* that reality and unreality, poetry and science, can be fully achieved and communicated'.[52] We shall also see that her major early work, *House of Incest* (1936), was influenced by German silent cinema. In the 1940s Nin was impressed by the films of Maya Deren, seeing *Meshes of the Afternoon* (1943) and *At Land* (1944), and subsequently acting in one of her films. She praised Deren's work as 'better in some ways than the early surrealist movies because there are no artificial effects, just a simple flowing of the threads of fantasy'.[53] This close film connection extended into the following decade when Nin's husband Hugh Guiler produced (using the name Ian Hugo) *Ai-Ye* and *Bells of Atlantis*. She claimed that the latter particularly had been influenced in its editing by *House of Incest*, complaining: 'I deserve half the credit for those films. I found the shipwreck and told him how to film it'.[54] Later in her life, after making an honourable exception for Surrealist film, she reflected that 'in most films, what takes place in our feelings, the imagery of our dreams around events, is rarely filmed'. For that reason she praised Ingmar Bergman because 'he refuses to establish boundaries. He feels that dream and action are interrelated, fantasy and madness, creation and destruction'. In short, 'his role is to make our subconscious visible'.[55] Nin could here be describing her own ambitions. In interview she explained: 'I think my work is well suited to film as we had intended film to be, which is to handle the inner life, the fantasy, the dream'.[56]

The complex visuality of Nin's stories owes much to her fascination with film. The title story of *Under a Glass Bell* (1944), probably as homage to Djuna Barnes, describes a young woman (Jeanne) living with her brothers in a baroque, over-furnished stately house. All the figures in the art-works decorating the rooms seem to have become frozen in mid-motion and the bell-jar of the title figuratively encloses the house and evokes the claustro-phobia of the narrative itself. Acting out an implicitly incestuous relationship, Jeanne and her brothers circle slowly around each other. Jeanne enters a room of mirrors: 'ceilings of mirrors, floors of mirrors, windows of quicksilver opening on windows of quicksilver [...] Woman imprisoned in the stillness of mirrors washed only by jellied colours'.[57] The narrative resem-bles the progression of a silent film. As the point of view follows Jeanne's eyes, our sense of space opens up into repetitious mirrored perspectives in which Jeanne's isolation is mocked by endless duplications of herself. Jeanne tries to see into herself, fails, and then tries to imagine death, by which point visualization has ended: 'Quickly, more quickly she turned to catch the face of her soul, but even when she moved at dream speed she saw the face of the actress, the small curtain closing inside of the pupil'. As depth is denied, she turns to death: 'She bowed nearer to catch the immobility, the death. But the caverns within the pupil of the eye diminish and close at the sight of death. The eye dead could not see the eye dead in the mirror'.[58] Jeanne's movements in this story suggest a progression into more and more internal spaces of the self. Notionally she is enacting a relationship with her brothers, but the privi-leged point of view is always hers. Ironically, in the innermost space – the room of mirrors – her otherness becomes so heightened that she yearns to close the gap between her image and subject position.

This story marks an introverted extreme form of a theme running through much of *Under a Glass Bell*, namely the drama of seeing.[59] 'Houseboat' describes a dreamlike sequence as a boat drifts down the Seine, offering new landscapes to the observer. In a displaced sexual fantasy ('Je suis le plus malade des surréalistes') Savonarola fixes the female protagonist with his 'dilated vision'. 'The All-Seeing' describes a chameleon-like artist who is constantly changing costumes and guises, and who again fixes the female narrator with his eye. Finally in 'The Eye's Journey' a painter inserts the hallmark of his transcendental vision on his canvases: 'Aware it was through the Eye that he had passed to reach this other side of the world, he always painted a small human eye in the corner, the secret door of his escape into the deep regions unknown to the surface of the eyes'.[60] The Eye functions like Nin's dream transitions, taking the painter into other regions in a flow. But the story traces the painter's gradual decline into paranoia, signalled visually as a contraction of his studio space, until he is carried away to an asylum where he loses his sight. Settings in these stories tend to be expressionistic of states of being or of desires. 'The Labyrinth' spatializes dream through symbolic spaces which shift variously from tunnel to cave and honeycomb. Here yet again there is no stable ground to the real.

A number of critics have stressed the performatory energy informing Anaïs Nin's writings. Helen Tookey, for instance, argues that she was constantly picking up and jettisoning selves.[61] If this is so, acting becomes a heightened version of experience not, as often happens, to contrast the inauthentic with its implied opposite, but rather to enact the rival impulses within the self. In 1938 Nin recorded how she and Miller went to see the Hollywood actress Luise Rainer in a film. Afterwards Miller praised the actress's grace and drew a comparison with Nin herself: 'You are all light and gaiety, but if one catches you unaware, one sees a tragic face', concluding that Nin possessed a 'mysterious dual character'. Nin's comment in her diary is revealing: 'Henry never understood me as well as at this moment'.[62]

The story 'Stella' (i.e. 'star': collected in the 1961 edition of *Winter of Artifice*) explicitly ties self-visualization to film acting. The film-star protagonist experiences a shock at watching her own performance:

> Stella sat in a small, dark room and watched her own figure acting on the screen. Stella watched her 'double' moving in the light, and she did not recognize her. She almost hated her. Her first reaction was one of revolt, of rejection. The image was not she. It was a work of artifice, of lighting, of stage setting.[63]

The private screening gives this confrontation between subjective and objectified selves a real psychological impact. From this point on Stella engages in a complex negotiation of her own screen image, which paradoxically is both like and not like her. It carries her shape ('figure') and features, yet has an 'air of the unformed', a softness awaiting the imprint of the viewer. The erotic implications of this perception are confirmed when Nin introduces Stella's lover Bruno who, she realizes, sees a 'dream of Stella', someone who can play the role of lover within his married life. Because Stella registers such a huge distance from her screen persona she sets about composing the setting of a star in her actual life, purchasing a huge bed surrounded by mirrors. But, instead of closing the gap between the perceiving and observed selves, the result is fragmentation: 'She is decomposed before the mirror into a hundred personages'.[64] Stella is caught between the conviction that no role can contain her and the dream of a grand role which will give supreme expression to her personality. Unable to resolve this impasse, her communicative powers atrophy: 'She appeared in a new story on the screen. Her face was immobile like a mask. It was not Stella. It was the outer shell of Stella'. Although this description essentially only recapitulates the division of the opening scene, the event is figured as a kind of death: 'People sent her enormous bouquets of rare flowers [...] Flowers for the dead, she murmured. With only a little wire, and a round frame, they would do as well'.[65]

The 'othering' of the camera in Nin's writings has an important psychological dimension. In her youth her father used to photograph her naked and after she had engaged in therapy with the French psychiatrist René Allendy she recorded that he 'freed me of the EYE of the father, of the eye of the camera which I have always feared and disliked as an *exposure*'.[66] This passage makes explicit the sexual dimension of the camera–eye for Nin and helps to explain why so often in her works entrapment is represented as subjection to an implicitly male-gendered gaze.

Nin's *House of Incest* and Miller's *Scenario*

Nin began to plan the narrative which was to be called *House of Incest* early in 1935. She later recorded that it began in dream, consisting of 'visionary symbolic dream sequences which were woven together', to shift the metaphor, through 'jump cutting' transitions.[67] In fact the narrative had a more immediate cinematic stimulus in the 1928 German film *Alraune*; during the early stages of composition Nin actually used this as her own working title.[68] The film – now regarded as an early classic of science-fiction cinema – describes the creation by artificial insemination (from a criminal in a prostitute) of a girl in the laboratory of a professor of genetics. This variation on the Frankenstein theme carries undertones of incest in the ambiguous relation of Alraune (played by Brigitte Helm) to her 'father'. Alraune's erotic nature seems to define her and to arise from the mystery of her origins. The latent incest in *Alraune* would have appealed to Nin, who had herself engaged in such a relationship with her own father, and she planned to compose three versions of Alraune in which she herself would be the third.[69] Nin rational-ized the subject of her emerging narrative as being 'based on the idea that the first love was always within the family and was always, in an emotional sense, incestuous'.[70] She showed drafts of this narrative to Miller, to Otto Rank and even to Antonin Artaud. Miller's reaction was both positive and active. In his annotations he wrote: 'All pictorial passages wonderful. Would make a film script'; and he proposed extensive revisions which would concentrate the dream section.[71]

Nin explained the organization of *House of Incest* to her father as follows: 'The characters are three different women who blend into one and are represented by one woman. Watery birth, symbolism, the imprisoned inner life, then deliverance into the light of day'.[72] The novel progresses serially through seven episodes whose opening lines establish a special meaning to seeing here: 'My first vision of earth was water veiled. I am of the race of men and women who see all things through this curtain of sea, and my eyes are the colour of water'.[73] This amniotic image blurs the organ of sight into the field of vision and Nin articulates this primal state as one of heightened, even hallucinatory vividness: 'Lost in the colours of the Atlantide, the colours running into one another without frontiers. Fish made of velvet, of organdie with lace fangs, made of spangled taffeta, of silks and feathers and whiskers, with lacquered flanks and rock crystal eyes, fishes of a withered leather with gooseberry eyes, eyes like the white of egg'.[74] Note here how fluidity has become a quality of vision whereby colours and objects merge together in an extended series of quasi-cinematic dissolves. In her dialogues with Henry Miller Nin insisted on 'giving scenes without logical, conscious explanations', thereby preserving an air of 'silent mystery'; and the model she produced to support her method was that of Buñuel's *Un Chien Andalou*.[75]

In Miller's dream sections from the *Tropics* and *Black Spring* we saw how he typically moved from observed visual data, through the grotesque to apocalypse. Nin, by contrast, establishes the field of consciousness as the narrative ground. Writing in 1946 in answer to those who found her writings disorienting, Nin declared: 'I place you in a world which is like the world of the dream, sparingly furnished only with the objects which have proved their symbolic value, and not their familiar value as objects which give us our daily gravitational security'.[76] *The House of Incest* opens by establishing the primacy of the narrating 'I' who engages in internal dialogues with her own alternative female projections: Sabina and Jeanne. Sabina is the personification of eroticism and here the narrator casts herself as mediator with her (male) audience: 'The soft secret yielding of women I carved into men's brains with copper words; her image I tattooed in their eyes'.[77] Sometimes the narrator acts as projector, sometimes as observer, and sometimes as visionary commentator. Miller's Whitmanesque 'I see… I see' formula finds its counterpart in Nin as she explores images of the self ('I see two women in me', 'I saw a city', for example). Here once again Artaud provides a relevant analogue. In *The Novel of the Future* Nin states: 'The poet, or the novelist who writes poetically, is what Antonin Artaud called the *voyant*. The seer. He has merely found a way to shut out the appearance of things and concentrate on the invisible, life of spirit and emotion'.[78] This is exactly what Nin attempts in *House of Incest*. The visionary here does not imply privileged access to a transcendental truth so much as a willed exclusion of external reality so that she can depict the self's quest for a way towards life.

Nin was mistaken in taking dissolves as the main transition device in *Un Chien Andalou*. In fact there are many more cuts as Buñuel jumps abruptly from image to image and from perspective to perspective. Nin tries to capture this quality of discontinuity by using textual gaps in some editions and by avoiding connectives at the beginnings of paragraphs. Buñuel's film opens with the notorious slicing open of an eye with a razor blade, which some critics have taken as a sexual act. Nin replaces such overt violence with a static image: 'there is a fissure in my vision and madness will always run through'.[79] Buñuel locates madness or at least obsession in his male character who is given the main point of view, as in the following sequence: 'Long shot of the young woman in the background and the man from the back moving towards her. He suddenly stops pursuing her, looks down and turns as though he were searching for something, then turns back on her. Quick shot of his face in close-up, looking more furious and sadistic than ever'.[80] In *Un Chien Andalou* the male gaze arrests and assaults, the eye being supported by the young man's arms. Since Buñuel admitted that he incorporated Freudian imagery into the film, the arm or hand becomes a displaced penis, whereas Nin concludes *House of Incest* with a female dancer who is figured without arms one moment, with them the next. Here the arms suggest desire for life rather than specifically sexual desire.

The climactic section of Nin's narrative comes when her second female projection Jeanne leads the narrator into the house of incest. If the house symbolizes the self, the scenes within capture the taboo nature of the relation depicted. Thus, 'in the house of incest there was a room which could not be found, a room without window, the fortress of their love, a room without window where the mind and blood coalesced in a union without orgasm and rootless like those of fishes'.[81] Within the figure of the search, rooms are linked by a chain which the narrator follows. Ironically, at this innermost room vision is doubly denied. Firstly, the room cannot be found and there-fore seen; secondly, whereas within the traditional metaphor of house-as-consciousness windows usually feature as eyes,[82] here there are none. Nevertheless, Nin expresses the narrator's evocation of incest through a series of visual discoveries; the unimaginable must be rendered in physical, symbolic terms. And at each stage images recur with their significance either shifted or made more explicit: the egg as a symbol of birth, Janus representations of women with 'two sides forever separate', and so on.[83]

In the later sections of Nin's novel Jeanne functions as a guide for the narrator, opening the doors on her love for her brother. In keeping with the narrative's dream logic, locations and duration itself shift constantly. In an episode of meta-reference to artistic representation, Jeanne's brother falls asleep in the room of her paintings: 'Jeanne, I fell asleep among the paintings, where I could sit for many days worshipping your portrait. I fell in love with your portrait, Jeanne, because it will never change'.[84] Here Nin introduces an allusion to *The Picture of Dorian Gray*, in which a character becomes his own animated portrait, fixed nevertheless at a point of youthfulness. Because *House of Incest* possesses a narrative voice the identity of the speaker at this moment blurs into the narrator's; there are no speech marks to distinguish it textually. The fact that beauty and obsessive love should be expressed through the figure of the portrait keeps Nin's primary emphasis on the eye and also draws the reader's attention to a motif of pathos running throughout *House of Incest*, namely that of transience. The narrator is haunted by death and loss, repeatedly describing herself as reconstituting images of lost concepts. We should not exaggerate the importance of the portrait described above, however, because its spatial structure contradicts one of Nin's articles of faith about dreams: they have no frames or boundaries. Neither should novels or films therefore. *Un Chien Andalou* plays ironically with endings by captioning its last scene 'IN THE SPRING' and showing the two lovers half-buried in a desert. The caption suggests a beginning but the scene draws our attention to a traditional image of time gradually swallowing up the characters. Nin pursues a less sombre strategy referring to a post-text in depicting a female figure 'dancing towards daylight'.

Once *House of Incest* was finished Miller and Nin began work on a scenario based on dream and parodying Nin's novel, for which the work would be divided up as follows: 'He [Miller] would create the universe of the dream, I the details. He drags in cosmic symbology, and I the individual'.[85] This work was to be based on the Surrealist principle which Nin summarized from Miller: 'If the films are the most successful expression of surrealism, then the scenario is what suits the surrealist stories and the dreams best'.[86] There is evidence in Nin's journals that this collaboration did not run smoothly. She disliked what she saw as the bogus intellectualism of some dream narratives and thought Miller made his dreams too definite whereas her own conviction was that the dream episodes should flow into each other. In 1936 *Scenario* was published as a 'Film with Sound' 'directly inspired' by Nin's *House of Incest*. Nin for her part was hurt by the final work, which she felt owed everything to *Alraune/House of Incest* but which contained nothing from it.[87]

Scenario repeats many themes and images from *House of Incest* including the motif of the split self. Two female figures appear, both named with reference to the mandrake symbol – Alraune and Mandra – and the narrative describes their emerging sexual relationship. Indeed, one difference between *Scenario* and *House of Incest* is that Miller makes sexuality a more explicit defining characteristic throughout. Alraune personifies erotic energy, Mandra – described as 'idol-like' – a more passive version of femininity. At one point they are represented as Siamese twins struggling to separate; at another Mandra talks to her unrecognized image in a mirror. As she kisses this image the latter becomes Alraune. The woman's two faces, one sad and one smiling, are, as we saw earlier, versions of how Miller conceived Nin herself.

House of Incest juggles such female figures in relation to the narrative voice and here we encounter one of the main differences between the two works. *Scenario* opens with the following scene:

> NIGHT. A tropical garden filled with pebbled paths. In the centre of the garden a small pond out of which rises a huge bowl filled with gleaming gold-fish. The heavy face of Alraune hovers over the garden like a mask. The face grows larger and larger until it fills the screen […] The eyes roll upward; they have the fixed stare of a drug addict. They grow round, large, glassy, then troubled, then wild. They twitch like the eyes of a Javanese dancer. They grow calm and fixed again, dreamy, like the eyes of an opium smoker.[88]

There is a studied use of exotic or oriental imagery in Miller's narrative; and like Nin, he uses the present tense to convey visual immediacy. But the main difference lies in Miller's use of the third person in the narrative. Where Nin gave us the perceptual fluctuations of the narrator herself, Miller presents his central character as brooding over her own world, within which the bowl represents the mental life. The cinematic analogy is absolutely explicit and situates the reader within an imagined scene of spectatorship. The close-up on a face with upturned eyes makes reference to *Un Chien Andalou* where the young man's shifts in mood are shown. The self-consciousness of Miller's method comes out later in *Scenario* when he uses fades and a scene 'slowly dissolves, blurs out like the edge of a dream'.[89] Although he strives after interiority, he proves to be less successful partly because his comparisons ('like a mask', 'like the eyes') keep situating his imagery within the world. It is as if we have entered an imaginary space but are constantly reminded of that fact.

Miller's change of narrative person involves a change in perspective and therefore of gender. Although the relation between the two female figures stands at the centre of Miller's narrative, they are constantly being held within a male gaze. Miller's narrative rhythm is to build up towards local climaxes – often erotic ones. Nin's concluding image of a dancer is appropriated and transformed into an erotic performance. Take the example of section III. Here Alraune 'pounces on Mandra hungrily', at which point the tempo accelerates. The containing space of the room opens out into a labyrinth; the thought-image of the bowl shows the fish darting around 'in fury and ecstasy'; and an abrupt cut moves us to the Freudian image of a man firing a gun. At this point thought collapses before erotic urgency – the fish bowl shatters – and Alraune's dance begins. This act is encoded as 'primitive' by taking place amid a context of 'naked savages' and then directed as spectacle towards a young man tied to the ground. As her frenzy mounts Miller reverses an image of her gaze through the eyes of the prostrate observer: 'her vulva looks like a tattooed eye'. Finally the moment of orgasm comes but with a 'flow of blood'.

The female figures are repeatedly positioned so as to be on show or reduced to their own genitals. To take one example, in section VII Mandra is tied to the mast of a boat, a gender inversion of Ulysses being protected from sirens, whereupon thousands of men converge on her. Then the mast shifts to the equally phallic mandrake, 'the pollen miraculously bursting into flower'.[90] The insistent recurrence of the mandrake is only one sign of a general suggestion that the male is needed to create vitality. Miller even introduces an important magus-figure, an astrologer whose room is accessed through the vaginal 'petals' of his door. At the heart of the female, it seems, lies the male creative principle. The astrologer also embodies intellectual lore: he experiments, his body contains a sophisticated machine, and he pores over the maps on his floor. In short, he appears to embody the mind denied Alraune and Mandra, who are depicted overwhelmingly in physical and sensuous terms. This may be the reason why Nin was so annoyed with Miller's *Scenario*. Although it borrows plenty of images and devices from *House of Incest*, it covertly privileges the male perspective throughout, whether as a gendered gaze or through the power figure of the astrologer. Given such a heavy tilt towards male enabling figures, it is not surprising that the collaboration between Miller and Nin did not work out.

Delmore Schwartz

Parker Tyler's study *The Hollywood Hallucination*, so admired by Henry Miller, describes the movie theatre as a 'place of waking dream, a psychoanalytical clinic for the average worker and his *day*- not his *night*, dreams!' He states baldly: 'Hollywood is the mass unconscious', and tries to explain the attractions of film through its appeal to fantasy: 'the darkness of the movie theatre is actually the night itself, the night of sleep and dreams. And the field of the screen is the lidded eye through which the mind that will not sleep [...] projects its memory and its wild intelligence'.[91]

We have seen how the writings of Miller and Nin are full of liminal images, thresholds into new spaces of dream or new dimensions of fantasy. Delmore Schwartz's famous 1935 story 'In Dreams Begin Responsibilities' uses the setting of a movie theatre in the way described by Tyler as a place of waking dream. On the eve of his twenty-first birthday the young narrator goes to see a film, apparently from 1909: 'This is a silent picture as if an old Biograph one, in which the actors are dressed in ridiculously old-fashioned clothes, and one flash succeeds another with sudden jumps. The actors too seem to jump about and walk too fast'.[92] This impression is both stylized and misleading. It sets up an apparent distance from the narrator's present, which is almost immediately brought into question. For, as the narration proper commences, it emerges that the narrator is watching his parents-to-be going on a date to Coney Island. As they discuss their future together and have their first disagreements, the narrator starts to cry (to the annoyance of an old lady sitting next to him) and then to shout out to the figures on the screen not to do what they are planning. Finally he becomes so disruptive that he is ejected from the cinema.

Schwartz evokes a complex layered reality in his story, in which the borders of illusion are constantly blurring. The opening description of the film, for instance, very quickly gives way to precise, realistically paced description which includes sound, and thereby resembles the technical aspects of a film from the 1930s. The following account of a fortune-teller's booth is typical: 'The place is too warm, and my father keeps saying that this is all nonsense, pointing to the crystal ball on the table [...] [the fortune-teller enters] But suddenly my father feels that the whole thing is intolerable; he tugs at my mother's arm, but my mother refuses to budge'.[93] The boy seems to be watching a fantasy spectacle of parental conflict, which he is powerless to affect. Like the dream-narratives of Miller and Nin, this account uses the present tense for immediacy despite the absence of the 'dreamer' himself. Laurence Goldstein has interpreted the story as a Freudian fantasy in which the old woman and the movie usher perform the role of the superego, a fantasy which dissipates at the end of the story when the boy leaves the place of fantasy and wakes to his first adult birthday. Although the description of his parents' outing is given in the present tense, suggestive of a film script, 'we confront the paradox that a cinematic imagination is displayed for the purpose of defeating the totalising power of spectatorial passivity'.[94] Unlike Parker Tyler's account of the movie house as a *shared* space of dream, the story dramatizes the boy's mental cinema as a visual spectacle at odds with the actual film and with the social experience of the audience. Film thus helps to complicate our attempts to identify the real here. If the boy is dreaming, the visual precision and realism of his parents' outing give it a disturbing actuality which contrasts with the description in 'Screeno', Schwartz's story about a movie lottery game. After the competition ends, 'the film went on in all its soft floating figures and pleasing movement'.[95] Here the distinction between actuality and fantasy is clear. It is the ambiguity of 'In Dreams', together with its disruptive shifts between different realities, which gives that story its power.

Notes

1   Benjamin, *Illuminations*, p. 239. Benjamin's statement (from 'The Work of Art in the Age of Mechanical Reproduction') occurs within a general discussion of how the movie camera introduces scale and proportion unavailable to the naked eye.
2   Henry Miller, *The Wisdom of the Heart*, p. 47.
3   Henry Miller, *Letters to Emil*, p. 34.
4   *Letters to Emil*, p.72; Robert Ferguson, *Henry Miller: A Life*, p. 104.
5   Jay Martin, *Always Merry and Bright*, p. 323.
6   Henry Miller, *The Cosmological Eye*, pp. 53, 55–56; 'Buñuel', p. 157. Miller used the latter essay to introduce himself to Anaïs Nin.
7   Henry Miller, 'Reflexions on *Exstasy*', in *The Cosmological Eye*, p. 63. Miller found the idea behind the film to be 'an automatic death, a DEATH IN LIFE' (p. 67: Miller's emphasis).
8   Gunther Stuhlmann, ed., *A Literate Passion*, p. 140.
9   Miller, *The Wisdom of the Heart*, pp. 49, 56, 57, 60.
10 Miller made an exception in the case of the 1936 Gary Cooper film *Mr Deeds Goes to Town*, which he found to be a successful portrayal of the 'common man' (*The Wisdom of the Heart*, p. 60).
11 Stuhlmann, ed., *A Literate Passion*, pp. 342, 347–48. Although the screenplay came to nothing, Miller subsequently wrote two essays on this novel.
12 *Hollywood Hallucination* was published by Simon and Schuster in 1944. Tyler was co-author with Charles Ford of the 1933 novel *The Young and Evil*, which became a gay underground classic. Set in Greenwich Village, the novel anticipates Tyler's emerging interest in the cinema by describing events with a scenic immediacy and with only minimal narrative commentary.
13 Henry Miller, 'Original Preface to *Hollywood's Hallucination*', in *Sunday after the War*, p. 39.
14 *Sunday after the War*, p. 54.
15 Hortense Powdermaker's *Hollywood: The Dream Factory – An Anthropologist Studies the Movie-Makers* was published in 1950.
16 Henry Miller, *The Air-Conditioned Nightmare*, p. 169.
17 Henry Miller, *Tropic of Cancer*, p. 241. Cf. Miller's *The Books in My Life*, p. 110: 'For me Walt Whitman is a hundred, a thousand, times more *America* than America itself'.
18 Henry Miller, *Tropic of Capricorn*, p. 23.
19 Miller, *The Wisdom of the Heart*, p. 174; *Tropic of Capricorn*, p. 69. Brassaï's sequences particularly caught Miller's attention: 'Brassaï strikes at the accidental modulations, the illogical syntax, the mythical juxtaposition of things' (*The Wisdom of the Heart*, p. 176).

Miller's recurring fantasy of becoming a disembodied eye resembles the displacement of the spectator's body described by Parker Tyler. For him, the impact of the movie camera lies in the fact that 'the eye itself has become a body capable of greater spatial elasticity than the human body' (*The Hollywood Hallucination*, p. 23).

20 *The Wisdom of the Heart*, pp. 179–80. Considering Brassaï's gaze, Miller borrows an image from *Un Chien Andalou*: 'you have the sensation of a razor operating on your own eyeball' (p. 174). Anaïs Nin complained to Miller about his self-effacement in *Black Spring*: 'But why do you give the EYES in the book to Brassaï, the photographer? They are your eyes, you are describing what you saw, not Brassaï' (*Journals*, vol. 1, p. 366; her emphasis).

21 *Tropic of Capricorn*, p. 213.

22 *Tropic of Cancer*, p. 14.

23 *Tropic of Cancer*, pp. 23–24.

24 Martin, *Always Merry and Bright*, p. 283; Henry Miller, *The World of Sex*, pp. 120, 101.

25 Stuhlmann, ed., *A Literate Passion*, p. 119.

26 *Tropic of Cancer*, p. 69.

27 Henry Miller, *Black Spring*, p. 25.

28 *Black Spring*, p. 10.

29 Elizabeth W. Bruss, 'Eye for I', p. 307.

30 *Black Spring*, p. 127. This section was also published in *The Cosmological Eye*, appropriately for a collection devoted to the visual sense.

31 *Black Spring*, p. 29.

32 *Black Spring*, p. 147.

33 Bruss, 'Eye for I', p. 305.

34 *Black Spring*, p. 148.

35 *Black Spring*, p. 161.

36 *Journals*, vol. 2, p. 248.

37 Anaïs Nin, *A Woman Speaks*, p. 86.

38 Djuna Barnes, *Interviews*, p. 121. Other figures interviewed by Barnes included Mimi Aguglia, Gabrielle Deslys, Lillian Russell, Lou Tellegen, Alla Nazimova and Helen Westley.

39 Barnes, *Interviews*, p. 123.

40 Coleman and Barnes both contributed to *transition*, where Nin would almost certainly have encountered their work.

41 Emily Holmes Coleman, *The Shutter of Snow*, pp. 190, 191. Coleman's title itself carries cinematic connotations.

42 Coleman, *The Shutter of Snow*, p. 192.

43 Andrew Field, *The Formidable Miss Barnes*, p. 146.

44 Barnes, *Selected Works*, p. 295.

45 Barnes, *Selected Works*, p. 259.

46 Barnes, *Selected Works*, pp. 261, 281.

47 Barnes, *Selected Works*, p. 283.

48 Laura Winkiel, 'Circuses and Spectacles: Public Culture in *Nightwood*', p. 18.

49 *A Woman Speaks*, p. 199.

50 Anaïs Nin, *The Novel of the Future*, p. 97.

51 Anaïs Nin, 'Realism and Reality', in *The White Blackbird*, p. 19; *The Novel of the Future*, pp. 75–76, 36.

52 Early diary entry quoted in Helen Tookey, *Anaïs Nin, Fictionality and Femininity*, p. 142. Tookey's study includes valuable points on the relation between self-writing and film in Nin.

53 *Journals*, vol. 4, pp. 77, 104. Nin later praised Deren as a 'very talented woman who really started the underground film' (*A Woman Speaks*, p. 107). Deren was married to Sasha Hammid who collaborated with Steinbeck in making *The Forgotten Village*.

54 *Journals*, vol. 5, pp. 59–60; Deirdre Bair, *Anaïs Nin: A Biography*, p. 363. Ian Hugo confirmed that *Bells of Atlantis* was explicitly modelled on *House of Incest* and that Nin played an important role in the composition of the film: 'The Making of *Bells of Atlantis*', in Evelyn J. Hinz, ed., *The World of Anaïs Nin*, pp. 77–80.

55 Anaïs Nin, *In Favour of the Sensitive Man*, pp. 87, 93. Nin states at the opening of the first of these essays: 'Antonin Artaud said that only films would be able to depict dreams, fantasies, the surrealist aspect of our experience' (p. 86).

56 *A Woman Speaks*, p. 199.

57 Anaïs Nin, *Under a Glass Bell*, p. 40.

58 *Under a Glass Bell*, p. 41.

59 In his reading of the collection Keith Cushman argues that Nin achieves a tight unity through the imagistic patterning of figures of entrapment, drowning, bondage (chains) and so on. He continues: 'The same motifs and images are used in both fantastic and realistic contexts with the net result of breaking down the distinction between fantasy and reality' ('The View from *Under the Glass Bell*', in Hinz, ed., *The World of Anaïs Nin*, p. 119.

60 *Under a Glass Bell*, p. 78.

61 Tookey, *Anais Nin*, pp. 12–13 and Chapter 3 *passim*. The latter chapter documents Nin's fascination with the actress-figure.

62 *Journals*, vol. 2, pp. 304–305.

63 Anaïs Nin, *Winter of Artifice*, p. 1. According to Philip K. Jason, 'Stella' was material dropped from an earlier novel, published in the 1961 edition of *Winter of Artifice* for the first time (*Anaïs Nin and her Critics*, p. 39).

64 *Winter of Artifice*, p. 19. The use here and elsewhere by Nin of the present tense reflects an attempt to convey the effect of a dream film diary. Robert A. Haller has noted, in relation to Nin's writings, the necessity that 'the diary film must be photographed at once, *during* the evnts depicted' ('Anaïs Nin and Film', p. 136).

65 *Winter of Artifice*, p. 35.

66 *Journals*, vol. 1, p. 95.

67 *The Novel of the Future*, pp. 119, 134.

68 The film was based on the 1911 novel *Alraune* by Hans Heinz Ewers and was also screened under the title *Unholy Love*.

69 Stuhlmann, ed., *A Literate Passion*, p. 127. The first version of Alraune was to be based on Henry Miller's wife June, but Nin then converted the latter's name into Djuna (another homage to Barnes) and separated that realist section of her narrative from *House of Incest*.

70 *A Woman Speaks*, p. 119.

71 *Journals*, vol. 1, pp. 276–77; Stuhlmann, ed., *A Literate Passion*, pp. 142–43.

72 Anaïs Nin, *Fire*, p. 356.

73 Anaïs Nin, *House of Incest*, p. 15.

74 *House of Incest*, p. 16.

75 *Journals*, vol. 1, p. 317.

76 Anaïs Nin, *The Mystic of Sex*, p. 26.

77 *House of Incest*, p. 22.

78 *The Novel of the Future*, p. 120.

79 *House of Incest*, p. 39.

80 Luis Buñuel, *L'Age d'Or and Un Chien Andalou*, p. 104.

81 *House of Incest*, p. 52.
82 In Poe's tale 'The Fall of the House of Usher', another narrative which focuses on inces-
    tuous brother–sister love, the house possesses 'vacant and eye-like windows'.
83 In her essay 'Realism and Reality' Nin wrote: 'I never include the concrete object or fact
    unless it has a symbolic role to play' (*The Mystic of Sex*, p. 24).
84 *House of Incest*, p. 61.
85 *Journals*, vol. 1, p. 277.
86 *Journals*, vol. 1, p. 316.
87 *Fire*, p. 117.
88 Miller, *The Cosmological Eye*, p. 75.
89 *The Cosmological Eye*, p. 91.
90 *The Cosmological Eye*, p. 97.
91 Tyler, *The Hollywood Hallucination*, pp. 244, 238, 231.
92 Delmore Schwartz, *In Dreams Begin Responsibilities*, p. 1.
93 Schwartz, *In Dreams Begin Responsibilities*, p. 8.
94 Goldstein, *The American Poet at the Movies*, p. 101.
95 Schwartz, *In Dreams Begin Responsibilities*, p. 200.

13

Nathanael West and the Hollywood Novel

The rise of the Hollywood film industry was closely followed from 1912 onwards by a growing number of novels engaging with what one critic has described as the 'hyperbolic cultural symbol' of the USA as a whole. For John Springer the Hollywood novel – a broad category that included romance, satire, and crime fiction – revolved around a central theme, the 'confusion of illusion and reality'.[1] My focus in this chapter, however, is not to repeat such surveys but rather to examine those Hollywood novels which appropriate or imitate the very representational techniques of the film medium they are describing. Again and again we shall see characters being drawn in to the complex process of commodification within the Hollywood system.

One of the earliest novels to do this was Harry Leon Wilson's *Merton of the Movies* (1922), which was greatly admired by Gertrude Stein, who made a point of visiting Wilson during her 1935 visit to Hollywood.[2] In *Everybody's Autobiography* she described it as the 'best description of America that has ever been done' and, as if that wasn't enough, the 'best book about twentieth century [*sic*] American youth'.[3] Wilson's novel describes the experiences of an Illinois assistant in a clothes shop whose obsession with film leads him to move to Hollywood where, after many setbacks reducing him to the brink of starvation, he finally achieves success as a movie star. In his discussion of this novel, John Springer draws our attention to the opening admission of uncertainty which is followed by a narration operating on at least two levels. For him the novel's ambiguity is compounded by the protagonist's 'misapprehension of himself and others, brought on by his identification with movie plots and characters'.[4] For Springer the novel is multivocal, incorporating the voices of film magazines, producers, etc.; but, even more importantly, Wilson demonstrates with considerable skill how Merton Gill's obsession with film leads to an unusually complex visual sensibility inadequately explained through the binary of illusion and reality.

The novel opens with a chapter called 'Dirty Work at the Border' in which is described a sexual melodrama whereby one Buck Benson defends the honour of Estelle St. Clair from the advances of Snake le Vasquez (aka

'Slimy Viper'). The male lead is played by none other than Merton in the climactic confrontation between the two men:

> 'Am I too late, Miss St. Clair?'
> Snake le Vasquez started at the quiet, grim voice.
> '*Sapristi!*' he snarled. 'You!'
> 'Me!' replied Buck Benson, for it was, indeed, no other.
> 'Thank God, at last!' murmured Estelle St. Clair, freeing herself from the foul arms that enfolded her slim young beauty and staggering back from him who would so basely have forced her into a distasteful marriage.[5]

Even such a short passage should demonstrate how Wilson is creating a narrative out of stereotypes. Although each character speaks, the action is primarily visual, a matter of gesture, movement and expression. In other words, the account resembles a description from a silent film. Reading this scene briefly resembles an imaginary viewing in which Merton simultaneously plays the role of audience and male lead. In every sense he is projecting an idealized movie scenario for himself.

Springer draws a comparison with a dime novel, but the more relevant analogy would be with a film magazine. Merton subscribes to publications which closely resemble *Photoplay*, the most popular magazine of the period.[6] Among its features were photo-essays on the stars (Merton is eager to learn whether one actress is married), scenario contests (entered by Merton and his fellow enthusiast Tessie), photographs of extras during shooting, and also summaries of actions transcribed from films. The latter supplies the paradigm which Wilson is following here. In the early pages of the novel the reader is invited to identify with Merton's imagined stardom, which in turn has been encouraged by the fantasies of access to the film business encouraged by publications like *Photoplay*.

This action – or we should say this dream – is rudely disrupted by the voice of reality, that of Merton's boss, telling him to get on with serving customers. Here prosaic actuality does not replace Merton's dream so much as complicate it, producing a hybrid narrative, neither dream nor reality but a confusion between the two. It emerges that Merton is not content to visit the cinema or subscribe to film magazines, but he also does photo sessions dressed up in his favourite cowboy costume. While his job is selling women's clothes, his costume mimics that of a star like Tom Mix and enables him to construct an idealized masculine image of himself. This is where the novel's importance emerges because in comic terms Wilson demonstrates how Merton dreams of being at one and the same time a star performer and his own audience. When he tries to mount a horse which throws him to the ground, Merton compensates for that indignity by composing a substitute scene in which he stars successfully: 'He saw himself approach Dexter, vault into the saddle, put spurs to the beast, and swiftly disappear down the street'.[7]

The only place where Merton can realize such ambitions is Hollywood, and the main body of the novel concerns his gradual discovery of the cinema system and his rise to success. In many scenes which anticipate Nathanael West's *The Day of the Locust* Merton registers the variety of characters in Hollywood and then the depthless nature of studio sets. Seen from behind, the latter are desubstantialized into 'fragile contrivances of button lath and thin plaster'.[8] Dualities multiply in this novel: between Merton's workaday and fantasy selves, between the frontage and back of such sets, and also between film techniques seen from a distance and then experienced. Wandering through the studios, he sees an actress in close-up and then not long afterwards actually experiences being in a close-up as he is filmed for a musical. In other words, one sign of Merton's enthusiasm for the movies is his capacity to imagine himself becoming converted into a film property. The novel makes complex play on the alternations between visual sequences in which Merton is the subject, the perceiving 'camera', and those in which he is seen on camera playing the jaundiced socialite and other roles. Merton's way of negotiating through situations involves the composition of imaginary cinematic scenarios in which he draws on a repertoire of possible roles and stories.

This exercise of his imagination compensates for Merton's helplessness within the Hollywood system and resituates him as a 'director'. This is what happens when he imagines a film of mealtimes back home in Illinois:

> He would pause to take superb close-ups of these, the corned beef on its spreading platter hemmed about with boiled potatoes and turnips and cabbage, and the corned beef hash with its richly browned surface. The thrilling climax would be the roast beef on Saturday night, with close-ups taken in the very eye of the camera, of the mashed potatoes and the apple pie drenched with cream. And there were close-ups of Metta Judson [the housekeeper], who had never seriously contemplated a screen career, placing upon the table a tower of steaming hot cakes, while a platter of small sausages loomed eloquently in the foreground.[9]

The scene has an obvious physical grounding in the fact that Merton's initial lack of success is being reflected in his shortage of food, but it is also striking how the scene is being imagined through the cinematic devices of close-up and spatial arrangement between foreground and background. Throughout the central sections of the novel, Wilson contrasts scenes registered, witnessed or 'directed' by Merton, in which the visual data is clear and coherently organized, and those actually acted by him in movies. In the latter scenes Merton is no longer supplying the point of view and these seem far more fragmented, incoherent and fleeting. The effect is as though he is performing in a larger action over which he has no say at all, which is exactly what is happening. Merton's fear is of turning into caricature, a dreaded possibility embodied in the unnamed but easily identifiable cross-eyed comedian Ben Turpin, whose image represents the antithesis to Merton's more glamorous stills of himself.[10]

Merton's alternation between subject and object of vision has its counterpart in the difference between scenes he composes for himself and those composed by others. In the opening imaginary melodrama he plays an idealized cowboy called Buck Benson, scarcely conscious of how he has become protagonist and his own best viewer. In the later chapters he imagines that he is playing out similarly dignified roles but when he sees the final film he realizes that he has unconsciously been performing in a comedy. Ironically, at this point he becomes a success and all his dreams become reality. Merton's initial estrangement from his own movie image reflects his discovery that in Hollywood he is no longer his own property. *Merton of the Movies* thus turns out to be an unusually apt title because the protagonist's imagination and performatory identity (he has no family background to speak of) are shaped and ultimately confirmed by the cinema. Merton's success is the confirmation of his cinematic view of experience. In that respect the novel focuses more closely on its individual protagonist and makes less play on spectacle than many Hollywood novels, including Carl Van Vechten's *Spider Boy* (1928).

Van Vechten visited Hollywood in 1927, where he met with King Vidor to discuss making a film adaptation of his novel *Nigger Heaven*.[11] While there he also met Theodore Dreiser, who was celebrating the sale of the movie rights to *An American Tragedy*. Van Vechten wrote a series of articles on Hollywood for *Vanity Fair*, in the first of which he exclaimed: 'Hollywood is incredible, fantastic, colossal'.[12] The tone of his enthusiasm is rather ambivalent, as though he were already afraid of being overwhelmed by the place, and he coped with the problem of explaining his role to others by claiming to be an 'idler' writing a novel about Hollywood. The following year the tangible proof of his story would be published. Van Vechten was conscious of negotiating the stereotypes of Hollywood that were already circulating and stressed that local parties were not orgies, and that Hollywood society was very hierarchical, with stars playing the role of an aristocracy. In his final article he shrewdly noted there was 'everywhere courtesy and fear'[13] – fear, because careers in Hollywood were so brief and precarious.

On his return to New York Van Vechten published his novel about Hollywood, *Spider Boy* (1928), which he punningly subtitled *A Scenario for a*

Moving Picture. The novel centres on one Ambrose Deacon, a successful
New York playwright who is lured to Hollywood by the chance to write film
scenarios. As he heads west by train Deacon encounters the first signs of the
place in a star who orders him to change his plans and meet her in Hollywood.
This sets a keynote for the whole novel in that Deacon is constantly being
given directions by others and caught up in the frenetic pace of Hollywood
life. Van Vechten creates a series of comic situations in which the comedy
arises from the incomprehension of his protagonist. To take one instance, on
his way back into Los Angeles after a party, Deacon gets a lift on a milk-float
and as he is trying to thank the driver, tumbles headlong in the street. Points
like this led Van Vechten's biographer Bruce Kellner to bemoan the novel's
'lamentable lapses into Max Sennett slapstick'.[14] But this is one of the points
to Deacon's Hollywood experience. Before going there, his experience of
cinema had been limited to films such as *The Birth of a Nation*, *The Cabinet
of Doctor Caligari* and those of Chaplin. Now he begins to realize the popular
nature of film and, even more importantly, Hollywood as a system in which
circulating images are all-important. Deacon's mishap is witnessed by a
director, who exclaims to him: 'I'd like to know [...] how you think *Golden
Dreams* will go in the movie houses when it becomes known to the fans that
Miss Starling's guest, Ambrose Deacon, the eminent playwright, is in the
habit of driving down Wilshire Boulevard on the box of a delivery wagon,
more, that he is bounced off this box to roll in the street like a keg of beer'.[15]

Deacon has by this point become included in the Hollywood spectacle so
completely that we can see the double ironies in Van Vechten's subtitle.
Spider Boy presents a 'moving picture' most immediately in the sheer pace of
events, which constantly veer into farce and slapstick. Deacon's ignorance of
Hollywood is expressed through his physical ineptness. Despite being a New
York sophisticate, in Hollywood he acts like an innocent abroad. Secondly,
his account could present a moving picture in that it describes a romance;
Deacon marries a star and the celebrations mark a high spot in the Hollywood
social calendar. But here again Van Vechten shifts the narrative towards farce
as Deacon becomes increasingly bemused by the spectacle of the occasion.
Apart from the sheer quantity of gifts and flowers, the wedding is even
attended by a troop of American Indians. It is obvious, then, that Van
Vechten is burlesquing a Hollywood romance, but without ridiculing film
itself; hence the self-reflexive dimension to his subtitle, which humorously
suggests that his narrative needs to be converted into film for its real meaning
to emerge.

One of Deacon's main discoveries in Hollywood is that writing becomes
commodified into stories which might be modified unpredictably and which
lose any connection with individual authorship. Classic novelists, he is told,
are just 'not suitable for the screen'.[16] In this way Van Vechten comically

indicates the hard lesson learnt by figures such as Faulkner, Fitzgerald and Aldous Huxley, who assumed that screenwriting would be an easy extension of their main career. Deacon is told: 'Picture stories ain't written, they're rewritten', and shortly afterwards he learns that his experiences in Hollywood would make good 'film material'. This is when the title *Spider Boy* is first suggested as indicating the 'pursuit of the male by the female'.[17] Van Vechten thus transposes a possible film title into the title of his own novel and by so doing comically recognizes the growing interdependence between the two media.

Spider Boy capitalizes on the ignorance of its protagonist whereas Carroll and Garrett Graham's *Queer People* (1930) describes the experiences of one Whitey, a shameless opportunist who demonstrates a capacity to exploit the advantages of every situation. John Springer has described the action as a 'grand tour' of Hollywood society, and indeed one of Whitey's assets foreshadows that of Nathanael West's Tod Hackett, namely his 'ability to view his woes from the standpoint of an unaffected and slightly amused spectator'.[18] Whitey learns Hollywood with extraordinary speed and part of this learning process involves recognizing the sheer chance involved in opportunities. The spectacle of Hollywood might be one of 'bedlam and chaos', but Whitey has no difficulty in weaving his way through situations of bewildering complexity.

His arrival in Hollywood is signalled by the following scene:

> A tremendous uproar was taking place across the street. A truck, bearing a huge generator, was providing power for giant arc-lights which played about the sky and into windows and spectators' eyes. One shop was ablaze with 'broad' lights. A wheezy tenor, boosted to gigantic proportions, was bawling over the radio. Perhaps three hundred persons were milling about in the street.[19]

Is a film being made? No, it is only the opening of 'some beauty shop'. In this scene Whitey discovers how the electronic media, the technical dimension to Hollywood, can boost a mundane event into a spectacle determined by sheer media 'size'. As in West, the studios do not contain or limit the masquerade of Hollywood. Only a small proportion of *Queer People* is devoted to films themselves; instead we are shown the jockeying for status in Hollywood society and glimpses of symptomatic Hollywood activities. Late in the novel Whitey witnesses an opening-night spectacle which anticipates the concluding scene in *The Day of the Locust*: 'Giant spot-lights pawed the sky and glared into the eyes of the spectators. Thousands of gaping movie fans jammed the streets to see the stars come in [...] Hawkers rented boxes and folding chairs to gapers. Hordes of uniformed police, who should have been pursuing bandits, kept the on-lookers in line'.[20] The potential for disorder here is far more muted than in West. Instead the Grahams present the spotlights as a technological gaze blinding the spectators and making their arrival futile. But the business of Hollywood is business and even the hawkers have their role to play.

Queer People has a comic energy totally missing in Elmer Rice's laboured satire of Hollywood, *A Voyage to Purilia* (1930). Rice attempts to portray the place as an anti-utopia characterized by self-deception and Puritanism, but in practice the result is a string of scenes pastiching cinematic subjects such as slapstick, the Yellow Peril (enacted by a sinister race called the 'Chinks'), the car chase, the Western, and so on. For Claude-Edmonde Magny, 'in this utopia, the social categories of the movies, their vision of the world, and even their modes of perception have taken possession of reality and moulded it extensively'.[21] One of the few points at which Rice attempts to apply cinematic methods occurs when the visitor-protagonist arrives at the Purilian metropolis, a thinly disguised version of Los Angeles. Without ever explaining why such rapid scenes would occur, Rice evokes the city through a montage of visual glimpses: 'Serrated skylines; great avenues black with traffic; a lofty cathedral; the interior of a vast and luxurious restaurant; a street lined with theatres; a huge office buzzing with hundreds of busy clerks; a dozen mighty ships at anchor; a colossal stadium crammed with cheering thousands [...] all these swirled before our startled eyes'.[22] Rice seems supremely indifferent to the motivation of visual representation, with the result that his sequence reads incoherently, jumping arbitrarily from aerial views to street scenes and interiors. There is no experiential sequence through the narrator's point of view and Rice's ignorance of film technique helps to explain why his novel fails to engage satirically with its purported subject. The same could never be said of Nathanael West.

Nathanael West: *Miss Lonelyhearts*

West's *The Day of the Locust* (1939), the supreme example of the Hollywood novel, was the result of almost a decade of work in the movie capital. West first went to Hollywood in 1933 and briefly secured a job as screenwriter for Columbia, afterwards returning to New York. In 1935 he returned to Los Angeles and wrote screenplays variously for Republic Productions, Columbia, RKO, and Universal. While in Hollywood he met writers such as Faulkner, John O'Hara, and Scott Fitzgerald; and his screenwriting brought him into contact with writers such as Horace McCoy.[23] In 1936 he delivered a paper on Hollywood to the Western Writers Congress called 'Makers of Mass Neurosis', now apparently lost.

Even before the completion of *The Day of the Locust*, which he began in

1936, West was weaving a cinematic consciousness into his fiction. *A Cool Million* (1934) burlesques the 'log cabin to white house' narrative by breaking its narrative down into segments. Each episode follows a pattern of establishing a situation, introducing a disruptive element which ridicules ceremonies and other scenes of solemnity by leading up to a sudden disruption, and a scenic climax which as often as not involves some kind of attack on the protagonist Lemuel Pitkin. T. R. Steiner has commented on West's method here as supplying the 'invisible frame'. In this novel West uses no style as such, supplying instead the 'skewing of speeches, the introduction of super-grotesqueries, the revelation of what happens after the jump–cut'.[24] For Steiner, West performs a function which resembles that of a film producer in minimizing verbal commentary and instead manipulating imagistic detail. The rags-to-riches paradigm which West ridicules presumes a logical continuity from episode to episode but West breaks down this sequence with end-of-scene climaxes which exploit the reader/viewer's incomprehension. Thus he facetiously uses comedy, melodrama (will the sinister Chinaman stab Lemuel?) and other effects to prevent the reader from identifying with Lemuel. The discontinuity from episode to episode undermines the paradigm by showing the ludicrous results of chance interventions, and each episode concludes with some fresh violence to Lemuel, so that by the end of the novel his physical substance has been grotesquely reduced.[25]

It was from two humorists that West learned the value of the short, objectively described scene which became the narrative unit for both *Miss Lonelyhearts* and *The Day of the Locust*. The first of these was S. J. Perelman, West's friend from Brown University and brother-in-law. Perelman had recoiled from Hollywood's 'tawdriness' when he first visited the place, but evidently his distaste did not last long, as he established himself as a screenwriter firstly with the Marx Brothers' *Monkey Business* (1931), subsequently collaborating with Laura West on further screenplays throughout that decade.[26] Perelman's prose writings were characteristically short comic sketches and at least two of these were devoted to Hollywood. 'Scenario' opens as though presenting a screenplay ('fade in, exterior grassy knoll, long shot') and then modulates into the monologue of a cheerfully cynical filmmaker who makes no bones about manipulating appearances to fool his audience or about the alcoholism of film stars. This piece is far less visual than 'Strictly from Hunger', which draws on Perelman's first experiences of Hollywood. Partly anticipating Aldous Huxley's Hollywood novel *Ape and Essence* (1949), this sketch undermines Perelman's naïve excitement at reaching the film capital by describing the 'suttee' as the producers and actors immolate themselves if their film fails.[27] Scene two is Hollywood Boulevard, where Perelman evokes masquerade: 'In a Chinese eatery cunningly built in the shape of an old shoe I managed to assuage the inner man with a chopped glove salad topped off with frosted cocoa. Charming platinum-haired hostesses in red pyjamas and peaked caps added a touch of colour to the surroundings.' Like West, he plays comically on the discontinuity between these visual images, and then describes a climactic sexual assault in the studios by a star: 'My scream of terror only egged her on, overturning chairs and tables in her bestial pursuit. With superhuman talons she tore off my collar and suspenders. I sank to my knees, choked with sobs, hanging on to my last shirt-stud like a drowning man. Her Svengali eyes were slowly hypnotizing me; I fought like a wounded bird – and then, blissful unconsciousness.'[28] In the first of these excerpts Perelman acts out the role of an observer bemused by the inconsistent masquerade going on around him, but in the second he enters the cinematic frame by acting out a role in sexual melodrama normally played by a female lead. The star, ludicrously named Diana ffrench-Mamoulian, confirms the stereotype of the *femme fatale* preying on the hapless Perelman, who tries to cling on to the signs of male decency (collar, studs, etc.) before he finally yields to this Hollywood vamp.[29] We shall see a similar progression in *The Day of the Locust* as Tod Hackett moves from attempted spectatorship to sexual involvement in Hollywood.

Perelman read the first chapters of *Miss Lonelyhearts* and complained to West that they were 'too psychological, not concrete enough'. He recommended that West put in 'more description of people and things'.[30] Essentially the same advice was given about *The Day of the Locust* by the publisher Bennett Cerf, who was instrumental in getting the novel accepted by Random House. The novel had originally been narrated by Claude Estee, a successful screenwriter, but Cerf asked West to change the narration into the third person. He also asked West to remove a lesbian scene and to tone down others. West agreed to all these revisions, admitting that he wanted Homer's torture to work by 'understatement and suggestion rather than brutal accent'.[31]

Both Perelman and Cerf recommended a descriptive method which concentrated on visual data and which allowed the drama of local scenes to emerge without explicit verbal prompting. In other words, both writers helped West to achieve the scenic sense which is the hallmark of his more mature fiction. Before we consider how this method bore fruit in *Miss Lonelyhearts*, we need to remember the changes West made to his narrative during composition. Originally intending to produce a 'novel in the form of a comic strip', he abandoned this plan but retained some features which he summarized as follows: 'Each chapter instead of going forward in time, also goes backward, forward, up and down in space like a picture. Violent images are used to illustrate commonplace events. Violent acts are left almost bald'.[32]

From the very beginning of West's conception, then, *Miss Lonelyhearts* was to be a heavily framed narrative. Its segmented montage structure, which in the final text exploits discontinuity through chapter captions and through the juxtaposition of incongruities, pulls ironically against its very subject of contact. By casting his protagonist as a problem columnist, West opens up an expectation or at least a hope that acts of communication will take place in cycles of appeal and response. In fact, it is a novel which breaks this cycle repeatedly and which shows violence and discontinuity to be characteristic of American life. The first incongruity in the novel lies of course in the fact that Miss Lonelyhearts is a man. As Jane Goldman has rightly argued, 'every time Miss Lonelyhearts is referred to in the third person masculine the crisis in gender categorisation and the very constructedness of gender is foregrounded'.[33] Image follows rhetoric throughout and Goldman's assertion could be further generalized to demonstrate how all aspects of identity are shown to be constructed. West establishes the need for a Miss Lonelyhearts through instances of the letters sent and then focalizes an image of him through his cynical editor Shrike: 'Although his cheap clothes had too much style, he still looked like the son of a Baptist minister. A beard would become him, would accent his Old-Testament look. But even without a beard no one could fail to recognize the New England puritan. His forehead was high and narrow. His nose was long and fleshless. His bony chin was shaped and cleft like a hoof'.[34] Appearance is problematic throughout *Miss Lonelyhearts* and what we encounter here is the first of many suggestions that clothes constitute a costume or disguise. They are skewed across his role in the newspaper, neither revealing nor concealing a type-identity which suppresses him as an individual. Before the protagonist's own visual perspective can be exploited he himself is contained – framed within a stereotype.

Instead of reinforcing identity, Jane Goldman argues that 'clothes themselves construct ideologically gendered roles'.[35] In fact, towards the end of the novel a girl literally becomes her party dress, which is addressed instead of her person. Not only that, gestures are shown to be discontinuous with verbal expression. Shrike's girlfriend Miss Farkis has a masculine handshake; the girl Betty has the manner (but not the experience) of a professional gambler; and Shrike's wife Mary performs a series of 'formal, impersonal gestures'. Shrike is the supreme exemplar of this discontinuity through a strategy taken from the cinema: 'He practised a trick used much by moving picture comedians – the deadpan'.[36] Thus, however animated his words become, his face remains a 'blank'.

The scene which most clearly thematizes West's method of segmentation occurs when Miss Lonelyhearts and Shrike's wife Mary go to a Latin bar called El Gaucho.[37] Mary 'goes Spanish' immediately, altering her gestures to suit the new setting. Miss Lonelyhearts registers a connection between the objects making up the décor of the bar and contemporary advertisements: 'Guitars, bright shawls, exotic foods, outlandish costumes – all these things

were part of the business of dreams. He had learned not to laugh at the advertisements offering to teach writing, cartooning, engineering, to add inches to
the biceps and to develop the bust'.[38] 'Business' is the key term here. Just as
the adverts separate off different skills and sections of the body, so the human
figures in this scene and in the novel generally fragment into disparate roles
and postures. Mary's dress reflects this process in resembling a steel carapace
which renders her a grotesque mechanism going through her pantomime of
automatic gestures. The protagonist here attempts to preserve a distance
between himself and the observed but, as happens with Tod in *The Day of the
Locust*, sexual desire breaks down this detachment. When Miss Lonelyhearts
takes Mary home he tears off her clothes in the vestibule. She clings on to her
coat and the 'covering' of speech under the pretext that her husband will get
suspicious, but even this might be part of an act. Miss Lonelyhearts never
gets over the threshold.

Because Miss Lonelyhearts acts as witness or observer in many scenes his
roles are repeatedly cued in by the actions of those he meets. When Fay Doyle
takes the sexual initiative by kissing him on the mouth, it is his turn to transform into a mechanism. From the very first glimpse of her he tries to bring
her figure under visual control by breaking it down into component parts
('legs like Indian clubs, breasts like balloons') and, despite her feminine
clothes, 'she looked like a police captain'.[39] In this image, as usual in West,
one part tugs against another. Fay's evident strength is encoded by Miss
Lonelyhearts as suggesting an energy he is used to associating with
masculinity.

Throughout the novel West shows how the media have commercialized
desire and rendered it banal or grotesque. Because the media have become an
unavoidable part of the environment they impose their messages so forcefully
that one possible reaction is recoil; standing in the street, bombarded with
sights and sounds that he cannot organize, Miss Lonelyhearts tries to
suppress his senses of sight and hearing. The cinema of course forms a crucial
part of this technologized environment; at one point we see a man apparently
on the verge of death going to see a movie called *Blonde Beauty*. More importantly, we should recognize how West draws on the techniques of the cinema
to portray his scenes. When Miss Lonelyhearts meets Fay Doyle's disabled
husband he focuses attention on his awkward Chaplinesque movements: 'He
used a cane and dragged one of his feet behind him in a box-shaped shoe with
a four-inch sole. As he hobbled along, he made many waste motions, like
those of a partially destroyed insect'. The insect analogy highlights a surreal
quality in the man's movements which ironically suppresses the fact that
every movement constitutes an attempt to communicate. Or again, when we
see his features in close-up their misalignment provokes a different comparison: 'He looked like one of those composite photographs used by screen

magazines in guessing contests'.[40] Once again Miss Lonelyhearts supplies the point of view and, in a defence mechanism, compares the living features with a printed image. As we saw earlier, West had decided to make his images 'bald', i.e. as striking as possible without extensive commentary, and here Miss Lonelyhearts implicates himself in a way of seeing as a consumer. Like the photographs in the film magazines, the disabled man presents a puzzle for him to decode. Once he makes contact with this figure he is drawn into the scenes with more immediacy and the last image of the novel, like a slapstick comedy but with an altogether more sombre context, shows Miss Lonely-hearts and the disabled man rolling down a flight of stairs.

The Hollywood Freak Show

Already we have encountered features of West's narrative which he will develop in *The Day of the Locust*: rapid vivid scenes with minimal verbal commentary and grotesque reversals and climaxes. A work which almost certainly helped him to develop his conception of the grotesque was Tod Browning's 1932 film *Freaks*. In her study of freak shows in America Rachel Adams declares: 'Freak shows are guided by the assumption that *freak* is an essence, the basis for a comforting fiction that there is a permanent, qualitative difference between deviance and normality, projected spatially in the distance between the spectator and the body onstage'.[41] The film *Freaks* engages with its eponymous subjects in such a way that this distance is closed up. It carries a pre-credits sequence explaining that 'the majority of freaks, themselves, are endowed with normal thoughts and emotions'.[42] The film proper opens and closes with sideshow scenes not in the original script in which a showman addresses the audience within and outside the film by warning: 'You laugh at them... and yet, but for the accident of birth, you may be as they are'. He then proceeds to display the 'most astounding living monstrosity of all time', gesturing towards a figure within a screened enclosure. Far from laughter, the spectators' reaction is one of horror, heightened by the fact that this figure was once normal. The film then moves into an extended flashback to show the events leading up to this transformation and finally reveals the figure as half woman, half chicken. The first scenes of the film thus explicitly address the issue of viewing freaks. Early in the narrative two men are strolling in woods near the circus. The one describes the freaks as monstrosities who should be put down at birth; the other accepts with reservations the analogy drawn with children by a chaperone.

In this way the film seems to be concerned with 'subverting the notion of normative standards altogether'.[43] However, in her analysis of the film Rachel Adams finds an underlying ambivalence towards the freaks. On the one hand, it appears to humanize the freaks; on the other, after the female acrobat turns against them (and her own fiancé) at her wedding celebrations, they become threatening antagonists in wreaking their revenge on her. In the most direct, physical way the action destabilizes the division between freakishness and normality through the transformation of the woman and, although it alludes to sideshows and vaudeville, 'yet at the same time, it makes problematic the kind of looking that such spectacles encouraged by experimenting with the camera's ability to manipulate perspective'.[44] Exactly the same point can be made about *The Day of the Locust*, which explicitly invites the reader to reconsider the monstrous in its opening chapter and which disperses the notion of freakishness throughout the movie capital.

When West went to Hollywood in the mid-1930s it is inconceivable that he did not encounter one of the most notorious films of the decade and it is likely that he borrowed the forename of his protagonist from the writer of the story (Tod Robbins) and the director of the 1932 film, Tod Browning.[45] As early as *A Cool Million* (1932) West was drawing on sideshows to shape his satires and according to his biographer he described Hollywood to his New York friends as a 'museum of curiosities'.[46] Towards the end of that novel the travelling 'Chamber of American Horrors' sums up the grotesqueries the protagonist has experienced at first hand. Like Barnum's, the show is disguised as a museum, whereas in fact it gathers together parodic images of contemporary know-how based again on disguise: 'The visitor saw flower pots that were really victrolas, revolvers that held candy, candy that held collar buttons and so forth'.[47] In anticipation of *The Day of the Locust*, West divorces appearance from use so completely that commodities become unpredictable and even unidentifiable objects. Similarly, the show's 'Pageant of America' presents a series of playlets exposing the unattractive side to American history, its foundations in racism and exploitation.

All Hollywood in *The Day of the Locust* could be compared to a freak show, but the analogy sheds light on two characters in particular: the diminutive Abe Kusich and Homer Simpson.[48] Abe is first seen by Tod one night when he emerges from a bundle of clothing. The lighting of the event is strategically managed: Tod 'struck a match, thinking it might be a dog wrapped in a blanket. When the light flared up, he saw it was a tiny man. The match went out and he hastily lit another. It was a male dwarf rolled up in a woman's flannel bathrobe. The round thing at the end was his slightly hydrocephalous head'.[49] The two matches pace the visual revelation of Abe from shape to features. Unlike the situation in the film *Freaks*, Abe is not contained within a show as an exhibit, but is a full participant in the commercial and sexual business of Hollywood. He follows the fashions, claims to have hot tips, and later becomes one of the rivals for Faye's sexual favours. West's visual perspective on him prevents the reader from dismissing Abe as a mere oddity.

The same is true of Homer Simpson. Tod establishes a way of seeing him which operates even when he is not present in scenes. Indeed, Homer himself occupies the same vantage point when observing his hands. Because they move with a life of their own they seem to be organisms separate from the rest of his body. The hypothetical observer of Homer slides easily into his own point of view on his body: 'He got out of bed in sections, like a poorly made automaton, and carried his hands into the bathroom. He turned on the cold water. When the basin was full, he plunged his hands in up to the wrists. They lay quietly at the bottom like a pair of strange aquatic animals'.[50] Throughout the novel West foregrounds his hands and those of other characters since visually they are potentially the most expressive limbs. Like Wing Biddlebaum in *Winesburg, Ohio*, Homer possesses hands with a disturbing energy of their own.[51]

Although hands are foregrounded throughout West's novel as part of his characters' performances, they represent opposing possibilities of action. The disabled man in *Miss Lonelyhearts*, for instance, possesses hands which become increasingly frenzied in his attempts to communicate. In the case of Homer, however, there is a more cinematic significance to the emphasis on his hands. Stephanie Sarver has demonstrated convincingly that in his portrayal of Homer West was drawing on the 1931 James Whale film of *Frankenstein*.[52] Homer's waking, described in the last quotation, suggests that he is coming alive and as the novel progresses he develops a more mechanical and stylized way of walking which once again resembles that of Frankenstein's monster. Sarver draws so many parallels that there can be no doubt of West's use of the film, although this use involves more than horror effects. Because Homer is a product of the Hollywood system, West suggests that the *latter* is monstrous. Homer is visually strange rather than terrifying and, through his hands, he embodies the suppressed violence ready to burst forth. Thus, we can acknowledge a similarity between the monster causing the death of a child in *Frankenstein* and the late episode with Adore Loomis. In the latter, though, West totally excludes any childhood innocence. On the contrary, Adore has been turned into a freak by his mother, who has trained him to perform a sexual act beyond his years. When he teases Homer in the crowd with a purse on a string, Homer vents his frustration on Hollywood by stamping the child to death. Then violence breeds violence and the crowd beat Homer to death. The concept of monstrosity is thus extended away from any individual and projected into the whole scene, which dramatizes Hollywood at its most destructive.

The Hollywood Masquerade: *The Day of the Locust*

For West Hollywood was primarily a place of simulation. This novel marks the culmination of a whole series of allusions in his writings to fakery in décor and behaviour. In an unpublished story (probably dating from the early 1930s) called 'Mr Potts of Pottstown' this perspective is applied to tourism. The eponymous American travels to Switzerland and at one point is startled to see a mountaineer strip off his false moustache and reveal himself to be from Mr Potts' home town. His message is stark: 'Switzerland is nothing but a fake, an amusement park owned by a very wealthy company. The whole show is put on for the tourist trade [...] It's all scenery'.[53] Transpose this account on to Hollywood and we have a compact summary of his view of the film capital.

West opens *The Day of the Locust* by apparently using one of the most common novelistic strategies, namely the description of an unfamiliar place, but from the very beginning he foregrounds simulation. Without giving the reader any locating statements, he describes a street scene: 'An army of cavalry and foot was passing. It moved like a mob; its lines broken, as though fleeing from some terrible defeat. The dolmans of the hussars, the heavy shakos of the guards, Hanoverian light horse, with their flat leather caps and flowing red plumes, were all jumbled together in bobbing disorder'.[54] This 'medium shot' cleverly focuses our eye entirely on the costumed figures and suspends our sense of context. West's play on incongruity – how can an army on horseback be riding through a modern American city? – invites, or rather compels, the reader to speculate on the relation between figures and place, visually establishing one of the main themes of the novel: violence and conflict.[55] West projects a general spectacle here but also draws our attention to costume (the headgear of the 'soldiers') and their disorder. If this is one mob, the novel concludes with another, a mob of spectators rather than performers.

From this initial spectacle West takes us to two street scenes, important for situating Tod within his field of vision (the cavalry are seen from a window), one demonstrating dress, the other building styles. In the first, Tod breaks down a crowd scene into individual instances of incongruity: a lady going shopping in a yachting cap, an insurance clerk going home in a Tyrolean hat, and so on. If these figures were not distinguished from each other a bogus sense of cohesion within the crowd would emerge. The distinction between crowd and mob in the novel is an important one. 'Mob' suggests a number of people gathered together in a chaotic and potentially violent way. Indeed, there is violence within this street scene as West pulls back the focus to include the urban poor. Our gaze is redirected to observers within the scene who have a sinister homogeneity: 'Scattered among these masqueraders were people of a different type. Their clothing was sombre and badly cut, bought from mail-order houses [...] When their gaze was returned, their eyes filled with hatred'.[56] Spectatorship thus becomes charged with bitterness and social envy. Far more is at stake than simple observation since West never allows us to forget the lure of Hollywood in feeding the dream of success.

The third description which is used to establish Hollywood for the reader is that of the architectural medley of Pinyon Canyon where Tod lives. Nature is acknowledged and immediately assimilated into the constructedness of the place as the evening light along the tops of hills and buildings is compared to a neon tube, and once again discontinuity is central: 'On the corner of La Huerta Road was a miniature Rhine castle with tarpaper turrets pierced for archers. Next to it was a highly coloured shack with domes and minarets out of the *Arabian Nights*'.[57] Since West through Tod notes the substance at the same time as the appearance, the material lightness, newness, and – by implication – temporary nature of these structures comes out strongly. Dwellings in Hollywood are the residential equivalent of costume, offering roles that their occupiers can adopt. Jonathan Veitch has noted that the 'cliched readymades of desire are so ubiquitous that even the architecture of the city comes to resemble the sets on the back lot'. This is made explicit when Tod walks across a lot, moving through Surrealistic sets which sometimes have no depth and certainly have no consistency with each other. The effect is totally visual but the description comes to resemble a dream as dimension and proportion shift unpredictably. Veitch continues: 'This manipulation of signs foregrounds an essential feature of West's settings. No environment is left neutral; environment is always converted into atmosphere, carefully dressed with the appropriate props. And *atmosphere prescribes performance*' (his emphasis).[58] There is no separation possible between domicile and behaviour since each is equally prescribed by the repertoire of roles located in Hollywood. Thus the screen writer Claude Estee (who was to be the protagonist in West's original plan) lives in an imitation Southern mansion which carries its own obligatory impersonation. Its swimming pool is a status symbol within which floats a simulated dead horse 'to amuse'. Homer lives in a 'queer' cottage, described as both 'Spanish' and 'Irish' though neither label fits. It resembles a set for Disney's *Snow White* in having an elaborately cute roof of mock thatch.

It is a premise of *The Day of the Locust* that Hollywood is a style of life spreading beyond the studios, and to ensure that this message comes across forcibly West uses a protagonist who is a film artist. Tod Hackett is a professional observer used throughout to give us angles of vision and to articulate the complex appearances of Hollywood. The fact that he is an artist rationalizes comparisons with Daumier, Goya and other painters, all of which encourage us to read the novel scenically. Involved commercially in the cinema but disenchanted with the system (rather like West himself), Tod applies a whole array of visual devices to convey the grotesque life of Hollywood. His project of composing a set of lithographs called 'The Dancers' represents an attempt to freeze local figures in 'stills' and thereby exercise some control over the spectacle confronting him. We shall see how this fails in the case of Faye Greener. Suffice it for the moment to say that characters come across as embodied roles. Earle, for instance, defines himself visually as a cowboy by standing every day in front of a saddlery store. This shop contains all his props (boots, spurs and so on) and his features are flattened out into a 'mechanical drawing', i.e. into a figure without depth, like a human 'flat'. It is Tod of course who registers these nuances of appearance.

Faye Greener is one of the most important characters in the novel in that she stands at the sexual centre of the action and embodies the contradictions of the Hollywood system so clearly.[59] She enters the novel via a film still from a farce in which she played a minor part. West suggests that Faye is a would-be actress, counterpointed initially against her father Harry who is a has-been. The echo in her name of Fay Wray, the star of *King Kong*, only adds to her status as a figure of simulation. Harry has enjoyed a certain success in vaudeville but has fallen victim to developments in the medium so that he has to carry around with him the testimonial of his former vaudeville role. This has in turn been modulated into the job of salesman for silver polish which he hawks from door to door. Instead of performing on the silver screen he sells a commodity devoted to appearance. Harry, in other words, has converted himself into a commodity; for him, performance and selling have become indistinguishable. His sales spiel is part of his performance and when he has a fit at Homer's the seizure is expressed in appropriately mechanical terms, like the motions of an over-wound toy. Amazingly, even in illness Harry continues to act, playing off his role as victim against his daughter. Harry quite literally acts himself into the ground; even in his coffin he is made up as if performing in a minstrel show.

Harry acts as a comic foil to Faye, who even sings to him when he is having a heart attack. Laurence Goldstein has rightly stressed their importance in the novel since both have constructed their behaviour entirely on the basis of spectatorship.[60] For them all experience involves a performance and an audience. The nearest Faye demonstrates to a subjective life is the stories she is constantly inventing for potential films. When he learns this, Tod describes his sensation in terms of theatre: 'Being with her was like being backstage during an amateurish, ridiculous play. From in front, the stupid lines and grotesque situations would have made him squirm with annoyance, but because he saw the perspiring stagehands and the wires that held up the tawdry summerhouse with its tangle of paper flowers, he accepted everything and was anxious for it to succeed'.[61] Transpose the analogy to the film studio and the comparison still stands. More importantly, despite recognizing Faye's ridiculous aspect, Tod is already showing signs of being drawn in to her performance. The stories which fascinate Tod resemble a file of possible roles for Faye and exemplify a status described by Guy Debord in *The Society of the Spectacle*: 'Media stars are spectacular representations of living human beings, distilling the essence of the spectacle's banality into images of possible roles'.[62] Faye never loses this banality of image because she has such a superficial conception of success, and also because we grow accustomed to thinking of her in the plural as a series of personae.

Initially at least, Faye comes across as modelled on the clichéd figure of the *femme fatale*, superficially resembling a female role popular in Hollywood as looking guilty but being innocent.[63] Initially Tod wonders whether she is working as a local call girl and West contrasts his worldly-wise view of Faye with Homer's more wide-eyed reaction to her appearance: 'Although she was seventeen, she was dressed like a child of twelve in a white cotton dress with a blue sailor collar. Her long legs were bare and she had blue sandals on her feet'.[64] Contrast this with her appearance in a draft of the novel and we can see how carefully West revised visual details:

> Faye was about seventeen years old and very pretty. She had wide straight shoulders, narrow hips and long legs. Under her tight sweater, her tiny breasts showed like the twin halves of a lemon. She had no hat on. Her 'platinum' hair was drawn tightly away from her face and gathered together in back by a narrow baby blue ribbon that allowed it to tumble loosely to her shoulders. The style of her coiffure had been copied from Tenniel's drawings of Alice.[65]

Both descriptions are implicitly gendered as from a male perspective, the second focalized through a specific observer. The latter moves conventionally from general outline to details and keeps the focus mainly on Faye's head. In the shorter final version the descriptive sequence follows the movement of Homer's gaze over Faye as he studiously avoids her face. The result is that her 'costume' is foregrounded as deceptively childlike and her sex-appeal tied initially to the only part of her body which is bare – her legs. Although Homer tries to avoid her eyes, West suggests that Faye's gaze is fixed on Homer to see what kind of effect she is getting from her audience.

As West's novel progresses, Faye's appeal becomes more overtly sexual. Immediately before the scene with Miguel in which Faye casts herself as the seductress, she addresses the group on how to make a career in Hollywood. Ironically, her gestures lose all connection with her words. The effect is as if her soundtrack is either too low or too unsynchronized and Faye becomes a purely visual spectacle: 'None of them really heard her. They were all too busy watching her smile, laugh, shiver, whisper, grow indignant, cross and uncross her legs, stick out her tongue, widen and narrow her eyes, toss her head so that her platinum hair splashed against the red plush of the chair back. The strange thing about her gestures and expressions was that they didn't really illustrate what she was saying'.[66] The elision of her words cues in her sexual mime with the Mexican which is performed with music to a male audience jockeying for her favours – hence the symbolism of the cock fight. Picking up on the significance of West's original title for the novel (*The Cheated*), Mathew Roberts has argued that *The Day of the Locust* 'must work to *identify* its reader with the position of a cheated and pathologized mass-cultural subject'. Tod, he goes on, is not only an authoritative critical figure within the novel, but he also desires Faye and is therefore able to identify with the cheated masses. Roberts finds a progression from representations of Faye as a denaturalized fetish object to an 'eroticized image' which reflects a loss of critical distance in Tod.[67]

The final scene of the novel, a first-night riot, draws Tod decisively into the cheated masses. It is not only an external scene but also one of exclusion and a scene which is described as predictable: 'The police force would have to be doubled when the stars began to arrive. At the sight of their heroes and heroines, the crowd would turn demoniac'.[68] And at that point it would turn into a mob. Because they are denied any sight of the stars the crowd turns inward. Its actions make a reprise of images we have seen earlier in the novel, displacing them onto other characters as if to imply their typicality. Tod is kicked in the backside just as Harry feigns in his performance; an old man molesting a girl repeats the action of Miguel with Faye; and the game played by Adore Loomis with a purse on the end of a string sums up the financial promise of Hollywood. Swept backwards and forwards, Tod almost passes out and loses his capacity to distinguish between the spectacle before him and his painting *The Burning of Los Angeles*. Sight and hearing become confused and, as he is lifted into a police car, Tod himself becomes a mechanism in the final climax of sound: 'The siren began to scream and at first he thought he was making the noise himself. He felt his lips with his hands. They were clamped tight. He knew then it was the siren. For some reason this made him laugh and he began to imitate the siren as loud as he could'.[69]

It is characteristic of West's attention to material conditions that the novel should end with a sound. *The Day of the Locust* contains many allusions to the defunct silent cinema, most obviously in the summarized pornographic film which breaks down. As Blake Allmendinger has shown, figures such as Harry and Homer resemble actors in performing silent mimes, whereas sound becomes a prominent feature of modernity.[70] However, sound is shown as a dissonance. We have already seen examples of visual incongruity and of mismatches between characters' appearance and speech (Adore Loomis' performance of a sexual adult is one of many examples). In the studio accident where the set collapses the apparatus itself 'screams'; voice is displaced onto inanimate objects, while characters become mechanisms, uttering machine-like sounds. It is entirely appropriate to West's view of Hollywood that the last human act in the novel should be an imitation. Through a series of grotesque scenes, many with their own violent climaxes, West appropriates the representational practices of Hollywood to turn them against his subject and to startle the reader into questioning those conventions.[71] His novel thus represents a more sustained embodiment of the strategy we found in the Delmore Schwartz story discussed at the end of the previous chapter. If it is true, as Richard Simon contends, that West's characters and plot were 'transposed from the movies and parodically reworked', then this would further explain the multiple resemblances and simulations projected throughout the novel.[72] As characters (Tod included) stumble from scene to scene, their disparities seem to preclude a 'director' supplying a linear continuity. The scenes instead build up a gradual montage of America's culture of the image and the celebrity in the 1930s.

Notes

1 Springer, *Hollywood Fictions*, pp. 11, 63. Springer's remains the best discussion of this fiction although earlier studies focusing on the dream of success (Jonas Spatz, *Hollywood in Fiction*) and on regionalism (Walter Wells, *Tycoons and Locusts*) are useful. Ian Hamilton's *Writers in Hollywood* (1990) is particularly useful on the politics of screenwriting and Richard Fine's *West of Eden* (1993) examines the notion of authorship in relation to the careers of 40 Hollywood writers. John Russell Taylor's *Strangers in Paradise* (1983) discusses the situation of émigré writers in Hollywood. Two essential bibliographical guides are Nancy Brooker-Bowers, *The Hollywood Novel* (1985), and Anthony Slide, *The Hollywood Novel* (1995).
2 George Kummer, *Harry Leon Wilson*, p. 116. Wilson came to Hollywood in 1920 to research his novel. Serialized in 1922 in the *Saturday Evening Post* and published in book form the same year, *Merton of the Movies* was adapted for the cinema under its original title in 1924 by Famous Players-Lasky, as *Make Me a Star* in 1932 by Paramount, and again under its original title in 1947 by MGM.
3 Stein, *Everybody's Autobiography*, p. 250.
4 Springer, *Hollywood Fictions*, pp. 65, 68.
5 Wilson, *Merton of the Movies*, p. 3.
6 *Photoplay* was founded in 1911. For a representative selection from its first decades of publication, see Barbara Gelman, ed., *A Photoplay Treasury*.
7 *Merton of the Movies*, p. 53.
8 *Merton of the Movies*, p. 74.
9 *Merton of the Movies*, p. 121.
10 In 1917 Turpin joined Mack Sennett's company. Vachel Lindsay praised Wilson's novel as a work in which fictional and cinematic techniques merged. He particularly praised the

irony of the ending as Merton is 'established for life in the business of making fun of himself' (Myron Lounsberry, ed., *The Progress and Poetry of the Movies*, p. 378).

11 Edward Burns, ed. *The Letters of Gertrude Stein and Carl Van Vechten*, vol. 1, p. 141.

12 Bruce Kellner, *Carl Van Vechten*, pp. 230–31; Carl Van Vechten, 'Fabulous Hollywood', p. 54.

13 'Hollywood Parties', pp. 47, 86, 90; 'Hollywood Royalty', pp. 38, 86; 'Understanding Hollywood', p. 78. In the last of these articles Van Vechten explains that he was helped in understanding Hollywood by reading Adela Rogers St Johns' 1925 novel *The Skyrocket*, which described the rise to stardom of a young woman called Sharon Kimm. The film based on the novel was released in 1926. St Johns wrote journalistic pieces on Hollywood and worked briefly as a screenwriter.

14 Kellner, *Carl Van Vechten*, p. 233.

15 Carl Van Vechten, *Spider Boy*, pp. 116–17.

16 *Spider Boy*, p. 48.

17 *Spider Boy*, pp. 194, 199–200.

18 Springer, *Hollywood Fictions*, p. 201; Carroll and Garrett Graham, *Queer People*, p. 35.

19 Graham and Graham, *Queer People*, p. 17.

20 Graham and Graham, *Queer People*, pp. 184–85.

21 Magny, *The Age of the American Novel*, p. 34.

22 Elmer Rice, *A Voyage to Purilia*, p. 119.

23 West's writer friends included the novelist John Sanford, who moved to Hollywood in 1936 and secured a post as screenwriter for Paramount, though with little success. McCoy worked for Republic with West, as did the novelist Samuel Ornitz. At the end of the 1930s West got to know Fitzgerald and sent him the galley proofs of *The Day of the Locust* (Dardis, *Some Time in the Sun*, pp. 150, 159). John O' Hara's stories about the movie capital are collected in *John O'Hara's Hollywood* (2007).

24 T. R. Steiner, 'A Confluence of Voices: West's Lemuel and the American Dream', in David Madden, ed., *Nathanel West: The Cheaters and the Cheated*, p. 158.

25 Jonathan Veitch sees an analogy between Lemuel's dismantling and old vaudeville routines (*American Superrealism*, p. 99).

26 Dorothy Herrmann, *S. J. Perelman: A Life*, p. 78; Christopher Adcock, 'S. J. Perelman', in Clark, ed., *American Screenwriters: Second Series*, p. 285. Perelman wrote for Paramount, Twentieth Century Fox, and MGM.

27 *Ape and Essence* is a post-nuclear narrative in the form of a film script with an introductory frame. Huxley's attitude to films shifted from initial distaste for the magnified images of human features they projected to professional involvement after he took up permanent residence in California in 1937. One of his most successful scripts was for MGM's *Pride and Prejudice* (1940). David Scott Dunaway's *Huxley in Hollywood* gives the definitive account of this phase of his career.

28 S. J. Perelman, *The Most of S. J. Perelman*, pp. 50, 52.

29 Her name echoes that of the Hollywood director Rouben Mamoulian.

30 Letter to Beatrice Mathieu, 12 April 1930, in Nathanael West, *Novels and Other Writings*, p. 769.

31 Letter to Bennett Cerf, 1938, in West, *Novels and Other Writings*, p. 783. Cerf's best-selling collection of comic sketches *Try and Stop Me* (1944) included a portrait of Samuel Goldwyn and 'Back to the Hollywoods' contained anecdotes about Dorothy Parker and others.

32 Nathanael West, 'Some Notes on Miss L.' [1933], in *Novels and Other Writings*, p. 401.

33 Jane Goldman, '"Miss Lonelyhearts and the Party Dress"'. West's original plan was to

give his protagonist the name Thomas Matlock; see Carter A. Daniel, 'West's Revisions of *Miss Lonelyhearts*', in Jay Martin, ed., *Nathanael West: A Collection of Critical Essays*, p. 53.

34 West, *Novels and Other Writings*, p. 61.

35 Goldman, '"Miss Lonelyhearts and the Party Dress"'.

36 West, *Novels and Other Writings*, p. 64.

37 Probably named after the 1928 Douglas Fairbanks film *The Gaucho*.

38 West, *Novels and Other Writings*, p. 83.

39 West, *Novels and Other Writings*, p. 89.

40 West, *Novels and Other Writings*, pp. 109, 110.

41 Rachel Adams, *Sideshow U.S.A.*, p. 6.

42 Transcribed from film. For commentary on Tod Browning, see David J. Skal and Elias Savada, *Dark Carnival*.

43 Adams, *Sideshow U.S.A.*, p. 72.

44 Adams, *Sideshow U.S.A.*, p. 65.

45 The film was the brainchild of Irving Thalberg. See Elias Savada, 'The Making of *Freaks*', for information on its composition and mixed reception. Tod Hackett's surname has occasioned some over-ingenious speculation about the suggestion that he is a 'hack' but Ian Hamilton argues that West simply borrowed the name of Albert Hackett, his friend the scenarist (*Writers in Hollywood*, p. 158).

46 Jay Martin, *Nathanael West: The Art of His Life*, p. 213.

47 West, *Novels and Other Writings*, p. 223.

48 West tried out a plan for a film based on an Eskimo family but the only trace of this plan is the appearance of the couple at Harry Greener's funeral; see West, 'Three Eskimos', in *Novels and Other Writings*, pp. 456–57.

49 West, *Novels and Other Writings*, p. 245.

50 West, *Novels and Other Writings*, p. 267.

51 In the story of Wing ('Hands') we are told: 'The hands alarmed their owner. He wanted to keep them hidden away' (Sherwood Anderson, *Winesburg, Ohio*, p. 28).

52 Stephanie Sarver, 'Homer Simpson Meets Frankenstein'. Richard Keller Simon sees West's narrative as a parodic deflation of the 1936 Frank Capra movie *Mr Deeds Goes to Town*, in which the individual fails to triumph over corruption ('Between Capra and Adorno', pp. 517–21). Apart from this film influence, Carvel Collins has documented extensive borrowings by West from *Sanctuary*, one of Faulkner's most cinematic novels ('Nathanael West's *The Day of the Locust* and *Sanctuary*'). Chip Rhodes finds influences on the novel from two films which West partly scripted: *The President's Mystery* (1936) and *Five Came Back* (1939) (*Politics, Desire, and the Hollywood Novel*, pp. 27–29).

53 West, *Novels and Other Writings*, p. 441.

54 West, *Novels and Other Writings*, p. 241.

55 One of West's much-quoted statements – 'in America violence is idiomatic' – occurs amid reflections on how violence has become routine in American life, partly thanks to media reports: 'Some Notes on Violence' (1932), in *Novels and Other Writings*, p. 399.

56 West, *Novels and Other Writings*, p. 242.

57 West, *Novels and Other Writings*, p. 243. The bewildering medley of architectural styles, signs and billboards is the first visual shock for the protagonist of Aldous Huxley's *After Many a Summer* (1939), who has just arrived from Britain.

58 Veitch, *American Superrealism*, p. 116.

59 Even her name sounds borrowed, taken perhaps from Fay Wray, one of the most famous female leads of the 1930s and star of *King Kong*. Fay Capeheart is the name of the first

starlet met by the protagonist of Horace McCoy's 1938 Hollywood novel *I Should Have Stayed Home*. 'Greener' suggests naivety and inexperience.

60 Goldstein, *The American Poet at the Movies*, p. 115.

61 West, *Novels and Other Writings*, p. 292.

62 Guy Debord, *The Society of the Spectacle*, p. 38.

63 This role is summarized by Richard Maltby as one played out in 'dramas of false appearances' (*Hollywood Cinema*, p. 44). West, like Horace McCoy in *I Should Have Stayed Home* (1938), stresses that sex is an integral part of Hollywood business. In total contrast, Dorothy Speare's *The Road to Needles* (1937) describes a Hollywood romance between a minor novelist and a dramatist-turned-screenwriter in such a way that neither the glamour of Hollywood nor the conventions of the romance novel are ever brought into question.

64 West, *Novels and Other Writings*, p. 281.

65 'Bird and Bottle' (1936), in Martin, ed., *Nathanael West: A Collection of Critical Essays*, p. 135. This piece eventually formed Chapter 14 of the novel.

66 West, *Novels and Other Writings*, p. 357.

67 Mathew Roberts, 'Bonfire of the Avant-garde', pp. 64, 67, 80. Karen Jacobs sees Tod's loss of distance as implicit as soon as he arrives in Hollywood, where he is confronted by a 'world of images which is apparently governed by its own laws and resists incorporation by a dominating gaze' (*The Eye's Mind*, p. 248). For her, there is an element of gynaephobia in Tod's fear of being consumed by feminine images (p. 255).

68 West, *Novels and Other Writings*, p. 379.

69 West, *Novels and Other Writings*, pp. 388–89. West's original ending would have completely lost this effect of climax in describing how Tod is taken home by the police; see 'Appendix VIII: The Original Final Chapter of *The Day of the Locust*', in Alister Wisker, *The Writing of Nathanael West*, p. 171.

70 Blake Allmendinger, 'The Death of a Mute Mythology'.

71 Robin Bly reads the novel as being caught in the double bind of showing complicity in the very representational methods it tries to critique ('Imitating the Siren').

72 Simon, 'Between Capra and Adorno', p. 522. Simon demonstrates West's allusions to contemporary films in impressive detail.

Bibliography

Original dates of publication for primary texts are given in square brackets.

Abel, Richard, 'American Film and the French Literary Avant-Garde (1914–1924)', *Contemporary Literature* 17/1 (Winter 1976), pp. 84–109.

Abramson, Leslie H., 'Two Birds of a Feather: Hammett's and Huston's *The Maltese Falcon*', in Richard Layman, ed., *Dashiell Hammett's 'The Maltese Falcon': A Documentary Volume* (Detroit: Gale, 2003), pp. 306–13.

Adams, Rachel, *Sideshow U.S.A.: Freaks and the American Imagination* (Chicago: University of Chicago Press, 2001).

Agee, James, *Agee on Film: Five Film Scripts* (Boston: Beacon Press, 1964).

— 'Art for What's Sake', *New Masses* (15 December 1936), pp. 48, 50.

— *Film Writing and Selected Journalism*, ed. Michael Sragow (New York: Library of America, 2005).

— *Let Us Now Praise Famous Men, etc.* (New York: Library of America, 2005).

— *The Collected Short Prose*, ed. Robert Fitzgerald (London: Calder and Boyars, 1972).

Alexander, William, *Film on the Left: American Documentary Film from 1931 to 1942* (Princeton: Princeton University Press, 1981).

Allmendinger, Blake, 'The Death of a Mute Mythology: From Silent Movies to the Talkies in *The Day of the Locust*', *Literature Film Quarterly* 16/2 (1988), pp. 107–11.

Anderson, David D., *Louis Bromfield* (New York: Twayne, 1964).

Anderson, Sherwood, *Perhaps Women* [1931] (Mamaroneck, NY: Paul P. Appel, 1970).

— *Winesburg, Ohio* [1919], ed. John H. Ferres (New York: Viking Press, 1966).

Arnheim, Rudolf, *Film As Art* (London: Faber and Faber, 1983).

Armstrong, Tim, *Modernism, Technology and the Body: A Cultural Study* (Cambridge: Cambridge University Press, 1998).

Arnold, Edwin T., 'The Motion Picture as Metaphor in the Works of F. Scott Fitzgerald', *Fitzgerald/Hemingway Annual 1977*, pp. 43–60.

— ed., *The Faulkner Journal: Faulkner and Film*, 16/1–2 (Fall 2000/Spring 2001).

Arthur, Anthony, *Radical Innocent: Upton Sinclair* (New York: Random House, 2006).

Asch, Nathan, *Pay Day* [1930] (Detroit: Omnigraphics, 1990).

Bair, Deirdre, *Anaïs Nin: A Biography* (London: Bloomsbury, 1996).

Baker, Carlos, *Ernest Hemingway: A Life Story* (Harmondsworth: Penguin, 1972).

Baldwin, James, *The Price Was Right: Collected Non-Fiction, 1948–1985* (London: Michael Joseph, 1985).

Barnard, Rita, 'Modern American Fiction', in Walter Kalaidjian, ed., *The Cambridge Companion to American Modernism* (Cambridge: Cambridge University Press), pp. 39–67.

Barnes, Djuna, *Selected Works* (London: Faber and Faber, 1980).

— *Interviews*, ed. Alyce Barry (Washington, DC: Sun and Moon Press, 1985).

Bassan, Maurice, *Hawthorne's Son: The Life and Literary Career of Julian Hawthorne* (Columbus: Ohio State University Press, 1970).

Bay-Cheng, Sarah, *Mama Dada: Gertrude Stein's Avant-Garde Theatre* (New York and London: Routledge, 2003).

Beja, Morris, *Film and Literature: An Introduction* (New York and London: Longman, 1979).

Benjamin, Walter, *Illuminations*, ed. Hannah Arendt (London: Collins/Fontana, 1973).

Benson, Jackson J., *The True Adventures of John Steinbeck, Writer* (London: Heinemann, 1984).

— 'The Background to the Composition of *The Grapes of Wrath*', in John Ditsky, ed., *Critical Essays on Steinbeck's 'The Grapes of Wrath'* (Boston: G.K. Hall, 1989), pp. 51–74.

— ed., *New Critical Approaches to the Short Stories of Ernest Hemingway* (Durham, NC: Duke University Press, 1990).

Benstock, Shari, *No Gifts from Chance: A Biography of Edith Wharton* (Harmondsworth: Penguin, 1995).

Bergreen, Laurence, *James Agee: A Life* (New York: E. P. Dutton, 1984).

Binggeli, Elizabeth, 'Burbanking Bigger and Bette the Bitch', *African American Review* 40.iii (Fall 2006), pp. 475–92.

Birchard, Robert S., 'Jack London and the Movies', *Film History* 1/1 (1987), pp. 15–38.

Blotner, Joseph, *Faulkner: A Biography*, 2 vols. (New York: Random House, 1974).

— *William Faulkner's Library – A Catalogue* (Charlottesville: University Press of Virginia, 1964).

Bly, Robin, 'Imitating the Siren: West's *The Day of the Locust* and the Subject of Sound', *Literature Film Quarterly* 32/1 (2004), pp. 51–59.

Bodeen, DeWitt, 'Films and Edith Wharton', *Films in Review* (February 1977), pp. 73–81.

Bordwell, David, *Narration in the Fiction Film* (Madison: University of Wisconsin Press, 1985).

— and Kristin Thompson, *Film Art: An Introduction*, 5th edn (New York: McGraw-Hill, 1997).

Boswell, Parley Ann, *Edith Wharton on Film* (Carbondale: Southern Illinois University Press, 2007).

Bowlby, Rachel, *Just Looking: Consumer Culture in Dreiser, Gissing and Zola* (New York and London: Methuen, 1985).

Bowser, Pearl, and Louise Spence, *Writing himself into History: Oscar Micheaux, his Silent Films, and his Audiences* (New Brunswick: Rutgers University Press, 2000).

Bowser, Pearl, Jane Gaines and Charles Musser, eds., *Oscar Micheaux and his Circle: African-American Filmmaking and Race Cinema of the Silent Era* (Bloomington: Indiana University Press, 2001).

Boyd, Thomas, *Through the Wheat* [1927] (New York: Award Books, 1964).

Branigan, Edward, *Narrative Comprehension and Film* (London: Routledge, 1992).

Bratton, Daniel, ed., *The Correspondence of Edith Wharton and Louis Bromfield* (East Lansing: Michigan State University Press, 2000).

Brooker-Bowers, Nancy, *The Hollywood Novel and Other Novels about Film, 1912–1982: An Annotated Bibliography* (New York: Garland, 1985).

Brown, Daniel R., 'The War Within Nathanael West: Naturalism and Existentialism', *Modern Fiction Studies* 20/2 (1974), pp. 181–202.

Brown, Rob, 'The Readies', *transition* 19–20 (June 1930), pp. 167–73.

Browne, Nick, 'Eisenstein in America: The First Phase', *Emergences: The Journal for the Study of Media and Composite Cultures* 12/2 (1 November 2002), pp. 181–97.

Bruccoli, Matthew J., *Some Sort of Epic Grandeur: The Life of F. Scott Fitzgerald*, revised edn (New York: Carroll and Graf, 1993).

—— *The Last of the Novelists: F. Scott Fitzgerald and 'The Last Tycoon'* (Carbondale: Southern Illinois University Press, 1977).

—— ed., *Conversations with Ernest Hemingway* (Jackson: University Press of Mississippi, 1986).

—— ed., *F. Scott Fitzgerald's Screenplay for 'Three Comrades' by Erich Maria Remarque* (Carbondale: Southern Illinois University Press, 1978).

—— ed., *The Only Thing That Counts: The Ernest Hemingway – Maxwell Perkins Correspondence* (Columbia, SC: University of South Carolina Press, 1999).

—— and George Parker Anderson, eds., *Tender is the Night: A Documentary Volume. Dictionary of Literary Biography Volume 273* (Detroit: Gale, 2003).

—— and J. E. Atkinson, 'F. Scott Fitgerald's Hollywood Assignments, 1937–1940', *Fitzgerald/Hemingway Annual 1971*, pp. 307–308.

—— and Judith S. Baughman, eds., *Conversations with F. Scott Fitzgerald* (Jackson: University Press of Mississippi, 2004).

—— and Margaret M. Duggan, eds., *Correspondence of F. Scott Fitzgerald* (New York: Random House, 1980).

Brunner, John, 'The Genesis of *Stand on Zanzibar* and Digressions', *Extrapolation* 11/2 (May 1970), pp. 34–43.

Bruss, Elizabeth W., 'Eye for I: Making and Unmaking Autobiography in Film', in James Olney, ed., *Autobiography: Essays Theoretical and Critical* (Princeton: Princeton University Press, 1980), pp. 296–320.

Bryher [Annie Winifred Ellerman], *The Heart to Artemis: A Writer's Memoirs* (London: Collins, 1963).

Buñuel, Luis, *L'Age d'Or and Un Chien Andalou*, trans. Marianne Alexandre (London: Lorrimer, 1968).

Burkdall, Thomas L., *Joycean Frames: Film and the Fiction of James Joyce* (New York: Routledge, 2001).

Burnett, W. R., *4 Novels: Little Caesar, The Asphalt Jungle, High Sierra, Vanity Row* (London: Zomba Books, 1984).

Burns, Edward, ed., *The Letters of Gertrude Stein and Carl Van Vechten, 1913–1946* (New York: Columbia University Press, 1986).

Cain, James M., *60 Years of Journalism*, ed. Roy Hoopes (Bowling Green, OH: Bowling Green State University Popular Press, 1985).

— *The Five Great Novels of James M. Cain* (London: Pan Books, 1985).

Caldwell, Erskine, *Call It Experience* [1951] (London: Heinemann, 1960).

— *With All My Might: An Autobiography* (Atlanta: Peachtree Publishers, 1987).

— and Margaret Bourke-White, *You Have Seen Their Faces* [1937] (Athens, GA: University of Georgia Press, 1995).

— and Margaret Bourke-White, *Say, is this the U.S.A.* (New York: Duell, Sloan and Pearce, 1941).

Carr, Virginia Spencer, *Dos Passos: A Life* (Garden City, NY: Doubleday, 1984).

Casey, Janet Galligani, *Dos Passos and the Ideology of the Feminine* (Cambridge: Cambridge University Press, 1998).

Castellito, George P., 'Imagism and Martin Scorsese: Images Suspended and Extended', *Literature Film Quarterly* 26/1 (1998), pp. 23–29.

Cather, Willa, 'Nebraska: The End of the First Cycle' [1923], in Guy Reynolds, ed., *Willa Cather: Critical Assessments* (Robertsbridge: Helm Information, 2003), vol. 1, pp. 41–47.

Cavell, Stanley, *The World Viewed: Reflections on the Ontology of Film* (Cambridge, MA: Harvard University Press, 1979).

Cendrars, Blaise, *La Fin du monde, L'Eubage, etc.* (Paris: Editions Denoël, 1960).

— *La Perle fiévreuse, Moganni Nameh, etc.* (Paris: Editions Denoël, 1960).

Cerf, Bennett, *Try and Stop Me: A Collection of Anecdotes and Stories, Mostly Humorous* (New York: Simon and Schuster, 1944).

Chandler, Raymond, *Raymond Chandler Speaking*, ed. Dorothy Gardiner and Kathrine Sorley Walker (Harmondsworth: Penguin, 1988).

Chaplin, Charles, *My Autobiography* (London: Bodley Head, 1964).

Charney, Leo, *Empty Moments: Cinema, Modernity and Drift* (Durham, NC: Duke University Press, 1998).

Charnov, Elaine S., 'The Performative Visual Anthropology Films of Zora Neale Hurston', *Film Criticism* 23/1 (1988), pp. 38–47.

Charyn, Jerome, *Movieland: Hollywood and the Great American Dream Culture* (New York: Putnam, 1989).

Chatman, Seymour, *Coming to Terms: The Rhetoric of Narrative in Fiction and Film* (Ithaca: Cornell University Press, 1990).

— 'What Novels Can Do That Films Can't (And Vice Versa)', in Gerald Mast, Marshall Cohen and Leo Braudy, eds., *Film Theory and Criticism: Introductory Readings*, 4th edn (New York and Oxford: Oxford University Press, 1992), pp. 403–19.

Clark, Randall, ed., *American Screenwriters: Second Series. Dictionary of Literary Biography Vol. 44* (Detroit: Gale Research, 1986).

Cohen, Keith, *Film and Fiction/The Dynamics of Exchange* (New Haven: Yale

University Press, 1979).

— ed., *Writing in a Film Age: Essays by Contemporary Novelists* (Niwot, CO: University Press of Colorado, 1991).

Cohen, Octavius Roy, *Bigger and Blacker* [1925] (Freeport, NY: Books for Libraries, 1970).

Cohen, Paula Marantz, *Silent Film and the Triumph of the American Myth* (New York: Oxford University Press, 2001).

Coleman, Emily Holmes, *The Shutter of Snow* [1930] (London: Virago, 1981).

Collins, Carvel, 'Nathanael West's *The Day of the Locust* and *Sanctuary*', *Faulkner Studies* 2/2 (Summer 1953), pp. 23–24.

Connor, Rachel, *H.D. and the Image* (Manchester: Manchester University Press, 2004).

Conrad, Joseph, *The Nigger of the 'Narcissus', etc.* (London: J. M. Dent, 1957).

Conron, John, *American Picturesque* (University Park, PA: Pennsylvania State University Press, 2000).

Coodley, Lauren, ed., *The Land of Orange Groves and Jails: Upton Sinclair's California* (Berkeley: Heyday Books, 2004).

Cooke, Alistair, ed., *Garbo and the Night Watchmen* (London: Secker and Warburg, 1971).

Corliss, Richard, *Talking Pictures: Screenwriters in the American Cinema* (Woodstock, NY: Overlook Press, 1985).

Crane, Stephen, *Tales of Adventure*, ed. Fredson Bowers (Charlottesville: Unioversity Press of Virginia, 1970).

— *Tales, Sketches, and Reports*, ed. Fredson Bowers (Charlottesville: University Press of Virginia, 1973).

— *The Red Badge of Courage*, ed. Sculley Bradley, Richmond Croom Beatty and E. Hudson Long (New York: W. W. Norton, 1962).

Crary, Jonathan, *Suspensions of Perception: Attention, Spectacle, and Modern Culture* (Cambridge, MA: MIT Press, 1999).

Crawford, Hugh, 'On the Fritz: Tom Kromer's Imaging of the Machine', *South Atlantic Review* 55/2 (1990), pp. 101–16.

Cripps, Thomas, 'Langston Hughes and the Movies: The Case of *Way Down South*', in John Edgar Tidwell and Cheryl R. Ragar, eds., *Montage of a Dream: The Life and Art of Langston Hughes* (Columbia, MO: University of Missouri Press, 2007), pp. 305–17.

— '*Native Son* in the Movies', in David Ray and Robert M. Farnsworth, eds., *Richard Wright: Impressions and Perspectives* (Ann Arbor: University of Michigan Press, 1973), pp. 101–15.

— *Slow Fade To Black: The Negro in American Film, 1900–1942* (London: Oxford University Press, 1977).

cummings, e. e., *A Miscellany Revised*, ed. George J. Firmage (New York: October House, 1965).

— *Eimi* [1933] (New York: William Sloane, 1949).

— *i: six nonlectures* [1953] (Cambridge, MA: Harvard University Press, 1972.

— *The Enormous Room* [1922] (Harmondsworth: Penguin, 1971).

Cunningham, Frank E., 'F. Scott Fitzgerald and the Problem of Film Adaptation', *Literature Film Quarterly* 28/3 (2000), pp. 187–96.

Dagenfelder, E. Pauline, 'The Four Faces of Temple Drake: Faulkner's *Sanctuary*, *Requiem for a Nun*, and the Two Film Adaptations', *American Quarterly* 28/5 (Winter 1976), pp. 544–60.

Dahlberg, Edward, *Bottom Dogs, From Flushing to Calvary, Those Who Perish, etc.* ['The Dahlberg Omnibus'] (New York: Minerva Press, 1976).

— *The Confessions of Edward Dahlberg* (New York: George Braziller, 1971).

Dardis, Tom, *Some Time in the Sun: The Hollywood Years of Fitzgerald, Faulkner, Nathanael West, Aldous Huxley, and James Agee* (New York: Scribner's, 1976).

Davis, Richard Harding, 'Billy and the Big Stick', *Somewhere in France* (New York: Scribner's, 1915), at http://www.fullbooks.com/Somewhere-in-France2.html/

— 'Breaking into the Movies', *Scribner's* 55 (March 1914), pp. 275–93.

Davison, R. A., 'The Publication of Hemingway's *The Spanish Earth*: An Untold Story', *Hemingway Review* 7 (1988), pp. 122–30.

Deal, Borden, *The Tobacco Men* (New York: Holt, Rinehart and Winston, 1965).

Debord, Guy, *The Society of the Spectacle*, trans. Donald Nicholson-Smith (New York: Zone Books, 1995).

Decharne, Max, *Hardboiled Hollywood: The Origins of the Great Crime Films* (Harpenden: No Exit Press, 2003).

DeKoven, Marianne, '"Why James Joyce Was Accepted and I Was Not": Modernist Fiction and Gertrude Stein's Narrative', *Studies in the Literary Imagination* 25/2 (Fall 1992), pp. 23–30.

DeMarco, Norman, 'Bibliography of Books on Literature and Film', *Style* 9/4 (1975), pp. 593–606.

Denzin, Norman K., *The Cinematic Society: The Voyeur's Gaze* (London: SAGE Publications, 1995).

Dessner, Lawrence Jay, 'Photography in *The Great Gatsby*', in Scott Donaldson, ed., *Critical Essays on F. Scott Fitzgerald's 'The Great Gatsby'* (Boston: G. K. Hall, 1984), pp. 175–86.

Dixon, Thomas, *The Clansman: An Historical Romance of the Ku Klux Klan* (New York: Doubleday Page, 1905).

— *The Fall of a Nation: A Sequel to The Birth of a Nation* (Chicago: M. A. Donoghue, 1916).

— *The Flaming Sword* [1939] (Lexington: University Press of Kentucky, 2005).

— *The Sins of the Father: A Romance of the South* [1912] (Lexington: University Press of Kentucky, 2004).

Dixon, Wheeler Winston, *The Cinematic Vision of F. Scott Fitzgerald* (Ann Arbor: UMI Research Press, 1986).

Docherty, Brian, ed., *American Crime Fiction: Studies in the Genre* (London: Macmillan, 1988).

Donald, James, Anne Friedberg and Laura Marcus, eds., *Close Up 1927–1933: Cinema and Modernism* (London: Cassell, 1998).

D[oolittle], H[ilda], *Asphodel*, ed. Robert Spoo (Durham, NC: Duke University Press, 1992).

— *Bid Me to Live* (London: Virago Press, 1984).

— 'Confessions and Letters: H.D.', *The Little Review* 12/2 (May 1929), pp. 38–40.

— 'Escape (January 1941)', in *Within the Walls* (Iowa City: Windhover Press, 1993), pp. 8–12.

— *Her* (London: Virago Press, 1984).

— *Kora and Ka* [1934] (New York: New Directions, 1996).

— *Nights* [1935] (New York: New Directions, 1986).

— *Notes on Thought and Vision* (San Francisco: City Lights, 1982).

— *Palimpsest* [1926] (Carbondale: Southern Illinois University Press, 1968).

— *The Gift: The Complete Text*, ed. Jane Augustine (Tallahassee: University Press of Florida, 1998).

— *Tribute to Freud*, revised edn (Manchester: Carcanet Press, 1985).

Dos Passos, John, *Century's Ebb: The Thirteenth Chronicle* (Boston: Gambit, 1975).

— *Novels 1920–1925* (New York: Library of America, 2003).

— *Occasions and Protests* (New York: Henry Regnery, 1964).

— *The Major Nonfictional Prose*, ed. Donald Pizer (Detroit: Wayne State University Press, 1988).

— *The Fourteenth Chronicle: Letters and Diaries*, ed. Townsend Ludington (London: Andre Deutsch, 1974).

— *Travel Books and Other Writings, 1916–1941* (New York: Library of America, 2003).

— *U.S.A.* [1938] (Harmondsworth: Penguin, 1976).

— 'Washington and Chicago II: Spotlights and Microphones', *New Republic* (29 June 1932), p. 179.

Dow, William, 'John Dos Passos, Blaise Cendrars, and the "Other" Modernism', *Twentieth Century Literature* 42/3 (1996), pp. 396–415.

Dreiser, Theodore, *An American Tragedy* (New York: Library of America, 2003).

— *Dreiser Looks at Russia* (London: Constable, 1928).

— *Dreiser's Russian Diary*, ed. Thomas P. Riggio and James L. W. West III (Philadelphia: University of Pennsylvania Press, 1996).

— *Hey, Rub-A-Dub-Dub! A Book of the Mystery and Wonder and Terror of Life* [1920] (London: Constable, 1931).

— 'Myself and the Movies', *Esquire* (July 1943), pp. 43–44.

— *Selected Magazine Articles* Vol. I, ed. Yoshinobu Hakutani (Cranbury, NJ: Associated University Presses, 1985).

— *Sister Carrie: An Authoritative Text, Backgrounds and Sources Criticism*, ed. Donald Pizer, 2nd edn (New York: W. W. Norton, 1991).

— *The American Diaries, 1902–1926*, ed. Thomas P. Riggio (Philadelphia: University of Pennsylvania Press, 1982).

DuBois, W. E. B., *Writings* (New York: Library of America, 1987).

Dunaway, David King, *Huxley in Hollywood* (New York: Harper and Row, 1989).

Dupee, F. W. and George Stade, eds., *Selected Letters of E. E. Cummings* (London: Andre Deutsch, 1972).

DuPlessis, Rachel Blau, *H.D.: The Career of that Struggle* (Brighton: Harvester Press, 1986).

Edel, Leon, 'Novel and the Cinema', in *The Theory of the Novel*, ed. John Halperin (New York: Macmillan, 1977), pp. 177–88.

Edmunds, Susan, *Out of Line: History, Psychoanalysis and Montage in H.D.'s Long Poems* (Stanford: Stanford University Press, 1994).

Edwards, Anne, *The Road to Tara: The Life of Margaret Mitchell* (London: Coronet, 1985).

Edwards, Justin, 'The Man with a Camera Eye: Cinematic Form and Hollywood Malediction in John Dos Passos' *The Big Money*', *Literature Film Quarterly* 27/4 (1999), pp. 245–54.

Eidsvick, Charles, 'Soft Edges: The Art of Literature, the Medium of Film', in John Harrington, ed., *Film and/as Literature* (Englewood Cliffs: Prentice-Hall, 1977), pp. 306–13.

Eisenstein, Sergei, *Film Form: Essays in Film Theory, and The Film Sense*, ed. and trans. Jay Leyda (Cleveland, OH: World Publishing, 1957) [each work paginated separately].

— *Film Essays*, ed. Jay Leyda (London: Dennis Dobson, 1968).

— *Immoral Memories: An Autobiography*, trans. Herbert Marshall (Boston: Houghton Mifflin, 1983).

— *Notes of a Film Director*, trans. X. Danko (New York: Dover, 1960).

Elias, Robert H., ed., *Letters of Theodore Dreiser: A Selection*, 3 vols. (Philadelphia: University of Pennsylvania Press, 1959) [paginated consecutively].

Eliot, T. S., *The Letters of T. S. Eliot. Volume I: 1898–1922*, ed. Valerie Eliot (New York: Harcourt Brace Jovanovich, 1988).

Elliott, Kamilla, *Rethinking the Novel/Film Debate* (Cambridge: Cambridge University Press, 2003).

Emerson, John, and Anita Loos, *How to Write Photoplays* (New York: James A. McCann, 1920).

Everett, Anna, *Returning the Gaze: A Genealogy of Black Film Criticism, 1909–1949* (Durham, NC: Duke University Press, 2001).

Fadiman, Regina K., *Faulkner's 'Intruder in the Dust': Novel into Film* (Knoxville: University of Tennessee Press, 1978).

— 'Hollywood's Use/Abuse of Faulkner', *Mississippi Quarterly* 42/3 (1989), pp. 333–37.

Farrell, James T., *The League of Frightened Philistines and Other Papers* [1945] (London: Routledge, 1948).

Faulkner, William, *Battle Cry*, ed. Louis Daniel Brodsky and Robert W. Hamblin (Jackson: University Press of Mississippi, 1985).

— *Country Lawyer and Other Stories for the Screen*, ed. Louis Daniel Brodsky and Robert W. Hamblin (Jackson: University Press of Mississippi, 1987).

— *Flags in the Dust*, ed. Douglas Day (New York: Random House, 1973).

— *Mosquitoes* [1927] (London: Picador, 1989).

— *New Orleans Sketches* (London: Sidgwick and Jackson, 1959).

— *Novels 1930–1935* (New York: Library of America, 1985).

— *Novels 1936–1940* (New York: Library of America, 1990).

— *Novels 1942–1954* (New York: Library of America, 1994).

— *The Penguin Collected Stories of William Faulkner* (Harmondsworth: Penguin, 1985).

— *Requiem for a Nun* [1951] (London: Chatto and Windus, 1965).

— *Sanctuary: The Original Text*, ed. Noel Polk (London: Chatto and Windus, 1981).

— *Selected Letters*, ed. Joseph Blotner (New York: Random House, 1977).

— *Stallion Road: A Screenplay*, ed. Louis Daniel Brodsky and Robert W. Hamblin (Jackson: University Press of Mississippi, 1989).

— *The De Gaulle Story*, ed. Louis Daniel Brodsky and Robert W. Hamblin (Jackson: University Press of Mississippi, 1984).

— *The Sound and the Fury: An Authoritative Text, Backgrounds and Contexts, Criticism*, ed. David Minter (New York and London, 1987).

Fauset, Jessie Redmon, *Plum Bun: A Novel without a Moral* [1928] (London: Pandora Press, 1985).

Fell, John L., *Film and the Narrative Tradition* (Berkeley: University of California Press, 1986).

Ferguson, Robert, *Henry Miller: A Life* (London and New York: Norton, 1991).

Field, Andrew, *The Formidable Miss Barnes: A Biography of Djuna Barnes* (London: Secker and Warburg, 1983).

Fielding, Raymond, *The March of Time, 1935–1956* (New York: Oxford University Press, 1978).

Fine, Richard, *West of Eden: Writers in Hollywood, 1928–1940* (Washington and London: Smithsonian Institution Press, 1993).

— 'Theodore Dreiser's "Revolt": An Unpublished Screenplay', *Literature Film Quarterly* 13/2 (1985), pp. 117–25.

Fitch, Noel Riley, ed., *In transition: A Paris Anthology* (London: Secker and Warburg, 1990).

Fitzgerald, F. Scott, *Babylon Revisited: The Screenplay* (New York: Carroll and Graf, 1993).

— 'Fitzgerald and the Hollywood Hacks', ed. James L. West, at http://www.timesonline.co.uk/article/0,,6870-685364,00.html

— 'Infidelity' [screenplay], *Esquire* 80 (December 1973), pp. 193–200, 290–304.

— 'Lipstick' [screenplay], *Fitzgerald/Hemingway Annual* (Detroit: Gale Research, 1978), pp. 5–33.

— *My Lost City: Personal Essays, 1920–1940*, ed. James L. W. West III (Cambridge: Cambridge University Press, 2005).

— *Novels and Stories 1920–1922* (New York: Library of America, 2000).

— *The Collected Short Stories* (Harmondsworth: Penguin, 1986).

— *The Great Gatsby*, ed. Matthew J. Bruccoli (Cambridge: Cambridge University Press, 1991).

— *The Love of the Last Tycoon: A Western*, ed. Matthew J. Bruccoli (Cambridge: Cambridge University Press, 1993).

— *Tender is the Night: A Romance* [1934], ed. Matthew J. Bruccoli (London: J. M. Dent, 1996).

Fitzpatrick, Kathleen, 'From *The Children* to *The Marriage Playground* and Back Again: Filmic Readings of Edith Wharton', *Literature Film Quarterly* 27/1

(1999), pp. 45–49.

Folks, Jeffrey J., 'William Faulkner and the Silent Film', *Southern Quarterly* 19/3-4 (1981), pp. 171–82.

Foner, Philip S., 'Upton Sinclair's *The Jungle*: The Movie', in Dieter Herms, ed., *Upton Sinclair: Literature and Social Reform* (Frankfurt am Main: Peter Lang, 1990), pp. 150–67.

Ford, Charles, and Parker Tyler, *The Young and Evil* [1933] (London: GMP, 1988).

Foster, Gretchen, 'John Dos Passos' Use of Film Technique in *Manhattan Transfer* and *The 42nd Parallel*', *Literature Film Quarterly* 14/3 (1986), pp. 186–94.

Fowler, Doreen, and Ann J. Abadie, eds., *Faulkner and Popular Culture: Faulkner and Yoknapatawpha, 1988* (Jackson: University Press of Mississippi, 1990).

Frank, Waldo, *In the American Jungle (1925–1936)* [1937] (Freeport, NY: Books for Libraries, 1968).

Freeman, Joseph, *An American Testament: A Narrative of Rebels and Romantics* [1936] (London: Victor Gollancz, 1938).

French, Warren, *Filmguide to 'The Grapes of Wrath'* (Bloomington, IN: Indiana University Press, 1973).

Friedberg, Anne, 'On H.D., Woman, History, Recognition', *Wide Angle* 5/2 (1982), pp. 26–31.

Friedman, Susan Stanford, *Penelope's Web: Gender, Modernity, H.D.'s Fiction* (Cambridge: Cambridge University Press, 1990).

Frohock, W. M., *The Novel of Violence in America*, 2nd edn (Dallas: Southern Methodist University Press, 1957).

Fuchs, Daniel, *The Golden West: Hollywood Stories* (Boston: Black Sparrow, 2005).

Furst, Lillian R., 'Innocent or Guilty? Problems in Filming Dreiser's *An American Tragedy*', *Connecticut Review* 9/2 (1976), pp. 33–40.

Fussell, Paul, *The Great War and Modern Memory* (New York and London: Oxford University Press, 1977).

Gallagher, Jean, 'H.D.'s Distractions: Cinematic Stasis and Lesbian Desire', *Modernism/Modernity* 9/3 (September 2002), pp. 407–22.

Garrett, George P., O. B. Hardison Jr and Jane R. Gelfman, eds., *Film Scripts One: Henry V, Streetcar Named Desire, The Big Sleep* [1971] (New York: Irvington, 1989).

Geduld, Carolyn, 'Film and Literature', *Contemporary Literature* 15/1 (1974), pp. 123–30.

Geduld, Harry M., ed., *Authors on Film* (Bloomington: Indiana University Press, 1972).

— and Ronald Gottesman, eds., *Sergei Eisenstein and Upton Sinclair: The Making and Unmaking of 'Que Viva Mexico!'* (Bloomington: Indiana University Press, 1970).

Gelman, Barbara, ed., *A Photoplay Treasury* (New York: Crown Publishers, 1972).

Gevirtz, Susan, *Narrative's Journey: The Fiction and Film Writing of Dorothy Richardson* (New York: Peter Lang, 1996).

Godden, Richard, *Fictions of Capital: The American Novel from James to Mailer* (Cambridge: Cambridge University Press, 1990).

— *Fictions of Labor: William Faulkner and the South's Long Revolution* (Cambridge:

Cambridge University Press, 1997).

Golbeck, Willis, Leon Gordon, et al., '*Freaks*: Script Synopsis' (MGM), at http://www.olgabaclanova.com/freaks_script_synopsis.htm/

Goldman, Jane, '"Miss Lonelyhearts and the Party Dress:" Cross-dressing and Collage in the Satires of Nathanael West', *Glasgow Review* 2 (2005), at http://www.arts.gla.ac.uk/SESL/STELLA/COMET/glasrev/issue2/goldm an.htm/

Goldstein, Laurence, *The American Poet at the Movies: A Critical History* (Ann Arbor: University of Michigan Press, 1994).

Graham, Carroll, and Garrett Graham, *Queer People* (New York: Vanguard Press, 1930).

Graham, Sheilah, *College of One* (London: Weidenfeld and Nicolson, 1967).

Gray, Richard, '*Sanctuary*, "Night Bird" and Film Noir', in Michel Gresset, ed., *Etudes Faulkneriennes I: Sanctuary* (Rennes: Presses Universitaires de Rennes, 1996) and at http://www.uhb.fr/faulkner/wf/articles/gray.html/

Grenier, Cynthia, 'The Art of Fiction: An Interview with William Faulkner – September, 1955', *Accent* 16 (Summer 1956), pp. 167–77.

Grimwood, Michael, *Heart in Conflict: Faulkner's Struggles with Vocation* (Athens, GA: University of Georgia Press, 1987).

Guest, Barbara, *Herself Defined: The Poet H.D. and her World* (London: Collins, 1985).

Guzzetti, Alfred, 'Narrative and Film Image', *New Literary History* 6/2 (1975), pp. 379–92.

Haas, Robert, 'The Story of Louis Pasteur and the Making of Zora Neale Hurston's *Their Eyes Were Watching God:* A Famous Film Influencing a Famous Novel?', *Literature Film Quarterly* 32/1 (2004), pp. 12–19.

Haberski, Raymond J., Jr, *It's Only a Movie! Films and Critics in American Culture* (Lexington: University Press of Kentucky, 2001).

Haller, Robert A., 'Anaïs Nin and Film: Open Questions', in Sharon Spencer, ed., *Anaïs, Art and Artists. A Collection of Essays* (Greenwood, FL: Penkevill, 1986), pp. 135–38.

Hamilton, Ian, *Writers in Hollywood, 1915–1951* (London: Heinemann, 1990).

Hammond, Paul, ed., *The Shadow and Its Shadow: Surrealist Writings on the Cinema*, 3rd ed. (San Francisco: City Lights, 2000).

Harrington, Evans, and Ann J. Abadie, eds., *Faulkner, Modernism, and Film: Faulkner and Yoknapatawpha, 1978* (Jackson: University Press of Mississippi, 1979).

Harrison-Kahan, Lori, 'Her "Nig": Returning the Gaze of Nella Larsen's *Passing*', *Modern Language Studies* 32/2 (2002), pp. 109–38.

Hart, Henry, ed., *American Writers' Congress* (New York: International Publishers, 1935).

Hayhoe, George F., 'Faulkner in Hollywood: A Checklist of his Film Scripts at the University of Virginia', *Mississippi Quarterly* 31 (1978), pp. 407–19; 'A Correction and Some Additions', 31 (1979), pp. 467–72.

Heath, Stephen, *Questions of Cinema* (London: Macmillan, 1981).

Hecht, Ben, *Rediscovering Ben Hecht, Volume I: Selling the Celluloid Serpent*, ed. Florice Whyte Koran (Washington, DC: Snickersnee Press, 1999).

Hemingway, Ernest, *A Farewell to Arms* [1929] (London: Arrow Books, 1994).

— *By-Line: Ernest Hemingway. Selected Articles and Dispatches of Four Decades*, ed. William White (Harmondsworth: Penguin, 1980).

— *Complete Poems*, ed. Nicholas Gerogannis (Lincoln, NE: University of Nebraska Press, 1979).

— *Dateline: Toronto: The Complete 'Toronto Star' Dispatches, 1920–1924*, ed. William White (New York: Scribner's, 1985).

— *Death in the Afternoon* [1932] (London: Jonathan Cape, 1966).

— *For Whom the Bell Tolls* [1941] (Harmondsworth: Penguin, 1962).

— *Selected Letters, 1917–1961*, ed. Carlos Baker (St Albans: Granada, 1981).

— *The Complete Short Stories: The Finca Vigia Edition* (New York: Charles Scribner's, 1987).

— *The Essential Hemingway* (St Albans: Triad/Panther, 1977).

— *The Spanish Earth* (Cleveland: J. B. Savage, 1938).

— *To Have and Have Not* [1937] (London: Grafton, 1988).

Hendrick, Paul, '"Brilliant Obscurity": The Reception of *The Enormous Room*', *Spring* 1 (1992), pp. 46–76.

Henninger, Katherine, 'Zora Neale Hurston, Richard Wright, and the Postcolonial Gaze', *Mississippi Quarterly* 56/4 (2003), pp. 581–95.

Herbst, Josephine, *The Starched Blue Sky of Spain and Other Memoirs* (New York: Harper Collins, 1991).

Herrmann, Dorothy, *S. J. Perelman: A Life* (New York: Putnam's, 1986).

Hinz, Evelyn J., ed., *The World of Anaïs Nin: Critical and Cultural Perspectives* (Winnipeg: University of Manitoba Press, 1978 and *Mosaic* (Winnipeg) 11/2 (Winter 1978)).

Hobhouse, Janet, *Everybody Who Was Anybody: A Biography of Gertrude Stein* (London: Arrow Books, 1986).

Hock, Stephen, '"Stories Told Sideways Out of the Big Mouth": John Dos Passos' Bazinian Eye', *Literature Film Quarterly* 33/1 (2005), pp. 20–27.

hooks, bell, *Black Looks: Race and Representation* (Boston: South End Press, 1992).

Hoopes, Roy, *Cain: The Biography of James M. Cain*, 2nd edn (Carbondale: Southern Illinois University Press, 1987).

Hopewell, Katherine, '"The Leaven, Regarding the Lump": Gender and Elitism in H. D.'s Writing on the Cinema', *Feminist Media Studies* 5/2 (2005), pp. 163–76.

Hotchner, A. E., *Ernest Hemingway's 'After the Storm': The Story plus the Screenplay and a Commentary* (New York: Carroll and Graf, 2001).

Howarth, William, 'The Mother of Literature: Journalism and *The Grapes of Wrath*', in David Wyatt, ed., *New Essays on 'The Grapes of Wrath'* (Cambridge: Cambridge University Press, 1990), pp. 71–99.

Howells, W. D., *London Films* (New York: Harper, 1905).

Hughes, Langston, *Collected Works of Langston Hughes. Volume 9: Essays on Art, Race, Politics, and World Affairs*, ed. Christopher C. De Santis (Columbia, MO: University of Missouri Press, 2002).

— *I Wonder As I Wander* [1956] (New York: Thunder's Mouth Press, 1986).

Humm, Maggie, *Modernist Women and Visual Cultures: Virginia Woolf, Vanessa Bell, Photography and Cinema* (Edinburgh: Edinburgh University Press, 2002).

Hurston, Zora Neale, *I Love Myself When I Am Laughing...A Zora Neale Hurston Reader*, ed. Alice Walker (New York: The Feminist Press, 1979).

— *Mules and Men* [1935] (New York: Harper and Row, 1990).

— *Their Eyes Were Watching God* [1937] (London: Virago Press, 1986).

Hussman, Laurence E., 'Dreiser's (Bad) Luck in Hollywood', *Dreiser Studies* 21/2 (Fall 1990), pp. 14–16.

— 'Squandered Possibilities: The Film Versions of Dreiser's Novels', in Miriam Gogol, ed., *Theodore Dreiser: Beyond Naturalism* (New York: New York University Press, 1995), pp. 176–200.

Hutchison, Beth, 'Gertrude Stein's Film Scenarios', *Literature Film Quarterly* 17/1 (1989), pp. 35–38.

Idol, John Lane, ed., *A Thomas Wolfe Companion* (Westport, CT: Greenwood Press, 1987).

Inge, M. Thomas, ed., *Conversations with William Faulkner* (Jackson: University Press of Mississippi, 1999).

Ivens, Joris, *The Camera and I* (Berlin: Seven Seas Publishers, 1969).

Jacobs, Karen, *The Eye's Mind: Literary Modernism and Visual Culture* (Ithaca: Cornell University Press, 2001).

Jacobs, Lewis, ed., *The Compound Cinema: The Film Writings of Harry Alan Potamkin* (New York: Teacher's College Press, 1977).

James, Henry, *The Art of the Novel: Critical Prefaces* (New York: Scribner's, 1962).

— *The Complete Tales: Volume 12, 1903–1912*, ed. Leon Edel (London: Rupert Hart-Davis, 1964).

Jason, Philip K., *Anaïs Nin and her Critics* (Columbia, SC: Camden House, 1993).

Jobst, John William, *Cinematic Technique in the World War I American Novel* (Ann Arbor: University Microfilms International, 1978).

Johnson, James Weldon, *Black Manhattan* [1930] (New York: Arno Press, 1968).

— *The Selected Writings of James Weldon Johnson*, ed. Sondra Kathryn Wilson, 2 vols. (New York: Oxford University Press, 1995).

Joshi, S. T., ed., *Mencken's America* (Athens, OH: Ohio University Press, 2004).

Joyce, James, *Ulysses*, ed. Jeri Johnson (Oxford: Oxford University Press, 1993).

Juncker, Clara, 'Dos Passos' Movie Star: Hollywood Success and American Failure', *American Studies in Scandinavia* 22/1 (1990), pp. 1–14.

Kaplan, Amy, *The Anarchy of Empire in the Making of U.S. Culture* (Cambridge, MA: Harvard University Press, 2002).

Kaplan, Carla, ed., *Zora Neale Hurston: A Life in Letters* (New York: Random House, 2003).

Kaplansky, Leslie A., 'Cinematic Rhythms in the Short Fiction of Eudora Welty', *Studies in Short Fiction* 33/4 (Fall 1996), pp. 579–89.

Karl, Frederick R., *William Faulkner: American Writer* (London: Faber, 1989).

Kawin, Bruce F., *Faulkner and Film* (New York: Frederick Ungar, 1977).

— 'Hawks on Faulkner: Excerpts from an Interview', *Post Script: Essays in Film and the Humanities* 22/1 (2002), pp. 3–22.

— *Telling It Again and Again: Repetition in Literature and Film* (Ithaca: Cornell University Press, 1972).

— ed., *Faulkner's MGM Screenplays* (Knoxville: University of Tennessee Press, 1982).

— ed., *To Have and Have Not* [screenplay] (Madison: University of Wisconsin Press, 1980).

Kazan, Elia, *A Life* (London: Andre Deutsch, 1988).

Kehl, D. G., 'Steinbeck's "String of Pictures" in *The Grapes of Wrath*', *Image* 17/1 (March 1974), pp. 1–10.

Kellman, Steven G., 'The Cinematic Novel: Tracking a Concept', *Modern Fiction Studies* 33/3 (1987), pp. 467–77.

Kellner, Bruce, *Carl Van Vechten and the Irreverent Decades* (Norman: University of Oklahoma Press, 1968).

Kennedy, Richard S., *Dreams in the Mirror: A Biography of E.E. Cummings*, 2nd edn (New York: Liveright, 1994).

Kessler, Carol Farley, *Charlotte Perkins Gilman: Her Progress toward Utopia with Selected Writings* (Liverpool: Liverpool University Press, 1995).

King, Michael, ed., *H.D. Woman and Poet* (Orono, ME: National Poetry Foundation, 1986).

King, Richard H. and Helen Taylor, eds., *Dixie Debates: Perspectives on Southern Culture* (London: Pluto Press, 1996).

Kliman, Bernice, '*An American Tragedy*: Novel, Scenario, and Film', *Literature Film Quarterly* 5 (1977), pp. 256–68.

Klotman, Phyllis, 'The Black Writer in Hollywood, Circa 1930: The Case of Wallace Thurman', in Manthia Diawara, ed., *Black American Cinema* (New York: Routledge, 1993), pp. 80–92.

Knight, Eric [Richard Hallas], *You Play the Black and the Red Comes Up* [1938] (Berkeley, CA: Black Lizard Books, 1986).

Koch, Stephen, *The Breaking Point: Hemingway, Dos Passos, and the Murder of Jose Robles* (New York: Counterpoint, 2005).

Kroeber, Karl, *Make Believe in Film and Fiction: Visual vs. Verbal Storytelling* (London: Palgrave Macmillan, 2006).

Kroeger, Brooke, *Fannie: The Talent for Success of Writer Fannie Hurst* (New York: Random House, 1999).

Kromer, Tom, *Waiting for Nothing and Other Writings*, ed. Arthur D. Casciato and James L. W. West III (Athens, GA: University of Georgia Press, 1986).

Kummer, George, *Harry Leon Wilson: Some Account of the Triumphs and Tribulations of an American Popular Writer* (Cleveland, OH: Press of Western Reserve University, 1963).

Landers, Robert K., *An Honest Writer: The Life and Times of James T. Farrell* (San Francisco: Encounter Books, 2004).

Latham, Aaron, *Crazy Sundays: F. Scott Fitzgerald in Hollywood* (New York: Viking, 1971).

Laurence, Frank M., *Hemingway and the Movies* (New York: Da Capo Press, 1982).

— 'Death in the Matinee: The Film Endings of Hemingway's Fiction', *Literature Film Quarterly* 2 (1974), pp. 44–51.

Leavelle, Charles, 'Brick Slayer is Likened to Jungle Beast', *Chicago Sunday Tribune* (5 June 1938), Part 1 p. 6.

Levin, Harry, *Contexts of Criticism* (New York: Atheneum, 1963).

Levine, Nancy J., '"I've Always Suffered from Sirens": The Cinema Vamp and Djuna Barnes' *Nightwood*', *Women's Studies* 16 (1989), pp. 70–88.

Lewis, R. W. B., and Nancy Lewis, eds., *The Letters of Edith Wharton* (London: Simon and Schuster, 1988).

Lewis, Wyndham, *Men Without Art* [1934] (Santa Rosa: Black Sparrow Press, 1987).

Lindsay, Vachel, 'The Art of the Moving Picture', in Dennis Camp, ed., *The Prose of Vachel Lindsay* (Peoria, IL: Spoon River Poetry Press, 1988), vol. 1, pp. 211–337.

— *The Progress and Poetry of the Movies: A Second Book of Film Criticism* (Lanham, MD: Scarecrow Press, 1995).

Litton, Alfred G., 'The Kinetoscope in *McTeague*: "The Crowning Scientific Achievement of the Nineteenth Century"', *Studies in American Fiction* 19 (1991), pp. 107–12.

London, Jack, *Hearts of Three* (London: Mills and Boon, 1918).

— *Novels and Social Writings* (New York: Library of America, 1982).

Loos, Anita, *Anita Loos Rediscovered: Film Treatments and Fiction*, ed. Cari Beauchamp and Mary Anita Loos (Berkeley: University of California Press, 2003).

Lorentz, Pare, *FDR's Moviemaker: Memoirs and Scripts* (Reno: University of Nevada Press, 1992).

— *Lorentz on Film: Movies 1927 to 1941* (New York: Hopkinson and Blake, 1975).

— *The River* (New York: Stackpole, 1938).

— 'The Screen', *Vanity Fair* (January 1934), pp. 45–46.

Lothe, Jakob, *Narrative in Fiction and Film: An Introduction* (Oxford: Oxford University Press, 2000).

Lounsberry, Myron, ed., *The Progress and Poetry of the Movies: A Second Book of Film Criticism by Vachel Lindsay* (Lanham, MD: Scarecrow Press, 1995).

Loving, Jerome M., *The Last Titan: A Life of Theodore Dreiser* (Berkeley: University of California Press, 2005).

Ludington, Townsend, 'The Ordering of the Camera Eye in *U.S.A.*', *American Literature* 49 (1977), pp. 443–46.

Lurie, Peter, *Vision's Immanence: Faulkner, Film, and the Popular Imagination* (Baltimore: Johns Hopkins University Press, 2004).

MacAdams, William, *Ben Hecht, The Man Behind the Legend: A Biography* (New York: Scribner's, 1990).

Macdonald, Dwight, *On Movies* (New York: Da Capo Press, 1981).

MacShane, Frank, *The Life of John O'Hara* (London: Jonathan Cape, 1980).

Madden, David, ed., *Nathanael West: The Cheaters and the Cheated. A Collection of Critical Essays* (Deland, FL: Everett/Edwards, 1973).

Magny, Claude-Edmonde, *The Age of the American Novel: The Film Aesthetic between the Two Wars*, trans. Eleanor Hochman (New York: Frederick Ungar, 1972).

Maine, Barry, ed., *Dos Passos: The Critical Heritage* (London and New York: Routledge, 1988).

— 'Steinbeck's Debt to Dos Passos', in Barbara A. Heavilin, ed., *The Critical Response to John Steinbeck's 'The Grapes of Wrath'* (Westport: Greenwood Press, 2000), pp. 151–61.

Maland, Charles J., *Chaplin and American Culture: The Evolution of a Star Image* (Princeton: Princeton University Press, 1989).

Maltby, Richard, *Hollywood Cinema* (Oxford: Blackwell, 2001).

— '"To Prevent the Prevalent Type of Book": Censorship and Adaptation in Hollywood, 1924–1934', *American Quarterly* 44/4 (1992), pp. 554–83.

Mandal, Somdatta, *Reflections, Refractions and Rejections: Three American Writers and the Celluloid World* (Leeds: Wisdom House, 2004).

Mandel, Charlotte, 'Garbo/Helen: The Self-Projection of Beauty by H.D.', *Women's Studies* 7 (1980), pp. 127–35.

— 'The Redirected Image: Cinematic Dynamics in the Style of H.D. (Hilda Doolittle)', *Literature Film Quarterly* 11/1 (1983), pp. 36–45.

March, William, *Company K* [1933] (New York: Arbor House, 1984).

Marcus, Laura, 'Literature and Cinema', in Laura Marcus and Peter Nicholls, eds., *The Cambridge History of Twentieth-Century English Literature* (Cambridge: Cambridge University Press, 2004), pp. 335–58.

— *The Tenth Muse: Writing about Cinema in the Modernist Period* (Oxford: Oxford University Press, 2007).

Margolies, Alan, 'F. Scott Fitzgerald's Work in the Film Studios', *Princeton University Library Chronicle* 32 (Winter 1971), pp. 81–110.

— '"Kissing, Shooting, and Sacrificing": F. Scott Fitzgerald and the Hollywood Market', in Jackson R. Bryer, ed., *The Short Stories of F. Scott Fitzgerald: New Approaches in Criticism* (Madison: University of Wisconsin Press, 1982), pp. 65–73.

Marsh, Joss Lutz, 'Fitzgerald, Gatsby and *The Last Tycoon*: The "American Dream" and the Hollywood Dream Factory', *Literature Film Quarterly* 20/1-2 (1992), pp. 3–13, 102–108.

Marshall, Scott, 'Edith Wharton on Film and Television: A History and Filmography', *Edith Wharton Review* 13/2 (1996), pp. 15–26.

Martin, Jay, *Always Merry and Bright: The Life of Henry Miller* (Santa Barbara: Capra Press, 1978).

— *Nathanael West: The Art of his Life* (New York: Carroll and Graf, 1980).

— ed., *Nathanael West: A Collection of Critical Essays* (Englewood Cliffs, NJ: Prentice-Hall, 1971).

Matterson, Stephen, 'A Life in the Pictures: Harold Pinter's *The Last Tycoon*', *Literature Film Quarterly* 27/1 (1999), pp. 50–54.

Maurois, André, *Man's Fate* [1934], trans. Haakon M. Chevalier (New York: Random House, 1961).

McAlmon, Robert, and Kay Boyle, *Being Geniuses Together, 1920–1930*, revised edn (London: Michael Joseph, 1970).

McCabe, Susan, *Cinematic Modernism: Modernist Poetry and Film* (Cambridge: Cambridge University Press, 2005).

McCoy, Horace, *4 Novels* (London: Zomba Books, 1983).

McGovern, Linda, 'The Man Behind the Curtain: L. Frank Baum and the Wizard of Oz', at http://www.literarytraveler.com/literary_articles/l_frank_baum.aspx/

McKay, Claude, *A Long Way from Home* [1937] (New York: Harcourt Brace and World, 1970).

— *Home to Harlem* [1928] (London: The X Press, 2000).

McLuhan, Marshall, *Understanding Media: The Extensions of Man* (London: Routledge and Kegan Paul, 1964).

Mellow, James R., *Constructed Lives: F. Scott and Zelda Fitzgerald* (London: Souvenir Press, 1985).

Mencken, H. L. *Prejudices: Sixth Series* (New York: Alfred A. Knopf, 1927).

Merz, Charles, *The Great American Band-Wagon* (New York: John Day, 1928).

Meyer, William E. H., Jr, 'From *The Sun Also Rises* to *High Noon*: The Hypervisual Great Awakening in American Literature and Film', *Journal of American Culture* 19/3 (Fall 1996), pp. 25–37.

Meyers, Jeffrey, 'Conrad's Influence on Modern Writers', *Twentieth Century Literature* 36/2 (Summer 1990), pp. 186–206.

— *Hemingway: A Biography* (London: Macmillan, 1986).

— ed. *Hemingway: The Critical Heritage* (London: Routledge and Kegan Paul, 1982).

Michaels, Walter Benn, 'An American Tragedy, or the Promise of American Life', *Representations* 25 (Winter 1989), pp. 71–98.

Micheaux, Oscar, *The Homesteader* [1917] (College Park, MD: McGrath, 1969).

Michelson, Annette, ed. *Kino-Eye: The Writings of Dziga Vertov*, trans. Kevin O'Brien (Berkeley: University of California Press, 1984).

Miller, Henry, *Black Spring* [1936] (London: John Calder, 1965).

— 'Buñuel, or Thus Cometh to an End Everywhere the Golden Age', *New Review* 1 (May–July 1931), pp. 157–59.

— *Letters to Emil*, ed. George Wickes (New York: New Directions, 1989).

— *Sunday after the War* (New York: Norton, 1944).

— *The Air-Conditioned Nightmare* [1945] (London: Granada, 1979).

— *The Cosmological Eye* (New York: New Directions, 1939).

— *The Wisdom of the Heart* [1941] (New York: New Directions, 1960).

— *The World of Sex and Max and the White Phagocytes* [1959] (London: Calder and Boyars, 1970).

— *Tropic of Cancer* [1934] (London: Grafton, 1989).

— *Tropic of Capricorn* [1936] (New York: Grove Press, 1961).

— *The Books in My Life* [1951] (London: Icon Books, 1963).

Millichap, Joseph R., *Steinbeck and Film* (New York: Frederick Ungar, 1983).

Mitchell, Greg, *The Campaign of the Century: Upton Sinclair's Race for Governor of California and the Birth of Media Politics* (New York: Random House, 1992).

Mitchell, Margaret, *Gone with the Wind* [1936] (London: Macmillan, 1938).

Moers, Ellen, *Two Dreisers* (London: Thames and Hudson, 1970).

Montagu, Ivor, *With Eisenstein in Hollywood* (New York: International Publishers, 1967).

Morissette, Bruce, *Novel and Film: Essays in Two Genres* (Chicago: University of Chicago Press, 1985).

Morsberger, Robert E., Stephen O. Lesser and Randall Clark, eds., *American Screenwriters: Dictionary of Literary Biography Vol. 26* (Detroit: Gale Research, 1984).

Morris, Adelaide, *How to Live/What to Do/H.D.'s Cultural Poetics* (Urbana: University of Illinois Press, 2002).

Moses, Gavriel, *The Nickel Was for the Movies: Film in the Novel from Pirandello to Puig* (Berkeley: University of California Press, 1995).

Mulvey, Laura, *Visual and Other Pleasures* (London: Palgrave, 1989).

Munson, Gorham, *The Awakening Twenties: A Memoir-History of a Literary Period* (Baton Rouge: Louisiana State University Press, 1985).

Munsterberg, Hugo, *The Film, a Psychological Study: The Silent Photoplay in 1916* (New York: Dover, 1970).

Murphet, Julian, and Lydia Rainford, eds., *Literature and Visual Technologies: Writing after Cinema* (Basingstoke: Palgrave Macmillan, 2003).

Murray, D. M., 'Faulkner, the Silent Comedies, and the Animated Cartoons', *Southern Humanities Review* 9 (1975), pp. 241–57.

Murray, Edward, *The Cinematic Imagination: Writers and the Motion Pictures* (New York: Frederick Ungar, 1972).

Nadel, Alan, 'Ambassadors from an Imaginary Elsewhere: Cinematic Convention and the Jamesian Sensibility', in Susan M. Griffin, ed., *Henry James Goes to the Movies* (Lexington: University Press of Kentucky, 2002), pp. 193–202.

Nagel, James, *Stephen Crane and Literary Impressionism* (University Park: Pennsylvania State University Press, 1980).

Nin, Anaïs, *A Woman Speaks: The Lectures, Seminars and Interviews of Anais Nin*, ed. Evelyn J. Hinz (Harmondsworth: Penguin, 1992).

— *Fire: The Unexpurgated Diary of Anais Nin, 1934–1937* (New York: Harcourt Brace, 1995).

— *House of Incest* (Chicago: Swallow Press, 1958).

— *In Favour of the Sensitive Man* (Harmondsworth: Penguin, 1992).

— *The Journals of Anaïs Nin*, ed. Gunther Stuhlmann (London: Quartet Books, 1973 [vol. 1: 1931–34], 1974 [vol. 2: 1934–39 and vol. 4: 1944–47], 1976 [vol. 5: 1947–55].

— *The Mystic of Sex: A First Look at D. H. Lawrence: Uncollected Writings, 1931–1974*, ed. Gunther Stuhlmann (Santa Barbara: Capra Press, 1995).

— *The Novel of the Future* (London: Peter Owen, 1969).

— *The White Blackbird and Other Writings* (Santa Barbara: Capra Press, 1985).

— *Under a Glass Bell and Other Stories* (Denver: Alan Swallow, 1948).

— *Winter of Artifice: Three Novelettes* (Athens, OH: Swallow Press/Ohio University Press, 1961).

Normand, Jean, *Nathaniel Hawthorne: An Approach to an Analysis of Artistic Creation*, trans. Derek Coltman (Cleveland, OH: Case Western University Press,

1970).

Norris, Frank, *McTeague, A Story of San Francisco: Authoritative Text, Contexts, Criticism*, [1899], ed. Donald Pizer, 2nd edn (New York and London: Norton, 1997).

— *The Octopus* [1901], (Harmondsworth: Penguin, 1986).

North, Joseph, ed., *New Masses: An Anthology of the Rebel Thirties* (Berlin: Seven Seas Publishers, 1972).

North, Michael, *Camera Works: Photography and the Twentieth-Century Word* (New York: Oxford University Press, 2005).

O'Hara, John, *John O'Hara's Hollywood*, ed. Matthew J. Bruccoli (New York: Carroll and Graf, 2007).

Oliver, Charles M., ed., *A Moving Picture Feast: The Filmgoer's Hemingway* (New York: Praeger, 1989).

Oliver, Lawrence J., 'Writing from the Right during the "Red Decade": Thomas Dixon's Attack on W. E. B. DuBois and James Weldon Johnson in *The Flaming Sword*', *American Literature* 70/1 (1998), pp. 131–52.

— and Terri L. Walker, 'James Weldon Johnson's *New York Age* Essays on *The Birth of a Nation* and the "Southern Oligarchy"', *South Central Review* 10/4 (Winter 1993), pp. 1–17.

Orgeron, Marsha, 'Rethinking Authorship: Jack London and the Motion Picture Industry', *American Literature* 75/1 (2003), pp. 91–117.

Ornitz, Samuel, *Allrightniks Row: 'Haunch Paunch and Jowl'* [1923] (New York: Markus Wiener, 1985).

Palmer, R. Barton, ed., *Nineteenth-Century American Fiction on Screen* (Cambridge: Cambridge University Press, 2008).

— *Twentieth-Century American Fiction on Screen* (Cambridge: Cambridge University Press, 2008).

Patterson, Louise Thompson, 'With Langston Hughes in the USSR', in David Levering Lewis, ed., *The Portable Harlem Renaissance Reader* (New York: Penguin, 1994), pp. 182–89.

Peary, Gerald, and Roger Shatzkin, eds., *The Classic American Novel and the Movies* (New York: Frederick Ungar, 1977).

— *The Modern American Novel and the Movies* (New York: Frederick Ungar, 1978).

Perelman, S. J., *The Most of S. J. Perelman* (London: Methuen, 1982).

Perlmutter, Ruth, 'Malcolm Lowry's Unpublished Filmscript of *Tender is the Night*', *American Quarterly* 28/5 (Winter 1976), pp. 561–74.

Perry, Margaret, ed., *The Short Fiction of Rudolph Fisher* (Westport, CT: Greenwood Press, 1987).

Phillips, Gene D., *Fiction, Film, and Faulkner: The Art of Adaptation* (Knoxville: University of Tennessee Press, 1988).

— *Hemingway and Film* (New York: Frederick Ungar, 1980).

Pirandello, Luigi, *Shoot! (Si Gira): The Notebooks of Serafino Gubbio, Cinemato-graph Operator* [1926], trans. C. K. Scott Moncrieff (New York: E. P. Dutton, 1934).

Pizer, Donald, *Dos Passos' U.S.A.: A Critical Study* (Charlottesville, VA: University

Press of Virginia, 1988).

— 'The Camera Eye in *U.S.A.*: The Sexual Centre', *Modern Fiction Studies* 26 (Autumn 1980), pp. 417–30.

— ed. *John Dos Passos' U.S.A.: A Documentary Volume. Dictionary of Literary Biography Vol. 274* (Detroit: Gale, 2003).

Porges, Irwin, *Edgar Rice Burroughs: The Man Who Created Tarzan*, 2 vols. (New York: Ballantine Books, 1976).

Powdermaker, Hortense, *Hollywood: The Dream Factory – An Anthropologist Studies the Movie-Makers* (Boston: Little, Brown, 1950).

Prenshaw, Peggy Whitman, ed., *Conversations with Eudora Welty* (Jackson: University Press of Mississippi, 1984).

Prigozy, Ruth, 'From Griffith's Girl to Daddy's Girl: The Masks of Innocence in *Tender is the Night*', *Twentieth Century Literature* 26/2 (1980), pp. 189–221.

Pudaloff, Ross, 'Celebrity as Identity: *Native Son* and Mass Culture', in Henry Louis Gates, Jr and K. A. Appiah, eds., *Richard Wright: Critical Perspectives Past and Present* (New York: Amistad Press, 1993), pp. 156–70.

Pyros, John, 'Richard Wright: A Black Novelist's Experience in Film', *Negro American Literary Forum* 9/2 (Summer 1975), pp. 53–54.

Rampersad, Arnold, *The Life of Langston Hughes*, 2 vols. (New York: Oxford University Press, 1986).

Rapf, Joanne E., '*The Last Tycoon* or "A Nickel for the Movies"', *Literature Film Quarterly* 16/2 (1988), pp. 76–81.

Regester, Charlene, 'African-American Writers and Pre-1950 Cinema', *Literature Film Quarterly* 29/3 (2001), pp. 210–35.

Rhodes, Chip, *Politics, Desire, and the Hollywood Novel* (Iowa City: University of Iowa Press, 2008).

Rice, Elmer, *A Voyage to Purilia* (London: Victor Gollancz, 1930).

Richardson, Robert, *Literature and Film* (Bloomington: Indiana University Press, 1969).

Riggio, Thomas P., ed., *Dreiser–Mencken Letters: The Correspondence of Theodore Dreiser and H. L. Mencken, 1907–1945*, 2 vols. (Philadelphia: University of Pennsylvania Press, 1986).

Ring, Frances, and R. L. Samsell, 'Sisyphus in Hollywood: Refocusing Scott Fitzgerald', *Fitzgerald/Hemingway Annual* 1973, pp. 93–104.

Robe, Chris, 'Eisenstein in America: The *Que Viva Mexico!* Debates and the Emergence of the Popular Front in US Film Theory and Criticism', *Velvet Light Trap* 54 (Fall 2004), pp. 18–31.

Roberts, Mathew, 'Bonfire of the Avant-Garde: Cultural Rage and Readerly Complicity in *The Day of the Locust*', *Modern Fiction Studies* 42/1 (1996), pp. 61–90.

Robinson, W. B., ed., *Man and the Movies* (Baton Rouge: Louisiana State University Press, 1967).

Rogin, Michael, '"The Sword Became a Flaming Vision": D. W. Griffith's *The Birth of a Nation*', *Representations* 9 (Winter 1985), pp. 150–95.

Rolfe, Lionel, *Literary L.A.* (San Francisco: Chronicle Books, 1981).

Ross, Harris, 'A Selected Bibliography of the Relationship of Literature and Film', *Style* 9/4 (Fall 1975), pp. 564–92.

Ross, Stephen J., ed., *Movies and American Society* (Oxford: Blackwell, 2002).

Rowley, Hazel, *Richard Wright: The Life and Times* (New York: Henry Holt, 2001).

Ruppert, Peter, Eugene Crook and Walter Forehand, eds., *Ideas of Order in Literature and Film* (Tallahassee: University Press of Florida, 1980).

Sandburg, Carl, *'The Movies Are': Carl Sandburg's Film Reviews and Essays, 1920–1928*, ed. Arnie Bernstein (Chicago: Lake Clairmont Press, 2000).

Sarver, Stephanie, 'Homer Simpson Meets Frankenstein: Cinematic Influence in Nathanael West's *The Day of the Locust*', *Literature Film Quarterly* 24/2 (1996), pp. 217–22.

Savada, Elias, 'The Making of *Freaks*', at http://www.olgabaclanova.com/the_making_of_freaks.htm/

Sayre, Joel, and William Faulkner, *The Road to Glory: A Screenplay*, ed. Matthew J. Bruccoli (Carbondale: Southern Illinois University Press, 1981).

Scholes, Robert, 'Narration and Narrativity in Film', in Gerald Mast and Marshall Cohen, eds., *Film Theory and Criticism: Introductory Readings*, 3rd edn (New York and Oxford: Oxford University Press, 1985), pp. 390–403.

Schulberg, Budd, *Some Faces in the Crowd* [1954] (London: Bodley Head, 1975).

— *What Makes Sammy Run?* [1941] (Harmondsworth: Penguin, 1978).

Schwab, Arnold T., 'Conrad's American Speeches and his Reading from *Victory*', *Modern Philology* 62 (1965), pp. 342–47.

Schwartz, Delmore, *In Dreams Begin Responsibilities and Other Stories* (New York: New Directions, 1978).

Seed, David, ed., *Essays and Studies 2005: Literature and the Visual Media* (Woodbridge and Rochester, NY: Boydell and Brewer, 2005).

Seidman, Barbara, '"Patronize Your Neighborhood Wake-Up-And-Dreamery": E. E. Cummings and the Cinematic Imagination', *Literature Film Quarterly* 13/1 (1985), pp. 10–21.

Seldes, Gilbert, 'The Cinema Novel', *The Seven Lively Arts* (New York: Harper, 1924), pp. 383–92.

Shi, David E., 'Transatlantic Visions: The Impact of the American Cinema upon the French Avant-Garde, 1918–1924', *Journal of Popular Culture* 14 (1981), pp. 583–96.

Shloss, Carol, *In Visible Light. Photography and the American Writer: 1840–1940* (New York: Oxford University Press, 1987).

Shulman, Robert, *The Power of Political Art: The 1930s Literary Left Reconsidered* (Chapel Hill: University of North Carolina Press, 2000).

Sidney, George R., 'William Faulkner and Hollywood', *Colorado Quarterly* 9 (1961), pp. 367–77.

Silverstein, Louis, 'Louis Silverstein's H.D. Chronology, Part Three (April 1919–1928)', at http://www.imagists.org/hd/hdchron3.html/

Simmonds, Roy, *John Steinbeck: The War Years, 1939–1945* (Lewisburg: Bucknell University Press, 1996).

Simon, Richard Keller, 'Between Capra and Adorno: West's *Day of the Locust* and the Movies of the 1930s', *Modern Language Quarterly*, 54/4 (1993) pp. 513–34.

Sinclair, Upton, *American Outpost: A Book of Reminiscences* (Pasadena, CA: Upton Sinclair, 1932).

— *The Brass Check* (Pasadena, CA: Upton Sinclair, 1920).

— *The Jungle* [1906], ed. Clare Virginia Eby (New York: Norton, 2003).

— *Upton Sinclair Presents William Fox* (Los Angeles: Upton Sinclair, 1933).

Sitney, P. Adams, *Modernist Montage: The Obscurity of Vision in Cinema and Literature* (New York: Columbia University Press, 1990).

Skal, David J. and Elias Savada, *Dark Carnival: The Secret World of Tod Browning, Hollywood's Master of the Macabre* (New York: Doubleday, 1995).

Sklar, Robert, *Movie-Made America: A Cultural History of American Movies* (New York: Vintage, 1976).

Slide, Anthony, *The Hollywood Novel: A Critical Guide to over 1200 Works with Film-Related Themes or Characters, 1912 through 1994* (Jefferson, NC: MacFarland, 1995).

— *American Racist: The Life and Films of Thomas Dixon* (Lexington: University Press of Kentucky, 2004).

— ed., *They Also Wrote for the Fan Magazines: Film Articles by Literary Giants from E. E. Cummings to Eleanor Roosevelt, 1920–1939* (Jefferson, NC: McFarland, 1992).

Smith, Grahame, *Dickens and the Dream of Cinema* (Manchester: Manchester University Press, 2003).

Snyder, Robert L., *Pare Lorentz and the Documentary Film* (Norman: University of Oklahoma Press, 1968).

Sobchack, Vivian C., '*The Grapes of Wrath* (1940): Thematic Emphasis through Visual Style', *American Quarterly* 31/5 (Winter 1979), pp. 596–615.

Soupault, Philippe, *Last Nights of Paris* [1931], trans. William Carlos Williams (New York: Full Court Press, 1982).

Spatz, Jonas, *Hollywood in Fiction: Some Versions of the American Myth* (The Hague: Mouton, 1969).

Speare, Dorothy, *The Road to Needles* (Cambridge, MA: Houghton Mifflin, 1937).

Spiegel, Alan, *Fiction and the Camera Eye: Visual Consciousness in Film and the Modern Novel* (Charlottesville: University Press of Virginia, 1976).

Spindler, Michael, 'John Dos Passos and the Visual Arts', *Journal of American Studies* 15 (1981), pp. 391–405.

Springer, John Parris, *Hollywood Fictions: The Dream Factory in American Popular Literature* (Norman: University of Oklahoma Press, 2000).

Stam, Robert, and Alessandro Raengo, eds., *A Companion to Literature and Film* (Oxford: Blackwell, 2004).

Stein, Gertrude, 'A Movie', in *A Primer for the Gradual Understanding of Gertrude Stein*, ed. Robert Bartlett Haas (Los Angeles: Black Sparrow, 1971), pp. 69–71.

— *Everybody's Autobiography* [1938] (London: Virago Press, 1985).

— 'Film: Deux soeurs qui ne sont pas soeurs', *La Revue Européenne* 5–7 (May–July 1930), pp. 600–601.

— *How Writing Is Written: Volume II of the Previously Uncollected Writings of*

Gertrude Stein, ed. Robert Bartlett Haas (Los Angeles: Black Sparrow Press, 1974).

— *Lectures in America* [1935] (London: Virago Press, 1988).

— *Paris France* [1940] (London: Brilliance Books, 1983).

— *Picasso: The Complete Writings*, ed. Edward Burns (Boston: Beacon Press, 1985).

— *The Autobiography of Alice B. Toklas* (London: John Lane, 1933).

— *The Geographical History of America or, The Relation of Human Nature to the Human Mind* [1936] (New York: Random House, 1973).

— *The Making of Americans* [1925] (London: Peter Owen, 1968).

— *Three Lives and Q.E.D.* [1909], ed. Marianne DeKoven (New York and London, 2006) (Harmondsworth: Penguin, 1990).

— *Writings and Lectures 1911–1945*, ed. Patricia Meyerowitz (London: Peter Owen, 1967).

Steinbeck, John, *America and Americans, and Selected Nonfiction*, ed. Susan Shillinglaw and Jackson J. Benson (New York: Viking, 2002).

— *Of Mice and Men* [1937] (London: Heinemann, 1971).

— *The Forgotten Village* (New York: Viking Press, 1941).

— *The Grapes of Wrath* [1939] (Harmondsworth: Penguin, 2000).

— *The Harvest Gypsies: On the Way to 'The Grapes of Wrath'* (Berkeley: Heyday Books, 1988).

— *Working Days: The Journals of 'The Grapes of Wrath,' 1938–1941*, ed. Robert J. DeMott (New York: Viking, 1989).

— *Zapata*, ed. Robert E. Morsberger (New York: Penguin, 1993).

Steiner, Wendy, *Exact Resemblance to Exact Resemblance: Literary Portraiture in Gertrude Stein* (New Haven: Yale University Press, 1979).

Stewart, Jacqueline, *Migrating to the Movies: Cinema and Black Urban Modernity* (Berkeley: University of California Press, 2005).

Stewart, L. D., 'Fitzgerald's Film Scripts of "Babylon Revisited"', *Fitzgerald/ Hemingway Annual 1971*, pp. 81–104.

Stoddart, Scott F., 'Redirecting Fitzgerald's "Gaze": Masculine Perception and Cinematic Licence in *The Great Gatsby*'. in Jackson R. Bryer, Alan Margolies and Ruth Prigozy, eds., *F. Scott Fitzgerald: New Perspectives* (Athens, GA: University of Georgia Press, 2000), pp. 102–14.

Stott, William, *Documentary Expression and Thirties America* (New York: Oxford University Press, 1973).

Stuhlmann, Gunther, ed., *A Literate Passion: Letters of Anaïs Nin and Henry Miller, 1932–1953* (London: Allison and Busby, 1988).

Suarez, Juan A., 'John Dos Passos' *U.S.A.* and Left Documentary Film in the 1930s: The Cultural Politics of "Newsreel" and "The Camera Eye"', *American Studies in Scandinavia* 31/1 (1999), pp. 43–67.

Swanberg, W. A., *Dreiser* (New York: Charles Scribner's, 1965).

Taylor, John Russell, *Strangers in Paradise: The Hollywood Emigres, 1933–1950* (London: Faber and Faber, 1983).

Taylor, Richard, *The Battleship Potemkin: The Film Companion* (London and New York: I. B. Tauris, 2000).

Tichi, Cecelia, *Shifting Gears: Technology, Literature, Culture in Modernist America* (Chapel Hill, NC: University of North Carolina Press, 1987).

Tintner, Adeline R., 'Henry James at the Movies: Cinematograph and Photograph in "Crapy Cornelia"', *Markham Review* 6 (1979) pp. 1–8.

Toklas, Alice B., *What is Remembered* [1963] (San Francisco: North Point Press, 1985).

Tookey, Helen, *Anaïs Nin, Fictionality and Femininity: Playing a Thousand Roles* (Oxford: Clarendon Press, 2003).

Totten, Gary, 'The Art and Architecture of the Self: Redesigning the "I"-Witness in Edith Wharton's *The House of Mirth*', *College Literature* 27/3 (Fall 2000) pp. 71–88.

Townsend, Kim, *Sherwood Anderson* (Boston: Houghton Mifflin, 1987).

Trotter, David, *Cinema and Modernism* (Oxford: Blackwell, 2007).

Turim, Maureen, *Flashbacks in Film* (New York and London: Routledge, 1989).

Turnbull, Andrew, ed., *The Letters of F. Scott Fitzgerald* (Harmondsworth: Penguin, 1968).

Tyler, Parker, *The Hollywood Hallucination* [1944] (New York: Simon and Schuster, 1970).

— and Charles Ford, *The Young and Evil* [1933] (London: GMP, 1988).

Urgo, Joseph R., '*Absalom, Absalom!*: The Movie', *American Literature* 62/1 (1990), pp. 56–73.

Van Vechten, Carl, 'Fabulous Hollywood', *Vanity Fair* (May 1927), pp. 54, 108.

— 'Hollywood Parties', *Vanity Fair* (June 1927), pp. 47, 86, 90.

— 'Hollywood Royalty', *Vanity Fair* (July 1927), pp. 38, 86.

— *Nigger Heaven* [1926] (Urbana: University of Illinois Press, 2000).

— *Spider Boy: A Scenario for a Moving Picture* (New York: Grosset and Dunlap, 1928).

— 'Understanding Hollywood', *Vanity Fair* (August 1927), pp. 45, 78.

Veitch, Jonathan, *American Superrealism: Nathanael West and the Politics of Representation in the 1930s* (Madison: University of Wisconsin Press, 1997).

Von Stroheim, Erich, *Greed*, ed. Joel W. Finler (London: Lorrimer, 1972).

Wagenknecht, Edward, *William Dean Howells: The Friendly Eye* (New York: Oxford University Press, 1969).

Wagner, Geoffrey, *The Novel and the Cinema* (Rutherford, NJ: Fairleigh Dickinson University Press, 1975).

Wagner, Linda W., ed., *Ernest Hemingway: Five Decades of Criticism* (East Lansing: Michigan State University Press, 1974).

— *Ernest Hemingway: Six Decades of Criticism* (East Lansing: Michigan State University Press, 1987).

Walker, Alexander, *Stardom: The Hollywood Phenomenon* (Harmondsworth: Penguin, 1974).

Warren, Robert Penn, 'Homage to *An American Tragedy*', in Harold Bloom, ed., *Theodore Dreiser's 'An American Tragedy': Modern Critical Interpretations* (New York: Chelsea House, 1988), pp. 21–36.

Weaver, Mike, *William Carlos Williams: The American Background* (Cambridge: Cambridge University Press, 1977).

Weinberger, Eliot, 'The Camera People', in Lucien Taylor, ed., *Visualizing Theory:*

Selected Essays from V.A.R., 1990–1994 (New York and London: Routledge, 1994), pp. 3–26.

Wells, Walter, *Tycoons and Locusts: A Regional Look at Hollywood Fiction of the 1930s* (Carbondale: Southern Illinois University Press, 1973).

Welsch, Janice R. and Syndy M. Conger, eds., *Narrative Strategies: Original Essays in Film and Prose Fiction* (Macomb: Western Illinois University Press, 1980).

Welty, Eudora, *Stories, Essays, and Memoir* (New York: Library of America, 1998).

— *The Eye of the Story: Selected Essays and Reviews* (New York: Vintage, 1979).

West, Dorothy, *The Richer, the Poorer: Stories, Sketches and Reminiscences* (New York: Doubleday, 1995).

West, Nathanael, *Novels and Other Writings* (New York: Library of America, 1997).

Westerhoven, James N., 'Autobiographical Elements in the Camera Eye', *American Literature* 48 (1976), pp. 340–64.

Westling, Louise, 'The Loving Observer of *One Time, One Place*', in Albert J. Devlin, ed., *Welty: A Life in Literature* (Jackson: University Press of Mississippi, 1988), pp. 168–87.

Wharton, Edith, *A Backward Glance* [1934] (London: Constable, 1972).

— *Collected Stories, 1911–1937* (New York: Library of America, 2001).

— *Ethan Frome and Summer* [1911, 1917] (London: Constable, 1965).

— *The Children* [1928] (London: Virago, 1985).

— *The House of Mirth: Authoritative Text, Backgrounds and Content Criticism* [1905], ed. Elizabeth Ammons (New York and London: Norton, 1990).

— *The Uncollected Critical Writings*, ed. Frederick Wegener (Princeton: Princeton University Press, 1996).

Wicks, Ulrich, 'Literature/Film: A Bibliography', *Literature Film Quarterly* 6 (Spring 1978), pp. 135–43.

Williams, Tony, *Jack London, The Movies: An Historical Survey* (Los Angeles: David Rejl, 1992).

Williams, William Carlos, *A Recognizable Image: William Carlos Williams on Art and Artists*, ed. Bram Dijkstra (New York: New Directions, 1978).

— *Imaginations* (New York: New Directions, 1971).

— *Selected Essays* (New York: Random House, 1954).

— *The Embodiment of Knowledge*, ed. Ron Loewinson (New York: New Directions, 1974).

— *White Mule* [1937] (London: McGibbon and Kee, 1965).

Wilson, Edmund, *Classics and Commercials: A Literary Chronicle of the Forties* (New York: Farrar, Straus, 1955).

Wilson, Harry Leon, *Merton of the Movies* [1922] (Berkeley, CA: Heyday Books, 2004).

Wilt, David, *Hardboiled in Hollywood: Five Black Mask Writers and the Movies* (Bowling Green, OH: Bowling Green State University Popular Press, 1991).

Winkiel, Laura, 'Circuses and Spectacles: Public Culture in *Nightwood*', *Journal of Modern Literature* 21/1 (Fall 1997), pp. 7–28.

Wisker, Alistair, *The Writing of Nathanael West* (Basingstoke and London: Macmillan, 1990).

Wolfe, Thomas, *The Hound of Darkness*, ed. John L. Idol, Jr (Chapel Hill, NC: Thomas Wolfe Society, 1986).

Wood, Gerald, 'From *The Clansman* and *Birth of a Nation* to *Gone with the Wind*: The Loss of American Innocence', in Dardon Asbury Pyron, ed., *Recasting 'Gone with the Wind' in American Culture* (Miami: University Presses of Florida, 1983), pp. 123–36.

Wranovics, John. *Chaplin and Agee: The Untold Story of the Tramp, the Writer, and the Lost Screenplay* (London: Palgrave, 2005).

Wright, Richard, *Early Works* (New York: Library of America, 1991).

— *Eight Men* (New York: Thunder's Mouth Press, 1987).

— *Native Son* [1940] (Harmondsworth: Penguin, 1983).

Young, Earl James, Jr and Beverly J. Robinson, eds., *The Life and Work of Oscar Micheaux* (San Francisco : KMT Publications, 2002).

Index